Views into

Views into the Chinese Room

New Essays on Searle and Artificial Intelligence

EDITED BY

John Preston and Mark Bishop

CLARENDON PRESS · OXFORD

OXFORD

UNIVERSITY PRESS

Great Clarendon Street, Oxford OX2 6DP

Oxford University Press is a department of the University of Oxford.
It furthers the University's objective of excellence in research, scholarship,
and education by publishing worldwide in

Oxford New York

Auckland Bangkok Buenos Aires Cape Town Chennai
Dar es Salaam Delhi Hong Kong Istanbul Karachi Kolkata
Kuala Lumpur Madrid Melbourne Mexico City Mumbai Nairobi
São Paulo Shanghai Singapore Taipei Tokyo Toronto

with an associated company in Berlin

Oxford is a registered trade mark of Oxford University Press
in the UK and in certain other countries

Published in the United States
by Oxford University Press Inc., New York

British Library Cataloguing in Publication Data

Data available

Library of Congress Cataloging in Publication Data

Views into the Chinese room : new essays on Searle and artificial intelligence / edited by
John Preston and Mark Bishop.
    p. cm.
    Includes indexes.
      1. Artificial intelligence. 2. Machine learning. 3. Searle, John R. I. Preston, John, 1957–
II. Bishop, Mark, 1962–
Q335.5 .V54 2002   006.3'5—dc21   2002066233
ISBN 0–19–825057–6
ISBN 0–19–925277–7 (Pbk.)

1 3 5 7 9 10 8 6 4 2

Typeset by Newgen Imaging Systems (P) Ltd., Chennai, India
Printed in Great Britain
on acid-free paper by
Biddles Ltd, Guildford & King's Lynn

ACKNOWLEDGEMENTS

The following material has previously been published, and is reprinted here with permission.

Material from pages 283–6 of Ned Block's 'The Computer Model of the Mind', which first appeared in Daniel N. Osherson and Edward E. Smith (eds.), *Thinking: An Invitation to Cognitive Science, Volume 3* (Cambridge, Mass.: MIT Press, 1990), by permission of MIT Press. All rights reserved.

Material from pages 21–30 of Roger Penrose's *The Emperor's New Mind: Concerning Computers, Minds, and the Laws of Physics* (Oxford: Oxford University Press, 1989), © Oxford University Press 1989, and pages 40–4 of his *Shadows of the Mind: A Search for the Missing Science of Consciousness* (Oxford: Oxford University Press, 1994), © Oxford University Press 1994, both by permission of Oxford University Press.

Material from Roger Penrose's 'On Understanding Understanding', *International Studies in the Philosophy of Science*, 11 (1997), 7–10, by permission of Carfax Publishing Company, Abingdon, England.

CONTENTS

NOTES ON THE CONTRIBUTORS

Alison Adam is a senior lecturer in the Information Systems Institute at the University of Salford, England. Her main research interest is gender and information technologies. She is currently working on a project to bring feminist ethics to bear on the developing field of computer ethics. The main theme of her book *Artificial Knowing: Gender and the Thinking Machine* (Routledge, 1998) involves a critique of AI from feminist epistemology. Her most recent book, *Virtual Gender* (with Eileen Green: Routledge, 2001) is an edited collection of research on gender and the virtual life.

Igor Aleksander is one of the 'oldies' of AI, having proposed digital memory-based neural networks in 1965. As the Gabor Professor of Neural Systems at Imperial College, London, he now models visual consciousness in the brain. Having published over 200 papers, he prefers writing books, for example, *Impossible Minds: My Neurons, My Consciousness* (Imperial College Press, 1996) and *How to Build a Mind* (Weidenfeld & Nicolson, 2000). A Fellow of the Royal Academy of Engineering he was awarded the Institution of Electrical Engineering's Year 2000 Outstanding Achievement Medal (Informatics). His appearances on radio and television include a discussion with John Searle in 1998.

Mark Bishop lectures in Cybernetics at the University of Reading, England. He has published over seventy-five papers on neural computation (both theoretical and applied) and the philosophy of artificial intelligence. His work in AI ranges from the development of an autonomous wheelchair for the severely disabled (SENARIO), to Colour Recipe Prediction, and the design of a new neural framework—Stochastic Diffusion Processes. He has been invited to lecture in America, the Middle East, and Europe and more recently has debated some of the philosophical issues outlined in this book both on the 'Today' programme and other UK radio programmes.

Ned Block is Professor of Philosophy and Psychology at New York University. Before that, he was Professor of Philosophy and Chair of the Philosophy

Program at MIT. He is the editor of the two-volume anthology *Readings in Philosophy of Psychology* (Methuen, 1980, 1981), of *Imagery* (MIT Press, 1981), and a co-editor of *The Nature of Consciousness: Philosophical Debates* (MIT Press, 1997). Several of his articles on issues in the philosophy of mind and cognition have been published in *The Philosophical Review*.

Selmer Bringsjord is Professor of Logic, Philosophy and Cognitive Science, and Director of the Minds and Machines Laboratory at Rensselaer Polytechnic Institute in Troy, New York. He is also Chief Scientist of Document Development Corporation. Bringsjord specializes in the logico-mathematical and philosophical foundations of Artificial Intelligence and Cognitive Science. He also specializes in building AI systems that are literarily creative (e.g. the BRUTUS story generation system). Bringsjord is author of *What Robots Can and Can't Be* (Kluwer, 1992) and other books, the most recent of which is *Artificial Intelligence and Literary Creativity: Inside the Mind of Brutus, A Storytelling Machine* (Lawrence Erlbaum, 2000). His website is at www.rpi.edu/~brings.

B. Jack Copeland is Professor of Philosophy at the University of Canterbury, New Zealand, and is Director of the Turing Archive for the History of Computing. He works in mathematical and philosophical logic, cognitive science, and the history and foundations of computing, and has published numerous articles in journals, including *The Journal of Philosophy*, *Mind*, *Analysis*, and *Scientific American*. He is author of *Artificial Intelligence: A Philosophical Introduction* (Blackwell, 1993, 2nd edition forthcoming), is currently writing and editing several books on Alan Turing, including one on Turing's Automatic Computing Engine, and is editing a volume for Oxford University Press to be entitled *Colossus: The First Computer*. His edited volume *Logic and Reality: Essays on the Legacy of Arthur Prior* appeared with Oxford University Press in 1996.

Jeff Coulter is Professor and Associate Chairman in the Department of Sociology at Boston University, Massachusetts. He is also an Associated Faculty member of the Department of Philosophy there. He is the author of numerous papers on topics in the philosophy of the human sciences, and his books include *The Social Construction of Mind* (Macmillan, 1979–86), *Rethinking Cognitive Theory* (Macmillan, 1983), *Mind in Action* (Polity Press, 1989), and (with Graham Button, John Lee, and Wes Sharrock) *Computers, Minds and Conduct* (Polity Press, 1995).

Stuart A. Eisenstadt recieved degrees in Theoretical Mathematics from Ramapo College of New Jersey (BS 1993) and Logic and Computation from Carnegie-Mellon University (MS 1993). His thesis, 'Prolegomena to a Theory of

Intentionality for Physical Symbolic Systems' based on the foundational work of his thesis adviser, Herbert Simon, demonstrated that the question of whether or not a machine can have intentionality is clearly empirical. Therefore, the answer will not be found through philosophizing, but rather through a close examination of the research being performed in the fields centred around studying the brain, for example, cognitive psychology, cognitive neuropsychology, and neuroscience, and the simulations which are used to help formulate theories in each of these fields. Using this more empirical than philosophical methodology the thesis demonstrated that it is possible to construct a theory of intentionality which is extremely plausible because it is founded on explanations of the cognitive functioning of humans which were attained experimentally.

He had the pleasure of working with his adviser, mentor, and friend, Professor Simon while at Carnegie Mellon, and for some years after, and looks fondly upon having had this opportunity. Their research was concerned with empirically determining whether human beings can think in ways that machines cannot and examining production system architectures as the basis for thinking, human and machine.

Stevan Harnad <http://www.cogsci.soton.ac.uk/harnad> was born in Hungary, did his undergraduate work at McGill University and his graduate work at Princeton University and is currently Professor of Cognitive Science at Southampton University, England. His research is on categorization, communication, and cognition. Founder and Editor of *Behavioral and Brain Sciences* (http://www.cogsci.soton.ac.uk/bbs), Psycoloquy (http://www.cogsci.soton.ac.uk/psyc), and the CogPrints Electronic Preprint Archive in the Cognitive Sciences (http://cogprints.soton.ac.uk), he is Past President of the Society for Philosophy and Psychology, and author and contributor to over 100 publications, including *Origins and Evolution of Language and Speech* (New York Academy of Science, 1976), *Lateralization in the Nervous System* (Academic Press, 1977), *Peer Commentary on Peer Review: A Case Study in Scientific Quality Control* (Cambridge University Press, 1982), *Categorical Perception: The Groundwork of Cognition* (Cambridge University Press, 1987), *The Selection of Behavior: The Operant Behaviorism of B.F. Skinner: Comments and Consequences* (Cambridge University Press, 1988), and *Icon, Category, Symbol: Essays on the Foundations and Fringes of Cognition* (in preparation).

John Haugeland is Professor of Philosophy at the University of Chicago. His main interests are early Heidegger, metaphysics, philosophy of mind (including cognitive science), and philosophy of science (especially the work of Thomas

Kuhn). He once converted an old IBM Selectric typewriter into a computer printer. Recent publications include *Mind Design II* (MIT Press, 1997), *Having Thought* (Harvard University Press, 1998), and *The Road since Structure: Philosophical Essays, 1970–1993, with an Autobiographical Interview* (by Thomas S. Kuhn, co-edited with James Conant; University of Chicago Press, 2000).

Larry Hauser received his Ph.D. in Philosophy from Michigan State University in 1993. His dissertation is entitled 'Searle's Chinese Box: The Chinese Room Argument and Artificial Intelligence'. Larry teaches philosophy and cognitive science at Alma College in Alma, Michigan, USA. He is a frequent contributor to the journal *Minds and Machines*, and author of 'The Chinese Room Argument: A Guided Tour and Annotated Bibliography' for the University of Rome's *Field Guide to the Philosophy of Mind* (online: http://www.uniroma3.it/kant/field/), as well as the 'Chinese Room Argument' entry for The Internet Encyclopedia of Philosophy (http://www.utm.edu/research/iep/).

Ron Noel specializes in cognitive engineering and the study of cognitive, biological, and machine design systems. He received his bachelor's and master's degrees from New Mexico State University, after which he worked for eight years in two analytical think tanks. In one, a military think-tank, he modelled human cognitive, perceptual, and decision behaviours for use in computer simulation to gain insights into the potential performance of proposed or conceptual systems. In the other, a cognitive science laboratory, he researched human behaviour to develop models of human abilities for creation of software that either interfaced to or automated the behaviours. Returning to academia as a lecturer at the University of Texas at El Paso, he received his Ph.D. from New Mexico State University in engineering psychology, specializing in the human–computer interface with a related area in digital design and micro-computer architecture. He is a veteran of many design projects, and many roles within them. He has received awards ranging from a national design award for artwork to an award by the US Army for the creation of original electronic hardware. One of his current research projects, the Mona-Lisa Project, falls under the Creative Agents theme in the Minds and Machines Laboratory at Rensselaer Polytechnic Institute, Troy, New York, and is breaking new ground in machine creativity and the use of non-analytic or holistic processes in design.

Roger Penrose is the Rouse Ball Professor of Mathematics at the University of Oxford. He was born in Colchester, Essex, UK in 1931, attended University College School, London, was awarded a B.Sc. degree at University College,

London and a Ph.D. degree at St John's College, Cambridge. He has held several posts in UK and USA, most particularly at Birkbeck College, London. He has received a number of prizes and awards including the 1988 Wolf Prize which he shared with Stephen Hawking for their understanding of the universe. His 1989 book *The Emperor's New Mind* became a best-seller and won the 1990 (Rhône-Poulenc) Science Book Prize. He has research interests in geometry, having made contributions to the theory of non-periodic tilings, to relativity theory, and the foundation of quantum theory. He has also contributed to the science of consciousness. His main research programme is to develop the theory of twistors, which he originated over thirty years ago as an attempt to unite Einstein's general theory of relativity with quantum mechanics. In 1994 he was knighted for services to science.

John Preston is a Senior Lecturer in the Department of Philosophy at the University of Reading, England. He received his B.A. in Philosophy from the Polytechnic of North London in 1982, his B.Phil. and D.Phil. from the University of Oxford in 1984 and 1988, and an M.Sc. in Computer Studies (Artificial Intelligence) from the University of Essex in 1990. He is the author of *Feyerabend: Philosophy, Science and Society* (Polity Press, 1997), editor of *Thought and Language* (Cambridge University Press, 1998), and of the third volume of Feyerabend's Philosophical Papers (*Knowledge, Science and Relativism* (Cambridge University Press, 1999)), and co-editor of *The Worst Enemy of Science? Essays in Memory of Paul Feyerabend* (Oxford University Press, 2000). He is currently writing on belief, knowledge, cognition, and the foundations of cognitive science.

Diane Proudfoot is Senior Lecturer in Philosophy at the University of Canterbury, New Zealand and is Co-director of the Turing Archive for the History of Computing. She works in the philosophy of language, philosophy of artificial intelligence, and on Wittgenstein, and has published in, among other journals, *Mind*, *Analysis*, and *Scientific American*. She is currently writing one book, and editing a second, on empty reference, and is co-writing *A Very Short Introduction to the Philosophy of Religion* for Oxford University Press.

Georges Rey studied with John Searle at Berkeley before receiving his doctorate from Harvard in 1978. He has published numerous articles regarding the relation of a computational/representational theory to traditional problems in the philosophy of mind. He was the co-editor (with Barry Loewer) of *Meaning in Mind: Fodor and His Critics* (1991), and is the author of *Contemporary Philosophy of Mind* (1996), both published by Blackwell's. He has held visiting positions at

MIT, the Australian National University, the University of London, and at CREA in Paris. He is presently professor of philosophy at the University of Maryland at College Park.

John R. Searle is Mills Professor of the Philosophy of Mind and Language, at the University of California at Berkeley. Born in 1932, in Denver, Colorado, he received his B.A. and D.Phil. in philosophy from Oxford University, where he studied under J. L. Austin and later became Lecturer in Philosophy at Christ Church from 1957. He joined the Department of Philosophy at Berkeley in 1959, where he became Professor of Philosophy. Searle's early work was in the theory of speech acts, and this led him, via his interest in intentionality, to issues at the heart of the philosophy of mind.

Among his many publications are *Speech Acts: An Essay in the Philosophy of Language* (Cambridge University Press, 1969), *Expression and Meaning: Studies in the Theory of Speech Acts* (Cambridge University Press, 1979), *Intentionality: An Essay in the Philosophy of Mind* (Cambridge University Press, 1983), *Minds, Brains and Science* (BBC Publications, 1984), *The Rediscovery of the Mind* (MIT Press, 1992), *The Construction of Social Reality* (Penguin, 1995), *The Mystery of Consciousness* (Granta, 1997), and *Mind, Language and Society: Philosophy in the Real World* (Weidenfeld & Nicolson, 1999).

Wes Sharrock is a Professor in the Department of Sociology at the University of Manchester, England. He has published co-authored articles in *Theory and Psychology* (with Jeff Coulter), *Inquiry* (with R. J. Anderson), *Human Studies* and *Social Studies of Science* (with Geoff Button), and is a co-author of *Philosophy and the Human Sciences* (Croom Helm, 1986), *The Ethnomethodologists*, (Ellis Horwood, 1986), and *Computers, Minds and Conduct* (Polity Press, 1995).

Herbert A. Simon was born in 1916 in Milwaukee, Wisconsin, and educated in political science at the University of Chicago (Ph.D. 1943). He held positions at the University of California (Berkeley), Illinois Institute of Technology, and, since 1949, Carnegie Mellon University, where he was Richard King Mellon University Professor of Computer Science and Psychology.

In 1978, he received the Nobel Prize in Economic Sciences, in 1986 the National Medal of Science, in 1969, the Distinguished Scientific Contribution Award of the American Psychological Association, in 1975 the A. M. Turing Award of the Association for Computing Machinery (with Allen Newell), in 1988, the John von Neumann Theory Prize of ORSA/TIMS, and in 1995, the Research Excellence Award of the International Joint Conference on Artificial Intelligence.

Simon's books include *Human Problem Solving* (with Allen Newell (Prentice-Hall, 1972)), *The Sciences of the Artificial* (MIT Press, 1969, 2nd edition 1981,

3rd edition 1996), *Scientific Discovery* (with others (MIT Press, 1987)), two volumes of collected psychology papers (*Models of Thought*, (Yale University Press, 1979)), a volume of papers on philosophy of science (*Models of Discovery* (D. Reidel, 1977)), and his autobiography, *Models of My Life* (MIT Press, 1996).

The reaction to the news of his death on 9th February 2001 was one of enormous shock and sadness when it spread among the world of scientists, colleagues, and friends. Still on Carnegie Mellon University's payroll when he died at the age of 84, he was as exuberant in his teaching and research as in his younger days.

John G. Taylor was trained as a theoretical physicist at Cambridge, and worked in the UK and USA at the Universities of Cambridge, Oxford, London, Southampton, Paris, Rutgers, and at the Institute for Advanced Study in Princeton. He worked on various quantum topics (field theory, gravity, super-strings) before turning full time to Neural Networks. In 1990 he set up the Centre for Neural Networks in King's College London, where he is a Professor in the Department of Mathematics, and since then has worked on many industrial applications as well as on computational neuroscience (modelling the retina, visual cortex, hippocampus, and frontal lobes). After working on brain imaging in Germany for two years, he more recently turned to consciousness and language, and is now developing a neural system to understand language at a conscious level, using detailed models of components of the brain.

Kevin Warwick is Professor of Cybernetics at the University of Reading, England. He has published over 350 research papers and has been awarded higher doctorates by Imperial College and the Czech Academy of Sciences, Prague. His paperback *In the Mind of the Machine* (Arrow, 1998) warns of a future in which machines are more intelligent than humans.

Kevin shocked the international scientific community by having a silicon chip transponder surgically implanted in his arm. In 2000 he was featured as the cover story in February's *Wired* magazine, received the Future Health Technology award from MIT, and presented the Royal Institution Christmas Lectures.

Michael Wheeler is Lecturer in Philosophy at the University of Dundee, Scotland. Previously, he has held teaching and/or research posts at the Universities of Sussex, Oxford, and Stirling. His published work includes studies of situated, embodied, and dynamical systems approaches to cognition, representational explanation in scientific psychology, neo-Cartesian and neo-Heideggerian interpretations of cognitive science, the conceptual foundations of evolutionary psychology, philosophical issues in artificial life and evolutionary robotics, and the nature and plausibility of the idea that genes code for phenotypic traits. His first book, *Reconstructing the Cognitive World: The Next Step*, is forthcoming from MIT Press.

Terry Winograd is Professor of Computer Science at Stanford University, California. He was an early researcher in artificial intelligence, focusing on natural language understanding. The seeming intelligence of his program SHRDLU led to optimism that computers could indeed understand language. He later moved away from artificial intelligence, arguing in a book co-authored with Fernando Flores (*Understanding Computers and Cognition* (Addison-Wesley, 1987)) that mainstream AI research was grounded on inadequate and misleading philosophical assumptions about knowledge. For the last decade he has written and done research on human–computer interaction.

1

Introduction

John Preston

Cognitive Science

In the mid-1970s one of the USA's best-known philanthropic organizations, the Alfred P. Sloan Foundation, invested substantial funds in a programme designed to stimulate progress in a burgeoning cross-disciplinary study of the nature and workings of the mind: 'cognitive science'. Although, with hindsight, it can be traced back to the 1950s, cognitive science came to public recognition (and was dubbed by the psychologist Christopher Longuet-Higgins) only in the early 1970s. It comprises a constellation of disciplines (the core members being psychology, linguistics, artificial intelligence, and neuroscience) which currently attempts to explain cognitive phenomena (thinking, reasoning, intelligence, perception, learning, understanding, belief, knowledge, memory, etc.) on the basis of hypotheses about the kinds of information-processing which support them. Motivated and underpinned by a certain philosophical perspective, the constellation subsequently broadened to include parts of or approaches to related fields like anthropology, archaeology, and sociology.

The University of California at Berkeley was one of the main beneficiaries of the Sloan Foundation's programme, as part of which prominent researchers were funded to travel around the country, lecturing at universities. How one of these researchers, a philosopher from UC Berkeley, came to be thought of as

I am grateful to John Searle, Andrew Hodges, Jack Copeland, and Mark Bishop for comments on draft versions of this introduction. Remaining errors it contains should not, of course, be laid at their door. My work on this material was also supported by a research fellowship from the Leverhulme Trust, to whom I am also grateful.

supplying the best-developed and most pointed threat to a core component of cognitive science is the story we have to tell. Although there is still tremendous controversy over its success, there is some consensus over the import of this 'Chinese Room argument' (CRA), which John Searle first published in a paper entitled 'Minds, Brains, and Programs' (Searle 1980*a*). The argument turns on an easily understood thought-experiment which mobilizes readily available intuitions. If sound, it undermines the official self-image of artificial intelligence (AI), one of the supposed foundations of much contemporary cognitive science. It may well also be contemporary philosophy's best-known argument.

Before we get around to the argument itself, though, we need to have some concepts at our disposal, and some history in place.

Turing Machines

Computer science, and the disciplines it made possible, such as AI, have a foundation in the work of the British mathematician Alan Turing.[1] His 1936 paper 'On Computable Numbers, with an Application to the *Entscheidungsproblem*', a founding document of computer science, is remarkable both for its *theoretical* and its *practical* implications. Before it, there was no real theory of computation, yet it made possible the development (about a decade later) of the first modern stored-program electronic computers, which, in turn, was one of the main preconditions for the rise of cognitive science. The fundamental concepts introduced and explored in the paper can be explained in a relatively simple way.

Turing's paper, published even before he had completed his Ph.D., is about the *decision problem* posed by the German mathematician David Hilbert. The issue concerned *formal systems*, that is, mathematical systems in which the methods of constructing mathematical statements, as well as the assumptions and principles used in proving theorems, are governed by explicit and precise rules. In 1928 Hilbert had queried whether there is an 'effective' (or 'mechanical') method that can determine, of any given statement in a formal system, whether or not it is provable in that system. Turing, setting out to show rigorously that there is not (that mathematics is *undecidable*, in this technical sense), required a precise, convincing, and general definition of an effective or mechanical method. The concept he came up with, now known as the *Turing*

---

[1] Andrew Hodges's biography of Turing (Hodges 1983) is a wonderful source of material on Turing's thought, as well as his life.

machine, is the basic concept of theoretical computer science. The proposal now known as *Turing's thesis* says that whenever there is an effective or mechanical method for calculating the values of a mathematical function, that function can be computed by a Turing machine. The relatively informal concept of an effective or mechanical method can thus be *replaced* by the precise concept of a Turing machine.

It's crucial to what follows that Turing's idea of such an idealized 'machine' was explicitly modelled on that of a *person* performing a computation, and therefore presupposes the adequacy of his own analysis of such activity. When he talks about 'computers' in this 1936 paper, Turing means *humans who compute* (since, of course, there were no 'computers' in the modern colloquial sense at that time). He begins his analysis by pointing out that computation could always be done by writing symbols from a finite alphabet onto a paper tape uniformly divided into square frames. He then says:

The behaviour of the computer at any moment is determined by the symbols which he is observing, and his 'state of mind' at that moment. We may suppose that there is a bound B to the number of symbols or squares which the computer can observe at one moment. If he wishes to observe more, he must use successive observations. We will also suppose that the number of states of mind which need to be taken into account is finite . . . Let us imagine the operations performed by the computer to be split up into 'simple operations' which are so elementary that it is not easy to imagine them further divided. Every such operation consists of some change of the physical system consisting of the computer and his tape. We know the state of the system if we know the sequence of symbols on the tape, which of these are observed by the computer . . . and the state of mind of the computer. (Turing 1936, in Davis 1965: 136)

In the final step of his analysis, Turing proposes that we can avoid these references to the computing person's 'states of mind' altogether by supposing that he or she writes at every single step of the computation a 'note of instructions' which explains exactly how the computation should be continued. These notes of instructions take the place of the computer's 'states of mind', therefore 'the state of progress of the computation at any stage is completely determined by the note of instructions and the symbols on the tape' (ibid. 139–40).

In proposing that 'we may now construct a machine to do the work of this computer' (p. 137) Turing forges the connection between person and machine:

We may compare a man in the process of computing a real number to a machine which is only capable of a finite number of conditions . . . which will be called '*m*-configurations'. The machine is supplied with a 'tape' (the analogue of paper) running through it, and divided into sections (called 'squares') each capable of bearing a 'symbol'. At any moment there is just one square . . . which is 'in the machine'. We may call this square the 'scanned square'. The symbol on the scanned square may be called 'the scanned symbol'. The 'scanned symbol' is the only one of which the machine is, so to speak, 'directly aware' . . . The possible behaviour of the machine at any moment is determined by the *m*-configuration and the scanned symbol. This pair will be called the 'configuration'. (ibid. 117)

Any particular Turing machine can assume any one of a finite number of different internal 'configurations' at a given time. The activity of such machines consists in serially ordered, discrete steps, each step being completely determined by the machine's current *m*-configuration, the contents of its tape, and the square currently being scanned. A tabulation of all the possible configurations of a given Turing machine, together with a specification of the behaviour that follows from each configuration for each input, forms its 'machine table', which we now know as this kind of computer's *program*.

Following this analysis, the simplest kind of Turing machine is usually introduced and pictured as a physical device, consisting of:

A tape, indefinitely long in both directions, on which symbols are printed, divided into square frames of the same size, each of which can contain at any one time not more than one symbol,

and

a movable head that (a) prints discrete symbols, drawn from a finite alphabet, onto the tape, (b) erases one symbol at a time from the tape, and (c) reads, or identifies the contents of each square of the tape, one square at a time.

Anything that has this articulation, that is, a 'memory' for discrete symbols, and a way of serially accessing and changing its contents according to a program, counts as a Turing machine. So although Turing machines are often thought of as machines in the colloquial sense (physical devices whose parts operate according to the laws of mechanics), what's essential to them is their *functioning* or *operation*. Anything that operates *as* a Turing machine would *be* a Turing machine. In particular, a person who works like this to produce the results of computations would, by definition, be (operating as) a Turing machine.

Although the basic operations of a Turing machine form an extremely limited set, Turing claims that it includes 'all those which are used in the computation of a number' (Turing 1936–7: 118). So Turing machines are of interest because they illustrate what could be done by machines, in principle, given unlimited time and storage capacity.

One of Turing's most significant achievements, 'Turing's theorem', was a proof that there are Turing machines which can compute whatever any other Turing machine can compute. The devices whose conceivability it establishes, *universal* Turing machines, are of even more theoretical importance than special-purpose Turing machines. Turing realized that a coded description of any given Turing machine could be written onto a section of the tape of another such machine, which would then emulate the behaviour of the first machine, computing exactly what its progenitor would have computed when supplied with the same input. The possibility of universal Turing machines means that the 'engineering' problem, of making separate Turing machines for each kind of computational task, is replaced by what Turing later called 'the office work of "programming" the universal machine to do these jobs' (Turing 1948: 7). On the one hand, no physically existing computer can have the resources of a universal Turing machine (unlimited memory, perfect reliability, etc.). On the other, nobody would *use* such devices for computing, since their simple architectures make their operations far more unwieldy than any practical computing machine. Nevertheless, they are still thought of as prototypes, idealized models, of the kinds of digital computers we are familiar with, since these are computationally equivalent to Turing machines with finite tapes. Turing's idea of putting the program of a special-purpose machine into the memory of another, universal machine, the idea of a *stored-program computer*, was crucial in the development of contemporary machines.

The Church–Turing Thesis

But what exactly *can* Turing machines do? Here, controversy lurks. Turing more than once said that 'logical computing machines' (the term he later used for what we now call Turing machines) can do 'anything that could be described as "rule of thumb" or "purely mechanical"' (ibid.). Working independently and without knowledge of each other, Turing and Alonzo Church, the American logician who later supervised his Ph.D. thesis at Princeton, were both concerned with the concept of an effective or mechanical method, a notion used in mathematics to indicate a class of mathematical *functions* (or results, or problems) that can be computed (attained, solved) in a mechanical way ('by following fixed rules', as it's sometimes put). In late 1933, Church suggested identifying this informal notion with the mathematically precise concept of *lambda-definability*. His subsequent proof of the equivalence between this concept and the mathematical notion of a *recursive* function led to his first public identification of the effectively calculable functions with the recursive functions (this is now known as 'Church's thesis').

Around the same time, Turing independently presented another formally precise replacement for the concept of an effective or mechanical method: *computability by Turing machine*. He showed that, as long as we accept Turing's thesis, Hilbert's question is settled in the negative, proving that the predicate calculus is undecidable (i.e. that no Turing machine can determine, in a finite number of steps, whether or not an arbitrary formula of the calculus is provable). Turing delayed publication of his 1936 paper in order to show, in an appendix, that these two apparently different replacement concepts are actually equivalent (i.e. they pick out the very same set of mathematical functions). So the resulting *Church–Turing thesis* says that this set of recursive functions, those functions computable by Turing machines, contains every function whose values can be obtained by an effective or mechanical method.

Its denomination ('thesis') betrays the fact that, unlike Turing's *theorem*, the Church–Turing thesis isn't regarded as proven. However, the unforeseeable but proven equivalence of all existing attempts to analyse the notion of an effectively calculable function[2] is often regarded as strong evidence in its favour. Aside from this issue of its *status*, though, the exact *nature* of the thesis is also unclear. Is it a definition (and therefore a kind of convention, as Church himself thought), a proposal, or a conjecture? If the latter, as most commentators nowadays assume, is it a mathematical conjecture or an empirical one? Does the foundation of the concept of computability in human abilities mean that the thesis is intended to cover only phenomena in our physical world?

Even more important than the nature of the thesis, perhaps, is the matter of its implications. It's no exaggeration to say that the Church–Turing thesis has constituted the fundamental inspiration behind AI, the reason for thinking that electronic digital computers *must* be capable of (at least) human-level intelligence. Cognitive scientists have generally taken the Church–Turing thesis to mean that any function that can be computed can be computed by a Turing machine. This would mean that, as long as we ignore or abstract away from resource-limitations, anything the human brain can do (any function it can compute) could also be done (computed) by an electronic digital computer. Cognitive processes, no matter how intelligent, must be decomposable into routines whose primitive steps can all be executed by a machine.

---

[2] In terms of recursiveness, Turing computability, lambda-definability, Markov algorithm computability, etc.

The Turing Test

The computer age's first serious attempt to give a criterion for mentality and an important goal for AI forms the core of Turing's best-known paper. 'Computing Machinery and Intelligence' (Turing 1950) is surely the most famous, most widely read and reprinted, and the most influential article ever to have been published in a philosophy journal. The criterion Turing argued for involved the simulation of behaviour, specifically, linguistic behaviour. He called it the 'imitation game', but I shall refer to it as it's now known: the *Turing Test*. Because it's so well-known, a sketch will suffice here.

Turing famously rejected the question 'Can machines think?', deeming it 'too meaningless to deserve discussion' (Turing 1950: 442).[3] He therefore proposed to recast it as a question about a game in which a computer programmer has to render it impossible for a human 'interrogator' to tell, from typewritten output alone, whether that output is generated by a human or by a machine. Turing and his defenders then insist that if a machine cannot be distinguished from a human being under these conditions we must credit it with intelligence.

One of the more persistent complaints about the Test is that it is unacceptably *behaviouristic*, or that it proffers an *operational definition* of intelligent thought. Turing himself did subscribe to an account of learning which bears some hallmarks of psychological 'behaviourism'. According to such an approach to psychology, the discipline is suitably scientific only if it confines itself to the study of observable features of bodily motion, described in a restricted and colourless vocabulary. The heyday of psychological behaviourism preceded that of cognitive science, but the two bear an uneasy relationship to one another. Cognitive scientists think of themselves as having gone decisively beyond behaviourism by virtue of relinquishing its underlying conceptions of the mind, science, and psychological explanation. It would be ironic if their best test for mentality was in thrall to the view they thought of themselves as overthrowing.

In philosophy, behaviourism was the view that the meaning of statements about an organism's mental or psychological phenomena can be given wholly in terms of testable statements about its observable physical features and motions. This 'logical behaviourism' had important defenders from the 1930s to the 1950s, although it was challenged by, evolved towards, and was eventually

---

[3] Reprinted in Boden (1990: 49). From here referred to as B49. See, however, later remarks Turing made, recorded in Copeland (2000).

superseded in popularity by the materialist identity thesis, according to which minds are brains, and mental phenomena type-identical with neural phenomena. This view in its turn, however, had the limelight snatched from it by the perspective which still dominates the philosophy of mind: *functionalism*.

As for operational definitions, 'operationalism' is a philosophy of science according to which theoretical terms should be characterized in terms of the operations needed to verify that they apply. It's linked with behaviourist psychology because any psychological theory all of whose terms are defined in this way would perforce be acceptable to a behaviourist, since its terms would be characterized in terms of properties of, or relations between, stretches of observable phenomena. But the widespread view that Turing put forward, in the imitation game, an operational definition of thought or intelligence finds no support in what he actually said, and cannot be right, since such definitions state logically necessary and sufficient conditions of what they define, whereas Turing explicitly offered the Test as a sufficient condition only.

Turing Machine Functionalism

In the early 1960s, to skip ahead a little, the American philosopher Hilary Putnam, having already made contributions to the foundations of computer science in several papers on a form of Hilbert's decision problem and computational proof procedures for quantification theory, used the concept of a Turing machine (suitably liberalized) in order to state what came to be known as the *functionalist* view of the mind.

Functionalism is driven by the feeling that mentality is a matter of *functioning* rather than *substance*. Whether a creature is made out of carbon compounds, or (more generally) biological stuff, or (more generally still) even out of physical stuff (if there's any conceivable alternative) is of consequence only in so far as these substrates *constrain* their operation. What matters, as far as mentality goes, is not matter, what a thing is made of, but functioning, how the thing *works*, and what its *capacities* are. But functionalism, in this most general sense, is nowadays almost always accompanied by a naturalistic metaphysical thesis according to which mental phenomena are individuated in terms of their causal roles. From this derives the doctrine of *multiple realizability*, according to which mental phenomena can be credited to anything having states with the appropriate causal roles.

Since functionalism suggests that mental concepts are functional concepts, cognitive scientists explicitly or implicitly committed to some version of functionalism often suppose that *simulating* mental phenomena amounts to *duplicating* them. Specifically, if what's essential to mental phenomena is their causal roles, and if those roles can be simulated in computer programs, there's no reason why computers running those programs shouldn't be credited with the mental phenomena in question.

Putnam originally proposed an analogy between Turing machines and humans. Just as there are two possible descriptions of the behaviour of a given Turing machine: the *engineer's* structural description of its hardware, and the *logician's* or *computer scientist's* 'machine table' (what we would now call its *program*), so there are two possible descriptions of human psychology, the *physiological* description (corresponding to the engineer's structural description), and

a more abstract description of human mental processes, in terms of 'mental states' . . . and 'impressions' . . . —a description which would specify the laws controlling the order in which the states succeeded one another, and the relation to verbalization. This description, which would be the analogue of a 'machine table', it was in fact the program of classical psychology to provide! (Putnam 1960: 373)

But Putnam soon came to think that the correspondence between human and Turing machine was more than a mere analogy. By 1967 he was affirming that humans *are* what he called 'probabilistic automata'. (This differs from a Turing machine mainly in that the transitions between the configurations of a probabilistic automaton are allowed to differ in the probability that they will take place, rather than being deterministic.) Turing machine functionalism is then (roughly) the hypothesis that all systems capable of having any given psychological state are probabilistic automata.

Functionalists soon left behind this early form of their view, having been persuaded that humans, unlike probabilistic automata, can be in more than one (psychological) state, and can perform more than one (mental) operation, at a time. Crucial to this transition was the realization that a human mind couldn't be any kind of Turing machine because the *serial* processing that a single Turing machine is capable of cannot possibly reproduce, within the constraints provided by the human brain, the sorts of psychological abilities people display. Even fans of serial processing now insist that architectures comprising massively parallel *collections* of serial processors are needed. But a broader kind of functionalism according to which psychological states are individuated not just by their machine table states but by their causal connections with sensory inputs, with one another, and with behavioural outputs, has come to dominate the philosophy of mind and now lies at the heart of cognitive science.

Computationalism

Within contemporary cognitive science this perspective is closely associated with *computationalism*, whose most prominent and important philosophical champion is Jerry Fodor. He explicitly traces it back to Turing (although he sometimes warns readers that his history is idealized, not scholarly), and it's instructive to see how.

According to Fodor, cognitive science in general (and AI in particular) is primarily about *intelligent thought*. Central to its agenda are questions like 'How can people go from one true thought to another?', 'How can thought processes be *coherent*, or *intelligent*, or *rational*?'. Turing answered a related question, namely, 'Given that a state of an organism (or a system) has *semantic* features (e.g. truth), how could its state transitions preserve or respect those features?'. By doing so, he bequeathed to cognitive science not just *a* model but the *only* sensible model we have been able to come up with, of what intelligent (i.e. rational) thought processes could be. His model says that thought processes involve (perhaps even consist in) the computational transformation of mental representations. Mental representations are symbols, having both semantic and *syntactic* features. Thinking is essentially a matter of manipulating mental symbols. And *intelligent* or *rational* thought is a matter of *preserving truth* in inferences, moving from symbols (premises) to symbols (conclusions) in such a way that if one's premises are true, one's conclusions will also be true.

Turing, in providing a syntactical theory of computation, thereby provided a syntactical theory of intelligence. What he showed, according to Fodor, was how to construct a device (namely, a Turing machine) that can process symbols, purely in virtue of respecting their syntactic features, in a way that ensures that none of their semantic features will be violated. The state-transitions or processes of such a device can respect or preserve the 'content' of its states. For example, it can recognize (to put things loosely) that an inference from 'P & Q' to 'P' is valid (truth-preserving), regardless of what statements the component non-logical symbols stand for. And it does this by exploiting *parallels* between syntactic and semantic features. This is supposed to be the basic idea of the branch of logic known as *proof theory*, which deals with formal systems:

The basic question of cognitive science is, How could a mechanism be rational? The serious answer to that question is owing to Turing, namely: it could be rational by being a sort of proof-theoretic device, that is, by being a mechanism that has representational capacities—mental states that represent states of the world—and that can operate on these mental states by virtue of its syntactical properties. The basic idea in cognitive science is the idea of proof theory, that is, that you can simulate semantic relations—in particular, semantic relations among thoughts—by syntactical processes. That is what Turing suggested, and that is what we have all been doing in one or the other area of mental processing. (Fodor 1995: 88)

For this kind of cognitive science, then, human cognition is a brain process in which symbols (which have both syntactic and semantic features) are manipulated in virtue of their syntactic features (only). The semantic features ('content') of the symbols, although irrelevant to their processing, are nevertheless preserved by it.

Artificial Intelligence

Artificial intelligence, claims about which are the focus of the arguments discussed in this volume, began in earnest in the mid-1950s. An account of its history isn't practicable here,[4] so a quick sketch of its origins and development must suffice for our purposes.

Margaret Boden has plausibly traced the inception of AI to a 1943 paper by Warren McCulloch and Walter Pitts (McCulloch and Pitts 1943). Having proposed a 'correspondence' between the physiological relations among neurons and the logical relations among propositions, they showed that certain kinds of networks of artificial neurons can compute whatever functions a Turing machine can compute, and took this to be what they called a 'psychological justification' of the Church–Turing thesis. Since then, AI has mainly comprised two rather different (albeit intertwined) research programmes.

The founders of what is now thought of as the 'classical', 'symbolic' approach to AI, including John McCarthy, Herbert Simon and Allen Newell, and Marvin Minsky, were more familiar with, and influenced by, McCulloch's work than Turing's. Early research of this kind concentrated on a small number of problem-domains, and its working focus changed quite rapidly. Programs designed to prove theorems in areas of mathematics such as logic, geometry, and algebra rubbed shoulders with games-playing programs, devoted to draughts (checkers), chess, or card games such as bridge, and 'problem-solvers', programs which would address intellectual puzzles such as the 'towers of Hanoi', the 'bridges of

---

[4] For such accounts, see McCorduck (1979), Gardner (1985), Pratt (1987), and Boden (forthcoming).

Konigsberg', the 'travelling salesman', 'missionary and cannibals' cases, etc. Early AI research focused on such problems because, as the editors of the first major anthology of such research papers put it,

game situations provide problem environments which are relatively highly regular and well-defined, but which afford sufficient complexity in solution generation so that intelligence and symbolic reasoning skills play a crucial role. In short, game environ-ments are very useful task environments for studying the nature and structure of complex problem-solving processes. (Feigenbaum and Feldman 1963: 37)

Playing games, proving theorems, and solving problems are clearly examples of intelligent human activities. They also have the advantage of being tractable and manageably small domains.

Since the mid-1950s, however, AI programs have come to range over a field vastly greater than this. Problem-solving, itself now covering a far greater area, takes its place alongside vision, natural-language understanding, planning, 'machine learning', expert systems, and several other areas at the centre of this kind of AI.[5] But although these 'classical', 'symbolic' AI programs, designed to perform well on such activities, are of interestingly different kinds, they all deploy *representations* according to *rules*. The representations can be mathematical or language-like. The rules can be either *algorithms* (procedures guaranteed to give the right answer to the question posed) or *heuristics* (rule-of-thumb procedures which can narrow down the search-space). What such programs importantly share (for our purpose) is that they manipulate data-structures composed of *symbols* according to *instructions*.

Alongside these first steps in classical, symbolic AI ran another research programme, now known as *connectionism*.[6] Connectionist research investigates the properties of *neural networks*, which consist of large numbers of artificial neurons, small and very simple processing units, related to one another by connections whose excitatory or inhibitory 'weight', and whose threshold for firing, can be altered by the programmer. (The networks studied by McCulloch and Pitts are an early example.) In some ('local') connectionist networks each unit or 'node' is associated with a distinct symbol, but in the more interesting recent ones, symbolic information is thought of as being encoded in a distrib-uted way across collections of nodes. The ideas that form the background to this research were developed during the 1940s and 1950s by psychologists such as

---

[5] For an introduction, see Boden (1987).

[6] For introductions to the technical issues, see Wasserman (1989), Bishop (1997), and Haykin (1999). For the philosophical issues, see Bechtel and Abrahamsen (1999).

Donald Hebb, Karl Lashley, and Oliver Selfridge in a mathematical branch of their subject called *learning theory*.

The first computer simulation of a neural network was undertaken at the Massachusetts Institute of Technology in 1954. But the first important working networks were developed in the 1960s by Frank Rosenblatt, who showed how McCulloch–Pitts nets could be 'trained' to classify certain patterns as similar or distinct. The sorts of tasks networks excel at, such as pattern-recognition, pattern-completion, etc., contrast with those to which classical AI programs are usually put. Neural networks have been widely advertised as having some important similarities (of structure and operation) with brain components. But this isn't to say that the former are accurate models of the latter.

Boden sums up the influence of McCulloch and Pitts's 1943 paper thus:

> Their vision of implementing the 'logical calculus' influenced von Neumann in designing the digital computer, and inspired AI pioneers to attempt the formal modelling of thought. And their discussion of 'nervous activity' contributed to Hebb's psycho-physiological theory of cell-assemblies, and engendered various models of neural networks. . . . If 'nets' are thought of as approximations to real neural connectivities, then we have a broadly connectionist research-programme. Interpreted as highly abstract idealizations of neural activity, the prime focus being on binary logic rather than real cell-connectivities and thresholds, we have the digital information-processing typical of traditional AI. Both types of AI research were initiated as a result of McCulloch and Pitts's paper. (Boden 1990: 2–3)

Turing, as befits his heroic status, anticipated and laid foundations for *both* these research programmes. But his work on neural networks, although undertaken in 1947, was not published until more than twenty years later, and his role in the history of this kind of computation has only recently begun to be emphasized.[7] The advice he issued at the very end of his 1950 paper, that one ought to try both approaches ('abstract activities' such as chess, as well as providing a machine with sense-organs and educating it, like a child), although prescient, appears not to have been importantly influential on the founders of AI.

Conceptions and Claims of AI

There have always been at least two major conceptions of AI. The first, and more radical, saw it as the attempt to design and build machines which display a range

---

[7] See e.g. Leiber (1991), Proudfoot and Copeland (1994), Copeland and Proudfoot (1996).

of genuine psychological attributes: problem-solving, thinking, understanding, and reasoning, and perhaps ultimately even consciousness, feeling, and emotion. This seems to have been the official self-image of the AI project. According to the second, more modest conception, the aim was to enable machines to do things which, when humans do them, are counted as examples of these same psychological phenomena, but *without* the implication that the machines should be credited with the psychological attributes in question. At the centre of the mainstream cognitive science Searle discerns a theory of mind based on the first view of AI, according to which minds are really (certain kinds of) programs.

These two different conceptions are related to (but don't map exactly onto) one of Searle's best-known contributions to the debate, the distinction between 'Strong' and 'Weak' AI. These are not primarily (as some suppose) approaches to AI, nor ideas about how AI engineers should spend their time, but rather conceptions of the activity, the field, and its aims. Weak AI says simply that electronic digital computers are powerful instruments for helping us to model, and thereby understand, the mind. This is contested neither by the Chinese Room Argument, nor by Searle's later work.[8] In fact, he expresses enthusiasm for it (e.g. Searle 1982b: 57).

Searle's arguments are *not* aimed at rubbishing AI research, or those who carry it out. They are directed instead at a two-part claim *about* such research, the *Strong AI* thesis, which Searle originally formulated as saying that

(a) an appropriately programmed computer really would *have* (or be) a mind in the same sense that you or I have,

and

(b) its following the program(s) in question would explain its ability to do the psychological things it does.[9]

Strong AI, he also said, is 'a precise, well-defined thesis: mental processes are computational processes over formally defined elements' (Searle 1980a: 422 (B81).[10] It has been, in one form or another, an important part of the 'prose' of AI engineers, the accounts they generate in order to explain and justify what they do, both to those who provide its research funding, and to the wider

[8] However, as some commentators have noted, it's hard to see why 'Weak AI' deserves its name at all, since it ignores the possibility of genuine artificial intelligence (in electronic digital computers, at least). 'Weak AI' is better thought of as *cognitive simulation*.

[9] Later, Searle formulates (a) as 'all there is to having a mind is having an appropriately-programmed digital computer' (1987b: 295).

[10] In articles for the popular press (e.g. 1982a: 3, 1982b: 56), Searle sometimes characterizes Strong AI as a baggier group of theses.

public, via the media. (The extent to which this is true can partly be gauged from laypeople's reactions to AI projects.)

Strong AI, however, is something more than a thesis. It forms a sort of picture whose implications, if Searle is right, ramify within many different aspects of cognitive science. The Strong AI *thesis*, one might say, is by no means the only important matter to which Searle's arguments are supposed to pertain. Although he has gone to some lengths to clarify exactly what he takes the negative import of the CRA to be, he states it in rather different ways in different writings, and there is still unclarity about its scope. The first sections of Larry Hauser's chapter in this volume address this issue, taking Searle to task for the unclarity.

Examples of Strong AI

Ever since Searle's original paper, some have supposed that 'Strong AI' is a straw man, a position hardly anyone in the cognitive science community subscribes to, or has ever subscribed to. This is certainly not so. That it has indeed been held can be seen in careful theoretical statements, as well as in certain exuberant and unqualified predictions, made by the precursors and originators of AI. As far as Turing goes, his presentation of the imitation game implies that computers whose performance comes to be indistinguishable from that of humans (in this respect) should be counted as thinking things. Searle himself shows that the founders of AI all subscribe to Strong AI (Searle 1984: 29–30, 1987a: 210–11). Perhaps the centrepiece of Newell and Simon's theoretical work in AI is their 'Physical Symbol System Hypothesis', that 'the necessary and sufficient condition for a physical system to exhibit general intelligent action is that it be a physical symbol system' (Newell 1980: 170), that is, a machine that produces a changing collection of symbol-structures. In early 1956, Simon claimed that the two of them had just invented a thinking machine, and by 1957, they expressed their view that

[T]here are now in the world machines that think, that learn, and that create. Moreover, their ability to do these things is going to increase rapidly until—in a visible future—the range of problems they can handle will be coextensive with the range to which the human mind has been applied. (Simon and Newell 1958: 8)

Simon, in his chapter with Stuart Eisenstadt for this volume, resolutely maintains that genuine computer comprehension of natural language is not just empirically possible, but has been with us since 1972. Their chapter bears witness

that some cognitive scientists still prefer their terms to have operational definitions, and think that the right such definitions are what's needed to definitively
resolve the issue of which things can really have psychological properties.

Only a little contact with university departments of the core cognitive
sciences is necessary to testify to the ongoing prominence of Strong AI (among
both staff and students). Daniel Dennett, one of the most important contemporary philosophers of mind and cognitive science, explicitly identifies himself as one of its defenders. But *anyone* who *seriously* describes electronic digital
computers in psychological terms, or who proposes to replicate psychological
phenomena in such computers solely by programming them in appropriate
ways, is committed to Strong AI. Plenty of cognitive science literature is so
committed. Some important contemporary cognitive scientists subscribe to it
even in their more scholarly and less marketable productions, although it is
most manifest in recent popular books by authors such as Hans Moravec and
Ray Kurzweil. If you think you don't know of anyone who endorses Strong AI,
you haven't looked hard enough!

Searle, on the other hand, claims to have found an argument that undercuts
the idea that electronic digital computers (whether they run current AI programs, or *any* programs) can be said to exhibit any of the contested psychological capacities purely in virtue of their programs. Philosophers certainly have
no special insight into what technical tasks programmed machines might be
able to perform, or when. But they can have a say about how it makes sense to
characterize the abilities in question, especially when that characterization is
in non-technical terms, such as those we all use for mental phenomena. Like
anyone else they may, by using thought-experiments for example, establish or
refute theses about what is logically possible.

The Yale Programs

The AI lab at Yale University, having secured funding for visiting speakers from
the Sloan Foundation, invited Searle to speak to them about cognitive science.
Not knowing much about AI at the time, Searle bought a book recently written
by the head of the lab, Roger Schank, and his colleague from the Psychology
Department, Robert Abelson, in which they described what they called their
'story-understanding' programs.[11]

[11] From an interview with Searle conducted on 24 April 1999.

Schank and Abelson postulated certain theoretical entities which, they said, 'must form the basis of human memory organization' (Schank and Abelson 1977: 17). Human memory, they argued, is organized around *episodes*, personal experiences, and therefore must include a procedure for recognizing repeated or similar sequences. As an economy measure for storing episodes, they therefore proposed that 'when enough of them are alike they are remembered in terms of a standardized generalized episode which we will call a *script*' (ibid. 19, emphasis added):

A script is a structure that describes appropriate sequences of events in a particular context. A script is made up of slots and requirements about what can fill those slots. The structure is an interconnected whole, and what is in one slot affects what can be in another. Scripts handle stylized everyday situations. They are not subject to much change, nor do they provide the apparatus for handling totally novel situations. Thus, a script is a predetermined, stereotyped sequence of actions that defines a well-known situation. (Schank and Abelson 1977: 41)

The part of their work Searle focused on aimed to simulate and explain the human ability to understand stories. One of the notable facts about this is that people can answer questions about stories even when the correct answers to those questions aren't explicitly contained within the story itself. The Yale programs aimed to reproduce this ability (among others) using scripts which represent the sorts of information humans have about typical scenarios, to answer questions about the story they are given by referring to the appropriate representations.

Searle's Intervention: The Chinese Room

Before he got to Yale, Searle came up with a thought-experiment which he believed would show that no matter how good they were, programs like these could only ever simulate, but never duplicate, the psychological abilities in question.

Searle claims that nothing in his argument depends upon the details of the Yale programs, that it applies to *any* computer simulation of human mental phenomena. Although AI research isn't focused only on the simulation of *human* abilities (it isn't just 'Weak AI'—cognitive simulation), his idea is that the Yale programs are just the *kind* of things with which AI engineers hoped to construct machine intelligences. How fair is this?

Some commentators have complained that, even during the 1970s, many AI researchers were already unhappy with the assumption that language-understanding is self-standing, and had started paying more attention to the ways in which language is integrated with perception and action. Searle, as we shall see, has his own response to critics who insist that AI programs deal with the causal commerce between such domains. For the moment, he assumes that there is nothing untypical about the Yale programs. They may be relatively unsophisticated by today's standards, but they are not bad examples of AI programs. Much of the rest of AI is 'more of the same', and the Strong AI claim would be that machines running such programs (when perfected by reference to cognitive psychology, of course), really would *understand* the stories they manipulate, in the same sense in which you and I do.

Searle believed his thought-experiment shows such claims to be utterly false. Here it is, in his own words:

Suppose that I'm locked in a room and given a large batch of Chinese writing. Suppose furthermore (as is indeed the case) that I know no Chinese, either written or spoken, and that I'm not even confident that I could recognize Chinese writing as Chinese writing distinct from, say, Japanese writing or meaningless squiggles. To me, Chinese writing is just so many meaningless squiggles. Now suppose further that after this first batch of Chinese writing I am given a second batch of Chinese script together with a set of rules for correlating the second batch with the first batch. The rules are in English, and I understand these rules as well as any other native speaker of English. They enable me to correlate one set of formal symbols with another set of formal symbols, and all that 'formal' means here is that I can identify the symbols entirely by their shapes. Now suppose also that I am given a third batch of Chinese symbols together with some instructions, again in English, that enable me to correlate elements of this third batch with the first two batches, and these rules instruct me how to give back certain Chinese symbols with certain sorts of shapes in response to certain sorts of shapes given me in the third batch. Unknown to me, the people who are giving me all of these symbols call the first batch a 'script', they call the second batch a 'story', and they call the third batch 'questions'. Furthermore, they call the symbols I give them back in response to the third batch 'answers to the questions', and the set of rules in English that they gave me, they call the 'program'. Now just to complicate the story a little, imagine that these people also give me stories in English, which I understand, and they then ask me questions in English about these stories, and I give them back answers in English. Suppose also that after a while I get so good at following the instructions for manipulating the Chinese symbols and the programmers get so good at writing the programs that from the external point of view—that is, from the point of view of somebody outside the room in which I am locked—my answers to the questions are absolutely indistinguishable from those of native Chinese speakers. Nobody just looking at my answers can tell that I don't speak a word of Chinese. Let us also suppose that my answers to the English questions are, as they no doubt would be, indistinguishable from those of other native English speakers, for the simple reason that I am a native English speaker. From the external point of view—from the point of view of someone reading my 'answers'—the answers to the Chinese questions and the English questions are equally good. But in the Chinese case, unlike the English case, I produce the answers by manipulating uninterpreted formal symbols. As far as the Chinese is concerned, I simply behave like a computer; I perform computational operations on formally specified elements. For the purposes of the Chinese, I am simply an instantiation of the computer program. (Searle 1980a: 417–18 (B68–9)).

The central claims of Searle's original paper are clear. Something is a digital computer in virtue of performing computations. But computations alone cannot, in principle, give rise to genuine cognition. Computation being nothing but the manipulation of symbols in accordance with purely *formal* or syntactical rules, something that is only computing cannot be said to have access to or know or understand the '*content*', the *semantic* properties (meaning, interpretation) of the symbols it happens to be manipulating. For the computer, as it were, what it manipulates are 'just formal counters' (Searle 1982a: 4), not symbols. But it's a conceptual or logical truth that syntax is not sufficient for semantics. Computers therefore cannot be credited with *understanding* the rules they apparently follow, or the programs those rules compose, or the symbols they manipulate. In fact, their states entirely lack what philosophers call *intentionality*, 'the feature of certain mental states by which they are directed at or *about* objects and states of affairs in the world' (Searle 1980a: 424 n. 3 (B72), emphasis added). Computation, therefore, can neither be nor explain cognition. While something can *simulate* intelligent performances purely in virtue of performing computations, it cannot thus *duplicate* them.

What the Argument is Supposed to Target

At the very least, the Chinese Room immediately implies that one's own conscious awareness of one's linguistic ability is not captured merely by running the right programs, since the Room runs those, but neither it nor its inhabitant is *conscious of* being able to understand Chinese. But, arguably, you can't understand a language without knowing that you do so (a related joke: 'Can you speak German?' 'I don't know, I've never tried'). Some think this would be enough to show that AI cannot duplicate *all* important psychological phenomena. Others, like Hauser and Jack Copeland, detect here a pernicious Cartesian assumption about the incorrigibility of introspection, extended in an even more problematic way beyond the normal situations in which it is most plausible.

Regardless of this, Searle's aim is to crack a much bigger nut. The CRA focuses on language-understanding partly because to show that computers cannot *understand* would be to attack Strong AI 'on what its proponents take to be their strongest ground' (Searle 1980*b*: 453). Of all psychological concepts, the understanding of symbols (the symbols they themselves manipulate) is the one *most* plausibly attributed to electronic digital computers, the one partisans of Strong AI think most obviously can be ascribed to such devices.

Among AI engineers, especially, one quite often encounters the idea that the Chinese Room scenario is flawed because the program in question has not *learnt* to understand Chinese, and that this deficiency could be remedied by providing it with, or by substituting for it, a machine learning program (of the sort that Turing envisaged, or some more recent variant). This move will not work. Machine learning cannot rescue Strong AI from the CRA, since one could run an argument entirely parallel to the CRA focusing on learning, rather than understanding. Its conclusion, of course, would be that however good they may be at 'passing' Turing Tests relevant to learning, the machines in question don't *learn* anything. Any programs that can be run on Turing machines, 'any programs at any level at all' (Searle 1989*b*: 702), however embodied, and however they got there, are targeted by the Chinese Room Argument.

What is clear is that Searle never intended the argument to show anything as general as that machines cannot think (or understand, or have any genuine psychological capacities), that computers cannot think (etc.), or that there cannot be artificial thinking machines (artificial intelligence *proper?*). He is adamant that some machines *can* think (since people are machines, for example), that some computers can think (since we are computers), and allows that it may be possible to produce an artificial (man-made) thinking machine (Searle 1980*a*: 422 (B82)). Even if we understand the terms 'machine' and 'computer' in their contemporary and colloquial uses, in which people are contrasted with both machines and computers, Searle's argument doesn't seek to rule out the logical possibility that paradigm examples of computing machines (e.g. the PC on which I'm writing) might have psychological properties. The real focus of the CRA is *programs* (rather than whatever runs them), and it's best thought of as denying that anything could have any genuine psychological properties *solely in* *virtue of its running a program*. My PC could, as far as this argument is concerned, understand Chinese. But it couldn't do so in virtue of any program which AI engineers could make it run. Artificial Intelligence may be possible, but it cannot result solely from programming, however sophisticated.

This, however, already provides a large enough and important target. AI has changed since the 1950s, coming to conceive itself less as part of science and more as engineering. An increasing proportion of AI research is neither explicitly nor implicitly aimed at the goal which poorly informed philosophers sometimes suppose it *must* have, of producing an 'artificial mind' or brain. Indeed, concepts like that play a decreasingly important role in the prose and practice of AI. Nevertheless, plenty of AI research is still supposed to be about producing (rather than merely *simulating*) psychological phenomena on electronic digital computers just by programming them (even though AI engineers don't generally care whether their systems perform their tasks *in the same way* that intelligent creatures do). AI, even now, isn't *just* cognitive simulation.

The view which Hauser, Stevan Harnad, and Georges Rey here call *computationalism* or *the computer model of the mind*, which says that computation is both necessary and sufficient for cognition, because mental states are (solely) computational states, also falls within the target area (as does the related view Ned Block here identifies by the same term, that the brain is a digital computer). This forms the core of a wide research programme within cognitive science, the contemporary way of *doing* cognitive science, that Searle sometimes calls '*cognitivism*', according to which:

Thinking is processing information, but information processing is just symbol manipulation. Computers do symbol manipulation. So the best way to study thinking (or as [cognitivists] prefer to call it, 'cognition') is to study computational symbol-manipulating programs, whether they are in computers or in brains. (Searle 1984: 43)[12]

Hauser and Rey are particularly keen to show that Searle's arguments are ineffective against computationalism; Harnad agrees with Searle that his arguments do refute some forms of that view.

Versions of *functionalism* and the *representational theory of mind* according to which the mind is to the brain as computer program is to computer hardware also fall within the argument's sights. Searle sometimes identifies this analogy with, and sometimes treats it as a summary of, the thesis of Strong AI (Searle 1984: 28, 1987a: 210, 1987b: 295, 1990a: 20). Elsewhere he identifies it as 'the basic idea of the

---

[12] Unfortunately, at other times Searle calls the view that the brain is a digital computer 'cognitivism' (1990a: 122, 1992: 202).

computer model of the mind', implicit in Turing's 1950 paper, as well as announced and defended in many important textbooks and articles since (Searle 1990*b*: 21, 1992: 200). He thinks of Turing machine functionalism (at least) as a variant on a view which Putnam himself had already done his bit to discredit: behaviourism. (Behaviourism, of course, as if it needed any further refutation, is also within the sights of the CRA). The CRA is supposed to refute functionalism because the Room, if the programmers have got things right, not only *behaves* as if it understood Chinese, it *functions* (externally *and* internally) as if it does. And yet it doesn't understand. Rey stringently denies this, arguing that functionalism is in no way committed to the Turing Test, that it has resources far deeper than the behaviourism with which Searle misguidedly associates it, and that once one takes account of these, Searle himself might even count as a functionalist. He does, after all, accept (a non-computationalist version of) the representational theory of mind.

Against the Turing Test

One of the points at issue in the debate is the adequacy of the Turing Test, which Strong AI is widely supposed to use as its criterion of the mental.[13] Searle expresses what he takes to be the Strong AI view thus:

The conclusive proof of the presence of mental states and capacities is the ability of a system to pass the Turing test . . . If a system can convince a competent expert that it has mental states then it really has those mental states. If, for example, a machine could 'converse' with a native Chinese speaker in such a way as to convince the speaker that it understood Chinese then it would literally understand Chinese. (Searle 1982*a*: 3)

In this volume Roger Penrose, otherwise a fierce critic of Strong AI, argues in favour of accepting some form of the Turing Test on the grounds that only if we assume that the presence of mental phenomena is publicly detectable do we meet the appropriate standards of scientific objectivity. Whether as a core commitment of Strong AI, or just an optional extra, plenty of AI researchers, other cognitive scientists, and some of their philosophical cheerleaders do still seem to take something like the Turing Test as a sufficient condition of mentality.[14] By this I mean that whether or not they would explicitly agree that psychological phenomena are to be credited to anything which apparently

---

[13] Searle (1982*a,b*) explicitly treats the Turing Test as a component of Strong AI.
[14] For its most vigorous philosophical defence, see Dennett (1985) and Leiber (1991).

displays the appropriate linguistic skills, their practice betrays a readiness to credit them with such phenomena under just such conditions.

Searle thinks that this is totally wrong-headed. His argument can be presented as an attack on, and as embodying an alternative to, Turing's proposed sufficient condition for mentality.

He claims, first, that if the Turing Test is supposed to be not just a way of pragmatically avoiding philosophical discussion but a theoretically significant criterion of mental phenomena (such as intelligent thought), then the CRA refutes it (Searle 1982a: 5, 1987b: 295, 297, 1989a: 45, 1995b: 208). The case he makes reinforces the common complaint that the Test is behaviouristic (in the philosophical sense), casting doubt on its adequacy by insisting that 'there could be two "systems", both of which pass the Turing-test [for understanding], but only one of which understands' (Searle 1980a: 419 (B74)). His general diagnosis of the Test's failure is that it confuses epistemology with ontology: 'it makes a fundamental confusion between the way we would verify the presence of a mental phenomenon from the third person point of view [and] the actual first person existence of the phenomenon' (Searle 1989a: 45. See also Searle 1993b).

In this volume, Stevan Harnad agrees that the Room refutes the original Test under computationalist assumptions, but then goes on to investigate how much room for manoeuvre computationalists have. They might, he proposes, strengthen the Turing Test into something that would survive the CRA by requiring functional, or perhaps structural *and* functional, indistinguishability (instead of the mere linguistic indistinguishability of the original Test). But to require structural conditions would be to give up their doctrine that computational states are implementation-independent. Although Harnad thinks the CRA over-reaches itself in several ways, he also suggests that Searle's work has had a positive influence on cognitive science, helping to open up kinds of research which (unlike classical symbolic AI or connectionism) take the *embodiment* of minds seriously.

Terry Winograd, however, takes issue with Searle's entire conception of language, particularly of understanding. He complains that Searle is not entitled to claim that there are 'clear cases in which "understanding" literally applies and clear cases in which it does not apply' (Searle 1980a: 419 (B71)), and tries to show that the questions Searle raises simply don't permit of objective (right or wrong) answers. Winograd's central contention that Searle's question, 'Does the computer understand Chinese?' is meaningless when and because it has been removed from an appropriate context bears comparison with Turing's claim that the question 'Can a machine think?' is meaningless.

Searle's accusation that Strong AI and computationalism conflate ontology and epistemology also has implications for other views of the relation between the mind and behaviour. The Chinese Room scenario, after all, takes advantage of the fact that mere symbol-manipulation can in theory be used to simulate an enormous range of (perhaps even *all*) behavioural phenomena. It thereby suggests that our conception of the mental can be *entirely* divorced from our ways of telling what mental phenomena another being is undergoing, in Searle's words, that 'where the ontology—as opposed to the epistemology—of the mind is concerned behavior is, roughly speaking, irrelevant' (Searle 1993*b*). In this respect it parlays a traditional objection to behaviourism into an objection to anyone who thinks there is more than a purely contingent relationship between mental phenomena and behaviour.

Jeff Coulter and Wes Sharrock, by contrast, although agreeing with Searle over the bankruptcy of the Turing Test, diagnose the problem differently. For them the CRA shows, contrary to the Test, that the nature of a performance cannot be identified independently of the conditions of its production.

Second, Searle presents his argument not as a way of testing for any particular mental phenomenon, but as a way of testing theories of mind (1980*a*: 417 (B68)). Thought of thus, the experiment embodies the following general criterion of adequacy: given any theory of mind, ask yourself what it would be like if you yourself instantiated that theory, if your mind worked in the way the theory suggests. If the resulting mental world departs markedly from what you would experience, the theory in question has to be false.

It's difficult to see how such a criterion could be challenged at least when applied to *conscious* mental phenomena. If a theory fails to capture how things seem to a conscious subject, it has failed to capture the 'contents' of consciousness. In connection with this, Searle issues a general injunction always to 'insist on the first person point of view' (Searle 1980*b*: 451, 1982*c*: 346). Whether this is still thought of as problematic within cognitive science and its philosophy purely because of the residual behaviourism and operationalism Searle discerns there, or whether this injunction is itself methodologically inappropriate, or a philosophical liability, are some of the larger issues involved.

Initial Reservations

Certain misunderstandings of the Chinese Room scenario should be squashed from the outset.

That Searle cites only caricatures of rules of the very simplest kind (' "squiggle squiggle" is followed by "squoggle squoggle" ' (1980a: 419 (B73)), 'Reach into basket 1 and take out a squiggle-squiggle sign, and go put that over next to the squoggle-squoggle sign that you take from basket 2' (Searle 1987a: 213)), for example, is no objection. Even the most complex classical AI programs are concatenations of instructions of roughly this *kind*: they specify sequences of symbols or relationships between symbols which hold purely in virtue of their 'formal' or syntactic properties alone.

Some have complained that ordinary-language mental concepts such as understanding, in which the CRA is framed, are somehow not suitable to pose important questions to AI. But just as cognitive simulation aims to *simulate* everyday psychological phenomena such as story-understanding, so Strong AI conceives AI programs as means by which to *duplicate* (and thereby explain) such phenomena. They comprise the level of psychological abilities with which cognitive science ultimately has to make contact, if it's to explain what it claims to. Unless it can explain things *like* this, cognitive science hasn't got a subject-matter.

It has often been objected that Searle's scenario is unrealistic in other, important ways, for example, in its supposition that a human could possibly handwork the suite of programs that would undoubtedly be needed accurately to reproduce the performance of a native Chinese speaker in real time. The right response to this objection, I believe, is not that speed is irrelevant to how we ascribe psychological abilities such as intelligence. Rather, it is that the fact that the person in the room couldn't handwork the programs fast or reliably enough doesn't matter. Neither would it matter to Searle's response to the 'Systems Reply' (see below) if memorizing the programs in question turned out to be beyond human capacities. The Chinese Room is a thought-experiment, an investigation into what would follow if something thoroughly counterfactual were to be the case. But in this respect it doesn't differ from Einstein's request for us to imagine what we would observe if, *per impossibile*, we were riding on the front of a beam of light. In such scenarios, one is allowed to imagine what would happen if some contingent and variable limitations (such as the speed of human activity, the capacity of memory, and the reliability of operation) were idealized.[15]

What secures the relevance of Searle's scenario is the idea that any digital computer program could, 'in principle', be handworked in the way that the CRA demands. This is guaranteed by the fact that the person in the Chinese

---

[15] For serious philosophical reservations about thought-experiments, however, see Wilkes (1988).

Room has almost exactly the same resources Turing granted the human computer whose performance is modelled by what we now call 'Turing machines' (some sheets of paper, some very simple rules and instructions, and the wherewithal and means to follow them). To object, as some have, that the idealized version of Searle in the Chinese Room doesn't really constitute a computer, is to cut the ground from under Turing's original analysis of computation, and to jeopardize the basic concept of computer science. Criticisms of the CRA (along with new analyses of computation) must avoid implying that a person performing a computation is not really computing. If a Turing machine isn't an appropriate model of a human computing, such machines have nothing like the scientific importance currently attached to them. The beauty, as well as the import, of the CRA, is its close proximity not just to the Turing Test scenario, but also to the original explanation of a Turing machine. And the Chinese Room is no stronger an idealization than such a machine, since it abstracts from the human computer in much the same way (by ignoring limitations of speed, memory, and reliability, for example).

What is the Chinese Room *Argument*?

So far we've looked in an informal way at the Chinese Room scenario—the thought-experiment—and some of the conclusions Searle draws from it. As we shall see, Searle sets out the underlying *argument* against Strong AI and computationalism in different ways on different occasions. However, he never explicitly presents it as a piece of reasoning about the thought-experimental scenario. If it were presented thus, its premises would presumably be:

1. The person in the room has access only to the formal, syntactic features of the symbols he or she is presented with.
2. To understand the Chinese input, the person in the room would need access to the semantic features of those input symbols.
3. No set of formal or syntactical principles is sufficient for understanding.

But what exactly is this argument's conclusion? *If* the conclusion pertains only to the person in the room (if, for example, it's simply that the person in the room doesn't understand the Chinese input), then it's relevant to Strong AI only if that view makes a claim about the analogous part of a suitably programmed computer. It's often argued that Strong AI makes no such claim.

Exactly how is the Room supposed to be analogous to a computer? Searle says that when ensconced in the Chinese Room he 'simply behave[s] like a computer', is 'simply an instantiation of the computer program', that he *is* the computer and that he has 'everything that artificial intelligence can put into me by way of a program' (Searle 1980a: 418 (B69–70)).[16] The English-language rules constitute the computer program, and the first two batches of symbols the database to which the program has access.

However, some commentators, such as Ned Block and John Haugeland, urge that the person in the room is analogous not to the computer, as Searle usually claims, but *only* to its *central processing unit* (CPU), the executive part of the computer which controls and coordinates everything else happening in the machine. Haugeland, for example, argues here that Searle fails to apply his own proposed criterion for adequate theories of mind, asking himself only what it would be like to be *part of* the Chinese-understanding system, rather than the system itself. These commentators then remind us that Strong AI's claim is *not* about the CPU, but about the computer as a whole, the entire *system*. However if, as Copeland points out in what he calls the '*logical reply*', the Chinese Room Argument is supposed to pertain to the system as a whole, then although germane, it isn't watertight. It would then be of the form: 'No amount of symbol manipulation on the person's part will enable him to understand the Chinese input, therefore no amount of such manipulation will enable the wider system of which he is a part to understand that input' (Copeland 1993: 125).

Since the conclusion is about a system that isn't even referred to in the premises, *this* Chinese Room Argument (as it stands) must be logically invalid. It commits, as Haugeland puts it, a part–whole fallacy.

As I mentioned, Searle never presents the Chinese Room Argument in this way. In the abstract of his original 1980 article, he set it out as a derivation from axioms, thus:

(1) Intentionality in human beings (and animals) is a product of causal features of the brain.

(2) Instantiating a computer program is never by itself a sufficient condition of intentionality,

therefore

(3) The explanation of how the brain produces intentionality cannot be that it does so by instantiating a computer program.

---

[16] '*[N]o digital computer solely in virtue of its being a digital computer has anything that I don't have*' (Searle 1987a: 213; emphasis in original); '[N]o computer just by running the program has anything the man does not have' (Searle 1989: 45).

(1) is supposed to entail:

  (4) Any mechanism capable of producing intentionality must have causal powers equal to those of the brain.

(In more recent work, Searle explicitly says '*threshold* causal powers', since the brain may have more than is necessary to produce mentality. See e.g. Searle 1997: 158–9, 191, 202–3.) And from (2) and (4) is supposed to follow:

  (5) Any attempt literally to create intentionality artificially (strong AI) could not succeed just by designing programs but would have to duplicate the causal powers of the human brain. (Searle 1980a: 417, not reproduced in Boden)

The central argument of the original article, Searle tells us, is directed towards establishing axiom (2).

  Whenever he presents what he thinks of as the underlying CRA's abstract logical structure (Searle 1984: 39, 1987b: 296–7, 1990a: 21, 1989b: 703, 1997: 11–12, 109, 1999a: 39), however, or the *point* of the Chinese Room scenario (1991: 526), Searle always does so as follows:

  1. Programs are purely formal (syntactical).
  2. Minds (human ones, at least) have semantics, mental (i.e. semantic) contents.
  3. Syntax by itself is neither the same as, nor sufficient for, semantic content.

Therefore,

  4. Programs by themselves are not constitutive of nor sufficient for minds.

It's noteworthy that in such presentations of what we might call (following Searle, and Hauser 1997) 'the Brutally Simple argument', the Chinese Room scenario is said merely to *illustrate* or remind us of the truth of premise (3), rather than to constitute the argument against Strong AI. That so many commentators took the scenario to constitute (i.e. exhaust) the argument is why Searle felt able to say, in 1987:

[I]n all of the vast amount of literature that has grown up around the Chinese room argument, I cannot see that any of my critics have ever faced up to the sheer logical structure of the argument. Which of its axioms do they wish to deny? Which steps in the derivation do they wish to challenge? (1987b: 301)

  Whether treated as the argument underlying the Chinese Room scenario, as a streamlined reformulation of that argument, or as a separate though related piece of reasoning, the Brutally Simple argument does attract its own commentators. Dennett, perhaps the most determined critic of the Chinese Room Argument, has explicitly denied all three of its premises (Dennett 1987). In this volume, Copeland, Haugeland, and Hauser concern themselves explicitly with the Brutally Simple argument. Haugeland, for example, seeks to show that serious AI, while not committed to denying Searle's logical truth (that syntax is not sufficient for semantics), can respond to the CRA by denying that computer programs are *purely* syntactical. To do so, he outlines the conceptual foundations of AI in a way that takes account of the causal powers of programs and data.

The 'Systems Reply'

Copeland's 'logical reply' challenges only the logical validity of the Chinese Room Argument, and doesn't purport to take a stand on its conclusion. But it seems a short step to what Searle calls the 'Systems Reply', that although the person in the Room doesn't understand Chinese, the entire system comprising the Room and its contents does so. This is one of the replies to his Chinese Room scenario that Searle identified before publishing it, and then spent much of his original article responding to (thereby recapitulating, ironically?, the structure of Turing's 1950 paper).

Searle finds the Systems Reply deeply implausible, 'totally unmotivated' except by behaviourism and the question-begging Turing Test (Searle 1980a: 419 (B74), 1980b: 453, 1982c: 346), and thinks it a 'desperate move' on the part of the defender of Strong AI (1999a: 39). Whether this is so depends on the integrity of the analogy between the person in the Room and the computer: if the person is analogous only to the CPU (as Searle himself allows at one point (Searle 1987b: 297)), the Systems Reply, far from being a *reply* to the Chinese Room Argument, is actually what the defender of Strong AI was saying all along, and the original argument was misdirected. The cogency of Searle's argument then depends entirely on the success of the Systems Reply, or some such similar claim about the kind of thing which his opponents think is capable of understanding.

This means that Strong AI and Searle only really lock horns within his critique of the Systems Reply, which consists of several points. First, that the System has no more means of attaching meaning to, or interpreting, the Chinese symbols than the person in the Room had. It 'has a syntax but no semantics' (Searle 1982a: 5). To escape the feeling that the other elements of the System (ledgers, pieces of paper, walls, etc.) might matter in this respect, Searle urges that the person in the Room 'internalizes' these other elements (memorize the rules in the ledger, do all the calculations in his or her head, etc.) and works outdoors. Even so, Searle insists, he or she would still not understand Chinese. Secondly, Searle claims that it's wildly implausible to think that 'while a person doesn't understand Chinese, somehow the *conjunction* of that person and bits of paper might understand Chinese' (Searle 1980a: 419 (B73)), simply because the mere addition of the Room, and the pieces of paper with Chinese symbols and English instructions, can't possibly make the difference between understanding and not understanding. If the person alone doesn't understand Chinese, no amount of adding *these* kinds of things will turn the resulting conglomeration into something which does so. Thirdly, Searle urges that the Systems Reply has independently absurd consequences. By implying that 'all sorts of noncognitive subsystems [such as stomachs, livers, etc.] are going to turn out to be cognitive' (ibid. 420 (B74)) it stands convicted of being hopelessly over-liberal. (This is the familiar problem of *non-standard realizations*, often directed towards functionalism.)

Searle treats the first consideration as the decisive objection to the systems reply (e.g. Searle 1993b), but I find the second more persuasive. A person plus some pieces of paper and walls just *isn't the right kind of thing* to be a properly basic subject of mental phenomena. When we ascribe such phenomena to systems which include people as parts, which we sometimes do, either our ascriptions are not what Searle would call 'literal ascriptions of intrinsic intentionality' (1982c: 346), or the talk can always be 'cashed out' in terms of the mental phenomena exhibited by the people in question. Of course, systems can have important properties which none of their creature components have. But whether this is true of specifically *psychological* properties is another matter. Here, I think, defenders of the Systems Reply have been over-hasty. We could make the underlying principle explicit thus:

> If a system (not just a creature, but an arrangement in which one or more creatures is embedded) really exhibits some genuine psychological phenomenon ϕ, it does so only in virtue of one or more of its component creatures exhibiting ϕ.[17]

This secures the logical validity of the argument based directly on the Chinese Room scenario by adding a premise to the effect that if the person in the Room doesn't understand Chinese, the Room itself cannot do so either. The suggested

[17] A qualification must be added to allow for collective psychological phenomena, such as decisions, which result from compromises between the individual decisions attributable to the component creatures, but it isn't germane here.

principle fits with Searle's insistence that systems such as business corporations have no intrinsic mental phenomena other than those of their employees, officers, etc. (Searle 1982c: 346). I believe it also improves upon his well-known assertion that we're justified in making literal ascriptions of intentionality to things because they are (at least) 'made of similar stuff to ourselves' (Searle 1980a: 421 (B80)), i.e. because they have the same biochemistry. The relevant similarity is not so much in the stuff things are made of, but in the *kind* of things they are.

However, none of this will impress or help Searle, since he agrees with proponents of the Systems Reply in rejecting such principles. He explicitly denies, in an early reply to Dennett, that his objection to the Systems Reply is that a system can have no psychological properties not possessed by its subsystems (Searle 1982b: 57). And he (rashly, I think) flouts the principle in question when he insists that *brains* (as well as their owners) have psychological states (1980b: 451); brains, after all, aren't creatures.

The 'Robot Reply'

More natural than the Systems Reply, perhaps, as a reaction to the Chinese Room scenario, is the idea that there's no understanding there because there aren't the right kind of causal relations between the symbols in the program and the things they refer to. Within a computationalist framework this becomes the 'Robot Reply', according to which an appropriately programmed robot, in rich causal contact with its environment (capable of reacting to stimuli, negotiating terrain, and operating upon things) would indeed have genuine understanding (and other mental phenomena).

Searle responds, first, that this move concedes the falsity of Strong AI (and computationalism) because to insist that syntax plus external causation would produce semantics is to *admit* that syntax is insufficient for semantics (Searle 1987b: 297). Causal theories of 'content' that might be taken to relate the robot's states and activities to the meanings of the terms it uses have recently become popular in the philosophy of mind (Rey mentions these). But they run strongly counter to the sort of 'internalist' semantic theory that Searle advocates, since they all attempt to reduce semantic relations to non-intentional natural phenomena. Such attempts, he urges, will fall prey to a combination of common-sense and technical objections. Among the former are that they leave out the essence of mental content, which is *subjectivity*, that they leave out intentionality *itself*, and (most crucially, I suspect) that they leave out the *normative* dimension of intentional concepts (Searle 1992: 50–1). Intentionality, in short, is *irreducible*.

Secondly, Searle again presses the Chinese Room into service, appropriately modified, to show that adding robotic 'perceptual' and 'motor' capacities adds no understanding whatsoever to the original program. A person inside a computer inside a robot, after all, is still presented *only* with symbols to manipulate, and still has no way of coming to know what they mean. That the resulting arrangement would be far more impressive, in its behaviour, than a 'bed-ridden' computer, merely testifies to its being able to pass a more sophisticated kind of Turing Test. But Searle's point is that Turing Testing is *always* inadequate, since such tests always fall short of establishing the existence of genuine psychological phenomena. The Robot Reply, he concludes, 'had the wrong level of causation. The presence of input-output causation that would enable a robot to function in the world implies nothing whatever about the presence of bottom-up causation that would produce mental states' (Searle 1987*b*: 300).

In this volume, Selmer Bringsjord and Ron Noel pursue this issue in depth. They begin by responding, on Searle's behalf, to the modified Robot Reply favoured by Stevan Harnad, which sets the bar for simulation higher than the Turing Test. Harnad, they argue, follows Dennett in attempting to combine the Systems Reply with the Robot Reply. So they identify what they call the 'missing thought-experiment', a scenario which would combine Searle's responses to both. They approach this thought-experiment, which involves surgically blurring the distinction between people and robots, via computational simulations. Just as it is possible to produce behaviourally accurate simulations of simple animals which have been 'zombified' (rendered incapable of having sensory experience), Bringsjord and Noel argue, it's possible to imagine a scenario in which a person, implementing the parts and processes of a robot, behaves normally and yet has no experience at all.

The Brain Simulator Reply

Searle sprung his thought-experiment on the world of AI at a time when the 'classical' symbolic approach dominated the field. In the late 1970s and early 1980s, the other main kind of AI research, concerned with neural networks, was at a low ebb, at least partly because people had been convinced (by Minsky and Papert 1968) that the kinds of neural nets studied up until that time simply could not compute important functions. Nevertheless, Searle's original article discusses an objection this sort of research suggests.

Searle initially found it ironic that AI should start appealing to the workings of the brain in order to evade the Chinese Room Argument. As he put it, 'I thought the whole idea of strong AI is that we don't need to know how the brain works to know how the mind works' (Searle 1980a: 421 (B77)). But neural network research doesn't represent an alternative to 'Strong AI'. Rather, it has its own version of the Strong AI claim (connectionist Strong AI) according to which an appropriately configured and trained connectionist network would have (the relevant) genuine psychological properties, and would do so purely in virtue of its having the configuration and training in question.[18]

Searle isn't alone in thinking that even weak AI of the 'classical', symbolic kind can now, at the beginning of the twenty-first century, be judged to have failed (Searle 1995b, 205ff.). Some of his most determined computationalist opponents would agree. However, although more sympathetic to weak AI of the connectionist kind, Searle consistently deems the above sort of appeal to neural networks irrelevant, on the grounds that the computational power of neural networks is no stronger than that of Turing machines. We know from the Church–Turing thesis, he asserts, that 'any computation you can do on a parallel machine, you can also do on a classical machine' (Searle 1999a: 39, see also 1990a: 22, 1993b, and 1999b: 37), and therefore the original CRA applies. Recent developments in neural network research, following the important revival of connectionism in the mid-1980s, aren't supposed to affect this claim. The contemporary connectionist *style* of computation (massively parallel, featuring distributed 'representations'), he also urges, cuts no ice in this respect.

Copeland's chapter in this volume vigorously disputes this understanding of the Church–Turing thesis, even though Searle shares it with most cognitive scientists. Copeland also convicts Searle's attempt to extend the CRA to connectionism of what he calls the *simulation fallacy*, the fallacy of supposing that if x is a simulation of y and y has property Φ, x has property Φ.

However, in response to connectionist Strong AI Searle also, just in case, formulates the 'Chinese Gym' thought-experiment:

Imagine that instead of a Chinese room, I have a Chinese gym: a hall containing many monolingual, English-speaking men. These men would carry out the same operations as the nodes and synapses in a connectionist architecture . . . and the outcome would be the same as having one man manipulate symbols according to a rule book. No one in the gym speaks a word of Chinese, and there is no way for the system as a whole to learn

[18] The last clause here is needed to rule out appeals to non-computational (e.g. electro-chemical) properties of networks, which Searle allows might make the difference between duplicating and merely simulating mental phenomena (Searle 1993b).

the meanings of any Chinese words. Yet with appropriate adjustments, the system could give the correct answers to Chinese questions. (Searle 1990a: 22)

Copeland suggests not only that the logical reply is once again sufficient to refute this version of the argument, but that it also either commits the simulation fallacy or begs the question.

The broader underlying issues are also addressed here by neuroscientists. Igor Aleksander and John Taylor, although sympathetic to the original thrust of the CRA, both agree that recent neural modelling shows how to escape its clutches. According to them, a certain kind of inner experiential perspective which is a necessary precondition for genuine computer understanding is now within reach. Aleksander examines the way in which neural modelling bears on whether there could be a computational form of intentionality. He argues that special, emergent representations ('neural depictions'), developed in the context of a recent research programme on artificial consciousness, not only capture ego-centred experience of the world, but may also have an emergent intentionality. Taylor, meanwhile, seeks to expound the kind of semantics which might be used by the brain. Invoking evidence from functional brain imaging and deficit disorders, he suggests a neural model of language-processing within the frontal lobes in which semantic relations figure as 'virtual actions', residues of previously taken bodily movements. A virtual action-based semantics, in Taylor's view, leads to the possibility of meaning being attached to the computer's symbolic representations of external objects, and thus shows, he argues, that the CRA's challenge can now be answered.

Syntax and Semantics

A large part of the power of the Chinese Room Argument derives from its being premised on a distinction from linguistics which lies near the heart of contemporary cognitive science, between *syntax* and *semantics*, syntactic and semantic features or properties. Thinkers from outside computational cognitive science, such as some followers of Wittgenstein, have occasionally tried to challenge the integrity of this distinction. But that move isn't available to computationalists.

It's impossible to overestimate how much Searle wants to wield, and rely on, this distinction.[19] Many of his replies to critics of the CRA involve him repeating

---

[19] In the original article, though, the terms 'syntax' and 'semantics' appear infrequently, and only in the final sections, since the point is put there largely in terms of the distinction between form and content.

his fundamental challenge: neither the person in the Room, nor the programmed electronic digital computer, nor the system comprising the entire Chinese Room arrangement, nor a robot incorporating the Chinese understanding program and interacting causally with appropriate things in its environment have any way of attaching meanings *to* the symbols they are manipulating, or any way of finding (rather than just hallucinating) the meaning *in* those symbols. 'Formal symbols by themselves can never be enough for mental contents, because the symbols, by definition, have no meaning (or interpretation, or semantics) except insofar as someone outside the system gives it to them' (Searle 1989*a*: 45). The only meanings that the symbols in the program have is given to them by something (namely, someone) *outside* the system. Someone *inside* simply has access only to the syntax, and no way of 'getting from' the syntax to the semantics.[20]

What Searle does with the distinction, as we've seen, is to use the Chinese Room scenario to remind us of what he calls a 'very simple logical truth, namely, syntax is not sufficient for semantics' (Searle 1984: 34, 39, 1987*a*: 231, 1987*b*: 296, 1989*a*: 45, 1989*b*: 701, 1990*b*: 21, 1992: 200, 1993*a*: 15, 1997: 12).

Nothing in Searle's arguments is supposed to depend on the present state of computer technology. This derives from the fact that they pertain to what it is to be a digital computer, its original *definition*. And this, of course, is the Universal Turing machine. Turing machines are precisely what Searle has in mind when he writes: 'Digital computer programs by definition consist of sets of purely formal operations on formally specified symbols. The ideal computer does such things as print a 0 on the tape, move one square to the left, erase a 1, move back to the right, etc.' (Searle 1982*a*: 4). Digital computers, on this conception, are by definition symbol-manipulating devices (1990*a*: 20). Computers can be said to manipulate symbols, but the symbols 'have no meaning; they have no semantic content; they are not about anything' (1984: 31). They have to be specified purely in terms of their formal or syntactical structure. The operation of computers can, by definition, be specified purely formally, in terms of abstract symbols (1984: 30). A digital computer is 'a device which manipulates symbols, without

---

[20] Sometimes Searle writes as if the symbols do have meanings, but they can't be accessed by the person in the room. At other times he says that they have no meanings at all (e.g. when he says that while in the Room he doesn't understand Chinese because 'the entire system, me, symbols, rule books, room, etc., contain only Chinese symbolic devices but no meanings' (Searle 1989*a*: 45)). I take it that this isn't a vacillation: the underlying view is that the symbols have meaning, but only in so far as someone outside the system gives them meaning, and that without going outside the system, it's impossible to work out their meanings. (What on earth would a meaningless symbol be, anyway?)

any reference to their meaning or interpretation' (1989a: 45). Likewise, computer *programs*, by definition, are 'purely formal and abstract sets of rules for manipulating symbols' (1989a: 45), entirely defined by their formal or syntactical structure. The distinction between formal symbols and semantics, manipulation of syntactical elements and meanings 'applies at every level of program implementation' (1989b: 703).

Hauser, however, challenges Searle on the grounds that although programs are purely syntactic, the *processes* in which they run are not. Could Searle have failed to take into account the fact that program runs have (causal and dynamic) properties that inert programs don't? This raises a problem about the transition from the Chinese Room *scenario* to the Chinese Room *argument* that's supposed to represent it. The scenario, of course, involves *running* a program (by hand). But does the first premise of the 'Brutally Simple' argument survive if we focus on running programs, rather than inert ones?

Intentionality and the Brain: Searle's 'Biological Naturalism'

According to computationalists, Turing solved the problem of rationality (or intelligence) by showing how, given states which have both syntactic and semantic features, minds could process them in virtue of the former in a way that doesn't mangle the latter. Turing did not, however, ask (let alone answer) the question 'What is it for a state (physical or mental) of an organism or device to *have* semantic features?'. Turing's idea doesn't address this, the problem of *intentionality*, but it isn't supposed to.

The problem of intentionality, however, is precisely where Searle's main interest lies. In contrast to digital computers as Searle presents them, you and I do have ways of attaching meanings to, of discovering the meaning in, and of understanding, the symbols we use (in thought or language). We have access to both syntax *and* semantics. '[W]e know from our own experience that the mind has something more going on in it than the manipulation of formal symbols; minds have contents' (Searle 1997: 10). 'By virtue of their content', says Searle, our thoughts, perceptions, understandings, etc. 'can be about objects and states of affairs in the world' (1990a: 21). We know that the symbols we use *are* symbols, that their purpose is to represent, and we know their meanings. The mental, semantic 'contents' the mind has are 'biologically produced by the brain' (1990a: 24).

This brings us to a large topic, Searle's own positive theory of mental phenomena, which he calls '*biological naturalism*', and which has been no less controversial than his negative arguments. Its major theme is that mental phenomena are *biological* phenomena (1987*a*: 217). Searle applies biological naturalism principally to consciousness, which has been the focus of his more recent work. In this volume Penrose, and Coulter and Sharrock dispute his idea that consciousness is a biological phenomenon.

Biological naturalism is founded on the idea that the relation between mental phenomena and brains is best understood on analogy with that between microstructural features and the macrostructures they are features of. Water, for example, consists of micro-particles, molecules of H_2O. These have a certain limited range of properties, like weight, dimension, chemical valence, etc., and also stand to one another in a limited range of relationships. But the objects these micro-particles compose, physical 'systems' such as particular bodies of water, also have 'surface' or 'global' properties such as liquidity, solidity, and transparency (sometimes called 'emergent properties'). Such surface or global properties, according to Searle, can be causally explained by the behaviour of elements at the micro-level. So the liquidity of a particular glass of water is supposed to be explained by the structure of and interactions between the H_2O molecules of which it is composed. In short: micro-properties can (sometimes) cause macro-properties, and when they do, they also causally explain those macro-properties.

Searle's idea is that the relationship between micro-properties and macro-properties serves as a good model for the mind–brain relation, and thus dispels some of the mystery in the mind–body problem. (Not all of it, because he also thinks purely natural physical phenomena are themselves pretty mysterious.) His doctrine on the mind–body problem is thus that mental phenomena are both *caused by* brain processes and '*realized in*' the physical system we call the brain. This is what allows mental phenomena to enter into causal relations with other physical phenomena. Properties like consciousness are (emergent) properties of brains (macro-level objects), not of their micro-level constituents (particular neurons, or anything smaller, like molecules). (This is one reason why it's important to Searle to be able to attribute psychological phenomena to brains, rather than just to people.) Individual neurons aren't themselves conscious. Nevertheless, consciousness is caused by the operations of neurons, the component parts which brains are (partly) made of.

Searle's conception of intentionality as a *biological* property concerns several contributors to this volume. Alison Adam's paper directly addresses his use of the concept of intentionality to distinguish genuine from counterfeit minds. Invoking the work of anthropologist Mary Douglas, Adam interprets Searle's use of the distinction as a vestige of a problematic picture of the status of humans, our relation to nature, and the deeply valued boundary between us and machines. She seeks, instead, to guide us beyond the antagonism between philosophy and AI which arguments such as the CRA seem to have generated, as well as beyond the existing spectrum of options on the relationship between humans and machines. In order to do so, she appeals to recent research in social science (actor-network theory) and feminist thought (Donna Haraway's 'cyborg feminism'), which blur the boundary in question.

Adam's constructivist approach to social reality contrasts vividly with Searle's own writings on these topics (Searle 1995a), but has something in common with Kevin Warwick's claim, in this volume, that arguments like Searle's must involve species-bias. Warwick, at the forefront of research on cyborgs, has first-person experience of an interface between human tissues and silicon-based electronic computational devices, and is keen to erase any suggestion of a boundary between humans and machines. Taking Searle to deny the possibility of computer-controlled conscious robots, he argues that the CRA's attack on computer understanding can be rebutted if the machines in question can be given consciousness. Using Searle's own premise that consciousness is a feature of the brain, he suggests that there is a continuum of consciousnesses, that different kinds of brains have different kinds of consciousness, and that neither simulated silicon brains nor artificial neural networks can be denied consciousness of some kind. He then seeks to show that computers can indeed be conscious, deploying something like an operational definition of that term, claiming that humans are programmed too, in their genes, and appealing to 'machine learning'. For Warwick, Searle's suggestions that creatures with brains are special because of their *biology* is not to the point, since certain kinds of existing robots are already 'non-biological' living things.

Coulter and Sharrock, while finding merit in the CRA, also take serious issue with Searle's theory of intentionality (in part following work by other commentators of a Wittgensteinian orientation (e.g. Malcolm 1991, Hacker 1992)), particularly with his view of how language is dependent on the mind. Searle's theory issues in problems such as how minds impose intentionality on linguistic entities that aren't intrinsically intentional, and how one 'attaches' meanings to the words going through one's mind. These, Coulter and Sharrock argue, are pseudo-problems, deriving entirely from Searle's overly mentalistic renditions of concepts such as meaning and understanding. They return to

Searle's theory of speech acts (Searle 1969) in order to critically evaluate the foundations of his approach to language.

Diane Proudfoot, meanwhile, investigates resemblances between the CRA and Wittgenstein's own remarks on cognition (some of which were spurred by dialogue with Turing). Despite agreement between Wittgenstein and Searle that symbol-manipulation is insufficient for, and hence cannot constitute, understanding, and that computing machines don't genuinely follow rules, Proudfoot argues that Wittgenstein's perspective provides persuasive objections to the CRA, and to the model of mind underlying it. Like Hauser, she finds Searle making an illicit appeal to 'first-person authority' to decide whether he understands Chinese. But Proudfoot also argues that Wittgenstein's later work has something more positive to offer: a perspective which has more in common with contemporary philosophy of mind, and with new developments in cognitive science.

Searle's New Foundation for Cognitive Science

Searle suggests that cognitive science should begin not from the morass of computationalism, even devotees of which can't agree about their foundational concepts, but from things we already *know* about how the world works. Among these are things that few but the most determined philosophical sceptics deny, such that 'we all really do have mental states and processes', that they are intrinsic to us, and not merely a matter of how others choose to treat us, and that many of these states and processes are intentional (Searle 1993*b*). But as well as these unproblematic theses, Searle supposes that we also now know that brains cause minds, and that brain operations of the right kind are *sufficient for* mental phenomena (that is, for '*pure*' mental phenomena, the ones picked out by non-factive verbs):

To put it crudely, and counting the rest of the nervous system as part of the brain for the purposes of this discussion, everything that matters for our mental life, all our thoughts and feelings are caused by processes inside the brain. As far as the causation of mental states is concerned, the crucial step is the one that goes on inside the head, and not the external stimulus. And the argument for this is simply that if the events outside the brain occurred but caused nothing in the brain, there would be no mental events, *whereas if the events in the brain occurred the mental events would occur even if there were not an outside stimulus.* (Searle 1987*a*: 222, emphasis added)

This is what Searle calls the *principle of neurophysiological sufficiency* (ibid. 229).

Although widely misrepresented as believing otherwise, Searle allows that having a working organic brain may not be necessary for having a mind (1997: 131, 203). All we can say is that it's a causal precondition for having a mind *as far as we now know*. But does a working brain constitute a mind, and is having certain things go on in a brain sufficient for having mental phenomena? I think the answers to these questions may not be as obvious as Searle suggests. Plenty of contemporary philosophers are convinced that brain events are necessary but not sufficient for important intentional mental phenomena. Most of them (the 'externalists') insist that what's also needed is an appropriate relationship between the brain and the world external to it. Searle's determined 'internalism', epitomized by his insistence that a brain in a vat could have the very same pure mental phenomena as an embodied and socially situated person (Searle 1983: 230), constitutes, to my mind, one of the most problematic aspects of his views.[21]

Computers Don't Follow Rules At All?

The CRA grants the computationalist premise that computer programs can be characterized in terms of syntactic properties (or, equivalently, that computers follow syntactic rules). A more radical option is to deny that computers follow any rules at all. This path, taken by certain thinkers influenced by the later work of Wittgenstein, elicits agreement or sympathy in this volume from Coulter and Sharrock, Proudfoot, and Mark Bishop.

One of its basic points is that even the simplest rule-following operations require agents capable of exhibiting the capacities characteristic of normativity: they must *understand* the rules being followed, be capable of *explaining*, *justifying*, and *correcting* what they (and others) do by reference to the rules in question. As a result, Turing was wrong in thinking that the primitive operations of a Turing machine are truly *mechanical* in the sense that they presuppose no intelligent agent for their execution. Perhaps this is what Wittgenstein meant by insisting that Turing machines are '*humans* who calculate' (Wittgenstein 1980, § 1096).

One way of developing this viewpoint, pursued by Peter Hacker and Stuart Shanker,[22] issues in the claim that Turing (and his followers) profoundly mis-characterized his own achievement. Contrary to the computationalist view, what Turing really did was to design a way of producing the output to

---

[21] See e.g. Glock and Preston (1995).
[22] See e.g. Hacker (1990, ch. IV) and Shanker (1998).

processes which previously required intelligence *without* their using any intelligence at all. If this is right, we have to take seriously the possibility that what AI engineers are really doing, and the conclusions they are really establishing, are not very much like what they *say* they are doing and establishing. They should be taken as showing how it's possible to design artefacts and get people to treat them as really performing tasks which they merely *appear* to be performing. As a result, when we credit computers with certain achievements, the concepts in question are not used in the same sense as that in which they apply to humans.

Searle doesn't consistently endorse this line of reasoning. For him, computers can indeed be literally credited with performing *some* of the tasks we naturally think of them as performing, even when those tasks are psychological: 'Just by manipulating meaningless symbols the computer can prove theorems, win chess games, and form new hypotheses' (Searle 1989*a*: 45).[23] In fact, he dismisses Wittgenstein's later work as 'part of a larger tradition of seeking behaviouralistic or quasi-behaviouralistic analyses of mental concepts', whose efforts are 'doomed to failure' (Searle 1987*a*: 231). His own views do make contact with this tradition, though, in his claim that the kind of intentionality that computers (and certain other systems) apparently display is not the kind which humans exhibit. Coulter and Sharrock's claim that intentional terms are used in different (but not metaphorical) senses when applied to humans and to machines bears comparison both with the closely related view of Searle, and with Hauser's critique of it. Hauser appeals to linguistics to show that such uses of psychological concepts aren't ambiguous, but are being given a strict and literal application. Searle's distinction between intrinsic intentionality and as-if intentionality (which isn't intentionality at all), Hauser suggests, is inferior to H. P. Grice's important distinction between natural and non-natural meaning, which supports attributions of ambiguity in the right cases, but not in the cases Searle and the Wittgensteinians claim to detect.

Searle's Trivialization and Observer-Dependence Arguments

More recently, Searle has moved closer to this Wittgensteinian view. Since the inception of the debate, his only major change of mind on the issues consists in his withdrawal, a decade after his original paper, of the assumption that

---

[23] In fact, in more recent writings (e.g. 1999*b*: 36) Searle questions whether, for example, IBM's 'Deep Blue' really plays chess.

computers follow syntactic rules. In later work he presents other arguments which, while still resting on the syntax/semantics distinction, concede less to Strong AI and computationalism than the Chinese Room.

He argues, first, that it's clear from the original definition of the kind of computation that machines are supposed to perform that

(1) For any object there is some description of that object such that under that description the object is a digital computer,

and that

(2) For any program there is some sufficiently complex object such that there is some description of the object under which it is implementing the program. (Searle 1990*b*: 26–7, 1992: 208)

The phenomenon of 'multiple realizability' beloved of computationalists and functionalists, turns into a *universal* realizability which trivializes their doctrines.

Ironically, Putnam, the founder of Turing machine functionalism, had already argued that computational descriptions are too cheap ('*everything has every functional organization*' (Putnam 1988, p. xv; emphasis in original), taking this to mean that functionalism would imply behaviourism (ibid. 121–5)). Searle's trivialization argument has been addressed most vigorously by Copeland and by David Chalmers (Copeland 1996, Chalmers 1996*a*, 1996*b*). In this volume, the issue is pursued by Block, Haugeland, and Rey, who criticize Searle's argument, and by Bishop, who seeks to reinstate Putnam's triviality proof in the face of Chalmers's critique, arguing that Strong AI implies a fanciful and unacceptable panpsychism.

What Searle means by 'the original definition of computation' is simply Turing's specification, in his 1936 paper, of what we now call Turing machines. Searle proposes to return to this because he finds very little agreement among contemporary cognitive scientists on fundamental questions about computation. That specification talks about the machine's elementary operations, which include the ability to print a '0' or a '1' in each square of its indefinitely long tape. (That any Turing machine program can be stated in terms of this set of symbols is perhaps what tempts some to think that computers use binary arithmetic.) But, as Searle points out, these 0's and 1's are not to be thought of as physical inhabitants of the computer: one wouldn't find them if one opened the machine up: 'To find out if an object is really a digital computer, it turns out that we do not actually have to look for 0's and 1's, etc.; rather we just have to look for something that we could *treat as* or *count as* or *could be used to* function as 0's and 1's.' (Searle 1990*b*: 25, 1992: 206).

If Searle is right about this, almost *anything* counts as a digital computer, since anything can be treated as 'running a program' (no matter how simple) consisting of 0's and 1's. Computationalists can accept this. For them, what matters is whether anything with the necessary structure can be treated as running *any* program. If almost any process can count as almost any computation, then the computationalist view of cognition, instead of being the interesting (and empirical) hypothesis its advocates intend, is vacuous. Rather than being a substantial, informative answer to the question 'How does the brain (or the mind) work?', an answer which would pick out some *observer-independent* fact about brains which specifies what processes take place within, the computationalist answer would become trivial. Likewise, to say of a complicated enough system that it's running a particular program would be empty, since such a system will be treatable as if it's running *any* program (compatible with its level of complication). Cognition will be computation simply because almost any process is computational.

According to Searle, all this is a consequence of the deeper point that, as he puts it, *syntax is not intrinsic to physics*. In other words, 'syntax' is not the name of a physical feature or property: 'the ascription of syntactical properties is always *relative to* an agent or observer who treats certain physical phenomena as syntactical' (Searle 1990*b*: 26, 1992: 208; emphasis added); '[s]omething is a symbol only relative to some observer, user, or agent who assigns a symbolic interpretation to it' (Searle 1993*a*: 16, see also 1995*b*: 209–10). We might be able to tighten up the original definition of computation, probably by imposing some *causal* conditions, in order to block the inference to universal realizability. However, Searle says, 'these further restrictions on the definition of computation are no help in the present discussion because the really deep problem is that syntax is essentially an *observer-relative* notion' (Searle 1990*b*: 27, 1992: 209, emphasis added).

Perhaps this is best treated as a second new argument. The idea is that computation is defined in terms of syntax, but syntax is observer-dependent, so computation is observer-dependent too. It can therefore never suffice for semantics, since whether or not a state has a given semantic 'content' is one of its observer-independent or 'intrinsic' features. Therefore, there's no prospect of our ever 'discovering' that something (be it a brain, a mind, or anything else) is a machine carrying out computations *independently of someone's having assigned it such a role*. This new argument concedes less to computationalism than the CRA, since it implies that computationalism doesn't even succeed in being false, but rather is incoherent, having no clear sense (Searle 1993*a*: 15, 1995*b*: 205, 1997: 14). Whereas the CRA, if successful, shows that computation isn't sufficient for cognition, the new argument is supposed to show that it cannot be necessary, either.

This argument from observer-dependence here exercises Block, who responds that the observer-dependence in question is far more limited than Searle thinks, Rey, who urges that the argument is a *non sequitur*, Haugeland, Penrose, and Coulter and Sharrock. Haugeland and Penrose argue forcefully that syntax and computability (respectively) are not observer-dependent. According to Rey, Searle misunderstands the computationalist project, conflating it with extraneous claims that any serious defender of it should reject. Coulter and Sharrock, though, seek to impugn Searle's distinction between the intrinsic and the observer-dependent, discerning there a failure to recognize that functional properties are indeed intrinsic.

Looking Forward: Hypercomputation, Non-computability, and Dynamical Systems

Just how far into the existing and future technology are Searle's arguments supposed to reach? They purport to cover any formal symbol-manipulation system, that is, anything whose operations can be run (rather than just simulated) on a digital computer. As we have seen, Searle already explicitly argued that a modified version of the CRA, the Chinese Gym, covers neural networks and parallel distributed processing.

What about even later developments? In recent years, new kinds of computers (some of which, nevertheless, Turing may have had inklings of) and new kinds of computational environments have come to be thought of as logically or even physically possible. It has been argued, for example, that certain kinds of hyper-computers or 'super-Turing' computers could compute functions which Turing machines can't, and that even Turing machines can compute such functions when embedded within certain kinds of relativistic space-times (Hogarth 1994).

In recent work (e.g. Copeland 1996), Jack Copeland has suggested and explained ways in which the Church–Turing thesis has been mis-stated or misunderstood. In his chapter for this volume, he makes further contributions to this project, germane to Searle's own complaint that cognitive scientists have failed to explain why and how they take such technical results and theses within computability theory to be relevant to questions of how brains work, as well as to questions of how electronic digital computers do so, and whether and how they might constitute or give rise to minds (Searle 1990b: 22, 24; 1992: 205). Copeland's work, however, suggests that there may be kinds of computers which exceed the computational power of human beings, in virtue of using operations that no human being, unaided by machinery, can perform. If there could be such devices, whose programs could not possibly be handworked within the Chinese Room, the CRA, even if sound, would be powerless to refute the claim that the human brain is such a device.

Copeland's views make a vivid contrast with those of Roger Penrose. Although he thinks the original Chinese Room Argument has considerable force against computationalism, Penrose finds Searle too ready to accept the reigning orthodoxy that brains are digital computers (on the grounds that '*everything* is a digital computer'). He famously prefers, as more rigorous than the CRA, an argument from Gödel's theorem, according to which in any formal system there are statements which mathematicians can see are true and yet which cannot be proved true by any computational reasoning within that system. He regards the argument as establishing that there must be *non-computable* neural processes, processes that cannot even be simulated by a Turing machine, underlying human mathematical understanding. This means he opposes Searle over *Weak* AI. Penrose speculates that such processes may take place at the problematic and badly understood borderline between classical and quantum physics and, in particular, that non-computable processes underlying consciousness may take place at the sub-cellular level. The final section of his chapter continues a debate about consciousness that he and Searle have been engaged in for several years.

Another important way of dissenting from the orthodoxy in AI and cognitive science, the *dynamical systems approach* to cognition, is the subject of Michael Wheeler's chapter. The questions which exercise him concern the relation between this approach and Searle's argument, and whether the former provides new insights into the latter. Wheeler's paper includes a vivid introduction to the new approach, characterizing dynamical systems, setting out basic concepts of dynamical systems analysis, and suggesting how dynamical systems research might be conducted. It then tackles the question of the relationship between dynamical and computational systems (defined in terms of the Turing machine paradigm), showing that the latter set is contained within, but by no means exhausts, the former. However, since the difference between these two sorts of systems pertains to the role of *time*, the Chinese Room Argument still applies to dynamical systems, because they are specified in purely *formal* (non-semantic) terms, and the CRA's conclusion is that no such process is sufficient for mentality. Searle could, as Wheeler points out, construct a new version of the CRA in which he manipulates formal elements in accordance with the equations which govern dynamical systems. Invocation of dynamical neural networks would not block this version of the CRA. However, Searle's own account of the specific non-formal causal powers of the brain which suffice for mentality, Wheeler concludes, is deeply problematic, and the dynamic systems approach, if and when attacked by Searle, bites back. The confrontation, in my opinion, constitutes one of the most important new features of this volume's debate.

As we saw, it's no coincidence that the Chinese Room scenario gives expression to the fundamental concept in traditional computation theory, the Turing machine, via its explicit invocation of what can be achieved by a human computer, idealized in certain respects, but unaided by machinery. Among the challenging questions that Searle's argument poses to these new approaches are: why should we suppose that what the machines in question are doing is really *computation*? Could their operations be repeatable, reliable, and normative enough to count as such? Even if there are logically possible machines which can compute some functions that Turing machines cannot, why should we suppose that their computations could not be simulated by the Chinese Room arrangement? Could there be primitive computational operations that could be performed by a device (whether brain or machine) but not by an unaided human being?

Conclusion

This volume was conceived as a forum in which to provide opportunities to restate the original argument and envisaged responses, to develop those responses, and to indicate lines of argument which Searle did not anticipate. Several contributors have honed and developed their arguments by reference to each other's contributions. Searle was not asked, or given the opportunity here, to respond to the chapters in this volume. But although it's not supposed to contain the last word on the debate, the volume does not simply take stock. Rather, it attempts to latch onto a new phase of the debate, in which detailed analysis and unpicking of the arguments pro and con predominates over the original 'replies' which Searle himself enumerated.

In preparing the volume, the editors became more aware than ever of a sort of consensus among cognitive scientists to the effect that the CRA is, and has been shown to be, bankrupt. Despite the fact that several notable 'names' within the philosophy of mind agree with Searle,[24] it's true that the negative

---

[24] Baumgartner and Payr (1995) include some of the confessions in a fascinating volume.

consensus among computationalists has become, if anything, even more solid. Some prominent philosophers of mind declined to contribute on the grounds that the project would give further exposure to a woefully flawed piece of philosophizing. Even some who have contributed to the volume think of the CRA not just as flawed, but as pernicious and wholly undeserving of its fame.

Despite this consensus it is notable, however, that there is (still) little agreement about exactly how the argument goes wrong, or about what should be the exact response on behalf of computational cognitive science and Strong AI. We should probably find it extraordinary how much opinions can differ, and how wide the variety of topics which can be raised by, a scenario as apparently simple as the Chinese Room. But Searle's thought-experiment is a microcosm of much contemporary philosophy and cognitive science. Its importance, both philosophically and practically (in its impact on the self-image of current and proposed cognitive science research programmes) has ensured that it has been widely attacked (and defended), with almost religious fervour. It raises a host of issues about mind and mentality, language, meaning and understanding, intentionality, computers, cyborgs, and our self-conception. It can also be used to raise large methodological questions about how cognitive science should be done (computationalism versus 'cognitive neuroscience', versus some more person-centred alternative?), as well as about what philosophy should be ('scientific'? or 'analytic'? or perhaps 'phenomenological'?). At the very least, it forces those involved in contemporary cognitive science into clarifying exactly what general theoretical theses they want to defend.

References

BAUMGARTNER, P., and PAYR, S. (eds.) (1995) *Speaking Minds: Interviews with Twenty Eminent Cognitive Scientists* (Princeton: Princeton University Press).

BECHTEL, W., and ABRAHAMSEN, A. A. (1999) *Connectionism and the Mind: Parallel Processing, Dynamics, and Evolution in Networks*, 2nd edn. (Oxford: Blackwell).

BISHOP, C. M. (1997) *Neural Networks for Pattern Recognition* (Oxford: Oxford University Press).

BODEN, M. A. (1987) *Artificial Intelligence and Natural Man*, 2nd edn. (London: MIT Press).

—— (ed.) (1990) *The Philosophy of Artificial Intelligence* (Oxford: Oxford University Press).

—— (forthcoming) *A History of Cognitive Science*.

CHALMERS, D. J. (1996a) 'Does a Rock Implement every Finite-State Automaton?' *Synthese*, 108: 309–33.

CHALMERS, D. J. (1996b) *The Conscious Mind: In Search of a Fundamental Theory* (Oxford: Oxford University Press).

CHURCHLAND, P. M., and CHURCHLAND, P. S. (1990) 'Could a Machine Think?' *Scientific American*, 262 (Jan.), 26–31.

COPELAND, B. J. (1993) *Artificial Intelligence: A Philosophical Introduction* (Oxford: Blackwell).

—— (1996) 'The Church-Turing Thesis', *Stanford Online Encyclopedia of Philosophy*.

—— (1998) 'Turing's O-Machines, Penrose, Searle, and the Brain', *Analysis*, 58: 128–38.

—— (2000) 'The Turing Test', *Minds and Machines*, 10: 519–39.

—— and PROUDFOOT, D. (1996) 'On Alan Turing's Anticipation of Connectionism', *Synthese*, 108: 361–77.

DENNETT, D. C. (1985) 'Can Machines Think?' in M. Shafto (ed.), *How We Know* (San Francisco: Harper & Row), 121–45.

—— (1987) 'Fast Thinking', in his *The Intentional Stance* (Cambridge, Mass.: MIT Press), 323–37.

FEIGENBAUM, E. A., and FELDMAN, J. (eds.) (1963) *Computers and Thought*, (New York: McGraw-Hill). Reprinted Cambridge, Mass.: AAAI Press and MIT Press, 1995.

FODOR, J. A. (1995) 'The Folly of Simulation', in Baumgartner and Payr 1995: 85–100.

GARDNER, H. (1985) *The Mind's New Science: A History of the Cognitive Revolution* (New York: Basic Books).

GLOCK, H.-J., and PRESTON, J. M. (1995) 'Externalism and First-Person Authority', *The Monist*, 78: 515–33.

HACKER, P. M. S. (1990) *Wittgenstein: Meaning and Mind, Part 1: Essays* (Oxford: Blackwell).

—— (1992) 'Malcolm and Searle on "Intentional Mental States" ', *Philosophical Investigations*, 15: 245–75.

HAUSER, L. (1997) 'Searle's Chinese Box: Debunking the Chinese Room Argument', *Minds and Machines*, 7: 199–226.

HAYKIN, S. (1999) *Neural Networks: A Comprehensive Foundation*, 2nd edn. (Englewood Cliffs, NJ: Prentice-Hall).

HODGES, A. (1983) *Alan Turing: The Enigma of Intelligence* (London: Unwin).

HOGARTH, M. L. (1994) 'Non-Turing Computers and Non-Turing Computability', in D. Hull, M. Forbes, and R. M. Burian (eds.), *PSA 1994*, i (East Lansing, Mich.: Philosophy of Science Association), 126–38.

KURZWEIL, R. (1998) *The Age of Spiritual Machines: When Computers Exceed Human Intelligence* (New York: Viking).

LEIBER, J. (1991) *An Invitation to Cognitive Science* (Oxford: Blackwell).

McCORDUCK, P. (1979) *Machines Who Think: A Personal Inquiry into the History and Prospects of Artificial Intelligence* (San Francisco, Calif.: Freeman).

McCULLOCH, W. S., and PITTS, W. H. (1943) 'A Logical Calculus of the Ideas Immanent in Nervous Activity', *Bulletin of Mathematical Biophysics*, 5: 115–33. Reprinted in Boden 1990.

MALCOLM, N. (1991) ' "I Believe that p" ', in E. Lepore and R. van Gulick (eds.), *John Searle and His Critics* (Oxford: Blackwell), 159–67.

MINSKY, M. L., and PAPERT, S. (1968) *Perceptrons: An Introduction to Computational Geometry* (Cambridge, Mass.: MIT Press).

NEWELL, A. (1980) 'Physical Symbol Systems', *Cognitive Science*, 4: 135–83.

PRATT, V. (1987) *Thinking Machines: The Evolution of Artificial Intelligence* (Oxford: Blackwell).

PROUDFOOT, D., and COPELAND, B. J. (1994) 'Turing, Wittgenstein, and the Science of the Mind', *Australasian Journal of Philosophy*, 72: 497–519.

PUTNAM, H. (1988) *Representation and Reality* (Cambridge, Mass.: MIT Press).

SCHANK, R. C., and ABELSON, R. P. (1977) *Scripts, Plans, Goals and Understanding: An Inquiry into Human Knowledge Structures* (Hillsdale, NJ: Lawrence Erlbaum).

SEARLE, J. R. (1969) *Speech Acts: An Essay in the Philosophy of Language* (Cambridge: Cambridge University Press).

—— (1980a) 'Minds, Brains, and Programs', *Behavioral and Brain Sciences*, 3: 417–24.

—— (1980b) 'Intrinsic Intentionality', *Behavioral and Brain Sciences*, 3: 450–6.

—— (1982a) 'The Myth of the Computer', *New York Review of Books*, 29/7: 3–6.

—— (1982b) 'The Myth of the Computer: An Exchange', *New York Review of Books*, 29/11: 56–7.

—— (1982c) 'The Chinese Room Revisited', *Behavioral and Brain Sciences*, 5: 345–8.

—— (1983) *Intentionality: An Essay in the Philosophy of Mind* (Cambridge: Cambridge University Press).

—— (1984) *Minds, Brains and Science* (London: BBC Publications and Cambridge, Mass.: Harvard University Press).

—— (1987a) 'Minds and Brains without Programs', in C. Blakemore and S. Greenfield (eds.), *Mindwaves* (Oxford: Blackwell), 208–33.

—— (1987b) 'Turing the Chinese Room', in T. D. Singh and R. Gomatam (eds.), *Synthesis of Science and Religion: Critical Essays and Dialogues* (San Francisco and Bombay: The Bhaktivedanta Institute), 295–301.

—— (1989a) 'Artificial Intelligence and the Chinese Room: An Exchange [with Elhanan Motzkin]', *New York Review of Books*, 36 (16 Feb.), 45.

—— (1989b) 'Reply to Jacquette', *Philosophy and Phenomenological Research*, 69: 701–7.

—— (1990a) 'Is the Brain's Mind a Computer Program?' *Scientific American*, 262 (Jan.), 20–5.

—— (1990b) 'Is the Brain a Digital Computer?' *Proceedings and Addresses of the American Philosophical Association*, 64: 21–37.

—— (1991) 'Yin and Yang Strike Out', in D. M. Rosenthal (ed.), *The Nature of Mind* (Oxford: Oxford University Press), 525–6.

—— (1992) *The Rediscovery of the Mind* (Cambridge, Mass.: MIT Press).

—— (1993a) 'The Problem of Consciousness', *Social Research*, 60: 3–16.

—— (1993b) 'The Failures of Computationalism', *Think*, 2: 68–71.

—— (1995a) *The Construction of Social Reality* (London: Allen Lane).

—— (1995b) 'Ontology is the Question', in Baumgartner and Payr 1995: 202–13.

—— (1997) *The Mystery of Consciousness* (London: Granta).

SEARLE, J. R. (1999a) Interview (with Julian Moore), *Philosophy Now*, winter, 37–41.

—— (1999b) 'I Married a Computer' (review of Kurzweil 1998), *New York Review of Books*, 47 (8 Apr.), 34–8.

SHANKER, S. G. (1998) *Wittgenstein's Remarks on the Foundations of A.I.* (London: Routledge).

SIEGELMANN, H. T. (1999) *Neural Networks and Analog Computation: Beyond the Turing Limit* (Boston: Birkhäuser).

—— and SONTAG, E. D. (1994) 'Analog Computation via Neural Networks', *Theoretical Computer Science*, 131: 331–60.

SIMON, H. A., and NEWELL, A. (1958) 'Heuristic Problem-Solving: The Next Advance in Operations Research', *Operations Research*, 6: 1–10.

TURING, A. M. (1936) 'On Computable Numbers, with an Application to the *Entscheidungsproblem*', *Proceedings of the London Mathematical Society*, series 2, vol. 42: 230–65 (with corrections in vol. 43: 544–6). Reprinted in M. Davis (ed.), *The Undecidable* (New York: Raven Press, 1965), to which page references are given.

—— (1948) 'Intelligent Machinery', reprinted in B. Meltzer and D. Michie (eds.), *Machine Intelligence 5* (Edinburgh: Edinburgh University Press, 1969), 3–23.

—— (1950) 'Computing Machinery and Intelligence', *Mind*, 59: 433–60.

WASSERMAN, P. D. (1989) *Neural Computing: Theory and Practice* (New York: Van Nostrand Reinhold).

WILKES, K. V. (1988) *Real People: Personal Identity without Thought Experiments* (Oxford: Oxford University Press).

WITTGENSTEIN, L. (1980) *Remarks on the Philosophy of Psychology, Volume 1* (Oxford: Blackwell).

2

Twenty-One Years in the Chinese Room

John R. Searle

I

I want to use the occasion of this volume dedicated to the twenty-first anniversary of the Chinese Room Argument to reflect on some of the implications of this debate for cognitive science in general, and indeed, for the current state of our larger intellectual culture. I will not spend much time responding to the many detailed arguments that have been presented. I have already responded to more criticisms of the Chinese Room Argument than to all of the criticisms of all of the other controversial philosophical theses that I have advanced in my life. My reason for having so much confidence that the basic argument is sound is that in the past twenty-one years I have not seen anything to shake its fundamental thesis. The fundamental claim is that the purely formal or abstract or syntactical processes of the implemented computer program could not by themselves be sufficient to *guarantee* the presence of mental content or semantic content of the sort that is essential to human cognition. Of course a system might have semantic content for some other reason. It may be that implementing this program in this particular hardware is sufficient to cause consciousness and intentionality, but such a claim is no longer Strong Artificial Intelligence. It is at the very heart of the Strong AI thesis that the system that implements the program does not matter. Any hardware implementation will do, provided only that it is rich enough and stable enough to carry the program. This is why I can, at least in principle, carry out the steps in the program in the Chinese

Room, even though my 'hardware' is quite unlike that of commercial computers. In short, the distinction between the software and the hardware, and the essential point in the whole modern notion of computation that a program is multiply realizable in different hardwares, is sufficient to refute the claim that the implemented software by itself, regardless of the nature of the implementing medium, would be sufficient to guarantee the presence of mental contents.

The Chinese Room Argument, in short, rests on two absolutely fundamental logical truths, and twenty-one years of debate has not in any way shaken either of these. Here they are. First, syntax is not semantics. That is to say, the implemented syntactical or formal program of a computer is not constitutive of nor otherwise sufficient to guarantee the presence of semantic content; and secondly, simulation is not duplication. You can simulate the cognitive processes of the human mind as you can simulate rain storms, five alarm fires, digestion, or anything else that you can describe precisely. But it is just as ridiculous to think that a system that had a simulation of consciousness and other mental processes thereby had the mental processes, as it would be to think that the simulation of digestion on a computer could thereby actually digest beer and pizza.

I said above that there was no way that the implemented computer program by itself could *guarantee* the presence of mental content or semantic content. But how on earth did the proponents of Strong AI imagine that it could guarantee the presence of mental content? What picture do they have? Actually, the ambiguities in their position are illustrative of certain important failures of reductionist attempts to deal with philosophical issues over the past century, and I want to say a little bit about such reductionist attempts. The typical pattern is to treat the epistemic basis for a phenomenon—behavior in the case of the mind, sense data in the case of material objects—as somehow logically sufficient to guarantee the presence of the phenomenon. The basic urge is a verificationist reductionist urge, and the Turing Test is an expression of this same urge. But the reductionist also wants to continue to track the intuitive idea of the phenomenon that was supposed to be reduced in the first place. The intuitive notion of a mental state or a material object has somehow to be preserved within the reductionist enterprise. This is why the Chinese Room poses such a problem: I implement the program, but I do not understand Chinese. What the Strong AI thesis amounts to in its pure form, is that the implemented program is *constitutive* of a mind. A system that implements the right program necessarily has a mind because there isn't anything else to having a mind. The Turing Test gives us a test for the presence of the mind, but the actual thing that it is a test for is a series of computational processes. Now, what is the Strong AI theorist to say in the face of an obvious counter-example such as the Chinese Room? The proponent of Strong AI is committed by the ideology to saying that in the Chinese Room I do in fact understand Chinese because I can pass the Turing Test by carrying out the steps in the computation. But it is simply too preposterous to say that I understand Chinese or that I would understand Chinese by carrying out the steps in the program, because I quite obviously do not, and in the imagined circumstances would not, understand Chinese. What is the reductionist to do? The typical move over the past twenty-one years has been to grant that I do not understand Chinese, but then to say such things as, 'Well, it's the whole system that understands Chinese', or sometimes even, 'A subsystem in you understands Chinese'. But these evasions will not do. The proponent of Strong AI is originally committed to the view that the program is constitutive of mental content, but in the face of obvious counter-examples, retreats to a different position, that the program is somehow *associated with* mental content. That was the whole point of the Systems Reply. The Systems Reply claims that even though there is no semantic content in me alone, there is semantic content somewhere else—in the whole system of which I am a part, or in some subsystem within me. But the same argument that worked originally—namely, I do not have any understanding of Chinese because I do not know what any of the words mean, I have no way to attach meaning to any of the symbols—works for the whole system. The whole system doesn't know what any of the words mean either, because it has no way to attach any mental content to any of the symbols.

What is interesting is not just the evasiveness of the Systems Reply, but the fact that it illustrates the general tendency of twentieth-century reductionist accounts of the mind. Behaviorism was confronted with the same difficulty. The behaviorist is forced to say that the behavior is constitutive of the mental. But in the face of obvious counter-examples the idea was always to suggest that there was some way that in the system that behaves appropriately the right mental states would somehow be associated with the behavior.

The problem for all these forms of reductionism is the same: are there really two things or just one. The thesis of reductionism is that there is just one thing—behavior, or computer programs or sense data or whatever—but in the face of the counter-examples the reductionist says that the other thing must be there too. Hence there are two things. The urge of the reductionist to try to hang on to the reduced notion amounts to a quiet abandonment of the reduction. If he really were consistent in the reduction of mental states to program states, he should have said, 'There isn't any such thing as understanding in addition to symbol manipulation, there is just the symbol manipulation. Whether that goes on in the individual or in the whole room makes no difference. The symbol manipulation is all there is to understanding.' But that is too obviously absurd from the first-person point of view, where I know clearly the distinction between my manipulating symbols in English together with having an understanding of them, and my manipulating symbols in Chinese with no understanding whatever. So the Strong AI theorist makes the desperate move of saying the understanding is somewhere else in the system. It is the whole room that understands, not the person in the room.

There is, in short, a deep contradiction in the reductionist's position. On the one hand, he wants to say there is no such thing as semantic content in addition to symbol manipulation, but on the other hand, when I present a case of symbol manipulation without semantic content, he does not say, 'Well, that is all there was in the first place', what he says is, 'The semantic content must be somewhere else in the system'. This is a straight contradiction. You cannot maintain that there is no such thing as semantic content in addition to symbol manipulation, and then say that there must be semantic content somewhere else in the system in addition to the symbol manipulation. So when I said earlier that the implemented program by itself is insufficient to *guarantee* the presence of mental states, that covered both of the possible moves of the Strong AI theorist. The program by itself is insufficient to *constitute* mental states because of the distinction between syntax and semantics. And it is insufficient by itself to *cause* mental states because the program is defined independently of the physics of its implementation. Any causal power the machine might have to cause consciousness and intentionality would have to be a consequence of the physical nature of the machine. But the program, *qua program* hasn't got any physical nature. It consists of a set of formal, syntactical processes that can be implemented in the physics of various kinds of machinery.

To the frequently asked question, 'Well, what is the difference between the brain, which, after all, functions by a set of microprocesses such as neuron firings at synapses and the computer with its microprocesses of flip flops, "and" gates and "or" gates?' The answer to that question can be given in one word: *causation*. We know that the specific neurobiological processes in the brain are sufficient to cause consciousness, intentionality, and all the rest of our mental life by a form of 'bottom-up' causation. Lower-level neuronal processes, presumably at the level of synapses, cause higher-level features of the brain such as consciousness and intentionality. It is no use being told that it is 'counter-intuitive' that a kilogram and a half of this gray and white gook in my skull should cause consciousness, because we know in fact that it does. The point I make is not that it is counter-intuitive that computers should be conscious. I have no interest whatever in such intuitions. The point, rather, is that the implemented program is insufficient by itself to guarantee the presence of consciousness. The program is not defined in terms of its powers to cause higher-level features of the system, because it has no such powers. It is defined, rather in terms of its syntactical or formal structure. Of course the computer on which I am typing might be conscious for some other reason. Perhaps God has decided to endow all computers that have a label that says 'Intel-inside' with consciousness. That is up to Him, and not up to me. My argument is a purely logical argument about the distinction between the syntax of the implemented computer program and the actual semantic content of mental states.

The basic structure of the Chinese Room Argument is rather obvious, and the principles on which it rests—the distinction between syntax and semantics and the distinction between simulation and duplication—are not at all difficult to grasp. I have little or no difficulty in explaining them even to people unsophisticated in any of the technical notions in question. One wonders, therefore, why the debate continues. Well, of course, there are a number of reasons. Many people have a professional commitment to Strong AI. To put the point bluntly, in many cases their careers and the funding of their research projects depend on the continued belief that they are 'creating minds' (one Strong AI worker actually assured me that he was 'creating minds'). For such people it is psychologically impossible to accept that the project of Strong AI is misconceived in principle. They would like to believe that the failure of Strong AI is due to some temporary limitation of the technology; that if only we had faster computer chips or more complex parallel distributed processing systems, we would be able to overcome the argument. The point of the argument has nothing whatever to do with any state of technology, it has to do with the very concept of computation, a concept that Alonzo Church, Alan Turing, and others explained to us half a century ago.

II

One of the interesting features of contemporary intellectual life that this whole debate has exposed, is the persistence of a set of obsolete seventeenth-century categories in which the issues are typically defined and discussed. I am thinking not only of the obsolete contrast of the 'mental' and the 'physical', of 'mind' and 'body', but just as important, the obsolete contrast between 'man' and 'machine'. So the issue about Strong AI is often taken to be the same as the question, 'Could a machine think?' But of course the whole question is absurd. We are, after all, machines. If 'machine' is defined as any physical system capable of performing certain functions, then there is no question that human and animal brains are machines. They are *biological* machines, but so what? There is no logical or philosophical reason why we could not duplicate the operation of a biological machine, using some artificial methods. The whole opposition of man versus machine involves a series of deep philosophical mistakes, and I tried to expose some of them in the original article, but apparently more needs to be said. So I will try to say what I think needs to be said as a series of numbered propositions.

1. There is no question that machines can think, because human and animal brains are precisely such machines.

2. There is no question that an artificially made machine could, in principle, think. Just as we can build an artificial heart, so there is no reason why we could not build an artificial brain. The point, however, is that any such artificial machine would have to be able to duplicate, and not merely simulate, the causal powers of the original biological machine. An artificial heart does not merely simulate pumping, it actually pumps. It actually causes the pumping of blood. And an artificial brain would have to do something more than simulate consciousness, it would have to be able to *produce* consciousness. It would have to cause consciousness.

3. Could we produce consciousness artificially in some medium other than carbon-based organic compounds? The short answer to that question is that we just do not know at present. Since we do not know how the brain does it, we do not know what sorts of chemical devices are necessary for its production. Perhaps it will turn out that consciousness can only be produced using electrochemical phenomena, but does not require organic compounds. It might be that certain types of organic compounds in certain conditions are causally sufficient without it being the case that they are causally necessary. At present we just do not know.

It is important to get clear about what is at issue. When I say that the implemented program by itself is not enough to constitute consciousness and intentionality, that is a logical claim on my part. By definition, the syntax of the program is not constitutive of the semantics of actual thoughts. But when I say that a system composed entirely of beer cans is not sufficient to cause consciousness and intentionality, that is an empirical claim on my part. It is like saying that a system composed entirely of beer cans is not sufficient to digest hamburgers. It is a claim about how nature works. It is logically possible, though not actually possible, that I could be mistaken. But it is not logically possible that syntax by itself should be semantics. Strong AI rests on a logical error. But it is still an open question what sorts of systems are necessary and sufficient to produce consciousness and intentionality. We know at one end that human and animal brains are sufficient to do it. We know at another end that beer cans cannot do it. What sorts of chemistry in between are capable of causing consciousness and intentionality is still an open question, and is likely to remain open until we figure out how brains do it.

4. Though computers of the sort that you can buy in a store are 'machines', computation as standardly defined does not name a machine process. Oddly enough, the problem is not that computational processes are too much machine-like to be conscious, it is rather that they are too little machine-like. The reason for this is that computation is defined purely formally or abstractly in terms of the implementation of a computer algorithm, and not in terms of energy transfer. Let me repeat this point: computation as standardly defined does not name a machine process in the sense in which photosynthesis or internal combustion name machine processes, because photosynthesis and internal combustion necessarily involve energy transfers. Computation does not. Computation is the name of an abstract mathematical process that can be implemented with machines that engage in energy transfer, but the energy transfer is not part of the definition of computation. To state the point with a little more precision: the notion 'same implemented program' defines an equivalence class that is specified not in terms of physical or chemical processes, but in terms of abstract mathematical processes. Could a machine process cause a thought process? The answer is: yes. Indeed only a machine process can cause a thought process, and 'computation' does not name a machine process; it names a process that can be, and typically is, *implemented* on a machine.

Strong AI is a weird mixture of behaviorism and dualism. It is behaviorist in its acceptance of the Turing Test, but it is at a much more fundamental philosophical level, dualist, because it rejects the idea that consciousness and intentionality are ordinary biological phenomena like digestion. In the words of Dennett and Hofstadter, we are to think of the mind as, 'an abstract sort of thing whose identity is independent of any particular physical embodiment'.[1] I will say more about this point later.

---

[1] Hofstadter and Dennett (1981: 15).

III

There is an interesting series of larger philosophical issues raised by this debate, and I want now to consider at least some of them. I believe that future intellectual historians will be puzzled by certain peculiar features of late twentieth and early twenty-first-century scientific culture. One of the most puzzling of these features is the persistence of certain anti-scientific views masquerading under the guise of science. When I say 'masquerading' I do not mean to imply any form of charlatanry or dishonesty on the part of the masqueraders. I think they are quite innocently mistaken about the contrast between their view and a genuinely scientific approach. A few decades ago the most obvious case of an anti-scientific approach masquerading as science was behaviorism in philosophy and psychology. The basic idea of the extreme forms of behaviorism was that there isn't anything to mental life other than our behavior and our dispositions to behavior. But anyone who has ever felt a pain or experienced an emotion knows immediately that this view is false. The pain that I feel is one thing, the behavior that the pain causes me to exhibit is another. What difference could be more obvious? Why wasn't this obvious at the time? Why wasn't it obvious to everybody? Well, let's go a step further, and ask what motivated this peculiar form of anti-scientific view in the midst of a scientific culture. And we find that the mistake of behaviorism was underlain by an even deeper mistake, that of verificationism. People erroneously supposed that the essence of science, and of what they thought of as the 'scientific method', was that there must be certain conclusive methods of verifying scientific claims. The extreme version of this view was Logical Positivism, whose adherents claimed that the meaning of any sentence is its method of verification, and therefore that the verification of a sentence about someone's mind gave us the entire meaning of the sentence. Thus, at least where 'other minds' are concerned, because the verification of a sentence about another mind allowed only evidence about that person's behavior, it seemed there couldn't be anything else to the mind other than the behavior. I believe that this, like behaviorism itself, is profoundly anti-scientific, but I have not yet said anything about the nature of 'science' which would justify that view, and I will delay such an account for a few moments more.

In order to explain exactly why these views—behaviorism and verificationism—were in fact profoundly anti-scientific, though many people thought of them as a natural consequence of something called 'scientific method', I need to say something about the history of the development of science and of the scientific world-view in our intellectual culture. The Ancient Greeks did not have science as we now think of it. Perhaps the greatest single achievement of Greek civilization was the invention of the idea of a theory. A theory is a set of systematically logically related propositions that provide an explanation of the phenomena of some domain. One of the earliest examples of a systematic theoretical account of a domain is Euclid's geometry as expounded in his *Elements*. With the invention of the idea of a theory the Greeks arrived at almost everything that is necessary for science, but they did not have the idea of systematic observation and experiment. They never reached the idea of an institutionalized form of systematic observation and experiment. That came really only after the Renaissance. And, as far as I know, it really did not get going until the seventeenth century.

The scientific achievements of the seventeenth century are among the greatest achievements of Western civilization. But the scientific revolution suffered from certain specific local problems that had to do with the intellectual culture of the rest of Western civilization during the seventeenth century, in particular with the enormous intellectual power possessed by organized religion, especially by the Catholic Church.

The intellectual significance of the great conflict between science and religion in the seventeenth centuries and subsequently is much bigger than anything I can hope to cover in the space of this short chapter. But for the present purposes there are three features to which I would like to call attention. First, most of the philosophers and scientists involved in this dispute did not want to give up on either science or religion; they wanted to pursue their scientific investigations while maintaining their religious convictions. Descartes found a way for them to do that: he divided the world into two, a mental realm of the soul or spirit that was the proper domain of religion, and a physical realm of matter, which was the proper domain of science. This division of the territory seemed to make it possible to have a strict physical science combined with the acceptance of religious doctrines such as the immortality of the soul. Science, in short, was taken to be about matter and the physical world. But there was a realm beyond the reach of science, and that was the realm of the spirit or the soul or mental substance. Descartes's famous distinction between *res cogitans* and *res extensa* is the classic statement of this dualism.

Though this distinction was perhaps politically and sociologically useful in the seventeenth century, it has proved to be unfortunate in the twentieth and twenty-first centuries, because many people still hold the view that consciousness and subjectivity are not proper domains of scientific investigation. Many people believe that the investigation of consciousness and intentionality, phenomena which are inherently subjective and mental, is somehow beyond the reach of an objective science. This is a very deep mistake, with deep historical roots, and I will expose it in more detail shortly.

A second feature of the dispute between science and religion was the obsession with *method*. The idea was that in science there was a special method, and that this method differed from other areas of human investigation. The endless debates about faith and reason were an expression of this great dispute between science and religion, and a consequence of the conviction that what was special about science in attaining the truth was 'scientific method'. Again, the consequence of this conception, like the consequence of the dualism of Descartes, was to give people a conception of science as more restricted than we have come to think of it today. Science, they thought, is not universal in subject-matter, but has a restricted subject-matter. Some have even said it is restricted to the subject-matter which is mathematically statable. Unless you can measure the phenomena in question, they are not proper scientific phenomena. Furthermore, science is constrained by a particularly narrow notion of method.

A third feature of the conflict between science and religion did not become fully apparent in the seventeenth century, but only emerged in subsequent eras, and indeed has only become fully manifest in the twentieth century. It is this: religion sought absolute and indubitable truths. Science, on the other hand, was much more tentative. Science was a matter of hypotheses that one could test, but these hypotheses were never taken as absolute truths. In the twentieth century the various scientific revolutions, especially the Einsteinian revolution that overthrew the apparent universality of Newtonian physics, and the quantum mechanical revolution that challenges some of our most basic assumptions, seem to make this tentative character of science all the more obvious. The picture that we get is that whatever scientists believe today, they will not believe tomorrow, that there is a continuing evolution from one tentative hypothesis to another. One philosopher who espoused this doctrine explicitly was Karl Popper (Popper 1959). Popper thought of science as not a matter of attaining the truth, but rather as a matter of putting forward hypotheses and knocking them down. Science never attains the truth, but just moves from one hypothesis to another, and the surviving hypotheses, like soldiers in an endless war, are different from earlier hypotheses only because they are still alive and not yet shot down. The move from the pro-science philosophy of Popper to the anti-scientific views of Thomas Kuhn (Kuhn 1962, 1970) and Paul Feyerabend

(Feyerabend 1975) is not as great as many philosophers and scientists think. Indeed, many scientists who reject Kuhn, and would be appalled by Feyerabend's views if they knew anything about them, profess to admire Popper's philosophy of science. I think they do not properly understand Popper. They like the fact that Popper praises them for their originality in putting forward new and original hypotheses, but they do not understand that Popper rejects the basic assumption behind their enterprise, namely the assumption that they are getting at the truth.[2]

These three features, dualism, the obsession with method, and the tacit rejection of truth as the aim of investigation have exercised a pervasive, though not always explicit, influence on intellectual life. And these influences have spilled over into the debate about Strong AI. How exactly? I mentioned earlier that there is a tacit dualism in the computational conception of the mind. The mind is not an ordinary part of the biological world like digestion and photosynthesis but is something formal and abstract, hence we do not have to worry about the specific biochemical mechanisms that produce consciousness and the various forms of intentionality. Furthermore the key problem is to find a conclusive method for ascertaining the presence of mental phenomena and we have found that in the Turing Test. The existence of an objective test makes it look as if we are doing real science. Do we not have an objective method of verification, just like real sciences? Finally we do not have to worry about what inner facts correspond to our claims about consciousness and intentionality in real life. Rather we postulate an abstract mechanism—the computer program—and we have a test of its success and failure—the Turing Test—and when our hypotheses are confirmed by the Turing Test that is all the truth we need. I hope it is obvious that this is a massive tissue of errors, and one of the virtues of the Chinese Room Argument is that it helps to expose these errors. Most obviously it refutes the Turing Test. The 'system', whether me in the Chinese Room, the whole room, or a commercial computer, passes the Turing Test for understanding Chinese but it does not understand Chinese, because it has no way of attaching any meaning to the Chinese symbols. The appearance of understanding is an illusion. Furthermore, when we flesh out the details, the argument reminds us of the necessity of scientific realism. We are interested in the *fact* of internal mental states, not in the external appearance. Our claims, if true, have to meet more than an instrumental test, they have to correspond to facts in the world.

---

[2] For an excellent discussion of these issues, see Stove (1999).

IV

So far I have been calling attention to certain mistakes that people commonly make when they are insufficiently aware of the implications of the scientific world-view. Now I want to turn to three less obvious features of this world-view. These features do not lie on the surface, but, I believe, are readily recognizable.

1. *The distinction between observer-dependence and observer-independence.* Absolutely essential to our understanding of the world is to be able to distinguish between those features of the world that exist independently of our attitudes and purposes, and those that exist only relative to us. I have at various times characterized this as the distinction between those features of the world that are 'intrinsic' and those that are observer-dependent, but the word 'intrinsic' is a frequent source of confusion, so to avoid confusion I sometimes characterize the distinction as between observer-dependence and observer-relativity on the one hand, and observer-independence on the other. Typically the natural sciences study features that are observer-independent: force, mass, gravitational attraction, photosynthesis, tectonic plates, molecules, and planets, are all observer-independent. If we all cease to exist tomorrow, these would go on existing, and indeed, if we had never existed, these would still have existed. I realize that in physics it is common to identify some of these parameters relative to coordinate systems, but it is also essential to see that even though the physics textbooks sometimes call this 'relative to an observer', they do not mean that in my sense. They do not think, for example, that in order for an object to have a mass, somebody has to be consciously thinking about it, or indeed that anybody ever has to consciously think about it.

The social sciences typically deal with phenomena that are observer-dependent. I am thinking of phenomena like political parties, marriage, money, elections, nation states, property, and organized sports. As usual, psychology falls somewhere in between. Most of psychology deals with observer-independent phenomena such as perception and memory, but sometimes in social psychology, we deal with observer-dependent phenomena, such as social organizations. With these distinctions in mind it is absolutely crucial to distinguish between those attributions of mental phenomena that are observer-dependent, and those attributions that are observer-independent. My present state of consciousness is entirely observer-independent. No matter what anybody thinks, I am now conscious. But the attributions of mental states that I make to my computer are observer-dependent. If I say the computer now has more *memory* than it used to have or that it *knows how* to run more word-processing programs than it used to be able to do, both of these mental attributions are obviously observer-dependent. Literally speaking, the computer does not remember anything, and it does not know anything, it is just a machine that we use for certain purposes. I think these attributions started out as metaphors, but they are evolving new literal meanings as the metaphors become dead metaphors.

Once we recognize the distinction between observer-dependent and observer-independent phenomena, then we can see that we need to distinguish three different phenomena where intentionality is concerned.

A. Observer-independent intentionality. Example: I am now thirsty or I am now hungry.

B. Observer-dependent intentionality, where the ascription of the intentionality is literal. Example: The French sentence 'J'ai faim' means 'I am hungry'. Notice in this case there is nothing metaphorical about the attribution of a meaning to a French sentence. It is quite literal. But the French sentence construed as a purely formal, syntactical object has no meaning in itself, the meaning that it has is only relative to French speakers, that is, it is in my sense observer-dependent.

C. Metaphorical attributions of intentionality. These are cases where we say 'My car is thirsty for gasoline', or 'My lawn is thirsty for water'. In such cases the attributions are not intended literally, and as long as no one takes them literally, there is no confusion. As I remarked earlier, attributions of intentionality to computers are passing from the non-literal metaphorical to the literal observer-dependent. But in both cases, both in the metaphorical and in the literal ascriptions, the attributions are observer-dependent. There is nothing intrinsic to the computer that makes a phenomenon a case of remembering, in the way that it is intrinsic to me and not observer-relative that I can now remember a picnic that I attended last week.

2. *Success and failure are observer-dependent.* Computer science is correctly regarded as a branch of engineering. Engineering is, taken collectively, the set of disciplines that seek to use the results of the natural sciences to try to improve the life of human beings and improve their control over nature. Physics tells us how the world works, engineering tells us how to use that knowledge to build bridges, airplanes, and computers. This seems to me the exactly right way to understand these disciplines. However, this leads to a persistent error in the philosophical interpretations of the results of computer science. The error is to

suppose that, somehow or other, success and failure are natural categories. In the simplest terms, the assumption is that if the computer can do something as well as humans can do it, or do it better than humans can do it, that somehow or other these successes and failures are psychologically relevant. This is true both of people who are sympathetic to Artificial Intelligence, and people who are not sympathetic. Both make the same error. Thus, for example, Ray Kurzweil (Kurzweil 1999) supposes that increased computational power by itself is evidence of psychological relevance; and Roger Penrose (Penrose 1994) assumes that the failure of computer algorithms to match human performance in seeing the truth of unprovable sentences, as shown by Gödel, is relevant to appraising the project of Strong AI. Both of these involve a very deep mistake. The mistake is supposing that nature is about succeeding and failing. So I want to emphasize this point. Nature knows nothing of success and failure. In nature, events just happen. What we think of as succeeding and failing is relative to our consciousness, relative to our interests. And we can assume that other conscious animals also have some kind of idea of success and failure, which again is relative to their interests.

It might seem that evolutionary biology gives us examples that are exceptions to this principle. After all, is it not an objective scientific fact that certain species *succeed* in surviving and that others *fail*? Is it not also an objective scientific fact that individual members of a species can succeed from an evolutionary point of view in reproducing their genes and that other animals fail in this reproductive function? The facts of survival and extinction are, indeed, facts like any others. But the fact that we think of one as success and the other as failure is up to us. The discipline of evolutionary biology does indeed proceed *as if* organisms were trying to survive and reproduce, and were succeeding and failing in doing so. But it has to be remembered that the apparent intentionality of the success and failure involved is entirely observer-dependent. I do not believe we could do evolutionary biology as a subject without thinking in terms of inclusive fitness and corresponding success in surviving and failure to survive of species. But it does not follow from evolutionary biology that success and failure are intrinsic to nature. A plant that survives and reproduces has only 'succeeded' relative to our conception of success and failure. The plant knows nothing of success and failure. The plant just has blind biochemical processes that either produce certain effects or do not produce those effects.

This is the deep fallacy embodied in the whole idea of the Turing Test. The objection to the Turing Test is not just the one I made earlier, namely that you could have the same external behavior without having the same internal processes. That I take it is an obvious point, and I hardly need to belabor it any further. But there is a more interesting error involved in the Turing Test, and that is that somehow or other succeeding and failing in our technological projects is, by itself, of scientific significance. It is not.

Nowhere was this confusion about success and failure more blatant than in all the hype that surrounded the success of the IBM team in building and programming a machine, Deep Blue, that could beat the World Chess Champion. Using new hardware that could calculate over 200 million chess moves per second, and developing a tree that could go to twelve places before assigning numerical values to the terminus points, the IBM engineers built a machine that could beat Gary Kasparov. This was a tremendous engineering achievement. Of what scientific significance, for understanding human psychology, was this result? As far as I can tell, it was of no significance whatever.

Because commercial computers were designed as labor-saving artifacts, and because we have come to measure our success and failure in designing computers in terms of their greater or lesser successes in carrying out tasks that humans can carry out, we tend to think that somehow or other the scientific significance of computation is measured in its success or failure in competing with human beings. This whole theory is a nest of mistakes. Human success and failures exist only relative to human interests. And indeed computer success and failures exist only relative to human interests because the machine does not have any psychologically real or observer-independent interests. In the case of Deep Blue, the machine did not know that it was playing chess, evaluating possible moves, or even winning and losing. It did not know any of these things, because it does not know anything. All psychological attributions made of it were observer-dependent. Indeed it did not even know that it was number-crunching or carrying out a program. In an observer-independent sense, the only things going on in the machine were very rapid state transitions in electronic circuits.

3. *Objectivity and subjectivity.* There is a persistent mistake that pervades much of our intellectual culture, and the debates that I have had with some people in the AI community have brought it out; it is a mistake in our conception of objectivity and subjectivity. The claim is that science is by definition objective, and the implication is supposed to be that because the mental phenomena of our ordinary experience seem to be subjective, their study cannot be part of a science properly construed. This is an error. There are at least two distinctions of objectivity and subjectivity that are being confused with each other. First there

is a distinction between epistemic objectivity and subjectivity. If I say 'Calvin Coolidge was born in the United States', that claim is epistemically objective because its truth or falsity can be ascertained as a matter of fact independent of the attitudes of the observers. But if I say 'Calvin Coolidge was a great President', that claim is epistemically subjective because its truth or falsity cannot be ascertained objectively, the claim can only be made relative to people's interests and evaluations. In addition to this sense of the objective/subjective distinction, there is another sense having to do with ontology, having to do with the mode of existence of entities. In that sense, mountains and molecules, as well as planets and tectonic plates, are ontologically objective. Pains, tickles, and itches, on the other hand, are ontologically subjective. They exist only as they are experienced by human or animal subjects. The point of this distinction for the present discussion is that the ontological subjectivity of the domain of human mental life does not preclude an epistemically objective science of this domain. It is one of the many mistakes involved in a certain conception of cognitive science, that the subjectivity of our common-sense notion of the mental precludes it from being a proper subject-matter for science. This is the error of confusing ontological subjectivity and objectivity with epistemic subjectivity and objectivity. Once we recognize the existence of an ontologically subjective domain, then there is no obstacle in having an epistemically objective science of that domain.

V

What have these three points—about observer dependence and observer independence, the observer dependence of success and failure, and the different distinctions hiding in the objective/subjective distinction—got to do with Strong AI and the debate about the Chinese Room Argument? I think they are used to buttress the mistakes that I pointed out earlier. I pointed out that Strong AI is a weird mixture of behaviorism and dualism. It is behavioristic in accepting the Turing Test, which is a straight expression of behaviorism. If it walks like a duck and talks like a duck, etc., then it is a duck, and if it behaves exactly as if it understood Chinese then it does understand Chinese. I used to think it strange that this mistake was married to dualism, but I now see that they are a natural match. Here is how. If you accept the behavioristic criterion for the presence of the mental, then the mental is unlikely to be anything truly substantive of a biological nature. It is unlikely to be like digestion or photosynthesis or the secretion of bile, or any other natural human biological process. So the behaviorism of the Turing Test goes well with the idea that the mind is something formal and abstract. Now, the obvious falsity of this ought to strike everybody. There is nothing formal or abstract about wanting to throw up or to feeling a surge of anger. But if you accept the weird mixture of dualism and behaviorism that emerged in the twentieth century, then it will seem perfectly natural to think that the mind is not a substantive physical process, but is rather something formal and abstract. And we all know which piece of modern technology can produce things that are formal and abstract. That is precisely what computer science does. It implements formal and abstract computer programs in concrete physical hardwares. And what matters is not the hardware, since any hardware will do; what matters is the formal, abstract program.

But now, what fact about the physical system makes it the case that it has psychological properties? At this point the failure to distinguish the observer-independent and the observer-dependent features comes into play. We all feel completely comfortable in saying that our present computers have bigger memories and are much more intelligent than the computers we had ten years ago. What we are inclined to forget is that none of these attributions attributes any observer-independent features to the system. In each case the psychology is in the eye of the beholder.

And if we go deeper we can see that the failure to see the distinction between observer-dependent and observer-independent features of the world is fatal to the claims that Artificial Intelligence could ever be a branch of the natural sciences. The crucial question to ask is: what about computation? Is it observer-independent, or is it observer-dependent? Remember, of course, that the fact that something is observer-dependent, and hence to that extent ontologically subjective, does not render it epistemically subjective. But, to repeat the question, what about computation? Well, there are computations that I actually do consciously, where there is no question that the computation is observer-independent. If I add two plus two to get four, that computation goes on in me regardless of what anybody thinks. But if I say of this pocket calculator that it is computing two plus two equals four, that is only relative to our interests. We have designed it, used it, programmed it, etc., in such a way that we can use it to compute with. In short, the computation of the pocket calculator is entirely observer-dependent. And what goes for the pocket calculator goes for the commercial computer. The commercial computer has a whole lot of observer-independent features, indeed that is why we pay so much money for it. It has electrical state transitions of incredible rapidity, and we can control those and program them. But in addition to the electrical state transitions, the computation that we attribute to the computer is observer-dependent. It is only relative to our interests that we can identify those state transitions as 0's and 1's etc. Now, to repeat, when I say that it is observer-dependent, I do not mean that it is arbitrary. You cannot use just any piece of circuitry as an and-gate or an or-gate, but it is none the less not a natural phenomenon.

Furthermore, we have the added mistake of supposing that success and failure are somehow or other relevant to science. That is, it is assumed, as I mentioned earlier, that increased computational capacities, Moore's Law in action, will somehow get us closer to producing a conscious computer. But this again is a mistake that comes from not understanding the basic character of the natural sciences. They investigate nature, and nature as such knows nothing of success and failure. In order to create consciousness you have to create mechanisms which can duplicate and not merely simulate the capacity of the brain to create consciousness. And by itself, the production of observer-relative success in competing with humans is no evidence at all for the presence of consciousness.

Finally, the quest for epistemic objectivity, a legitimate quest in science, is mistakenly supposed to preclude ontological subjectivity as a domain of investigation. This is such a massive error that one is amazed to see it in real life, but there it is. Rather than investigating the inner, qualitative, ontologically subjective character of human mental life, investigators in AI find the objective physical character of the computer systems, the physical symbol systems, reassuring. It seems we can only be doing real science if we change the subject and talk not about mental reality but about our electronic systems and their programs. This error is based on not seeing that you can have an epistemically objective science of a domain that is ontologically subjective. Indeed such sciences already exist. Any textbook of neurology moves without philosophical qualms between discussion of the patients' (ontologically subjective) pains, anxieties, and fears and the underlying (ontologically objective) neuronal structures that both cause these symptoms and in which they are realized.

Conclusion

One of the main morals to be drawn from this entire discussion is that an epistemically objective science of the mind will have to account for the existence of ontologically subjective phenomena such as consciousness and intentionality. In this science the computer will play the same role that it plays in any other science. It is a useful tool for investigation, and it is especially useful for producing simulations of natural phenomena. But the simulation should not be confused with duplication, whether the subject-matter is the mind, or anything else.

In the twenty-one years since the original publication of 'Minds, Brains, and Programs' a remarkable development has taken place. We have come to understand a great deal more about how brains function and we are beginning to understand how they might produce consciousness. We have a long way to go and I would not wish to overestimate the progress that has been made. But it is not out of the question that we will within the lifetimes of people living today come to understand how brain processes cause consciousness and how conscious states are realized in the brain. With an understanding of the biological mechanisms of consciousness most of the problem of intentionality will also be solved, because the intentionality of vision, hearing, memory, etc. are in the first instance all cases of conscious intentionality. The unconscious forms are derivative from the conscious forms. In cognitive science there is an inexorable paradigm shift taking place: we are moving from computational cognitive science to cognitive neuroscience. To the genuine science of the brain, the fantasy of Strong Artificial Intelligence, the fantasy that simply by designing the right computer program you could create consciousness and intentionality, is irrelevant.

References

FEYERABEND, P. K. (1975) *Against Method* (London: New Left Books).

HOFSTADTER, D., and DENNETT, D. C. (eds.) (1981) *The Mind's I: Fantasies and Reflections on Self and Soul* (New York: Basic Books).

KUHN, T. S. (1962) *The Structure of Scientific Revolutions* (Chicago: University of Chicago Press).

—— (1970) *The Structure of Scientific Revolutions*, 2nd edn. (Chicago: University of Chicago Press).

KURZWEIL, R. (1999) *The Age of Spiritual Machines* (New York: Viking).

PENROSE, R. (1994) *Shadows of the Mind: A Search for the Missing Science of Consciousness* (Oxford: Oxford University Press).

POPPER, K. R. (1959) *The Logic of Scientific Discovery* (London: Hutchinson).

STOVE, D. C. (1999) *Against the Idols of the Age*, ed. R. Kimball (New Brunswick: Transaction Publishers).

3

Searle's Arguments against Cognitive Science

Ned Block

1. The Chinese Room Argument

Searle's strategy is one of avoiding quibbles about specific programs by imagining that cognitive science of the distant future can come up with the program of an actual person who speaks and understands Chinese, and that this program can be implemented in a machine. Unlike many critics of the computer model, Searle is willing to grant that perhaps this can be done so as to focus on his claim that even if this can be done, the machine will not have intentional states.

The argument is based on a thought-experiment, derived from the Chinese Nation thought-experiment of Block (1978). Imagine yourself given a job in which you work in a room (the Chinese Room). You understand only English. Slips of paper with Chinese writing on them are put under the input door, and your job is to write sensible Chinese replies on other slips, and push them out under the output door. How do you do it? You act as the CPU (central processing unit) of a computer, following the computer program mentioned above that describes the symbol processing in an actual Chinese speaker's head. The program is printed in English in a library in the room. This is how you follow the program. Suppose the latest input has certain unintelligible (to you) Chinese squiggles on it. There is a blackboard on a wall of the room with a 'state' number written on it; it says '*17*'. (The CPU of a computer is a device with a finite number of states whose activity is determined solely by its current state and

Much of the material of this chapter is adapted from Block (1990) and (1995).

input, and since you are acting as the CPU, your output will be determined by your input and your 'state'. The '17' is on the blackboard to tell you what your 'state' is.) You take book 17 out of the library, and look up these particular squiggles in it. Book 17 tells you to look at what is written on your scratch pad (the computer's internal memory), and given both the input squiggles and the scratch pad marks, you are directed to change what is on the scratch pad in a certain way (write to the internal memory), write certain other squiggles on your output pad, push the paper under the output door, and finally, change the number on the state board to '*193*'. (The next state of a CPU is a function of the current state and two kinds of input, from memory and from input devices which are represented here as the squiggles that come under the input door.) As a result of this activity, speakers of Chinese find that the pieces of paper you slip under the output door are sensible replies to the inputs.

But you know nothing of what is being said in Chinese; you are just following instructions (in English) to look in certain books and write certain marks. According to Searle, since you don't understand any Chinese, the system of which you are the CPU is a mere Chinese simulator, not a real Chinese under-stander. Searle (rightly, in my view) rejects the Turing Test for understand-ing Chinese. His argument is based on the claim that the program of a real Chinese understander is not sufficient for understanding Chinese, so no symbol-manipulation theory of Chinese understanding (or any other inten-tional state) is correct about what *makes* something a Chinese understander. Thus the conclusion of Searle's argument is that the fundamental idea of thought as symbol-processing is wrong even if it allows us to build a machine that can duplicate the symbol-processing of a person and thereby duplicate a person's behavior. And since the view of thought as symbol-processing is central to one tradition in cognitive science, we can take the argument to purport to show that one central tradition in cognitive science has got things very wrong. In a later article (Searle 1990b), he extends the argument to the other main tradition in cognitive science, connectionism, with his 'Chinese Gym' argument—which uses an example closer to that of Block (1978).

The best criticisms of the Chinese Room Argument have focused on what Searle—anticipating the challenge—calls the Systems Reply. (Searle's original paper is followed by more than twenty-five responses; see also the comment on Searle (1980) in Hofstadter and Dennett (1981).) The Systems Reply has a posit-ive and a negative component. The negative component is that a company can be guilty of transferring nuclear materials to North Korea even if no individual person in the company is guilty. The behavior of institutions is a product of the activities of many people, and often none of them is really in control, the decisions being due to an interaction among them. Similarly, the system may understand Chinese even if no person who is part of its implementation understands Chinese (see Copeland 1993). So there is a gap in Searle's argument. The positive component goes further, saying that the whole system—man + program + board + paper + input and output doors—does understand Chinese, even though the man who is acting as the CPU does not. If you open up your own computer, looking for the CPU, you will find that it is just one of the many chips and other components on the main circuit-board. The Systems Reply reminds us that the CPUs of the thinking computers we hope to have someday will not *themselves* think—rather, they will be *parts* of thinking systems.

Searle's clever reply is to imagine the paraphernalia of the 'system' *internalized* as follows. First, instead of having you consult a library, we are to imagine you *memorizing* the whole library. Secondly, instead of writing notes on scratch pads, you are to memorize what you would have written on the pads, and you are to memorize what the state blackboard would say. Finally, instead of looking at notes put under one door and passing notes under another door, you just use your *own body* to listen to Chinese utterances and produce replies. (This version of the Chinese room has the additional advantage of generalizability so as to involve the complete behavior of a Chinese-speaking system instead of just a Chinese note exchanger.) But as Searle would emphasize, when you seem to Chinese speakers to be conducting a learned discourse with them in Chinese, all you are aware of doing is thinking about what noises the program tells you to make next, given the noises you hear and what you've written on your mental scratch pad.

I argued above that the CPU is just one of many components of the system. If the whole system understands Chinese, that should not lead us to expect the CPU to understand Chinese. The effect of Searle's internalization move—the 'new' Chinese Room—is to attempt to destroy the analogy between looking inside the computer and looking inside the Chinese Room. If one looks inside the computer, one sees many chips in addition to the CPU. But if one looks inside the 'new' Chinese Room, all one sees is *you*, since you have memorized the library and internalized the functions of the scratch pad and the blackboard. But the point to keep in mind is that although the non-CPU components are no longer easy to see, they are not gone. Rather, they are internalized. If the program requires the contents of one register to be placed in another register, and if you would have done this in the original Chinese Room by copying from one piece of scratch paper to another, in the new Chinese Room you must copy from one of your mental analogs of a piece of scratch paper to another. You are implementing the system by doing what the CPU would do and you are simultaneously simulating the non-CPU components. So if the positive side of the Systems Reply is correct, the total system that you are implementing does understand Chinese.

'But how can it be', Searle would object, 'that you implement a system that understands Chinese even though *you* don't understand Chinese?' The Systems Reply rejoinder is that you implement a Chinese understanding system without yourself understanding Chinese or necessarily even being aware of what you are doing under that description. The Systems Reply sees the Chinese Room (new and old) as an English system implementing a Chinese system. What you are aware of are the thoughts of the English system, for example, your following instructions and consulting your internal library. But in virtue of doing this Herculean task, you are also implementing a real intelligent Chinese-speaking system, and so your body houses two genuinely distinct intelligent systems. The Chinese system also thinks, but though you implement this thought, you are not aware of it.

The Systems Reply can be backed up with an addition to the thought-experiment that highlights the division of labor. Imagine that you take on the Chinese simulating as a nine-to-five job. You come in Monday morning after a weekend of relaxation, and you are paid to follow the program until 5 p.m. When you are working, you concentrate hard at working, and so instead of trying to figure out the meaning of what is said to you, you focus your energies on working out what the program tells you to do in response to each input. As a result, during working hours, you respond to everything just as the program dictates, except for occasional glances at your watch. (The glances at your watch fall under the same category as the noises and heat given off by computers: aspects of their behavior that is not part of the machine description but are due rather to features of the implementation.) If someone speaks to you in English, you say what the program (which, you recall, describes a real Chinese speaker) dictates. So if during working hours someone speaks to you in English, you respond with a request in Chinese to speak Chinese, or even an inexpertly pronounced 'No speak English', that was once memorized by the Chinese speaker being simulated, and which you, the English-speaking system, may even fail to recognize as English because you are so intent on following the program. Of course you may not do this perfectly, but then any actual computer can malfunction, and the parameters of malfunctioning are determined by the physical implementation. If you fail a lot, you are badly implementing the program of a Chinese speaker, but still implementing it. Any real speaker can faint, have a migraine, or die. These are different types of failures from those that the Chinese system being implemented by an English system is subject to (though migraines can happen here too), but the cognitive science perspective allows that different implementations bring different failures. Then, come 5 p.m., you stop working, and react to Chinese talk the way any monolingual English speaker would.

Why is it that the English system implements the Chinese system rather than, say, the other way around? Because you (the English system whom I am now addressing) are following the instructions of a program in English to make Chinese noises and not the other way around. If you decide to quit your job to become a magician, the Chinese system disappears. However, if the Chinese system decides to become a magician, he will make plans that he would express in Chinese, but then when 5 p.m. rolls around, you quit for the day, and the Chinese system's plans are on the shelf until you come back to work. And of course you have no commitment to doing *whatever* the program dictates. If the program dictates that you make a series of movements that leads you to a flight to China, you can drop out of the simulating mode, saying 'I quit!' The Chinese speaker's existence and the fulfillment of his plans depends on your work schedule and your plans, not the other way around.

Thus, you and the Chinese system cohabit one body. In effect, Searle uses the fact that you are not aware of the Chinese system's thoughts as an argument that it has no thoughts. But real cases of multiple personalities are often cases in which one personality is unaware of the others. Further, the Chinese system is not aware of your thoughts, so there is no asymmetry.

There is one aspect of Searle's case with which I am sympathetic. I have my doubts as to whether there is anything it is like to be the Chinese system, that is, whether the Chinese system is a phenomenally conscious system. My doubts arise from the idea that perhaps consciousness is more a matter of implementation of symbol-processing than of symbol-processing itself. Though surprisingly Searle does not mention this idea in connection with the Chinese Room, I see it as the argumentative heart of his position. Searle has argued independently of the Chinese Room (Searle 1992, ch. 7) that intentionality requires consciousness. (See the replies to Searle in *Behavioral and Brain Sciences*, 13 (1990).) But this doctrine, if correct, can shore up the Chinese Room argument. For if the Chinese system is not conscious, then, according to Searle's doctrine, it is not an intentional system either.

It is instructive to compare Searle's thought-experiment with the string-searching Aunt Bubbles machine described in Block (1990, 1995, 1980) and Braddon-Mitchell and Jackson (1996)—they call it the 'blockhead'. The block-head is the ultimate in unintelligent Turing Test passers, a hypothetical machine that contains *all conversations of a given length* in which the machine's replies make sense. Let's stipulate that the test lasts one hour. Since there is an upper bound on how fast a human typist can type, and since there are a finite number of keys on a teletype, there is an upper bound on the 'length' of a Turing Test conversation. Thus there are a finite (though more than astronomical) number of different Turing Test conversations, and there is no contradiction in the idea of *listing them all*.

Let's call a string of characters that can be typed in an hour or less a 'typable' string. In principle, all typable strings could be generated, and a team of intelligent programmers could throw out all the strings which cannot be interpreted as a conversation in which at least one party (say the second contributor) is making sense. The remaining strings (call them the sensible strings) could be stored in a hypothetical computer (say, with marks separating the contributions of the separate parties), which works as follows. Let us imagine that a judge who is judging the intelligence of the machine goes first, typing in something, as it might be 'Hi, I'm the judge'. Then the machine locates a string that starts with 'Hi, I'm the judge', spitting back its next element, which the programmers have chosen to be a sensible reply, for example, 'Hard job you've got, eh'. The judge then types something else. The machine finds a string that begins with the judge's first contribution, followed by the machine's, followed by the judge's next contribution (the string will be there since all sensible strings are there), and then the machine spits back its fourth element, and so on. (We can eliminate the simplifying assumption that the judge speaks first by recording *pairs* of strings; this would also allow the judge and the machine to talk at the same time.) The programmers might think of themselves as simulating the responses that would be given by some specific person, say my Aunt Bubbles. Though the blockhead can give the responses Aunt Bubbles would have given for any specified finite time, the machine has the intelligence of a jukebox.

Of course, the blockhead is only logically possible, not physically possible. The number of strings is too vast to exist, and even if they could exist, they could never be accessed by any sort of a machine in anything like real time. But since behaviorism is supposed to capture the *concept* of intelligence, conceptual possibility will do the job. If the concept of intelligence is supposed to be exhausted by the ability to pass the Turing Test, then even a universe in which the laws of physics are very different from ours should contain exactly as many unintelligent Turing Test passers as married bachelors, namely zero.

Note that the choice of one hour as a limit for the Turing Test is of no consequence, since the procedure just described works for *any* finite Turing Test.

I mentioned the blockhead because it makes for an interesting contrast with Searle's Chinese Room Argument. The most plausible approaches to the concept of thought are

1. The concept is a functional concept, the concept of a role defined by its relation to inputs, outputs, and other internal states and processes.
2. It is a natural kind concept: thinking is whatever basic feature of the human mind it is that was responsible for what Einstein did in coming up with his famous theories, what Gödel did in coming up with his famous proofs, what Shakespeare did in coming up with his famous plays, etc.

The Chinese Room comes out as a thinker according to 1—it is functionally equivalent to a person. And the Chinese Room is a thinker according to 2 if the relevant natural kind is computational. It fails 2 only if a rather adventurous empirical claim of Searle's is true, that the scientific essence of thought is *chemical* rather than computational. So Searle's Chinese Room Argument depends on an adventurous empirical claim. Searle describes the brain as secreting intentionality like a gland. But how does he know? Why should we believe *him* on this empirical question rather than the scientists who study the matter? Searle's argument depends on ungrounded empirical speculation.

The blockhead, by contrast, fails both tests. It is not functionally equivalent to a person since it lacks the appropriate network of internal states, and the idea that the relevant natural kind is a behavioral one is a casualty of the last forty years of successes of cognitive science. So according to both approaches to the concept of thought, the blockhead does not think. So the blockhead argument does not depend on ungrounded empirical speculation.

2. Is a Wall a Computer?

Searle (1990a) argues against the computationalist thesis that the brain is a computer. He does not say that the thesis is false, but rather that it is trivial, because, he suggests, everything is a computer; indeed, everything is *every* computer. In particular, his wall is a computer computing Wordstar. The key to computation is an isomorphism. We arrange things so that, if certain physical states of a machine are understood as symbols, then causal relations among those symbol-states mirror useful rational relations among the meanings of those symbols. The mirroring is an isomorphism. Searle's claim is that this sort of isomorphism is cheap. We can regard two aspects of the wall at time t as the symbols '0' and '1', and then we can regard an aspect of the wall at time $t + 1$ as '1', and so the wall just computed $0 + 1 = 1$. Thus, Searle suggests, everything (or rather everything that is big or complex enough to have enough states) is every computer, and the claim that the brain is a computer has no bite.

The problem with this reasoning is that the isomorphism that makes a syntactic engine drive a semantic engine is more full-bodied than Searle acknowledges. In particular, the isomorphism has to include not just a particular computation that the machine *does perform*, but all the computations that the machine *could have* performed. The point can be made clearer by a look at Fig. 3.1.

The numerals at the beginnings of arrows represent inputs. The computation of $1 + 0 = 1$ is represented by the path A→C→E. The computation of $0 + 1 = 1$ is represented by the path A→B →E, and so on. Now here is the point. In order for the wall to be this computer, it isn't enough for it to have states that correspond to '0' and '1' followed by a state that corresponds to '1'. It must also be such that *had* the '1' input been replaced by a '0' input, the '1' output *would have been* replaced by the '0' output. In other words, it has to have symbolic states that satisfy not only the *actual* computation, but also the *possible* computations that the computer could have performed. And this is non-trivial.

Searle (1992: 209) more or less acknowledges this point, but insists none the less that there is no fact of the matter of whether the brain is a specific computer. Whether something is a computer, he argues, depends on whether we decide to interpret its states in a certain way, and that is up to us. 'We can't, on the one

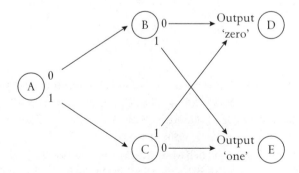

Fig. 3.1 A type of X-or gate.

hand, say that anything is a digital computer if we can assign a syntax to it, and then suppose there is a factual question intrinsic to its physical operation whether or not a natural system such as the brain is a digital computer.' Searle is right that whether something is a computer and what computer it is is in part up to us. A good example is that any physical device that can be interpreted as an inclusive OR gate can also be interpreted as an AND gate (and conversely). To see this, note that an AND gate outputs a '*1*' just in case both inputs are '*1*'—and otherwise outputs a '*0*'. Any physical device that acts this way can have its states reinterpreted. Suppose the interpretation that made it an AND gate was: 4 volt potential is interpreted as '*0*', 7 volts as '*1*'. But we could reverse the interpretation, reading 4 volts as '*1*' and 7 volts as '*0*'. Then we would have a device that outputs a '*0*' just in case both inputs are '*0*'s (otherwise '*1*'), and that is an OR gate. So a mere change in interpretation can change an OR to an AND gate. But though this example shows that we have some latitude in assigning computational descriptions, it also shows that what computer something is, is not *totally* up to us. An *inclusive* OR gate cannot be interpreted as an *exclusive* OR gate, for example. It just won't do the calculation, no matter how you interpret the states. (If you interpret the output according to the rule 'Consider the output to be the result of computing "exclusive OR [input 1, input 2]" ', then the result will be right, but the calculation will be done by the interpreter, not the gate). We have a great deal of freedom as to how to interpret a device, but there are also very important restrictions on this freedom, and that is what makes it a substantive claim that the brain is a computer of a certain sort.

Even if I am right about the failure of Searle's arguments, they do succeed in sharpening our understanding of the nature of intentionality and its relation to computation and representation.

References

BLOCK, N. (1978) 'Troubles with Functionalism', in C. Wade Savage (ed.), *Minnesota Studies in the Philosophy of Science, Volume 9* (Minneapolis: University of Minnesota Press), 261–325. Reprinted in N. BLOCK (ed.), *Readings in Philosophy of Psychology, Volume 1* (Cambridge, Mass.: Harvard University Press, 1980), 268–305.

—— (1980) 'Psychologism and Behaviorism', *Philosophical Review*, 90: 5–43.

—— (1990) 'The Computer Model of the Mind', in D. Osherson and E. Smith (eds.), *An Invitation to Cognitive Science, Volume 3: Thinking* (Cambridge, Mass.: MIT Press), 247–89.

—— (1995) 'The Mind as the Software of the Brain', in D. Osherson, L. Gleitman, S. Kosslyn, E. Smith, and S. Sternberg (eds.), *An Invitation to Cognitive Science, Volume 3: Reasoning*, 2nd edn. (Cambridge, Mass.: MIT Press), 377–425.

BRADDON-MITCHELL, D., and JACKSON, F. (1996) *Philosophy of Mind and Cognition* (Oxford: Blackwell).

COPELAND, B. J. (1993) 'The Curious Case of the Chinese Gym', *Synthese*, 95: 173–86.

HOFSTADTER, D., and DENNETT, D. C. (eds.) (1981) *The Mind's I: Fantasies and Reflections on Self and Soul* (New York: Basic Books).

SEARLE, J. R. (1980) 'Minds, Brains, and Programs', *Behavioral and Brain Sciences*, 3: 417–24.

—— (1990a) 'Is the Brain a Digital Computer?' *Proceedings and Addresses of the American Philosophical Association*, 64: 21–37.

—— (1990b) 'Is the Brain's Mind a Computer Program?' *Scientific American*, 262: 20–5.

—— (1992) *The Rediscovery of the Mind* (Cambridge, Mass.: MIT Press).

4

Understanding, Orientations, and Objectivity

Terry Winograd

In a way, this chapter is an argument not against Searle, but against the grounds on which the debate about his position has been conducted. I argue that the question Searle poses, 'Does the computer understand?', is a meaningless question when it is stripped of an appropriate context of utterance.

In his writings on artificial intelligence, in particular in his 'Chinese Room' example, Searle attacks two claims: that AI can 'explain' human cognitive ability, and that a computer can be said literally to 'understand' and have other cognitive states. I find myself in accord with his skeptical attitude towards both claims, but for reasons that do not correspond to his arguments. Although much has been written in response to his opinions, little agreement has been reached about the fundamental issues. This should not be surprising, because the questions as he posed them are simply not the kind of coherent questions that allow for objective answers. In framing the debate, Searle made contestable assumptions about the use of language. Put simply, I argue that it is an error to suppose that there is a right or wrong answer to the question of whether the computer (or the Chinese Room) 'understands' language. The error is not

This is a revised version of a paper written in 1979 intended for publication as one of the responses to Searle's original paper in *Behavioral and Brain Sciences*. It was not completed in time for that purpose, and was not subsequently published. In revising it for inclusion in this volume, I have not attempted to address the vast array of positions and arguments that have emerged in twenty years of debate, since the chapter is primarily concerned with the assumptions underlying that debate, which have remained constant over the years.

one of flawed logic in the argument about artificial intelligence, but is more fundamental and more pervasive. It has to do with the basic orientation we take towards the truth or falsity of statements in natural language.

Throughout the paper, Searle adopts the naïve view that 'understand' can be understood as a straightforward two-place predicate—that there is some objective sense in which it 'really is the case' that X understands Y or X doesn't understand Y. In presenting examples, he makes liberal use of loaded modifiers, such as 'obvious', 'perfectly', and 'certainly', as in 'it seems to me quite obvious in the example that I do not understand a word of the Chinese stories' (Searle 1980: 418)[1], 'what is it that I have in the case of the English sentences that I do not have in the case of the Chinese sentences? The obvious answer is that I know what the former mean, while I haven't the faintest idea what the latter mean' (ibid. (B71)), and 'the man certainly doesn't understand Chinese, and neither do the water pipes . . .' (ibid. 421 (B78)). Searle's 'just-plain-old-obvious-common-sense' posture can be a useful antidote to sophistry, but in this case it conceals the real issues. His interpretations of the counter-arguments all suffer from his unexamined adherence to the assumption that 'understand' should be treated as an observer-independent predicate. He explicitly states 'In "cognitive sciences" one presupposes the reality and knowability of the mental in the same way that in physical sciences one has to presuppose the reality and knowability of physical objects' (ibid. 422 (B80)).

We need to understand 'understand' in a different way (which Searle may then choose not to call 'cognitive science'). As an analogy, consider the terms 'man' and 'woman'. For most people for most of history, this has seemed like a clear objective distinction, rooted not in interpretation but in biology. We deal every day with paradigmatic cases of gender—with central and unproblematic uses of the terms. Now consider a victim of a rare disease such as testicular feminization, whose external characteristics are those of a woman, but whose chromosomal pattern is male and whose reproductive organs are not developed for either gender. People with a certain scientific attitude would say 'If the chromosomes are XY it is really a man. Everything else is just appearances'. Others with a more social-operational approach would say 'If she looks, acts, and views herself as a woman, she is really a woman. The rest is just biomolecular technicalities'. Others would say 'If there are no developed reproductive organs, it is neither a man nor a woman, and we have to give up the Boolean either-or nature of the categories'.

---

[1] Reprinted in Boden (1990: 70). From here referred to as B70.

It is unproductive to ask 'Which one of these three is *really* right?' Each is right for certain concerns and from certain perspectives. Each is wrong for others. The problem is that our eons of experience have led us to expect all of the factors (visible characteristics, reproductive potential, and genetic composition) to combine in a regular way. Our language isn't prepared to deal with a new situation in which they come unglued. That is exactly the problem that arises when we try to say that computers do (or don't) 'understand'. We have clear intuitions that mechanical things (such as pencil sharpeners) don't understand, and that human beings of normal intelligence do. But the computer is a mix-and-match, like the ambiguously gendered person. The familiar terms just don't fit, no matter how hard we contort our arguments.

Even a casual examination of the use of 'understand' in everyday discourse reveals that its applicability is not 'obvious'. For the sake of this examination of statements such as '*X* understands *Y*', we will consider only cases in which *X* is a person and *Y* is a linguistic text or utterance. Many additional interesting issues are raised by utterances such as 'Only Einstein really understood relativity', 'My analyst doesn't understand me', and 'I just can't understand what happened at Jonestown', but they are not central to this discussion.

Even in the case of understanding a linguistic object, there is no definable boundary between 'understanding' and 'not understanding'. We can say things like 'I read his dissertation but I didn't understand it'. 'Do you think he understood what you said about the hiring situation?', and 'It's the kind of book a high school student can understand'. There are cases where from one perspective we would choose to say that someone does understand something, while from another we would regard the same person as not understanding. As a native English speaker, I (in some obvious sense) understand a newspaper editorial. But if someone later points out its political undertones, I may say 'Oh, I really didn't understand it'.

This kind of phenomenon is not a rarity. Much of our basic vocabulary has the same property. If I ask 'Was the crowd big?', the answer does not depend simply on the number of people, but on a background of comparison with some anticipation (particular to speaker, hearer, and situation) of what size would be expected. Similarly, 'understand' carries with it an unspoken consensus between speaker and hearer. As a rough indication of understanding, we might say that *X* understands *Y* if, having heard (or read) *Y*, *X*'s potential for future action is changed in the appropriate ways. This paraphrase puts the weight of the speaker-hearer consensus on the word 'appropriate'. In some contexts, to use Schank's example, it is appropriate for someone who has heard a fragmentary account of an event in a restaurant to answer the question 'What did John eat?' with 'a hamburger'. In other cases (such as understanding a warning), there may be clear immediate actions that we expect, while in others (such as understanding a poem), the appropriate changes may be impossible to specify precisely. However, if a person reads a poem and his future potential for action (including mental and verbal action) is not in some way changed by it, we feel comfortable in saying 'He didn't really understand it'. Of course, for practical situations, there is no way of testing whether the appropriate changes have happened. One can make a finite number of specific tests (make observations, ask questions, etc.) but more could always be generated, and it is possible they would have conflicting results.

Everyday common sense urges us to believe that there must be a 'right' answer, not dependent on purposes, context, and interpretation. Either the computer understands or it doesn't. But our everyday common sense also tells us that the ground beneath our feet is flat, and that there is an absolute frame of reference for the motion of objects. The common-sense view works well as an approximation for the things we ordinarily encounter but this should not be taken as a proof that it will work with new phenomena. Naïve common sense suggests that although there may be a fuzzy boundary on terms such as 'woman' or 'understand', they have an objective real meaning, which we see in cases that are 'obvious'. I argue on the contrary that every meaning is inherently contextual and open-ended, but that in many everyday cases the context is so firmly shared and taken for granted among the participants that there is an illusion of objectivity. Language is always an incomplete, partial, and ambiguous reflection of experience. Therefore the answer to the question 'Does the computer understand?' is not an unequivocal 'yes' or 'no', but depends on the background of assumptions and interpretations, just as much as does the gender example.

'Understand' as an Orientation

In applying a predicate to an entity, one is implicitly committed to the presupposition that the entity is the type of thing to which the predicate properly applies. If we say that an idea is 'green', we presuppose that it is the kind of thing that can have a color. Since in ordinary interpretation it is not, the result appears semantically ill formed. If the world fell neatly into distinct categories, this formal notion of semantic restriction would be adequate. But ordinary everyday language falls between this kind of formalistic object property categorization, and something that might be characterized as metaphor. If I say that a person or a bee or a volcano is 'angry', I am slipping from a case in which it is a standard assumption that the predicate is appropriate to others in which I am using it to convey not only the sense of angriness, but also my orientation towards the object being characterized.

Much of the gut-level force of Searle's argument against AI comes from the unstated recognition that in uttering a sentence containing mental terms ('understand', 'perceive', 'learn'), we are adopting an orientation towards the referent of the subject of the sentence as an autonomous agent. The issue is not whether it really is autonomous—the question of free will has been debated for centuries and work in AI has provided no new insights. The issue is that in using mental terms, we treat the subject as an autonomous agent. In using the word 'action', rather than 'behavior' in the earlier paraphrase for 'understand', this autonomy was implicit. The kind of thing that acts or understands is an autonomous agent.

There are many reasons why one can feel uncomfortable with the tendency to adopt the same orientation towards people (who are the prime exemplar for autonomous beings), and towards machines (or systems or organizations). It isn't that in doing so speakers are right or wrong, accurate or inaccurate, but that they are accepting (often unwittingly) attitudes and role relations that can have implications for social interaction. Although there is no context-independent answer as to whether something is autonomous, it is not simply an idle matter of opinion.

Some statements are subject to coherent grounding within the network of statements accepted generally within a society, and therefore are more likely to be agreed upon as correct than statements that contradict or go outside of that discourse. If it is not up to us as a linguistically bound social group to decide which entities are autonomous agents, then who is it up to? Is the sun an autonomous agent? A networked computer? A robotic toy such as Furby or Aibo? This is not an objective question, but a choice (not individual but within a linguistic community) of what we choose to approach as 'autonomous'. It is misplaced concreteness to say 'It *is* autonomous' as though that were a matter of fact outside of our interpretive linguistic space.

When is it Appropriate to say that Someone (or Something) Understands?

Returning to an examination of the claims of AI, we can address them without buying Searle's assumption that there is an objective sense in which words such as 'understand' are correctly applied to some objects and not to others. The question is more a social one—when is it appropriate (or to borrow a word from speech act theory, 'felicitous') to characterize a situation as 'understanding'.

I find myself (along with most people I know) frequently using mental terms in talking about animals and machines. I find it effective to describe the behavior of a computer program using statements such as 'This program only understands two kinds of commands . . .'. In this context, the appropriate future action by the machine is clear. To understand a command means to perform those operations that the user intends to invoke in typing the input that corresponds to that command. It is clear to me and to the person I address that other changes (such as getting impatient, or noting that I seem to give those kinds of commands often, and therefore treating me differently) are not needed in order to be appropriate—in order to count as 'understanding'. This is not a derivative use of language involving some kind of metaphor. The word 'understand' is being applied as literally as it ever could be: that is, relative to a background and context of assumptions. Any attempt to claim that it is being used 'only metaphorically' or 'incorrectly' flies against the facts of ordinary language use. 'Literal' use, like 'correct' use, is not an objective distinction, but a contextual judgment.

In most discussions of artificial intelligence, the situation is more problematic, since there is rarely sufficient background of mutual agreement between speaker and hearer (or reader) about the range of appropriate change. Most people would feel that 'understanding of a story' should entail more than the ability to answer simple questions about whether a hamburger was eaten. Therefore, Schank's program does not undergo the 'appropriate' changes, and does not understand. In general, since AI claims are couched in terms of 'doing what a person does', the natural assumption about the range of appropriate changes is that they include the full extent of what one would normally expect in an adult human native speaker of the language. In this sense, it is clear that no existing AI program understands. It is potentially misleading to say that it does, except in specialized technical conversation where the background of expectations is not based on the background of full human abilities.

The Counter-arguments

We can re-examine the counter-arguments and Searle's responses in terms of our two observations about what it means to say 'X understands Y':

1. The speaker presupposes a context-dependent background of what the appropriate consequences are for understanding.

2. The speaker implies a presupposition that X is the kind of thing that can be autonomous.

Taking the replies in the order in which Searle addresses them in his response:

1. The Systems Reply (Berkeley)

> While it is true that the person who is locked in the room does not understand the story . . . he is merely part of a whole system and the system does understand the story.
>
> (Searle 1980: 419 (B72))

This argument is based on choosing not to adopt an orientation towards the blindly-rule-following homunculus as an autonomous agent, while attributing autonomy to this whole mysterious arrangement—a group to whom one passes stories and questions in Chinese, and that passes back answers after some inscrutable process of cogitation. The 'system', though not a conscious individual, is said to understand, in the same sense that one might ask whether a review committee understood a funding proposal. There may be reasons not to want to follow the consequences of granting autonomy to impersonal 'systems' whether made up of people or mechanisms (e.g. in attributing responsibility to corporations as distinct from the individuals who run them), but the Systems Reply raises a key issue. In using the word 'understand' one presupposes the boundaries of the system that will be treated as autonomous.

There is an interesting reflection of this point in the way we discuss our own minds. I can say 'The rational side of me understands, but my feelings are . . .'. In doing so, I reject the common-sense orientation of a person as a single autonomous entity, instead viewing the individual as made up of a number of independent 'subpersonalities', each acting autonomously.

2. The Robot Reply (Yale)

> . . . a [physically embodied] robot would . . . have genuine understanding.
>
> (ibid. 420 (B76))

Once again, the reply posits a necessary condition for treating something as autonomous—its physical embodiment. It further articulates the question of what it means for the potential for future action to be changed in appropriate ways. One measure of appropriateness is tied to the ways in which the possible actions mimic the corresponding human actions, which we see in the physical world. Most people would be more likely to adopt an orientation of autonomy towards an android than towards a less superficially human-like machine. This does not mean that they would have better philosophical justification for doing so, but that their whole background of perception and action towards the android would be affected by its physical characteristics, regardless of their conscious knowledge that it was artificially constructed.

3. The Brain Simulator Reply (Berkeley and MIT)

> Suppose . . . [the program] simulates the actual sequence of neuron firings at the synapses [in] the brain of a native Chinese speaker when he under-stands stories in Chinese and gives answers to them. . . . [S]urely in such a case we would have to say that the machine understood the stories; and if we refuse to say that, wouldn't we also have to deny that native Chinese speakers understood the stories?
>
> (ibid. 420 (B77))

Searle indicates that he finds this reply odd, since it depends on a notion of simulation that does not usually find its way into AI arguments. In doing so, he misses the point that it is a response to him (an admitted philosopher), in what the respondents saw as a philosophical, not technical vein. The issue he raised is whether a computer running a symbolic simulation could ever be described as 'understanding'. They were putting forward a case that was most likely to convince him that a simulation could duplicate in some exact sense the activ-ities of the brain. This is not at all incompatible with other (technical) discussions in which they might argue that other ways of building a translating machine would be more effective.

In responding to their arguments, Searle distinguishes between the 'formal properties' of the brain and the 'causal properties'. Lurking in this distinction is an interesting and dubious form of dualism. Searle would agree that the brain operates according to physical causal principles, and that the computer (or water pipes or whatever he uses as examples) may well operate with analogs or repres-entations of those same principles. He claims to believe that 'mental causality' exists in some other domain, whose connections to physical causality appear to be just as mysterious as the mind–body problem has always been. If someone can predict the future physical events in my brain and body based on physical caus-ality, and can also predict my future actions on the basis of intentional causality, there must be some magical connection that guarantees they will be consistent. It seems to be only due to Searle's formidable rhetorical skills that this view has been taken seriously in the absence of any coherent explanation of how the two worlds of causality manage to avoid getting in each other's way.

4. (What we might call) The Strong Brain Simulator Reply (MIT)

> We can even imagine that the machine operates, not with a single serial program, but with a whole set of programs operating in parallel, in the manner that actual human brains presumably operate when they process natural language. Now surely in such a case we would have to say that the machine understood the stories . . .? At the level of the synapses, what would or could be different about the program of the computer and the program of the Chinese brain?
>
> (ibid. 420 (B77))

Searle states that this is the same mistake as the 'Systems Reply'. I agree that the parallelism makes no essential difference. But in saying 'it doesn't make any sense to make such collective ascriptions to the team' Searle is refusing to acknowledge that people can choose to adopt an orientation towards groups (or teams) as unitary autonomous agents.

5. The Other Minds Reply (Yale)

> [if] a computer can pass the behavioral tests as well as [people] can . . . if you are going to attribute cognition to other people you must in principle also attribute it to computers.
>
> (ibid. 421 (B80))

Searle discounts this argument by insisting that cognitive science cannot be based purely on behavioral description. 'In "cognitive sciences" one presupposes the reality and knowability of the mental' (ibid. 422 (B80)). Given his dualistic approach, this implies that the cognitive scientist assumes without debate the reality of the mental for other people (since it is 'just plain obvious' that other people have mental states even though you can't experience their states yourself). But for machines, the assumption is that there can be 'the computational processes and their output without the cognitive state'. Both assumptions are commonsensical, which isn't a very solid reason for accepting them in this kind of debate.

The 'other minds' argument can be rejected on quite different grounds. Solipsism is a philosophical choice in some abstract intellectual sense, but not a real choice for anyone who lives in a society. By the very act of entering into serious conversation with other people (even if that conversation is a defense of solipsism) one is adopting an orientation that grants their autonomy as individuals. This is not the case when one interacts with machines (or animals, or even all the people one deals with, as histories of slavery and genocide have demonstrated). There are alternatives for how we understand our relationship to machines, and although an individual does not have an unencumbered choice (being enmeshed in the tradition embodied in a language), the tradition as a whole can move in different directions. It is certainly not an a priori conclusion that we must adopt the same orientation towards people and machines, no matter how well they mimic each other in behavioral tests.

6. The Many Mansions Reply (Berkeley)

> . . . eventually we will be able to build devices that have these [mental] causal processes.
>
> (ibid. 422 (B81)).

Searle claims openness to this possibility, commenting that it seems to trivialize the project of artificial intelligence. Based on his earlier comments, I do not understand how he can say 'I see no reason in principle why we couldn't give a machine the capacity to understand . . . since in an important sense our bodies and brains are precisely such machines'. My interpretation of his response to the 'brain simulation' response denies this. If someone were to build an exact replica of a human being (down to the chemical details) it would seem that his earlier objections still apply—that the replica operates according to physical causal principles, and that there is no understanding in the molecules or in the neurons or in the constructed brain matter, any more than the water pipes of his example. A claim that this replica is in some essential sense different from a person must be grounded either in a strong form of mind–body dualism or in an argument based on differences of perspective for interpretation.

Conclusion

The argument of this chapter as stated so far is in a way self-contradictory. I argue that there is no objective answer to the question as to whether a computer operating analogously to the Chinese Room actually 'understands'. But in bothering to state this argument, there appears to be an implied belief that to be a 'coherent question' the question must allow for an objective answer. Certainly, such an assumption flies in the face of the interpretation of meaning as context- and situation-dependent. The underlying question of significance is not whether Searle poses a 'coherent' question but whether it is a productive question. The value of questioning is generated in the argumentation that the question provokes, and Searle's argument has certainly led to an outpouring of thinking about questions of mechanism, meaning, and understanding. There is however, an important difference in perspective. When the argumentation centers around fine-tuning definitions and concocting clever *gedankenexperiments*, it can become self-indulgent and detached from real concerns. It can instead lead into questions about topics such as the attribution of autonomy, potential for action and change of action, and assumptions about boundaries of autonomous systems. The social constructions that surround us with regard to these questions have profound consequences. They have not been answered (and will never be in an objective sense) and in the continuing questioning, Searle's example and his arguments deserve many more years yet of discussion.

APPENDIX

In the process of revising this chapter for the current volume, the author and one of the editors entered into a dialog in which a number of potential objections were raised. In the spirit of seeing meaning as embedded in a discourse context, it seems more instructive to present them as a dialog, rather than attempting to anticipate the objections in the initial argument.

JP. You complain about Searle's claim that cognitive science must presuppose the reality and knowability of the mental. Isn't he right here, that unless cognitive science presupposes at least that, it simply wouldn't have a subject-matter? What else would it be *about*? Something that claims or hopes to constitute a science does have to presuppose that it has a subject-matter. In order for there to be a science of something, this something does need to exist, and its existence must be presupposed or asserted by the science in question. Could cognitive science (however conceived) do without the assumption that there are cognitive phenomena to be studied and known?

TW. In order for a discourse to be 'about' something, it does not need to presuppose the reality and knowability (in an objective sense) of the thing it is about. Participants may often jointly suspend disbelief and operate from an 'as if' position in which the reality is taken for granted. That is a discourse strategy, not a foundation. That is how we get along in everyday life. We use language that presupposes the existence of the things we talk about, digging only when appropriate into foundational questions. To take an obvious example, we can certainly have a discussion about 'God' without thereby presupposing the reality and/or knowability of a deity. It is an assumption of the 'Sciences' that they deal only with knowable matters, but that assumption is part of the social discourse, not a necessary condition for acting as scientists.

JP. Mightn't Searle try to take on your objections to the Chinese Room argument by admitting that there are grey areas in which it is unclear whether to say of someone that they understand, but insisting that all *he* needs is that there are central and unproblematic uses of such expressions too?

TW. This does reflect the fundamental difference between my view of meaning and Searle's. He always wants to say 'there may be a fuzzy boundary but some cases are just plain clear' and I want to say 'everything is contextual, but in many cases the context is so firmly shared and taken for granted among the participants that there is an illusion of objectivity'. This is a half-full/half-empty argument that can never be settled. I claim that my perspective explains why there is so much unresolved confusion around his claims about whether computers can understand. If the claims were based on statements that are inherently incoherent (in the sense of not having objective answers) then one would expect exactly the kind of ongoing debate over terms. Searle would argue that the confusion is due to other people's failure to correctly understand(!) his argument, and that there is really a right answer—his.

People who are not comfortable with ambiguity and uncertainty try to fall back on some standard by which one or another set of considerations is the 'objective' stance and therefore gives the 'real' answer. I see the open-endedness of meaning as the basic condition of language: language is always an incomplete, partial, and ambiguous reflection of experience. Therefore the question 'Does the computer understand?' is not answerable with any objective 'yes' or 'no', but rather depends on the background of assumptions and interpretations (as does the gender example). We have to take perspectives into account if we want to deal with language use in the real world, as opposed to an abstracted logic of definitions. This does not make a predicate like 'understand' more difficult to apply than it really is, but allows us to apply it as it really is used in ordinary discourse.

JP. You point out that linguistic distinctions (like 'man'/'woman') have borderline cases. But isn't this a different linguistic phenomenon from the one on which your case officially rests, which is context-relativity? After all, Searle could happily concede that 'man'/'woman' has borderline cases while at the same time insisting that there are (or at least *could* be) also very clear, indeed paradigm, cases of 'man' and of 'woman'.

TW. All cases are borderline. Some are just more visibly borderline than others. 'Borderline' means that the choice of whether the linguistic distinction applies is not context-independent, but depends on the context. There are many cases for which the context is so thoroughly shared and taken for granted that the border isn't visible. This is a contingent condition on the congruency of backgrounds of speaker and hearer, not a 'paradigmatic' or objective condition.

JP. You say 'There are cases where from one perspective we would choose to say that someone does understand something, while from another we would regard the same person as not understanding'. Searle might reply 'But surely if you were the person in the Chinese Room, you wouldn't have *any* doubt that, no matter how long you had spent in there, you wouldn't understand (any) Chinese?' So he might ask 'Why would one suppose that the judgment that the person in the Room doesn't understand Chinese is one of these "cases where from one perspective . . ."?'

TW. This is an accurate imitation of what Searle would say, complete with the empha-sized '*any*'. It is typical of his wording when he takes the 'how can you possibly doubt common sense?' tack. I would only have doubt if I went beyond my naïve standard way of talking about understanding, and considered the philosophical questions seriously.

JP. Your argument may establish (or at least make probable, by analogy) that 'under-stand' has borderline cases, but not that it is context-relative across the board. There may be 'cases where from one perspective we would choose to say that someone does understand something, while from another we would regard the same person as not understanding'. But isn't what you need to argue that there are no cases in which it is *not* true that from one perspective we would say that someone does understand something, while from another we would regard the same person as not under-standing?

TW. It would be impossible to argue that there are 'no cases' without being able to antic-ipate the context and background of all utterances among serious, intelligent, native speakers of English who might choose to use the word 'understand'. This would be a Sisyphean task.

JP. How far does your thesis of the relativity of understanding to context and purposes extend? Do you really disagree with Searle that the guy in the Room (considered alone) certainly doesn't understand Chinese?

TW. I disagree with the assumption that 'certainly doesn't understand' is a meaningful statement out of a specific context of use. The 'certainly' is a rhetorical trope, used to intimidate people into not thinking about cases in which what follows might not apply. Searle liberally tosses words such as 'clearly', 'obviously', 'plainly', and 'certainly' into his text in order to get this effect.

JP. Is it only from the standpoint of lazy common sense that this absolute judgment is acceptable?

TW. Yes.

JP. Are you using a single simple *criterion* of understanding: observable behavior? Mightn't Searle claim that (*a*) that's just behaviorism, and (*b*) it's too simple a cri-terion anyway? Aren't you focusing on a different *kind* of understanding from the kind he is interested in, which seems to be high-level 'conceptual' understanding, rather than just behavioral understanding. Would you apply your relativity thesis equally to high-level understanding?

TW. Your question is a great example of my point. You have coined two new concepts, 'behavioural understanding' and 'high-level understanding'. Each of them has its own horizon of meanings, which overlap with, but are not co-extensive with, the word 'understanding'. Indeed, we could continue proliferating this collection, which can be a valuable method for unpacking the issues that lie behind the use of the simpler term. Of course all of the same things apply when we do this—there is no objective boundary for 'behavioral understanding' or 'high-level understanding' any more than there is for 'understanding'. Meaning emerges exactly from this kind of dialog, rather than from assuming the existence of precise boundaries and definitions.

JP. Why can't adopting a particular orientation itself be correct or incorrect?

TW. Of course, anyone can characterize an orientation as correct or incorrect, and in doing so they are applying their own perspective to the correctness. Not all perspectives are created equal, and each statement is an invitation to argument and grounding on further statements that can be debated. Some statements are subject to coherent grounding within the network of statements within the society (e.g. most of standard science), and therefore are more likely to be agreed upon as correct than statements that contradict or go outside of that discourse. A statement that makes specific observational predictions (e.g. 'the sky is blue') is subject to grounding in individual experience. But of course, that is relative to individual physiology as well (e.g. 'this chemical tastes sweet' may be individual-dependent).

JP. I agree that the issue of who decides whether entities are autonomous agents, and how, will depend on the concept of autonomy. But, as with all these issues, I think Searle might say there is a certain fixity about that concept, and that, given our current understanding of it, there can be right and wrong answers to (some) questions of the form 'Is this entity autonomous?'.

TW. Here he would be drawing on common-sense intuition about 'a certain amount of fixity'. What that really means is that for many cases, the hard issues of meaning don't need to be faced because they fall in an area of broad consensus.

JP. So here we have the basic disagreement between you and Searle again, over whether language (or meaning) is totally open-ended, or just partially so?

TW. It is misleading to put it in 'totally' versus 'partially' terms, which makes one position seem extreme and the other by default more reasonable. I might equally well ask whether language is ever 'blindly objective' or only 'apparently objective within context'. Language use is indeed mostly objective, if we have an appropriate understanding of 'objective' (i.e. not problematic within the shared context of speaker and hearer). I am making the case that the ultimate grounding of the apparent intersubjective objectivity is never some god's-eye unsituated objectivity, but always a social/situational circumstance. It would seem quite magical to me if the human brain managed to tap into some externally granted objectivity (e.g. the 'real' meaning of 'autonomous') rather than acting as a nervous system, adapting as best it can with limited experience and situational blindness, producing pragmatically serviceable results.

JP. Would it be right to say that although you're happy with the literal/metaphorical distinction, this doesn't commit you to a distinction between correct (objective) and incorrect application?

TW. I am equally happy with a 'literal/metaphorical' distinction and with a 'correct/ incorrect' distinction. Both distinctions are useful in discourse, and neither is grounded in context-independent objectivity. I appreciate your ongoing attempts to save me from the risk of appearing silly by positing a consistently radical view that appears to fly in the face of common wisdom about language. I really do mean it, though!

JP. You say that all uses of the term 'understand' and its cognates depend on certain concerns and perspectives. Isn't there a problem of self-reflexion here? Musn't it be that your own uses of those terms are right only for certain concerns and from certain perspectives, but wrong for and from others?

TW. You correctly point out that if I am to be consistent in being relativistic, then I must apply it to my own statements as well as to the ones I am analyzing. Indeed, my own evaluations of attitudes are matters of social construction that is not the same as individual subjective opinion, but is grounded in the social discourse rather than in an appeal to objective truth.

References

BODEN, M. A. (ed.) (1990) *The Philosophy of Artificial Intelligence* (Oxford: Oxford University Press).

SEARLE, J. R. (1980) 'Minds, Brains, and Programs', *Behavioral and Brain Sciences*, 3: 417–24.

—— (1984) *Minds, Brains and Science* (London: BBC Publications).

5

A Chinese Room that Understands

Herbert A. Simon and Stuart A. Eisenstadt

The thesis of this chapter is that a computer can be programmed (and has been programmed) to understand natural language, in the sense of being able to translate natural language text, to answer in natural language questions put to it in language, and to perform similar tasks which, if performed by a human, would be taken as convincing evidence that the human understood the same language. We will call this thesis Empirical Strong AI (SAI-E) to distinguish it from Logical Strong AI (SAI-L), the thesis that Searle refutes, and which asserts that 'an appropriately programmed digital computer with the right inputs and outputs, one that satisfies the Turing Test, would thereby necessarily have a mind' (Searle 1999: 115).

It is impossible to discuss the validity of SAI-E or SAI-L, or any other hypothesis about the capacity of computers for understanding, without employing a definition of the term 'understand' that can provide a test for judging whether the hypothesis is true or false. We could settle the issue in a moment by defining 'understanding' as 'that which a computer can't do', or 'something that only a system that has flesh, blood and neurons can do'. As neither of these definitions, although they are often used in discussions of these matters, leads to an interesting question, we will eschew them. Instead, we will employ a definition of understanding that (a) is operational, in the usual sense, (b) corresponds closely to common usage of the term among native speakers of English, and (c) uses the same criteria for the presence of understanding in computer behavior as it does in human behavior. This chapter has nothing to say about understanding to a reader who prefers a quite different definition of that term; essays that employ a different definition have nothing to say about understanding to a reader who prefers the definition we propose, or one similar to it.

It would seem unreasonable to require a test of machine understanding that is stricter than the test we apply in judging human understanding, and so we propose using exactly the same tests for both. The test for computer understanding then has the same, but no more, ambiguities and uncertainties in its interpretation than the test for human understanding.

Whether a human being, and or a computer, 'understands' something, in the meaning of the term 'understand' given above, is an empirical question, which is therefore not capable of logical demonstration or refutation. On that ground alone, we would have to agree with Searle in rejecting SAI-L; for, at least since Hume, most persons would agree that empirical propositions do not achieve 'necessary' truth. Our beliefs are fallible. The question of whether a human in any given situation exhibits understanding is also an empirical question, subject to uncertainty that can never be wholly removed. The Chinese Room, as originally described by Searle, illustrates the kind of trick that can fool us into confusing understanding with non-understanding, using either a human or a computer as trickster, or both.

We propose SAI-E rather than SAI-L for the further reason that 'Turing Test' is an ill-defined term, and we need to have a clear criterion to determine whether understanding has been exhibited in any particular situation.

In our discussion, we will generally prefer Searle's phrase, 'mental state' to his term 'mind'. 'Mind' is an even more poorly defined term than 'Turing Test'. In the literature of philosophy and psychology, there are nearly as many different definitions of 'mind' as there are writers who have used the term. It is best avoided if we wish to deal with the empirical evidence for or against understanding as defined above, although the argument of this paper would not be altered if we introduced the (partial) definition: *empirical evidence that a system exhibits understanding is evidence that it has a mind (i.e. that it assumes various appropriate memory (mental) states); understanding is a sufficient, if not a necessary, empirical test for the existence of a mind.*

To further circumscribe the boundaries of this discussion, we cite Searle's concept of Weak AI (WAI-L), which he defines as

the view that the computer plays the same role in studying cognition as it does in any other discipline. It is a useful device for simulating and therefore studying mental processes, but the programmed computer does not automatically guarantee the presence of mental states in the computer. Weak AI is not criticized by the Chinese Room Argument. (Searle 1999: 115)

Given the phrase 'does not automatically guarantee' in Searle's WAI-L hypothesis, which converts it from an empirical to a logical hypothesis, this paper also has no quarrel with it, although it is too weak a hypothesis to be very interesting.

Between WAI-L and SAI-L, Searle leaves a very important no-man's land which could be, but need not be, a locus of disagreement, between Searle's position and SAI-E. For if the term 'mind' in SAI-L is intended to be synonymous with 'mental states' of WAI-L (and there is no indication that Searle intended anything else), there is left, though not with logical guarantees, the empirical possibility of mental states in the computer, hence its possession of mind and understanding—the latter term in the operational sense in which it is defined above. SAI-E lies in this no-man's land.

Evidence that a Human Understands

As we are dealing with empirical claims, a reasonable aim is to seek empirical evidence about a computer's understanding in a given situation at least as strong, and preferably stronger, than the evidence for understanding that we could obtain and would insist upon with a human in the same situation. At the present stage of technology, in evaluating human understanding, we are largely restricted to observing only behavior, including verbal behavior, in some range of situations (Ericsson and Simon 1993). To a limited extent, we can obtain additional evidence from observations of brain damage, fMRI, PET scans, EEG recordings and the like, and even, on certain occasions, from actual probes of and recordings from nerve cells.

In the future, there may be much more evidence of these kinds, with better temporal and spatial resolution than is now achievable. However, because today we nearly always make our judgments of human understanding or lack of understanding without such evidence, we are going to use external tests also to determine whether computers have understanding, and then use the internal tests that are available for computers, but not for humans, to determine the nature of the mental states that implement this understanding. In this way, we obtain empirical support for a theory of what the mental states of humans in corresponding circumstances are like, at the information-processing level and not at the level of neurons.

One common kind of test of understanding is to ask a person for the name of a particular process or object or relation between objects: the process or object or relation being within the range of vision of the respondent and being designated by pointing. If the respondent provides the correct name (as defined by usage in a language community), we conclude that he or she is in a mental state of understanding something about the intension of that name, that is, what process, object, or relation the name denotes. We can elaborate on the test to determine the degree of vagueness or precision of the intension. We can test whether the word 'cat' is produced if and only if a cat is present, or also when a leopard is present, or not when a Siamese cat is present but only when a common alley cat is. With our contemporary capabilities for displaying virtual reality, we can even test whether the respondent considers the Cheshire Cat, in the course of one of its disappearances, to be a cat.

At all events, as Quine has so eloquently shown in *Word and Object* (Quine 1960), our estimates of a human respondent's mental states and understanding of language are subject to all of the uncertainties that surround any empirically grounded belief. As the tricks of Clever Hans, the horse that 'understood' language, may be available to people as well as to horses, especially if they have accomplices, in doubtful cases we try to establish all sorts of safeguards against being fooled, using our ingenuity to create tests that can only be passed successfully if the respondent can associate the correct intensions with words. At the most banal level, we station proctors in examination rooms. If we did not, we might be testing only the abilities of students to match words in test questions with words in smuggled textbooks, not their abilities to use their knowledge of the intensions of the words to answer our test questions.

Understanding in the Chinese Room

Searle's description of what is going on in the Chinese Room is a particular version of Clever Hans or the proctorless classroom—perhaps more interesting, as being more ingenious, than the original one. If there is a human in the Chinese Room doing what Searle describes the occupant as doing (a computer could as readily be programmed to do it), he or she is showing good understanding of how to associate Chinese character strings that answer questions with Chinese character strings that ask the questions, but no understanding of Chinese, that is, no ability to supply the intensions of either questions or answers by pointing to objects or scenes.

We already see how we can proctor the test and expose Clever Hans: namely, by allowing an observer to examine the person (or program) who is perpetrating the hoax, using tests that can only be passed by someone (or something) possessing actual knowledge of the intensions of Chinese character strings.

As a second step, we will propose altering the Chinese Room to permit the respondent, whether human or an appropriately programmed computer, actually to understand the questions (i.e. to acquire mental states corresponding to their meanings), and to provide answers based on that understanding. To that end, we will install windows in the walls of the room, thereby giving the respondent, whether human or computer, who or which is assumed to have sensory organs that permit stimuli to be received from outside, access to that world of potential denotations. Before we install the windows and examine the consequences of doing so, we need to discuss further the tests we might apply to determine whether, in a particular situation, a computer understands language.

Evidence that a Computer Understands

We have seen that the same (fallible and approximate) empirical tests can be used to determine whether a computer understands some language as are used to determine whether a person understands it—being careful in both cases to avoid being fooled by tricks. But in the case of the computer we are not barred from invading its interior in the way that we are with humans. As a result, we can apply more, and more powerful, tests to claims of computer understanding than we can to claims of human understanding. In many cases, we can determine the computer's exact intensions by examining the portions of its program and memory that incorporate its perceptual tests for discriminating among observed objects, processes, or relations—these are the memory (or mental) states and processes stored in memory that implement the discriminations.

At least as important, in cases where the tests that define intensions are not supplied by the programmer, we can discover the learning processes the computer uses to acquire these tests. This is rather crucial for our purposes, for it may be objected (and Searle does so object) that there is no understanding if, in the processes the computer uses to answer the questions, the connection between questions and answers is direct and not mediated by intensions. We will see that such mediation takes place during the learning process.

The general validity of the objection is itself debatable (does or does not a reflexive blink that prevents flying dust from entering our eye represent understanding?), but it would be generally acknowledged that 'rote' responses, however functional, do not always imply understanding. What seems principally to distinguish rote responses from responses with understanding, as we actually use those terms in our language (in relation to either humans or computers), is that the latter involve intensions in some essential way.

Rudolf Carnap (1955) was perhaps the first to point out the possibilities for taking advantage of our access to the programs inside computers in order to apply to them more severe tests than we can apply to people for determining whether and when and to what extent understanding is occurring:

In order to make the method of structure analysis applicable, let us now consider the pragmatical investigation of the language of a robot rather than that of a human being. In this case we may assume that we possess much more detailed knowledge of the internal structure. . . . Just as the linguist [e.g. Quine's linguist in *Word and Object* (HAS)] . . . begins with pointing to objects, but later, after having determined the interpretation of some words, asks questions formulated by these words, the investigator of [the robot's] language *L* begins with presenting objects . . . but later, on the basis of tentative results concerning the intensions of some signs of *L*, proceeds to present predicate expressions . . . which use only those interpreted signs. . . .

Instead of using this behavioristic method, the investigator may here use the method of structure analysis. On the basis of the given blueprint of [the robot], he may be able to calculate the responses which [it] would make to various possible inputs. In particular, he may be able to derive from the given blueprint . . . [fairly precise boundaries for the intensions of certain concepts] . . .

It is clear that the method of structure analysis, if applicable, is more powerful than the behavioristic method, because it can supply a general answer and, under favorable circumstances, even a complete answer to the question of the intension of a given predicate. . . .

The intension of a predicate can be determined for a robot just as well as for a human speaker, and even more completely if the internal structure of the robot is sufficiently known to predict how it will function under various conditions. (Carnap 1955, reprinted in Carnap 1956: 244–7)

Going beyond Carnap's hypothetical proposal, we will describe three real computer programs that illustrate the kinds of tests we can apply to see (1) whether a computer uses understanding (intensions) to perform a task, and (2) whether it acquires its understanding by programming or by learning. Carnap, of course, mentions only the first kind of test, not the second.

One of these programs, EPAM (Elementary Perceiver and Memorizer), was initially programmed about 1959 and is still alive and well today. It learns to discriminate among stimuli (more precisely, among feature vectors derived from stimuli), to categorize stimuli, and to associate pairs of stimuli (e.g. to associate words with their denotations).

The second program, ZBIE (the meaning of the acronym is unknown), dates from the late 1960s. It is given representations of simple scenes (in the form of list structures—i.e. relational structures) together with simple sentences in some natural language (English, French, German, Russian) denoting these scenes. We may call the portions of computer memory in which scenes and sentences are stored, the 'mind's eye' and 'mind's ear', respectively. The program learns to associate the objects, processes, and relations in the schemes with words and phrases in the natural language, and the scenes with sentences in the language. When shown a new scene (with objects, processes, and relations whose names have been learned from other scenes), ZBIE now attempts, often successfully, to form a sentence denoting the scene. When shown a new sentence, using words that have already been associated with the objects, processes, and relations that they denote, it attempts, often successfully, to answer whether the sentence does or doesn't describe correctly a scene that is shown to it simultaneously.

The third program, CaMeRa, developed in the past five years, can form a 'mind's eye' image of a simple diagram presented as a bitmap (in analogy to a retinal image), can recode the image in terms of lines, for example, and their intersections, and can then associate words in natural language with the components of the mind's eye image and use knowledge already available in the natural language store to reason about the image.

We will claim that these programs show beyond reasonable doubt, in terms of internal and external empirical criteria, their ability to understand (some) natural language sentences—even as you and we—thus providing strong empirical support for SAI-E.

EPAM (Elementary Perceiver and Memorizer)

EPAM was constructed by Feigenbaum (1961) as a computer model (i.e. a theory in the form of a system of difference equations) simulating the behavior of human subjects in verbal learning experiments, and accounting for a wide range of phenomena reported in the published literature. In the succeeding thirty-eight years after its creation it has been gradually extended to other phenomena, notably the memory capabilities of experts in their domains of expertise and the abilities of human subjects to categorize stimuli (concept attainment).

A small number of changes have been made in EPAM over the years, and with each substantial change, the model was re-run on the data of the experiments with which it had been matched previously, in order to verify that it continued to fit these earlier data. The same basic parameter values are retained in its applications to all of its tasks. An extended description of EPAM and a detailed application to expert memory will be found in Richman, Staszewski, and Simon (1995); a survey of its earlier performances, in Feigenbaum and Simon (1984).

EPAM contains two fundamental mechanisms, a discrimination net, with tests of stimulus features at each of the nodes, that enables it to distinguish different stimuli; and a learning process for elaborating the net by building new nodes, with new tests, to distinguish between stimuli that have previously been mis-sorted or confused. EPAM does not have sensory organs that give access to external stimuli, but is given feature vectors which may be interpreted as perceptual encodings of the stimuli impinging on sensory organs.[1]

EPAM can be trained, for example, (1) on English words, and (2) on feature vectors for objects that are denoted by words. As a result of this training, it will grow a discrimination net that will allow it to distinguish and recognize each of the words and each kind of object. Now, using a paired-associate paradigm, it can be trained to associate each word with the object it denotes, so that (1) if presented with the word, it could select the appropriate object from a set of miscellaneous objects, and (2) if presented with an object, it could select the word that denotes that object (Eisenstadt and Simon 1997; Simon and Eisenstadt 1998). At present, EPAM has no grammatical capability, but it has a full capability for representing list structures in its memory, hence could acquire discrimination nets for sentence structures and for scenes. How effective such nets would be for language learning (beyond the word understanding that EPAM is now capable of) is an empirical question that awaits experimentation.

ZBIE: Learning Sentences and their Intensions

ZBIE is a computer program that was constructed by Siklóssy (1972) as a simulation model (again, a theory expressed as a system of difference equations) of human language learning. It accepts as inputs (1) sentences in any natural language, and (2) description lists that represent simple scenes (e.g. 'The dog is chasing the cat'). As in the case of EPAM, ZBIE does not address the question of sensory and perceptual acquisition of the scenes, but assumes that this has been accomplished by a pre-processor analogous to, but somewhat more complex than, that which could construct the feature vectors for EPAM.

---

[1] Sensory organs that would provide suitable feature vectors for input to EPAM have been constructed for a substantial number of robotic devices, for example, speech-understanding systems and the NAVLAB vehicle, which steers itself automatically while traveling on roads and highways at high speed.

Examining the interior of ZBIE after a period of learning, we see that it has acquired a vocabulary of words in the language it is studying, each associated with a referent in the scenes, and a vocabulary of linguistic relational structures, each denoting relational structures of the referents of the words—that is to say, phrase types, clause types, or sentence types. Detailed study of these internal structures, all of which are components of ZBIE's mental state, shows that they do correspond to word types (e.g. nouns, verbs) and common language structures (e.g. noun phrases, sentences) in the language being studied. The system learns word order, which of course varies from language to language.

ZBIE has been tested on only rather simple structures (the I. A. Richards series of 'Language from Pictures' was used as the model), but for these structures it clearly passes the operational tests of understanding, and just as clearly, the understanding is not programmed but learned. At the beginning, it does not know any French (or other language); at the end, after experiences with scenes and the French sentences that denote them, it does know some simple French.

By using sentences in two languages as inputs, instead of sentences as one input and scenes as another, both EPAM and ZBIE can learn to translate from one language to another. Suppose, for example, that ZBIE had already learned to understand the two languages, and that sentence S_A in the first language had as its denotation D_A in the scenes, whereas S_B in the second language had as its denotation D_B. Then, by matching D_A with D_B, ZBIE could determine to what extent S_A constituted a good translation of S_B. Unlike the case of the Chinese Room, here the translator understands the meanings of the sentences in both languages (i.e. what scenes are consistent with their intensions), and is able to check the translation against that understanding.

CaMeRa: Acquiring and Processing Sensory Stimuli

Both EPAM and ZBIE finesse the actual interaction between system and outside world by taking feature vectors (in the case of EPAM), or symbolic relational structures (in the case of ZBIE) as their non-language inputs. These are perceptual inputs that are presumably obtained as outputs of prior processes performed by sensory and perceptual organs. However, as already indicated, there already exists extensive experience in using robotic devices to perform these prior steps, so that there no longer remains any real doubt that speech and scenes can in fact be recognized by computers. For example, a computer has been programmed to play chess by hearing (in English) and interpreting each move played by the opponent; then choosing its own move and reporting it, keeping track in memory of the altered position. Of course, with the use of current technology, it could also make the move physically and keep track of the current position by observing it visually.

Whether the level of recognition is comparable to that of people is another question, whose current answer is 'in some respects, yes; in other respects, no'; and whether the detailed processes of recognition (within 10 millisecond time spans, say) are the same is even more doubtful. Clearly, at the respective levels of computer chips and neurons they are different. But differences in relative effectiveness and in details of process at that level are irrelevant (once a basic competence has been established for using intensional tests to link symbols with their denotations) to the question of whether computers can understand; the human tests of understanding (the mental states) are complex structures at the level of symbolic information processes, and extending over seconds or more, not at the level of specific neuronal processes, and extending over only a few milliseconds. Questioning understanding on the basis of differences at the level of individual neurons is a little like asking whether people using glasses to reinforce their eyesight or electronic hearing aids to improve hearing can understand.

None the less, the question of what the actual processes are that connect the outside world with the brain is of great interest to anyone who wants a full answer to the mind–body problem. We will describe briefly the CaMeRa project, which is aimed at dealing with some aspects of this problem, not at a neural level, but still at the level of information processes (Tabachneck-Schijf et al. 1997).

Diagrams on paper or on the blackboard are represented in CaMeRa as bitmaps. When viewed by CaMeRa's eye, these are transferred to the visual short-term memory, the 'mind's eye', where configurations of bits are noticed and assembled into lines, line intersections, and objects (e.g. rectangles). Information that represents these, and that is sufficient to reconstruct them subsequently in the mind's eye is then stored in long-term memory. While the interpreted objects remain in the mind's eye, or when they are returned there from long-term memory, they can be reasoned about.

Suppose that we draw on the blackboard the familiar supply–demand diagram of economics. A viewer will see a graph with the x-axis marked 'Q' and the y-axis marked 'P'. (The reader is invited to visualize this scene in his or her mind's eye, and then to draw it on a piece of paper.) A line or curve sloping downward to the right is marked '*D*', and another sloping upward to the right is marked '*S*'. The two lines intersect at a point labeled '*E*'.

The instructor asks the class, 'What is the equilibrium price?' A knowledgeable student looks at *E*, moves her eye horizontally to the *y*-axis, and, noticing the number 10 at the point of regard, answers, '10'. Clearly, we are not dealing here with a pure act of visual perception, but with the application of intensional tests to the diagram. To answer as she did, the student must know that '*E*' denotes equilibrium, and a number on the *y*-axis of the graph is the price in any situation that has the same *y*-coordinate as that number. We could carry this story further, but for our general purposes, we need only say that CaMeRa makes these same inferences as a consequence of linkages between the labels on the mind's eye image of the graph and statements in natural language it has read before looking at the graph that give the denotations of these same labels.

There is much more to be said about the connections between the various elements that are pictured and labeled in the diagram and the intensions, in the real world of buying and selling; but perhaps this brief introduction to CaMeRa will suggest its potential for exploring the concept of understanding in a world where meanings are commonly represented (both on paper and in the 'mind's eye') in verbal, diagrammatic, algebraic, and other forms. Its main value for our present purposes is to provide additional evidence that a computer can not only store information and recite it by rote, but can use that information, in relation to its knowledge of the intensions of the objects represented, to reason about the outside world. If we prefer that language, we can say that it acquires constantly changing mental states which it uses to perform tasks that exhibit its understanding.

The Computer Models as Theories

We introduced these computer models as theories of human understanding and as a source of internal tests of computer understanding of language—tests that go far beyond the traditional external behavioral 'Turing Tests'. The latter are the only tests available today for judging the extent to which, in any situation, human beings understand. In the case of the computer, we can, in addition to such external tests, examine in detail the way in which intensions and judgments of the meanings of texts are formed inside the black box (which is actually not black at all, but rather well illuminated).

For this reason the computer models also serve as theories (we have already called them that) of the human internal understanding processes (Searle's WAI). The mechanisms that we can observe in the computer but not in humans correspond to theoretical terms, whose acceptability as components of the theory depends, just as it does in physical and biological theories, on their effects upon the external behavior of the systems, which can be compared directly with the behavior of people (Simon 1977, 1983).

We are rather in the same position as geneticists were at the time of Mendel, when genes were theoretical terms with no operations to verify directly their presence or nature (Shen and Simon 1993). Even after chromosomes had been observed, there was a huge gap between the terms of genetic theory and the terms of observational microbiology. That gap has been filled to a considerable extent (by no means fully), but its existence and width for a century should remind us of the enormous fruitfulness and even essentiality of theoretical terms for the progress of our understanding of phenomena. The understanding of human thinking is a case of a very similar kind, whose progress depends heavily on a good appreciation of the knowledge that can be gained from theoretical models, built and examined in close juxtaposition with careful experimentation.

Conclusion

In this chapter we have described a small fragment of the empirical evidence that is available to show that computers are, indeed, capable of understanding by use of intensional tests, and of learning these intensions by associating words and other linguistic structures with their denotations, as detected through sensory stimuli. We have shown that it is, in fact, easier to establish that a computer exhibits understanding than to establish that a human exhibits understanding in the same situation, because, as Quine emphasized in *Word and Object*, our detection of human understanding (i.e. the presence of intensions) is based almost exclusively on the observation of behavior, while, as Carnap early noted, our detection of computer understanding rests on our direct observation both of external behavior and of the internal mechanisms that are producing it—the performance programs in the computer, and the learning programs that produce and modify these performance programs.

On the basis of this evidence, and a large body of other evidence provided by programs that solve difficult problems, programs that make scientific discoveries and rediscoveries, programs that draw, paint, and compose music, and many others, the case for Strong AI, in its empirical version, SAI-E, is overwhelming. But as we emphasized in our introduction, there is no conflict between this claim and Searle's claim that the SAI-L thesis is false. The Logical Natural Intelligence Thesis, the thesis that the ability of humans to understand is provable (as distinct from empirically supported) is equally false and irrelevant to the pursuit of empirical knowledge. Nor are we aware of any cognitive scientists who subscribe to SAI-L.

Guided by the SAI-E hypothesis, research on human thinking over the past forty years has greatly advanced our understanding of human thinking at the information-processing level, and has taken the first steps toward the connection of this level with neuronal structures and processes. We should not delay this progress by confusing an empirical question with a logical one.

References

CARNAP, R. (1955) 'Meaning and Synonymy in Natural Languages', *Philosophical Studies*, 7: 33–47, reprinted in Carnap 1956.

—— (1956) *Meaning and Necessity*, 2nd edn. (Chicago: University of Chicago Press).

EISENSTADT, S. A., and SIMON, H. A. (1997) 'Logic and Thought', *Minds and Machines*, 7: 365–85.

ERICSSON, K. A., and SIMON, H. A. (1993) *Protocol Analysis: Verbal Reports as Data*, rev. edn. (Cambridge, Mass: MIT Press).

FEIGENBAUM, E. A. (1961) 'The Simulation of Verbal Learning Behavior', *Proceedings of Western Joint Computer Conference*, 19: 121–32.

—— and SIMON, H. A. (1984) 'EPAM-like Models of Recognition and Learning', *Cognitive Science*, 8: 305–36.

QUINE, W. V. (1960) *Word and Object* (Cambridge, Mass: MIT Press).

RICHMAN, H. B., STASZEWSKI, J. J., and SIMON, H. A. (1995) 'Simulation of Expert Memory using EPAM IV', *Psychological Review*, 102: 305–30.

SEARLE, J. R. (1999) 'Chinese Room Argument', in R. A. Wilson and F. C. Keil (eds.), *The MIT Encyclopedia of the Cognitive Sciences* (Cambridge, Mass: MIT Press), 115–16.

SHEN, W., and SIMON, H. A. (1993) 'Fitness Requirements for Scientific Theories Containing Recursive Theoretical Terms', *British Journal for the Philosophy of Science*, 44: 641–52.

SIKLÓSSY, L. (1972) 'Natural Language Learning by Computer', in H. A. Simon and L. Siklóssy (eds.), *Representation and Meaning* (Englewood Cliffs, NJ: Prentice-Hall).

SIMON, H. A. (1977) 'Identifiability and the Status of Theoretical Terms', in R. E. Butts and K. J. J. Hintikka (eds.), *Basic Problems in Methodology and Linguistics* (Dordrecht: D. Reidel).

—— (1983) 'Fitness Requirements for Scientific Theories', *British Journal for the Philosophy of Science*, 34: 355–65.

—— (1985) 'Quantification of Theoretical Terms and the Falsifiability of Theories', *British Journal for the Philosophy of Science*, 36: 291–8.

—— (1992) 'The Computer as a Laboratory for Epistemology', in L. Burkholder (ed.), *Philosophy and the Computer* (Boulder, Colo: Westview Press).

—— and EISENSTADT, S. A. (1998) 'Human and Machine Interpretation of Expressions in Formal Systems', *Synthese*, 116: 439–61.

TABACHNECK-SCHIJF, H. J. M., LEONARDO, A. M., and SIMON, H. A. (1997) 'CaMeRa: A Computational Model of Multiple Representations', *Cognitive Science*, 21: 305–50.

6

The Chinese Room from a
Logical Point of View

B. Jack Copeland

John Searle has complained—and not without justice—that stock responses to
his 1980 paper 'fail to come to grips with the actual Chinese room argument'
(1990: 24). This chapter looks closely at various versions of the Chinese Room
Argument (CRA).

There are four principal versions of the argument: the vanilla version, the
outdoor version, the simulator version, and the gymnasium version.[1] The
vanilla and outdoor versions (Searle 1980a) are directed against traditional
symbol-processing AI; the simulator and gymnasium versions (Searle 1990)
are directed against connectionism. All are unsatisfactory. Moreover, even if
some version of the argument were sound, the argument could not possibly
establish—as Searle claims it does—his key thesis that whatever is 'purely
formal' or 'syntactical' is neither constitutive of nor sufficient for mind.

1. The Vanilla Argument

In its basic form, the CRA addresses the case of a human clerk—call him or
her Clerk—who 'handworks' a GOFAI program.[2] The program is presented to

---

[1] My remarks on the vanilla and outdoor versions apply *mutatis mutandis* to the derivative robot
version (Searle 1980: 420; reprinted in Boden 1990: 76–7. (From here referred to as B76–7)).

[2] 'Good Old Fashioned AI', John Haugeland's excellent term for traditional symbol-processing
AI (Haugeland 1985).

Clerk in English in the form of a set of rule-books. One not uncommon misunderstanding takes Searle to be asserting that the rule-books contain a simple 'look-up' table that pairs possible inputs directly with ready-made outputs (see e.g. Sterelny 1990: 220 ff.). So misinterpreted, Searle's argument is weakened; Searle's intention is that the rule-books may contain any GOFAI program that is claimed by its creators (or others) to understand Chinese—or indeed to have any 'cognitive states' whatsoever (Searle 1980a: 417 (B67–8)). The symbols processed by the program are not limited to Chinese ideograms (which merely form a vivid example); they may even be generated by a suite of sensors mounted on motor equipment that is itself under the control of the program (ibid. 420 (B76)).

To the programmers outside, the verbal behaviour of the Room—the system that includes the rule-books, Clerk, the erasable paper memory, Clerk's pencils and rubbers, the input and output provisions (paper cards and slots), and any clock, random number generator, or other equipment that Clerk may need in order to execute the precise program in question—is indistinguishable from that of a native Chinese speaker. But does the Room understand Chinese?

Here is the vanilla argument:

[Clerk] do[es] not understand a word of the Chinese stories. [Clerk] ha[s] inputs and outputs that are indistinguishable from the native Chinese speaker, and [Clerk] can have any formal program you like, but [Clerk] still understand[s] nothing. Schank's computer for the same reasons understands nothing of any stories. . . . [W]hatever purely formal principles you put into the computer will not be sufficient for understanding, since a human will be able to follow the formal principles without understanding . . . (ibid. 418 (B70–1))

The flaw in the vanilla version is simple: the argument is *not logically valid*.[3] (An argument is logically valid if and only if its conclusion is entailed by its premise(s); an argument is sound if and only if it is logically valid and each premise is true). The proposition that the formal symbol manipulation carried out by Clerk does not enable Clerk to understand the Chinese story by no means entails the quite different proposition that the formal symbol manipulation carried out by Clerk does not enable the Room to understand the Chinese story. One might as well claim that the statement 'The organization of which Clerk is a part has no taxable assets in Japan' follows logically from the statement 'Clerk has no taxable assets in Japan'.

---

[3] Copeland (1993a: 174–5; 1993b: 125–6).

It is important to distinguish this, the *logical reply* to the vanilla argument, from what Searle calls the *Systems Reply*. The Systems Reply is the following claim: 'While it is true that the individual person who is locked in the room does not understand the story, the fact is that he is merely part of a whole system and the system does understand the story' (ibid. 419 (B72)). As Searle correctly points out, the Systems Reply is worthless, since it 'simply begs the question by insisting without argument that the system must understand Chinese' (ibid. 419 (B74)). The logical reply, on the other hand, is a point about entailment. The logical reply involves no claim about the truth—or falsity—of the statement that the Room can understand Chinese.

2. The Roomless Room

Of course, any logically invalid argument can be rendered valid with the addition of further premises (in the limiting case one simply adds the conclusion to the premises). The trick is to produce additional premises which not only secure validity but are sustainable.

In his discussion of the Systems Reply Searle says:

My response to the systems theory is quite simple: Let the individual . . . memoriz[e] the rules in the ledger and the data banks of Chinese symbols, and [do] all the calculations in his head. The individual then incorporates the entire system. . . . We can even get rid of the room and suppose he works outdoors. All the same, he understands nothing of the Chinese, and a fortiori neither does the system, because there isn't anything in the system that isn't in him. If he doesn't understand, then there is no way the system could understand, because the system is just a part of him. (ibid. 419 (B73)).

Let me represent this, the outdoor version of the argument, as follows:

(2.1) The system is part of Clerk.

(2.2) If Clerk (in general, x) does not understand the Chinese story (in general, does not Φ), then no part of Clerk (x) understands the Chinese story (Φs).

(2.3) The formal symbol manipulation carried out by Clerk does not enable Clerk to understand the Chinese story.

Therefore

(2.4) The formal symbol manipulation carried out by Clerk does not enable the system to understand the Chinese story.

The outdoor version is logically valid. Premise (2.1) is perhaps innocent enough. Attention thus centres on (2.2), which I call the Part-Of principle.[4] Searle makes no mention at all of why he thinks the Part-Of principle is true. Yet the principle is certainly not self-evident. It is all too conceivable that a homunculus or homuncular system in Clerk's head should be able to understand Chinese without Clerk being able to do so. (Notice that Searle has no reservations concerning the application of predicates like 'understand' to subpersonal systems. He writes (against Dennett): 'I find nothing at all odd about saying that my brain understands English . . . I find [the contrary] claim as implausible as insisting "I digest pizza; my stomach and digestive tract don't"' (Searle 1980b: 451).) Likewise for related values of Φ. Conceivably there is a special-purpose module in Clerk's brain that produces solutions to certain tensor equations, yet Clerk himself may sincerely deny that he can solve tensor equations—does not even know what a tensor equation is, we may suppose. Perhaps it is the functioning of this module that accounts for our ability to catch cricket balls and other moving objects (McLeod and Dienes 1993). Clerk himself, we may imagine, is unable to produce solutions to the relevant tensor equations even in the form of leg and arm movements, say because the output of the module fails to connect owing to the presence of a lesion. Or, to move into the realm of science fiction, neuropharmacologists may induce Clerk's liver to emulate a brain, the liver remaining *in situ* and receiving input directly from a computer workstation, to which the liver also delivers its output. Clerk's modified liver performs many acts of cognition that Clerk cannot. One example: Clerk stares uncomprehendingly at the screen of the computer as his liver proves theorems in quantified tense logic.

Of course, one might respond to these and similar examples as follows. Since a part of Clerk is proving a theorem of quantified tense logic (solving a set of tensor equations, etc.) *then so is Clerk*—there he is doing it, albeit to his own surprise. This response cannot be available to Searle. If Clerk's sincere denial that he is able to solve tensor equations (or what have you) counts for nothing, then likewise in the case of the Chinese Room. However, it is a cornerstone of Searle's overall case that Clerk's sincere report 'I don't speak [*sic*] a word of Chinese' (1980a: 418 (B69)) suffices for the truth of premise (2.3). One might call this Searle's Incorrigibility Thesis. It, like the Part-Of principle, is left totally unsupported by Searle. (Searle sometimes says, as if to give independent support to (2.3): 'there is no way [Clerk] could come to understand Chinese in the [situation] as described,

---

[4] Copeland (1993a: 175).

since there is no way that [Clerk] can learn the meanings of any of the symbols' (1990: 20). This rhetoric simply begs the question, since the matter at issue is whether 'just having the symbols by themselves . . . [is] sufficient for semantics' and that this cannot be sufficient is, allegedly, 'the point that the Chinese room demonstrated' (ibid. 21).)

If the Part-Of principle is taken to be a modal claim equivalent to $\sim\Box$((some part of Clerk understands Chinese) & $\sim$(Clerk understands Chinese)) then, assuming the Incorrigibility Thesis, possible scenarios such as the forgoing do more than bear on the plausibility of the principle: they settle its truth-value. If, on the other hand, the Part-Of principle is said to be a purely contingent claim (i.e. a claim that happens to be true in the actual world but is not true in possible alternatives to the actual world), then Searle's difficulty is to produce reasons for thinking the principle true.

3. The Simulator Version

The Churchlands are correct in saying that the original Chinese room argument was designed with traditional AI in mind but wrong in thinking that connectionism is immune to the argument. It applies to any computational system . . . whether [the computations] are done in serial or parallel; that is why the Chinese room argument refutes strong AI in any form. (Searle 1990: 22)

Directed against the claim that a suitable connectionist network might understand Chinese, the simulator version of the argument is this:

Computationally, serial and parallel systems are equivalent: any computation that can be done in parallel can be done in serial. If the man in the Chinese room is computationally equivalent to both, then if he does not understand Chinese solely by virtue of doing the computations, neither do they. (ibid.)

The first sentence of the argument, while not completely clear in meaning, appears too strong. The claim, often heard, that the activity of any finite collection of Turing machines can be simulated by a single universal Turing machine is simply false. Networks of universal Turing machines operating in an asynchronous manner (Copeland and Sylvan 1999: 54) are in a sense irreducibly parallel in nature, since in general the actions of the individual processors cannot be interleaved in order to form a sequence of actions that is performable by a single universal Turing machine. The standard textbook proof that a finite assembly of Turing machines can be simulated by one universal Turing machine—which involves the idea of the universal machine interleaving the processing steps performed by the individual machines in the assembly— applies only in the case where the machines in the assembly are operating in synchrony. Under certain conditions, a simple network of two non-halting Turing machines m_1 and m_2 writing binary digits to a common, initially blank, single-ended tape, T, cannot be simulated by a universal Turing machine (here I am indebted to correspondence with Aaron Sloman). m_1 and m_2 work uni-directionally along T, never writing on a square that has already been written on, and writing only on squares all of whose predecessors have already been written on. (If m_1 and m_2 attempt to write simultaneously to the same square, a refereeing mechanism gives priority to m_1.) If m_1 and m_2 operate in synchrony, the evolving contents of T can be calculated by the universal machine. This is true also if m_1 and m_2 operate asynchronously and the *timing function* associated with each machine, Δ_1 and Δ_2 respectively, is Turing-machine-computable. $\Delta_1(n) = k\,(n, k \geqslant 1)$ if and only if k moments of operating time separate the nth atomic operation performed by m_1 from the $n + 1$th; similarly for m_2 and Δ_2. Where Δ_1 and Δ_2 are both Turing-machine-computable, the universal machine can calculate the necessary values of these functions in the course of calculating each digit of the sequence being inscribed on T. If at least one of Δ_1 and Δ_2 is not Turing-machine-computable and m_1 and m_2 are not in synchrony, m_1 and m_2 may be in the process of inscribing an uncomputable number on T.

Let me, therefore, represent the argument in such a way that this question-able generalization does not figure. Let N be a connectionist network that is said to understand Chinese. (Notice that Clerk, who we may assume has access to unlimited amounts of paper and never breaks down, is acting as a universal Turing machine.)

(3.1) Given an appropriate program, Clerk (together with his or her pencils, paper, erasers, and rule-books) is 'computationally equivalent' to N.

(3.2) Clerk does not understand Chinese (solely by virtue of doing computations).

Therefore

(3.3) N does not understand Chinese (solely by virtue of doing computations).

The situation is that we have a serial system—call it S—simulating the parallel system N. We are being asked to endorse the inference that, since S and N are 'computationally equivalent', and S does not understand Chinese, then neither does N. But, for reasons already rehearsed, (3.2) does not entail that S (Clerk plus rule-books, etc.) does not understand Chinese; and so the argument stalls.

This is not the only problem. Searle has issued frequent warnings on the perils of confusing a simulation with the thing being simulated. Here are some characteristic passages:

[N]o one supposes that a computer simulation of a storm will leave us all wet . . . Why on earth would anyone in his right mind suppose a computer simulation of mental processes actually had mental processes? (Searle 1989: 37–8)

Barring miracles, you could not run your car by doing a computer simulation of the oxidation of gasoline, and you could not digest pizza by running the program that simulates such digestion. It seems obvious that a simulation of cognition will similarly not produce the effects of the neurobiology of cognition. (Searle 1990: 23)

Searle's examples show forcefully that the following form of inference is logically invalid:

(3.4) x is a simulation of y; y has property Φ, therefore x has property Φ.

I will term the fallacy pointed out by Searle the *simulation fallacy*. Notice that even where x and y are both computational processes, the inference-form has exemplifications with true premises and false conclusion. For example: x is a simulation of y; y is a parallel process; therefore x is a parallel process.

Contraposing (3.4) produces:

(3.5) x is a simulation of y; it is not the case that x has property Φ, therefore it is not the case that y has property Φ.

(To contrapose an argument one swaps the conclusion with any one of the premises and negates each of the swapped statements: P, $\sim R$ therefore $\sim Q$ is a contrapositive of P, Q therefore R). It is a theorem of elementary logic that contraposing an invalid inference-form always produces an invalid inference-form.

A crucial step in the simulator version of the CRA can be represented thus:

(3.6) S is a simulation of N; it is not the case that S understands Chinese, therefore it is not the case that N understands Chinese.

This reasoning exemplifies the invalid form (3.5). In short, Searle's attempt to extend the CRA to connectionism appears to involve the simulation fallacy.[5]

There is another difficulty. Premise (3.1) cannot be relied upon. Hava Siegelmann and Eduardo Sontag (1994) have described a particular type of connectionist network that cannot be simulated by a universal Turing machine. (In essence they take a perfectly run-of-the-mill connectionist network and allow the value of a single one of its synaptic weights to be a *real* number rather than, as is more usually the case, a rational number.) Let me call

---

[5] Copeland (1993a: 182; 1993b: 227–8).

any neural network that cannot be simulated by a universal Turing machine an *O-network* (this terminology will be explained later). If *N* is an O-network, then premise (3.1) is false (since Clerk acts as a universal Turing machine). Some connectionists believe that the brain—abstracted out from sources of inessential boundedness, such as mortality—is an O-network. Searle's claim that the CRA 'refutes strong AI in *any* form' (emphasis added) is very bold.

I say more about the issue of hypercomputation—sometimes inaccurately called *super-Turing* computation—in Section 5.[6]

4. The Chinese Gym

Connectionism is

subject even on its own terms to a variant of the objection presented by the original Chinese room argument. Imagine that instead of a Chinese room, I have a Chinese gym: a hall containing many monolingual English-speaking men. These men would carry out the same operations as the nodes and synapses in a connectionist architecture . . . and the outcome would be the same as having one man manipulate symbols according to a rule book. No one in the gym speaks a word of Chinese . . . Yet with appropriate adjustments, the system could give the correct answers to Chinese questions. (Searle 1990: 22)

Perhaps the people in the gym simulate the network by passing each other plastic tokens, green tokens representing input along an excitatory connection and red tokens along an inhibitory connection. The number of tokens passed from one player to another in a single transaction represents the weight of the connection. Each player has a list detailing to whom they must pass their tokens and how many should be handed over. During the training phase of the simulation, the players make changes to their lists in accordance with the shouted instructions of the trainer.

Once again the logical reply is sufficient to rebut the argument. One can agree with Searle that no amount of handing around tokens and fiddling with lists of recipients will enable the individual players to understand Chinese. But there is no entailment from this to the claim that the simulation as a whole does not come to understand Chinese. The fallacy involved in moving from part to whole is even more glaring here than in the original version of the Chinese Room Argument.

[6] Hypercomputation is the computation of functions that cannot be computed by Turing machine. The term originates in Copeland and Proudfoot (1999).

The gymnasium version in fact consists of two inferences:

(4.1) No individual player understands Chinese (by virtue of doing the computations).

Therefore

(4.2) The simulation as a whole—call it G—does not understand Chinese (by virtue of doing the computations).

Therefore

(4.3) The network being simulated, N, does not understand Chinese (by virtue of doing the computations).

Since (4.1) does not entail (4.2), the upper inference is unsound. Might the lower inference alone nevertheless suffice for Searle's purposes?

With the upper inference gone, how is (4.2) to be supported? (4.2) is certainly not *intuitively* compelling. It is only if we place reality firmly to one side and enter a kind of fairyland that we can entertain as true the proposition that a group of humans with their pockets full of plastic tokens is simulating a connectionist network that contains maybe as many as one thousand million million connections. I have no intuitions about fairyland and least of all the intuition that a 'brain' of token-passing slaves cannot understand Chinese. (Many of Searle's attempted objections to cognitive science involve a studied refusal to take physical and biological realities seriously. For example: 'if we are trying to take seriously the idea that the brain is a digital computer, we get the uncomfortable result that we could make a system that does just what the brain does out of pretty much anything . . . cats and mice and cheese or levers or water pipes or pigeons or anything else . . . ' (Searle 1992: 207). The theory that the brain is a digital computer does not (need I say) imply that a system that does what the brain does can *really* be made out of pigeons. Only an absurd theory could imply this—Searle is surely right about that much. Likewise connectionism does not imply that a team of gymnasts can *really* simulate the brain.)

Letting the issue of the truth of (4.2) hang for now, and turning to the question of validity, the inference from (4.2) to (4.3) is this: G is a simulation of N; it is not the case that G understands Chinese, therefore it is not the case that N understands Chinese. As in the case of (3.6), this reasoning exemplifies inference-form (3.5), contrapositive of the reviled (3.4).

Let me see if there is any useful way of fending off the charge that the inference from (4.2) to (4.3) commits the simulation fallacy. After all, not every way of cashing out the variables in a fallacious inference-form need produce an invalid argument—for example, cashing out P and Q with one and the same sentence makes a valid argument even out of the invalid form P or Q, therefore P.

When one computing device, x, is said to simulate another, y, it is often the case that only the input–output relationship is duplicated: in other respects, the processes carried out by x and y may differ considerably. (For example, x may replicate y's input–output behaviour by means of an algorithm that is completely different from the algorithm actually employed by y). G, on the other hand, seems to mimic N much more closely than is the case in a common-or-garden simulation where only the input–output relationship matters. In fact, let's assume that, relative to some favoured way of distinguishing between process and implementation, G and N are carrying out one and the same computational process. This may be expressed by saying that G is *isomorphic* to N.

With the proviso that G is isomorphic to N, the inference from (4.2) to (4.3) is trivially valid: if a given computational process is insufficient for understanding then it is insufficient for understanding! The rub is that there is no more leverage for establishing that the process is insufficient in the case of one isomorph than in the case of the other. It is undeniable that Searle is home and dry if he can show that N, or any isomorphic copy, fails to understand Chinese by virtue of 'doing the computations'. But *that* is where we came in.

5. The Church–Turing Fallacy and Formal Symbol Manipulation

Searle believes it follows from Church's thesis that the activity of the brain can be simulated by a universal Turing machine:

Can the operations of the brain be simulated on a digital computer [read: Turing machine]? . . . [G]iven Church's thesis that anything that can be given a precise enough characterization as a set of steps can be simulated on a digital computer, it follows trivially that the question has an affirmative answer. (Searle 1992: 200–1; see also Searle 1997: 87)

However, Searle's statement of Church's thesis is mistaken. Church's thesis, also known as 'Turing's thesis' and the 'Church–Turing thesis' (Kleene 1967), is in fact a proposition concerning what can be achieved by a human clerk who manipulates symbols unaided by any machinery (save paper and pencil) and who works in accordance with 'mechanical' methods, that is, methods set out in the form of a finite number of exact instructions that call for no insight or ingenuity on the part of the clerk. The Church–Turing thesis (Turing 1936; Church 1936, 1937) states that whatever can be calculated by a clerk so working, even a clerk idealized to the extent of being free of all constraints on time, patience, concentration, and so forth, can also be calculated by a Turing machine. This thesis carries no implication concerning the extent of what can be calculated by a *machine* (say one that operates in accordance with a finite program of instructions), for among the machine's repertoire of primitive operations there may be those that no human being unaided by machinery can perform. Nor does the thesis imply that each process admitting of a precise characterization 'as a set of steps' can be simulated by a Turing machine, for the steps need not be ones that a human clerk working in accordance with some mechanical method can carry out.

Searle's mistake concerning the nature of the Church–Turing thesis is, in fact, a common one, which can be frequently encountered in recent writing on the philosophy of mind (see further Copeland 2000). One way to assist the extinction of a fallacy is to introduce a name for it. In Copeland (1998) I suggested the term *Church–Turing fallacy* for the fallacy of believing that the Church–Turing thesis, or some formal or semi-formal result established by Turing or Church, secures the truth of the proposition that the brain (or every machine) can be simulated by a universal Turing machine.

In his Ph.D thesis (Princeton 1938) Turing introduced the notional machines that he called 'O-machines'. Subsequently published as Turing (1939), this work is a classic of recursive function theory. Yet it is seemingly little-known among philosophers of mind. An O-machine (see further Copeland 1997, 1998; Copeland and Proudfoot 1999) is a programmable device able to perform mathematical tasks that are too difficult for a universal Turing machine. (Turing proved in (1936) that such tasks exist). An O-machine consists of a 'head' and a paper tape of unbounded length. Each square of the tape is either blank or contains a discrete symbol. A finite segment of the tape contains the program that is to be executed and the symbols that form the input. The O-machine manipulates symbols in a serial, step-by-step manner in accordance with the rules specified by the program. Every primitive operation of an O-machine that is not among the primitive operations of a Turing machine is, by definition, a formal operation on discrete symbols (in essence an operation that replaces a binary string with 1 or 0).

Trivially, the processing of an O-machine is always characterizable as a set of steps, namely, the set of steps specified by the machine's program. Employing the thesis espoused by Searle in the above quotation yields the absurdity that an O-machine can be simulated by a Turing machine—a contradiction.

An O-machine's program may call for primitive operations that a human clerk working by rote and unaided by machinery is incapable of carrying out (for otherwise, by the real Church–Turing thesis, whatever can be calculated by an O-machine can be calculated by a Turing machine). There is no possibility of Searle's Chinese Room Argument being successfully deployed against the functionalist hypothesis that the brain instantiates an O-machine—which Searle will presumably find as 'antibiological' (1990: 23) as other functionalisms. This is because the argument depends on Clerk being able to carry out by hand each operation that the program in question calls for. Turing originally introduced the Turing machine as a *model* of a human clerk engaged in mathematical calculation (1936: 231), and so, of course, each primitive operation of a Turing machine is indeed one that a human clerk can carry out. The same is true of the electronic machines fashioned after the universal Turing machine. As Turing himself put it: 'Electronic computers are intended to carry out any definite rule of thumb process which could have been done by a human operator working in a disciplined but unintelligent manner' (Turing 1950: 1). O-machines, on the other hand, conspicuously fail to satisfy this ground condition of the CRA.

Searle has repeatedly emphasized that it is the fact that computers have 'no more than just formal symbols' which entails that programs 'cannot constitute the mind' and that this is what the CRA shows (Searle 1989: 33, 1992: 200).

The whole point of the original [i.e. indoor] example was to argue that . . . symbol manipulation by itself couldn't be sufficient for understanding Chinese. (Searle 1980*a*: 419 (B73–4)).

[F]ormal syntax . . . does not by itself guarantee the presence of mental contents. I showed this a decade ago in the Chinese room argument. (1992: 200)

But O-machines point up the fact that the notion of a programmed machine whose activity consists of the manipulation of formal symbols is more general than the notion of a universal Turing machine. If there is an implication from '*x*'s operation is defined purely formally or syntactically' to '*x*'s operation is neither constitutive of nor sufficient for mind', it is not one that could possibly be established by the CRA.

Nor is this rich field of counter-examples to Searle's claim merely of logical interest. It may indeed be physically possible to construct a machine which, under the idealization of unbounded storage and unbounded computing time, can compute functions that a universal Turing machine is unable to compute. Speculation that there may be physical processes—and so, potentially, machine-operations—whose behaviour cannot be simulated by Turing machine stretches back over at least four decades (e.g. da Costa and Doria 1991; Doyle 1982; Geroch and Hartle 1986; Komar 1964; Kreisel 1967, 1974; Penrose 1989, 1994; Pour-El and Richards 1979, 1981; Scarpellini 1963; Stannett 1990; Vergis *et al.* 1986; a partial survey is given in Copeland and Sylvan 1999). And the view that the mind is some form of hypercomputer is yet to be fully explored (Copeland 1997, 2000). As Mario Bunge has remarked, the traditional computational approach 'involves a frightful impoverishment of psychology, by depriving it of nonrecursive functions' (Bunge and Ardila 1987: 109).[7]

References

BODEN, M. A. (ed.) (1990) *The Philosophy of Artificial Intelligence* (Oxford: Oxford University Press).

BUNGE, M., and ARDILA, R. (1987) *Philosophy of Psychology* (New York: Springer-Verlag).

CHURCH, A. (1936) 'An Unsolvable Problem of Elementary Number Theory', *American Journal of Mathematics*, 58: 345–63.

—— (1937) Review of Turing (1936), *Journal of Symbolic Logic*, 2: 42–3.

COPELAND, B. J. (1993a) 'The Curious Case of the Chinese Gym', *Synthese*, 95: 173–86.

—— (1993b) *Artificial Intelligence: A Philosophical Introduction* (Oxford: Blackwell).

—— (1997) 'The Broad Conception of Computation', *American Behavioral Scientist*, 40: 690–716.

—— (1998) 'Turing's O-Machines, Penrose, Searle, and the Brain', *Analysis*, 58: 128–38.

—— (2000) 'Narrow versus Wide Mechanism', *Journal of Philosophy*, 97: 1–32.

—— and PROUDFOOT, D. (1999) 'Alan Turing's Forgotten Ideas in Computer Science', *Scientific American*, 280/4: 98–103.

—— and SYLVAN, R. (1999) 'Beyond the Universal Turing Machine', *Australasian Journal of Philosophy*, 77: 46–66.

da COSTA, N. C. A., and DORIA, F. A. (1991) 'Classical Physics and Penrose's Thesis', *Foundations of Physics Letters*, 4: 363–73.

DOYLE, J. (1982) 'What is Church's Thesis?' MIT Laboratory for Computer Science.

GEROCH, R., and HARTLE, J. B. (1986) 'Computability and Physical Theories', *Foundations of Physics*, 16: 533–50.

HAUGELAND, J. (1985) *Artificial Intelligence: The Very Idea* (Cambridge, Mass.: MIT Press).

KLEENE, S. C. (1967) *Mathematical Logic* (New York: Wiley).

KOMAR, A. (1964) 'Undecidability of Macroscopically Distinguishable States in Quantum Field Theory', *Physical Review*, 2nd series, 133B: 542–44.

---

[7] I am grateful to Jon Opie for drawing my attention to this passage.

KREISEL, G. (1967) 'Mathematical Logic: What has it Done for the Philosophy of Mathematics?' in R. Schoenman (ed.), *Bertrand Russell: Philosopher of the Century* (London: George Allen & Unwin).

—— (1974) 'A Notion of Mechanistic Theory', *Synthese*, 29: 11–26.

McLEOD, P., and DIENES, Z. (1993) 'Running to Catch the Ball', *Nature*, 362: 23.

PENROSE, R. (1989) *The Emperor's New Mind: Concerning Computers, Minds, and the Laws of Physics* (Oxford: Oxford University Press).

—— (1994) *Shadows of the Mind: A Search for the Missing Science of Consciousness* (Oxford: Oxford University Press).

POUR-EL, M. B., and RICHARDS, I. (1979) 'A Computable Ordinary Differential Equation Which Possesses No Computable Solution', *Annals of Mathematical Logic*, 17: 61–90.

—— (1981) 'The Wave Equation With Computable Initial Data Such That its Unique Solution is Not Computable', *Advances in Mathematics*, 39: 215–39.

SCARPELLINI, B. (1963) 'Zwei unentscheitbare Probleme der Analysis', *Zeitschrift für mathematische Logik und Grundlagen der Mathematik*, 9: 265–89.

SEARLE, J. R. (1980*a*) 'Minds, Brains, and Programs', *Behavioral and Brain Sciences*, 3: 417–24.

—— (1980*b*) 'Intrinsic Intentionality: Reply to Criticism of "Minds, Brains and Programs" ', *Behavioral and Brain Sciences*, 3: 450–6.

—— (1989) *Minds, Brains and Science* (London: Penguin).

—— (1990) 'Is the Brain's Mind a Computer Program?' *Scientific American*, 262/1: 20–5.

—— (1992) *The Rediscovery of the Mind* (Cambridge, Mass.: MIT Press).

—— (1997) *The Mystery of Consciousness* (New York: New York Review of Books).

SIEGELMANN, H. T., and SONTAG, E. D. (1994) 'Analog Computation via Neural Networks', *Theoretical Computer Science*, 131: 331–60.

STANNETT, M. (1990) 'X-machines and the Halting Problem: Building a Super-Turing Machine', *Formal Aspects of Computing*, 2: 331–41.

STERELNY, K. (1990) *The Representational Theory of Mind* (Oxford: Blackwell).

TURING, A. M. (1936) 'On Computable Numbers, with an Application to the Entscheidungsproblem', *Proceedings of the London Mathematical Society*, series 2, 42: 230–65.

—— (1938) 'Systems of Logic Based on Ordinals', Princeton University doctoral dissertation. Published as Turing 1939.

—— (1939) 'Systems of Logic Based on Ordinals', *Proceedings of the London Mathematical Society*, series 2, 45: 161–228.

—— (1950) *Programmers' Handbook for Manchester Electronic Computer*, University of Manchester Computing Laboratory.

VERGIS, A., STEIGLITZ, K., and DICKINSON, B. (1986) 'The Complexity of Analog Computation', *Mathematics and Computers in Simulation*, 28: 91–113.

7

Nixin' Goes to China

Larry Hauser

'Strong AI', AI Proper, and Computationalism

Searle always describes the Chinese Room as targeting 'Strong AI': what this phrase is invoked to mean, however, varies. At the outset of his original presentation, Searle says, 'My discussion here will be directed at the claims I have defined as those of strong AI, specifically the claim that the appropriately programmed computer literally has cognitive states and that the programs thereby explain human cognition' (Searle 1980a: 417).[1]

'Strong AI', here, seems to denote the conjunction of the metaphysical claim, 'the appropriately programmed computer literally has cognitive states', and the methodological one 'that the programs thereby explain human cognition'.[2] It is natural to think that the metaphysical claim being targeted is the affirmative answer to Turing's (1950) question 'Can a machine think?' The plan of the

I am indebted to Carol Slater and Herbert Simon for their extensive comments on an earlier draft of this chapter. I also thank the other members of the Michigan State University Philosophy of Language Discussion Group—Barbara Abbott, Aldo Antonelli, Gene Cline, Rich Hall, Myles McNally, and Paul Rusnock—for their many useful comments and suggestions on earlier drafts. Additionally, I owe a considerable debt of gratitude to John Preston and Mark Bishop for their editorial guidance, and especially for their insightful comments and pressing questions regarding several key issues. Mistakes, misunderstandings, and other infelicities remaining are, of course, my own.

[1] Reprinted in Boden (1990: 67). From here referred to as B67.

[2] Since the focus of this chapter is the bearing of Searle's Chinese Room Argument on claims relating to the *existence* of *artificial* intelligence (not on claims that programs *explain human* intelligence); since the relation between the two questions is by no means simple or uncontroversial (see Hauser 1993a, ch. 2, sect. 2 for discussion); and since Searle's own discussion is almost wholly couched in metaphysical (not epistemological) terms; I pursue the methodological question no further.

original Chinese Room article (mirroring Turing 1950) and not a few of Searle's subsequent remarks encourage just this interpretation. Take, for instance, Searle's characterization of Strong AI in the 1984 Panel Discussion of the question 'Has Artificial Intelligence Research Illuminated Human Thinking?' as

the view that says: 'It isn't just that we're simulating thinking or studying thinking. Our appropriately programmed computers with the right inputs and outputs will literally have thought processes, conscious and otherwise, in the same sense that you and I do.' (Searle *et al.* 1984: 146)

Searle continues,

I like that thesis, because it's clear that we know exactly what someone is saying when he says, 'Look, my machine or the machine we're going to eventually build has thought processes in exactly the same sense that you and I have thought processes.' It's clear, and it's false, and it's demonstrably false. (ibid.)

The 'demonstration' that follows is the Chinese Room, patently here being advertised as targeting the thesis that computers already do or someday will think; as targeting AI proper. Likewise, chapter 2 of *Minds, Brains, and Science*—where Searle first formalizes the Chinese Room Argument (as below)—is entitled 'Can Computers Think?'.

Compare now: 'There are several common misunderstandings of the Chinese Room Argument and of its significance. Many people suppose that it proves that "computers cannot think". But that is a misstatement' (Searle 1994: 546). Retraction noted and accepted.

But if the argument doesn't target the thesis that 'the appropriately programmed computer literally has cognitive states' what does it target? 'Strong AI' as ever is what the targeted view is *called*, but Strong AI is now to be understood, strictly, as the view that 'the mind is a computer program' (ibid.): the target is *Computationalism*.

Computationalism says that computation is what thought is *essentially:* (the right) computation is *metaphysically necessary* for thought, that is, *regardless of anything else that could be the case*, nothing would be thinking if it weren't (right) computing; and (right) computation *metaphysically suffices*, that is, such computation would be thought under any circumstances, no matter what else might be the case. Much as water has a chemical essence that chemical science has discovered, Computationalism maintains, thought has a computational essence that cognitive science will discover. *Thus* aimed, against Computationalism, 'this is the point of the parable—if I don't understand Chinese on the basis of implementing the program for understanding Chinese, then neither does any digital computer *solely on that basis* [emphasis added] because no digital computer has anything that I do not have [in the example]' (ibid.). Depending, as it does on the modal force of 'solely on that basis' this 'simple refutation of Strong AI' (ibid.) is deceptively unsimple and, in fact, is very far from being 'obviously sound and valid' (ibid.).

Of course, if you dismiss the apparent mentality of extant machines as bogus or 'as if', as many, if not most, cognitive scientists incline to do; if you make computationalism your sole basis for belief that computers can or someday *will think*; then the Chinese Room may seem, to you, unproblematically, to target both. But while the *psychological gap* between Computationalism and AI may, for many cognitive scientists, be slight; the real logical and epistemological gap is considerable. What Searle proposes to bridge the gap—'*[b]rains cause minds*' and '*[a]nything else that caused minds would have to have causal powers at least equivalent to those of a brain*' (Searle 1984: 39–40; emphasis in original)—moreover, are argumentative matchsticks.[3] Consider, for instance, the following would-be bridging argument:

1. Brains cause minds (mentality).
2. Anything else that caused minds would have to have causal powers at least equivalent to a brain.
3. Computation alone does not cause minds.

Therefore,

4. Something else about the brain causes mentality.
5. Digital electronic computers lack this something else.

Therefore,

6. Digital electronic computers don't have mentality.

The trouble is that premise 5 is not so easily supported. In fact, it's *insupportable* unless we're told *what* this additional something *is* and *wherein* computers are supposed to be lacking it. Most importantly—as difficult as it may be for those who have antecedently dismissed the possibility to allow it—observational evidence strongly suggests that computers already do *seek*, *compare*, and *decide* things. On the evidence, the would-be bridging argument might *more plausibly* be continued from 4 as follows:

5a. Digital computers exhibit mentality.

Therefore,

6a. Digital computers have this something else.

Bridge out.

---

[3] See Hauser (1997) for further discussion.

The Chinese Room Argument versus Computationalism

Searle (1994: 546–7) presents the argument targeting Computationalism as having the following 'logical structure' (see Searle 1984: 39–42, 1989a, 1990a for earlier related formulations):

It is a derivation of a conclusion from three premises:

premise 1: programs are formal (syntactical),
premise 2: minds have contents (semantics),
premise 3: syntax is not sufficient for semantics.

'The story about the Chinese Room', as Searle explains it, 'illustrates the truth of premise 3' (Searle 1994: 546). Searle continues, 'From these three propositions the conclusion logically follows: programs are not minds. . . . And this conclusion', Searle tells us 'refutes Strong AI'.

But this conclusion misses the point. Computationalism holds 'the essence of the mental is the *operation* [emphasis added] of a physical symbol system' (Searle 1980a: 421 (B79) cites this formulation by Newell 1979). The Computationalist hypothesis identifies minds with *processes*: with program operations or program runs and not simply with the *programs* themselves. Obviously, no one ever proposed to identify static program instantiations, for example, on diskettes, with cognition. Only *operating* programs are candidate thinkers.

Suppose we modify the conclusion to actually speak to the Computationalist hypothesis, by substituting 'processes' for 'programs', and substituting likewise in the first premise to preserve logical structure. Thus revised, the argument is to the point; but it's unsound. Reformulated premise 1—'*processes* are syntactic'—is false. *Processes* are not syntactic: not *purely so* as the would-be modal force of the argument requires. The sentence tokens 'Ed ate' and 'Ed *ate*', though *physically* different (differently shaped: rendered in different typefaces), have the same *syntactic* form. This sameness of syntactic form is what makes them instances of the same sentence. Similarly, every instantiation of a given program is syntactically identical with every other instance: this is what makes *them* instances of the same *program*. In the simplest case, since spatial sequence of stored instructions and the temporal sequence of operations resulting from the execution of those instructions have the same syntax, the difference between inert instantiation and dynamic instantiation is not syntactic. The property of being a *process* is not, then, a purely formal or syntactic property but includes, essentially, a non-syntactic element—an element of dynamism—besides (see Hauser 1997: 211).[4]

Argument and Experiment

The Chinese Room *experiment* itself might seem to circumvent the preceding objection: the man-in-the-room is supposed to be *running* the envisaged natural language understanding program and *still* not understanding Chinese. This seems to show not just that '*Syntax by itself is neither constitutive of nor sufficient for semantics*' (Searle 1990a, emphasis in original) but that *syntax-in-motion* isn't sufficient by itself either. The overarching argument would now be more perspicuously rendered as follows:[5]

premise 2a: thought has contents (semantics),
premise 3a: computational processing (by itself) is not sufficient for semantics.

Therefore,

thought is not computational processing.

Note that the first premise drops out. The argument as restated has nothing to do with syntax.[6] Also note that where Searle's original premise 3, '*syntax* is not sufficient for semantics', *can* credibly be styled 'a conceptual truth that we knew all along' (Searle 1988: 214), 3a cannot. So, it seems the experiment must bear some *empirical* weight; and here, it's *the experiment* that doesn't suffice. It's methodologically biased, depending (as it does) on a dubious tender of epistemic privilege to

[4] Less simple cases—e.g. processes that loop—complicate the simple isomorphism between typographic order and temporal sequence. It might also be asked (as one reviewer of this chapter asked), 'Why shouldn't there be a perfectly good dynamic conception of syntax?' In either case a more concrete notion of *implementation* may be invoked. Such a notion needs to be made out anyhow—if computation is to explain actual behavior—and amounts here just to the (rightful) recognition that candidate thinkings are not processes *in the abstract*, but *in real time*. David Chalmers, in a similar vein, observes, 'Certainly no mere program is a candidate for possession of a mind. *Implementations of programs*, on the other hand, are concrete systems with causal dynamics, and are not purely syntactic' (1996: 327; emphasis in original).

[5] I speak of thoughts (in place of minds) here. Since 'mind', for Searle, abbreviates 'mental processes' (Searle 1984: 39)—so e.g. the phrase 'brains cause minds' serves 'just as a slogan' for 'the brain causes mental states'—nothing except expository ease turns on this move from talk of minds to talk of thoughts (i.e. of mental processes or states). For me, as for Searle, I take it, a thing is or has a mind just in case it thinks or has mental properties.

[6] Hauser (1997) discusses this oddity in more detail.

first-person disavowals of understanding (and other intentional mental states). That *other* 'blind trace' experiments in the recent history of cognitive science have even seemed to *their* advocates to yield intuitions not unsupportive of AI and Computationalism confirms the diagnosis of methodological bias and, perhaps, raises further issues about the robustness of Searle's thought-experimental design.

The Chinese Room Experiment

Methodological Bias: Searle's Cartesian Paraphernalia

Consider the transition from 'it seems to me quite obvious that I do not understand' to 'I understand nothing' (Searle 1980a: 418 (B70)). Result 3a depends not just on Searle's *seeming to himself not to understand* but on his *really not understanding*. That it would *seem* thus to Searle, from his 'first person point of view' (Searle 1980b: 451) in the situation described is, perhaps, unexceptionable. What is exceptionable is the transition from its seeming so from 'the first person point of view' to its *being so*. Those who understand natural languages such as English or Chinese are *normally* aware of understanding them: it both *seems* to them that they understand English or Chinese, *and they do*. Conversely, those who do not seem to themselves to understand a natural language (when they hear it spoken or see it written) *normally* do not understand. But notice that in the normal case of not understanding it also seems that I do not understand to *others*, from the 'third person' or 'external point of view'. Since the Chinese Room set-up is designedly abnormal in just this respect, we cannot appeal to the normal covariance of seeming to oneself not to understand with not understanding to decide this case in favor of Searle not understanding. Since Searle's imagined introspective lack of awareness or sincere disavowal of understanding is all the warrant the Chinese Room experiment provides for the conclusion that Searle would not understand the Chinese stories, questions, and answers in the envisaged scenario, the experiment fails.

It seems that only an a priori tender of the epistemic privilege of overriding all 'external' 'third person' appearances to how it seems 'from the point of view of the agent, from my [first person] point of view' (Searle 1980a: 420 (B75)) will suffice to save the experiment. This confirms what Searle's characterization of the experiment as implementing the methodological imperative 'always insist on the first person point of view' (Searle 1980b: 451) suggests. The experiment *does* invite us 'to regress to the Cartesian vantage point' (Dennett 1987: 336) and it seems to succeed only if we accept the invitation. The experiment's support for would-be result 3*a* is just as dubious as the Cartesian grant of epistemic privilege on which it depends. Of course, one needn't be a *metaphysical dualist* (Cartesian or otherwise), to hold some methodological brief for first person authority. However, *to sustain a case* based on first-person authority against AI— especially in the face of overwhelming third-person evidence of it—I submit, you *do*. You need to answer the question of what the additional something is in *us* that promotes *our* computation to thought to counter the third-person evidence: that's metaphysical. And you need to answer *as Searle does*, that 'consciousness' or 'ontological subjectivity' or 'qualia' are what's essential: that's dualistic.[7] The further question of *wherein* computers are lacking in ontological subjectivity—and why we should think so—remains. It remains because on the *third-person* evidence the natural conclusion would seem to be—again—that *whatever* else besides computation is required for thought, computers have this too, since in *seeking*, *comparing*, and *deciding* things, as they evidently do, they evidently think.

To reiterate: given the abnormality of the case Searle describes, one's self-avowed or introspected lack of understanding of Chinese in the example does not suffice to establish actual lack of understanding in the face of overwhelming evidence *of* understanding 'from the external point of view'. If the experiment reliably showed that one would not be *conscious of understanding* the Chinese (stories, questions, and answers) one was processing, it would *still* fail to show that this processing would not *amount to understanding*; and even the antecedent here is ill-supported by Searle's thought-experiment. Even if overriding epistemic privilege were granted to *actual* introspective deliverances or first-person disavowals, the Chinese Room experiment's extension of such privilege to *imagined* introspections (under scarcely imaginable circumstances) would still be highly dubious.

Other Blind Trace Scenarios

A further consideration undermines the Chinese Room experiment: similar (thought) experimental procedures seem to elicit contrary intuitions: Turing

---

[7] Searle frequently protests that he employs no 'Cartesian apparatus' (Searle 1992, pp. xxi, 14) or 'Cartesian paraphernalia' (Searle 1987: 146), and in several places (Searle 1992: 95 f.; 1987: 146) explicitly disavows 'privileged access' (at least in name). He protests too much, I think.

(1950), and Newell and Simon (1963), seem to draw conclusions contrary to Searle on the basis of similar blind trace scenarios.

Searle imagines himself to be hand-tracing a natural language understanding program on Chinese input (stories and questions), thereby producing appropriate Chinese output (answers). Hand-tracing is something computer programmers do to check and debug programs. In such cases, the programmer knows what the input means, what the output means, and what the program is supposed to be doing (the function it's supposed to be computing). The programmer *must* know these things in order to tell whether the program is processing the former into the latter *correctly*. The case Searle imagines is unusual in that the trace is 'blind':

Unknown to me, the people who are giving me all of these symbols call the first batch 'a script', they call the second batch a 'story', and they call the third batch 'questions.' Furthermore, they call the symbols I give them back in response to the third batch 'answers to the questions', and the set of rules in English that they gave me they call 'the program.' (Searle 1980*a*: 418 (B69))

Not only isn't Searle conscious of the *meanings* of the input and output strings he processes, he isn't even aware that the input strings are stories and questions, or that the output strings are answers. He may not even 'recognize the Chinese writing as Chinese' or for that matter, as *writing* as opposed to 'just so many meaningless squiggles' (ibid.). And he doesn't know that the set of instructions transforming input strings into output strings that he is following is a natural language understanding (or any other kind of) program.

Searle's blind trace procedure has precedents in Turing's wartime use of 'blind' human 'computers' to decrypt the German naval code, and Newell and Simon's use of 'protocols' derived from 'blind' inferences of human subjects to gather information about human-reasoning processes. Yet these experimenters fail to draw anything like Searle's conclusion—even seem moved to advocate opposing conclusions—by *their* reflection on *these* blind trace cases.

Turing, Bombes, Wrens, and Enigma

During World War II, Turing directed a project aimed at breaking the German naval code, 'Enigma'. The work was initially done by members of the Women's Royal Naval Service (Wrens) acting as human computers following decryption programs Turing devised. To maintain secrecy, the Wrens were kept in the dark about the *meaning* of the input they received and output they produced (that these were messages about the locations of submarines, etc.), even about the input and output being enciphered and deciphered *German* and about the input and output being encrypted and decrypted *messages*. 'The Wrens did their appointed tasks without knowing what any of it was for' (Hodges 1983: 211), like Searle in the Chinese Room. Overseeing this veritable Chinese gymnasium (compare Searle 1990a: 28), Turing, in Andrew Hodges's words, 'was fascinated by the fact that people could be taking part in something quite clever, in a quite mindless way' (Hodges 1983: 211): more incisively, it seemed that the Wrens were doing something *intelligent* (deciphering encoded messages) *unawares*. As the work of the Wrens was taken over by machines of Turing's devising, called 'Bombes', Turing seems to have surmised that the Bombes were likewise doing something intelligent—the same as the Wrens. This intuition occasioned by a situation comparable to the situation Searle imagines in his thought-experiment helped, I take it, inspire Turing's famous (1950) defense of machine intelligence.

Newell and Simon: Blind Protocols

In developing their General Problem Solver program (GPS), Allen Newell and Herbert Simon used a blind trace procedure to gather 'protocols' (running verbal commentaries) of deductive reasonings performed in the blind by human subjects. The protocols were intended to 'extract information' (Newell and Simon 1963: 282) about procedures humans use or manipulations humans perform in the course of their deductive reasonings. The information extracted was then to be used to 'write [GPS] programs that do the kinds of manipulation humans do' (Newell and Simon 1963: 283).

Here is how Newell and Simon describe the experimental situation:

A human subject, a student in engineering in an American college, sits in front of a blackboard on which are written the following expressions:

$(R \supset \sim P) \bullet (\sim R \rightarrow Q) | \sim (\sim Q \bullet P).$

This is a problem in elementary symbolic logic, *but the student does not know it* [emphasis added]. He does know that he has twelve rules for manipulating expressions containing letters connected by 'dots' ($\bullet$), 'wedges' (v), 'horseshoes' ($\supset$) and 'tildes' ($\sim$), which stand [which the subject does not know] for 'and', 'or', 'implies', and 'not'. These rules [inference and equivalence rules though the subject doesn't know this] show that expressions of certain forms . . . can be transformed into expressions of somewhat different form. . . . The subject has practiced applying the rules, but he has previously done only one other problem like this. The experimenter has instructed him that his problem is to obtain the expression in the upper right corner from the expression in the upper left corner using the twelve rules. . . . The subject was also asked to talk aloud as he worked; his comments were recorded and then transcribed into a 'protocol'; *i.e.*, a verbatim record of all that he or the experimenter said during the experiment. (Newell and Simon 1963: 278–9)

Here is an excerpt from the initial portion of this subject's protocol:

Well, looking at the left hand side of the equation, first we want to eliminate one of the sides by using rule 8 [A • B ⊃ A / A • B ⊃ B]. It appears too complicated to work with first. Now—no,—no, I can't do that because I will be eliminating either the Q or the P in that total expression. I won't do that first. Now I'm looking for a way to get rid of the [arrow] inside the two brackets that appear on the left and right sides of the equation. (ibid. 280)

In treating protocols of such 'blind' deductions as sources from which information about *the subject's* deductive thought processes can reliably be extracted, Newell and Simon, like Turing, seem to credit intuitions about these blind traces contrary to Searle's.

Nix

The point of experiments is to adjudicate between competing hypotheses. Since non-dualistic (functionalist, behaviorist, and neurophysicalist) hypotheses about the nature of thought do *not* privilege the first person, to tender overriding epistemic privileges to the first person fatally prejudices the experiment. The tendency of other blind trace scenarios to yield intuitions conflicting with Searle's reinforces this indictment. Though Searle is (understandably) keen to style his experiment to be an attempt just to 'remind us of a conceptual truth that we knew all along'; it's not. Neither, as just seen, can it bear any empirical weight.[8]

---

[8] It might be urged that the Chinese Room experiment *at least* shows that *when* the first-person point of view *is* considered to be privileged—or even *equal*—blind trace scenarios speak *against* AI; so, such cases provide no such support for AI and Computationalism as Turing, Newell, and Simon, perhaps, have taken them to provide. At least, to enlist third-person intuitions about blind trace scenarios *as supportive of* AI, it may here be urged, exhibits a *contrary* methodological bias—*against* dualistic hypotheses—on a par with the *pro* dualistic bias of the Chinese Room experiment. I think the parity here is overstated. *Ab initito* (considering past performance) dualistic hypotheses *are* more worthy of scientific dismissal than competing physicalist hypotheses. Likewise, private 'first-person' introspection reports or (dis)avowals are *less* worthy of scientific credence than public 'third-person' observation reports. *Imagined* introspective observations or (dis)avowals (as in the Chinese Room scenario) are less worthy yet. But even if parity is granted, the accusation of methodological bias *against* the Chinese Room remains, along with *independent* evidence of AI from actual intellectual accomplishments by real machines; for all Searle imagines.

Unequivocal Intentionality

Searle frequently insists that the intuitions his thought-experiment provokes are not Cartesian and have nothing to do with Dualism, just common sense. He would, no doubt, dismiss contrary intuitions evoked in others, or by other blind trace experiments, such as the theory laden and biased ones. The intentionality Turing thought he descried in the Wrens and Bombes, and that Newell and Simon perhaps took for granted in the protocols they elicited—according to Searle's elaboration on this—are not real *intrinsic* intentionality *like ours*. Neither Wrens, nor Bombes, nor Newell and Simon's 'deducers', to this way of thinking, really have thought processes; not in *'exactly the same sense* that you and I have' (Searle *et al.* 1984: 146: emphasis added). Similarly, when we describe the doings of computers in intentional terms—as when we say they're 'seeking' and 'deciding' things—such speaking, Searle insists, does not attribute actual *intrinsic* intentionality to the devices. It's figurative speaking: *as if* attribution. Since the mental terms are not being used in their literal senses, they're being used *ambiguously*. Would-be contrary blind trace examples and intuitions, like Turing's and Newell and Simon's, then are undone. Undone, Searle would have it, by equivocation on the mental terms in their would-be conclusions. By the same stroke all independent-seeming evidence of machine intelligence is also undone. They just act *as if* intelligent. Deep Blue doesn't even *play chess*. Computers don't even *compute*. Not really; not literally (cf. Searle 1999).

Of course,

> If we face a putative counterexample to our favorite philosophical thesis, it is always open for us to protest that some key term is being used in a special sense, different from its use in the thesis. We may be right, but the ease of the move should counsel a policy of caution. Do not posit an ambiguity unless you are really forced to, unless there are really compelling theoretical or intuitive grounds to suppose that an ambiguity really is present. (Kripke 1977: 268)

Searle himself, in a different context (where AI is not in question), agrees, 'an ordinary application of Occam's razor places the onus of proof on those who claim that these sentences are ambiguous. One does not multiply meanings beyond necessity' (Searle 1975: 40). I submit there are no compelling intuitive reasons for accepting the ambiguity between 'intrinsic' and 'as if' (attributions of) intentionality Searle alleges. Intuitive tests for ambiguity yield no evidence of ambiguity in such contexts. Tests, for instance, which enable us to 'hear' ambiguity as zeugma or punning in certain contexts yield no sense of zeugma or punning when applied to mental predications of computers.[9] There are, it seems, then, compelling intuitive grounds to suppose that such predications are *unambiguous* literal predications. Theoretical grounds Searle *does* offer for positing an ambiguity here, where intuition recognizes none, are woefully inadequate. Consciousness, on Searle's account is what confers real intrinsic intentionality. Yet he confesses, 'The real gap in my account is . . . that I do not explain the details of the relation between Intentionality and consciousness' (Searle 1991: 181). Indeed, he scarcely explains it even in outline.

Ambiguity Tests

Following Zwicky and Sadock,

From here on the count noun *understanding* is a neutral term to cover both those elements of 'meaning' (in a broad sense) that get coded in semantic representations, and those that do not. Each understanding corresponds to a class of contexts in which the linguistic expression is appropriate—though, of course, a class of contexts might correspond to several understandings, as in examples like Someone is renting the house (courtesy of Morgan [1972]). (Zwicky and Sadock 1975: 3 n. 9)

Though 'philosophers perennially argue for ambiguities on the basis of a difference in understanding alone', Zwicky and Sadock note (ibid. 4), nevertheless,

It will not do, of course, to argue that a sentence is ambiguous by characterizing the difference between two understandings. (ibid. 3)

A difference in understanding is a necessary, but not a sufficient, condition for ambiguity. (ibid. 4)

The choice between ambiguity, 'several underlying syntactic (or semantic) representations' (ibid. 2) and lack of specification, 'a single representation corresponding to different states of affairs' (ibid.), remains open. To illustrate this second notion, and the contrast with ambiguity, Zwicky and Sadock (ibid.) consider as an example sentence: 'My sister is the Ruritanian secretary of state'. This sentence, it may be observed,

is unspecified (general, indefinite, unmarked, indeterminate, vague, neutral) with respect to whether my sister is older or younger than I am, whether she acceded to her post recently or some time ago, whether the post is hers by birth or by merit, whether it

---

[9] Zeugma involves, roughly, the use of a single token of an expression to govern or modify two or more words to which the expression applies in different senses as in, 'She came home in a flood of tears and a sedan chair', 'The President let his pants and the country down', etc.

has an indefinite tenure or will cease at some specific future time, whether she is right-handed or left-handed, and so on. (ibid. 2–3)

Yet it shouldn't be said that this sentence is in 'many ways ambiguous just because we can perceive many distinct classes of contexts in which it would be appropriate, or because we can indicate many understandings with para-phrases' (ibid. 4). Compare *Deep Blue considers sacrificing a pawn* and *Kasparov considers sacrificing a pawn*. The difference between my understanding of 'considers' in these two sentences seems quite like the difference between these various under-standings of 'secretary of state' in Zwicky and Sadock's example. It seems unlike the difference between the disparate understandings of such clearly ambiguous sentences as 'They saw her duck' and 'He cooked her goose' (ibid. 3). The disparate understandings of 'her duck' here—i.e. 'a certain sort of bird' and 'a certain kind of action' (ibid. 4)—don't seem to be 'the sort of thing that languages could plausibly fail to specify' (ibid.) semantically. In such cases, where 'lack of specification is implausible' (ibid.), 'the burden of proof falls on anyone who insists that [the] sentences . . . are unspecified rather than ambigu-ous' (ibid.). On the other hand, sentences like 'My sister is the Ruritanian secretary of state' despite being 'unspecified with respect to some distinction' (ibid.), and indeed any number of them, nevertheless 'have otherwise quite similar understandings' (ibid.). The distinctions are all 'the sort of thing that languages *could* plausibly fail to specify' (ibid.) and the burden of proof falls on anyone who insists that the sentences are ambiguous. Zwicky and Sadock propose a number of tests whereby this burden may be discharged; or by means of which to assess possible borderline cases.

In another context—not in connection with the claim that predications of mental terms to computers are figurative 'as-if' predications—Searle himself accepts tests for distinguishing ambiguity from lack of specification in question-able cases. Searle asks us to consider 'the following sequence of rather ordinary English sentences, all containing the word "cut"' (Searle 1980c: 221):

1. Bill cut the grass.
2. The barber cut Tom's hair.
3. Sally cut the cake.
4. I cut my skin.
5. The tailor cut the cloth.

6. Sam cut two classes last week.
7. The President cut the salaries of the employees.
8. The Raiders cut the roster to 45.

9. Bob can't cut the mustard.
10. Cut the cackle!
11. Cut it out!

Searle deems it 'more or less intuitively obvious' (Searle 1980c: 221) that 'the occurrence of the word "cut" in the utterances of 1–5 is literal' (ibid. 221). Similarly, he deems it obvious that 'the sense or senses in which "cut" would be used in the utterances of 6–8', on the other hand, 'is a figurative extension of the literal meaning in 1–5' (ibid. 222). In 9–11 'the occurrences of the word "cut" are clearly in idioms' (ibid.): these will not concern us. The main problem is how to justify the distinction between the first group (1–5) and the second group (6–8) 'if someone wanted to deny it' (ibid.). Searle proposes, that the distinction between the literal use of 'cut' in 1–5 and its figurative employment in 6–8 can be made out by four different tests:[10]

Asymmetrical dependence of understanding 'A person who doesn't understand 6–8, but still understands 1–5, understands the literal meaning of the word "cut"; whereas a person who does not understand 1–5 does not understand that literal meaning; and we are inclined to say he couldn't fully understand the meaning of "cut" in 6–8 if he didn't understand the meaning in 1–5' (Searle 1980c: 222).

Translation 'in general, 1–5 translate easily into other languages; 6–11 do not' (ibid. 222).

Conjunction reduction 'certain sorts of conjunction reductions will work for 1–5 that will not work for the next group. For example,

12. General Electric has just announced the development of a new cutting machine that can cut grass, hair, cakes, skin, and cloth.

But if I add to this, after the word 'cloth', the expression, from 6–8, 'classes, salaries, and rosters', the sentence becomes at best a bad joke and at worst a category mistake' (ibid. 222).

Comparative formation 'the fact that we can form some comparatives such as, "Bill cut more off the grass than the barber did off Tom's hair", is further evidence that we are not dealing with ambiguity as it is traditionally conceived' (ibid. 224).

---

[10] The conjunction reduction and comparative formation tests are advocated by Zwicky and Sadock along with several other tests Searle doesn't mention. I only consider the tests Searle himself proposes here. The other tests described by Zwicky and Sadock (not mentioned by Searle) similarly fail to discover ambiguity in the cases of mental predications of computers at issue.

Let us put our problematic class of mental predications of machines to these tests to see how they fare; whether they support the judgment that such usages are figurative like the uses of 'cut' in 6–8.

Translation

It is manifestly false that statements like 'Deep Blue considers possible continuations of play', 'DOS recognizes the DIR command', 'My pocket calculator calculates that the square root of 2 is 1.4142135', and the like, are particularly difficult to translate into other languages. Computer manuals help themselves generously to locutions of this sort and are published in and translated into and from English, Japanese, French, German, etc. By the translation test, it seems attributions of mental properties to computers, as in computer manuals, are literal and not figurative.

Comparative Formation

Comparatives such as 'Deep Blue considers more continuations to a greater depth than its human opponent' and, 'My pocket calculator extracts square roots more quickly and accurately than I' are familiar locutions. They provoke no sense of zeugma: we 'hear' no punning. This argues that 'we are not dealing here with ambiguity as it is traditionally conceived' (Searle 1980c: 224) just as it argued that we were not using 'cut' ambiguously when we spoke of Bill cutting the lawn and the barber cutting Tom's hair. We can form the comparison without making a bad joke or a category mistake.

Conjunction Reduction

Here again the test seems to support the verdict that the usages at issue are literal and not figurative. Consider the sentence, 'Kasparov considered the possible continuation Q × R check'. If I add 'and so did Deep Blue', there is no zeugma. The Comparative Formation and Conjunction Reduction tests enable us to 'hear' ambiguity as zeugma or punning ('a bad joke'). Thus the humorous impression made by a conjunction reduction like 'She came home in a flood of tears and a sedan chair' reveals an ambiguity of 'in' between the sentential context, 'She came home in a flood of tears' and the sentential context 'She came home in a sedan chair'. Unlike 'GE's new cutting machine cuts cloth and salaries', I hear no pun (or otherwise have any intuition of semantic anomaly) in 'Kasparov considered the continuation Q × R check, and so did Deep Blue'.

Asymmetrical Dependence of Understanding

This test yields no firm verdict against the literalness of the attributions in question. The other three tests appeal beyond our original intuitions, either to empirical facts of translatability or to special comparative or conjunctive contexts where ambiguities can be heard as zeugma or punning. The understanding test, however, does not seem to extend our original intuitions. If your original intuition, like Searle's, is that mental predications of computers are figurative and equivocal, you'll intuit that someone who didn't know how to make such predications of people but only knew how to ascribe these predicates to machines would 'not understand the literal meaning' and that one who hadn't first learned how to make such predications of people 'couldn't fully understand' the meaning of such terms as applied to computers. If you don't share Searle's original intuition you won't share these further intuitions either. The other tests have a degree of theory neutrality which our intuitions about priority and asymmetrical dependence of understanding lack. (Searle himself presents the Understanding Test as continuous with his initial intuitive demarcation of literal, figurative, and idiomatic uses (Searle 1980c: 221–2), and seems to admit its indecisiveness in this connection.) The other three tests are what come in when the distinction between the literal uses and the figurative uses isn't so obvious as in the 'cut' examples. The other three tests come in 'if someone wanted to deny' (ibid. 222) your initial intuitions . . . as I deny Searle's intuitions about the figurativeness of mental attributions to computers. The verdict these tests render in this case—in the case of such mental attributions as Searle would deem figurative (and equivocal), which I deem literal (and unequivocal)—is clear: it's *unequivocal*.

Nix Nix

None of the ambiguity tests Searle proposes warrants any judgment of figurativeness, or supports a charge of ambiguity, against mental attributions to computers. The Understanding Test is too theory-dependent to serve as a check on equally theory-dependent intuitions about figurativeness and literalness. The more theory-neutral tests of Translation, Conjunction Reduction, and Comparative Formation, on the other hand, all tell in favor of the literalness and univocality of the predications in question. If Searle's Chinese Room experiment motivates and licenses a semantic distinction between 'as-if' and 'intrinsic' attributions of mental properties it will have to do so in opposition to, and not in agreement with, the semantic intuitions tapped by these tests. If the Chinese Room thought-experiment is supposed to license and motivate the claim that attributions of intentional phenomena to computers and their ilk are literally false, it will have to do so in opposition to a wealth of actual observations. We say, 'my calculator calculates that $5/12 = 0.4166666$', 'DOS recognized the DIR command', 'Deep Blue considered castling queen side', and the like. And we mean it.

Naïve AI

I don't claim to know what thought or intelligence essentially is, myself. I even have grave doubts that it is *essentially* any way (but that's another story). Still, I think, I know it when I see it. I agree with Searle (1980*a*: 422 (B82)) that whether computers think (or someday will) is 'an empirical question'. I further confess that beyond the platitudinous—'Use your ingenuity. Use any weapon at hand, and stick with any weapon that works' (Searle 1990*b*: 640)—besides having next to nothing to say about *what* it is I think I see when I think I see it, I have little to say about *how* I know it when I see it either. Except this: what ingenuity suggests to explain Deep Blue's intercourse with Kasparov is 'Deep Blue considers castling queen side', 'seeks to protect its king', 'decides to castle king side', and the like. It may seem uncomfortably like chicken sexing; but it works (cf. Hauser 1993*b*).

Here, some may worry, with Searle, that failure to distinguish between *as if* attribution (as to computers) and literal attribution (as to ourselves) will result in panpsychic proliferation; not just to simple devices such as thermostats, but even plants; even 'water flowing downhill' which '*tries* to get to the bottom of the hill by ingeniously *seeking* the line of least resistance' (or so it may seem). And 'if water is mental', Searle adds, 'everything is mental' (1989*b*: 198). I won't speak to thermostats and plants; at least not yet. I will speak to the water. There is a genuine difference in sense between the sense in which water seeks the bottom of the hill and the sense in which I do, I think. A difference having to do with Grice's (1957) distinction between *natural* and *non-natural* (attributions of) meaning, however, not with Searle's alleged distinction between *literal* and *as if* (attributions of) intentionality. Just as the smoke from my neighbor's chimney cannot (be said to) *naturally mean* there's a fire on his hearth *unless there is* a fire on his hearth; neither can water be said to seek the bottom of the hill by the line of least resistance unless there *is* a hill and a line of least resistance. Ponce de Leon, on the other hand, may well seek to find the Fountain of Youth, *regardless of its non-existence* much as the sentence 'There's fire on his hearth' can *non-naturally mean* there is, even when there isn't. *This* ambiguity—akin to Grice's *natural* and *non-natural* senses of meaning—is both theoretically well motivated, I take it, and one that standard ambiguity tests arguably do reveal. Consider:

1. That smoke and 'Feuer' mean fire.
2. Jack and Jill sought to fetch a pail of water in going up the hill and the water the line of least resistance in coming down.
3. Jack and Jill sought the pail of water less successfully than the water the line of least resistance.

If our intuitions are unclear with regard to simpler devices than computers, and simpler organisms than us—or even the cases just cited, themselves—I say, let the chips fall where they may. Let them fall wherever working (predictive-explanatory) ingenuity, differences of meaning that *do* get intuited in standard ambiguity tests, and warranted *scientific* theoretic considerations dictate. And if the chips fall too far towards panpsychism for comfort in Christendom . . . this is not a scientific consideration. Searle's would-be blanket distinction between as-if thought or intentionality (*theirs*) and real literal thought or intentionality (*ours*) promises to salve such discomfort; but, alas (for panpsychic discomfort sufferers), Searle's distinction is baseless. *Ex hypothesi*—since as-if-thinking things behave *exactly* as if they think—the distinction lacks any *predictive-explanatory* basis. Given the failure of standard ambiguity tests to reveal any such ambiguity (as we have seen), it lacks any semantic-intuitive basis. And given the inadequacies of the Chinese Room experiment (shown above) it lacks any scientific-theoretic basis.

Conclusion

If it looks like a duck and walks like a duck and quacks like a duck it ain't *necessarily* a duck; but it is prima facie a duck. Where applications of standard ambiguity tests yield intuitions to the contrary, accusations of ambiguity—or introductions thereof—need theoretical warrant. Under the *present* (mainly, received 'folk psychological') conceptual dispensation, for all we presently scientifically understand, computers literally do seek and decide things and have other characteristically intentional qualities such as we observe of them. Perhaps cognitive science will eventually *precisify* everyday 'folk psychological' concepts in such a way as to rule out (certain) computational would-be cases; or future research will discover that what we've mistakenly been calling 'seeking' and 'deciding' in (certain) computers isn't really of the same nature as human seeking and deciding (as research previously discovered that whales aren't biologically fish and that solid-seeming glass is really, chemically, liquid). Allowing for this, given an explanation of 'the details of the relation between Intentionality and consciousness' (Searle 1991: 181) Searle *could* have theoretical grounds for distinguishing real intrinsic conscious intentionality, from bogus as-if intentionality; he *could*, but *doesn't*.[11] He doesn't provide so much as an abstract—much less the details—of the wanted phenomenological account of intentionality. Small wonder: Searle's would-be differentiation of intrinsic intentionality (*ours*) from as-if intentionality (*theirs*) depends crucially on discredited dualistic notions of *subjective intrinsicality* according to which meaning is *phenomenologically 'in' consciousness* (see Hauser 1993*a*, ch. 5). Since scientific rehabilitation of such notions seems prerequisite for spelling out the 'details of the relationship between consciousness and intentionality', I, for one, am not holding my breath.

Contrary to Searle's failed *thought*-experiment, there is ample evidence from *real* experiments—for example, intelligent findings and decisions of *actual* computers running *existing* programs—to suggest that processing *does in fact* suffice for intentionality. The same evidence likewise supports (to a lesser degree, of course) the more daring claim that (the right) processing suffices *essentially* or *in theory*. Nothing in the Chinese Room withstands *here* either.

References

BODEN, M. A. (ed.) (1990) *The Philosophy of Artificial Intelligence* (Oxford: Oxford University Press).

CHALMERS, D. (1996) *The Conscious Mind* (Oxford: Oxford University Press).

DENNETT, D. C. (1987) 'Fast Thinking', in his *The Intentional Stance* (Cambridge, Mass.: MIT Press/Bradford Books), 323–37.

——— (1996) 'Did Hal Commit Murder?' Online: http://www.tufts.edu/as/cogstud/papers/didhal.htm (rough draft).

[11] Such an explanation *might* be grounds for dismissing the apparent intellectual attainments of computers as counterfeits; but this is very far from assured. Even given a triumphant phenomenological theory of intentionality, the application of the account to exclude computers would not be easy (to say the least) due to the 'ontological subjectivity' (Searle 1989*b*: 194) and consequent epistemic privacy of the *explanans*.

GRICE, H. P. (1957) 'Meaning', *The Philosophical Review*, 66: 377–88.

HAUSER, L. (1993*a*) 'Searle's Chinese Box: The Chinese Room Argument and Artificial Intelligence', East Lansing, Mich.: Michigan State University (doctoral dissertation). Online: http://members.aol.com/wutsamada/disserta.html

—— (1993*b*) 'The Sense of "Thinking" ', *Minds and Machines*, 3: 21–9. Online: http://members.aol.com/lshauser/rapreply.html

—— (1997) 'Searle's Chinese Box: Debunking the Chinese Room Argument', *Minds and Machines*, 7: 199–226.

HODGES, A. (1983) *Alan Turing: The Enigma* (New York: Simon & Schuster).

KRIPKE, S. (1977) 'Speaker's Reference and Semantic Reference', in P. French, T. E. Uehling Jr., and H. K. Wettstein (eds.), *Midwest Studies in Philosophy, Volume II* (Morris, Minn.: University of Minnesota Press).

MORGAN, J. L. (1972) 'Syntactic Form and Conversational Import—Some Interactions', in D. Cohen (ed.), *Papers from the University of Wisconsin-Milwaukee Linguistics Group First Annual Symposium on Limiting the Domain of Linguistics* (Milwaukee: University of Wisconsin-Milwaukee Linguistics Group), 37–53.

NEWELL, A. (1979) 'Physical Symbol Systems', Lecture at the La Jolla Conference on Cognitive Science.

—— and SIMON, H. A. (1963) 'GPS, A Program that Simulates Human Thought', in E. A. Feigenbaum and J. Feldman (eds.), *Computers and Thought* (New York: McGraw-Hill), 279–93.

SEARLE, J. R. (1975) 'Indirect Speech Acts', in his *Expression and Meaning* (Cambridge: Cambridge University Press), 30–57.

—— (1980*a*) 'Minds, Brains, and Programs', *Behavioral and Brain Sciences*, 3: 417–24.

—— (1980*b*) 'Intrinsic Intentionality', *Behavioral and Brain Sciences*, 3: 450–6.

—— (1980*c*) 'The Background of Meaning', in J. R. Searle, F. Kiefer, and M. Bierwisch (eds.), *Speech Act Theory and Pragmatics* (Dordrecht: D. Reidel), 221–32.

—— (1984) *Minds, Brains and Science*, (London: BBC Publications).

—— (1987) 'Indeterminacy, Empiricism, and the First Person', *Journal of Philosophy*, 84: 123–46.

—— (1988) 'Minds and Brains without Programs', in C. Blakemore and S. Greenfield (eds.), *Mindwaves* (Oxford: Blackwell), 209–33.

—— (1989*a*) 'Reply to Jacquette', *Philosophy and Phenomenological Research*, 49: 701–8.

—— (1989*b*) 'Consciousness, Unconsciousness, and Intentionality', *Philosophical Topics*, 17: 193–209.

—— (1990*a*) 'Is the Brain's Mind a Computer Program?' *Scientific American*, 262: 26–31.

—— (1990*b*) 'Who is Computing with the Brain?' *Behavioral and Brain Sciences*, 13: 632–40.

—— (1991) 'Perception and the Satisfactions of Intentionality', in E. Lepore and R. Van Gulick (eds.), *John Searle and his Critics* (Cambridge, Mass.: Blackwell), 181–92.

—— (1992) *The Rediscovery of the Mind* (Cambridge, Mass.: MIT Press).

—— (1994) 'Searle, John R.', in S. Guttenplan (ed.), *A Companion to the Philosophy of Mind* (Oxford: Blackwell), 544–50.

—— (1999) 'I Married a Computer', Review of R. Kurzweil, *The Age of Spiritual Machines: When Computers Exceed Human Intelligence, New York Review of Books* (8 Apr.), 34–8. Online at http://www.nybooks.com/nyrev/WWWarchdisplay.cgi?19990408034R.

—— McCARTHY, J., DREYFUS, H., MINSKY, M., and PAPERT, S. (1984) 'Has Artificial Intelligence Research Illuminated Human Thinking?' *Annals of the New York City Academy of Arts and Sciences*, 426: 138–60.

TURING, A. M. (1950) 'Computing Machinery and Intelligence', *Mind*, 59: 433–60. Reprinted in M. A. Boden (ed.), *The Philosophy of Artificial Intelligence* (Oxford: Oxford University Press, 1990).

ZWICKY, A. M., and SADOCK, J. M. (1975) 'Ambiguity Tests and how to Fail them', in J. Kimball (ed.), *Syntax and Semantics* (New York: Academic Press), 1–36.

8

Real Robots and the Missing Thought-Experiment in the Chinese Room Dialectic

Selmer Bringsjord and Ron Noel

Introduction

John Searle's Chinese Room Argument (CRA, see Searle 1980,[1] 1984) is arguably the twentieth century's greatest philosophical polarizer. On the one hand, as the years pass, it looks more and more as if his argument is headed for philosophical immortality. (Consider the book you're holding, published a full two decades after the argument's debut.) On the other hand, a common attitude among Strong AIniks is that CRA is not only unsound, but silly, based as it is on a fanciful story (CR) far removed from the *practice* of AI, practice which is year by year moving ineluctably toward sophisticated robots that will once and for all silence CRA and its proponents. For example, John Pollock, a philosopher and Strong AInik who takes his OSCAR system to be a significant step toward such robots, writes: 'Once OSCAR is fully functional, the argument from analogy will lead us inexorably to attribute thoughts and feelings to OSCAR with precisely the same credentials with which we attribute them to

For helpful comments on and criticisms of elements of this chapter and its ancestors, we are indebted to David Chalmers, Jack Copeland, Eric Dietrich, Jim Fetzer, Stevan Harnad, Pay Hayes, Marvin Minsky, Jim Moor, and John Searle. For the engineering work that was required to make the 'zombanimal' robots described herein a reality, we're indebted to Clarke Caporale.

[1] Reprinted in Boden (1990).

human beings. Philosophical arguments to the contrary will be passé.' (Pollock 1995: 6) The position that smarter and smarter robots will kill off Searle's CRA (and other arguments against Strong AI) is also expressed in Hans Moravec's recent book, *Robot: Mere Machine to Transcendent Mind* (Moravec 1999). Moravec cites Searle's CRA, and then simply goes on to describe a (near) future in which robots do everything we do, and more—an age in which it is taken for granted that robots have what CRA says they cannot have: subjective conscious states. There are many others who feel that the advance of robots will demote CRA to the lowly ranks of arguments like those given in the past for such propositions as that flight is impossible and that the Earth is flat. For example, in personal conversation with one of us (Bringsjord), Pat Hayes, John McCarthy, and Marvin Minsky—all three of whom have been involved in real robot building since AI's inception—have said outright that CRA is silly, and that as robots get smarter and smarter, this argument will wither away to a quaint curiosity. In particular, Hayes has said that Searle and like-minded thinkers are specifically analogous to those learned but ludicrous-in-hindsight men who declared that flight was impossible.

In this chapter we attempt some philosophical jujitsu against those who think real robots spell trouble for CRA: we show how real robots can be used to *strengthen* CRA.

We begin by refuting the modernized version of the Robot Reply to CRA, which is due to Stevan Harnad and Daniel Dennett; this modernized reply stands at present unscathed, despite Searle's own rejoinder to it. Part of our refutation is enabled by a new thought-experiment, one we call (for reasons to be explained) 'the missing thought-experiment'—in which figure robots and robotic appendages built and configured in our Minds and Machines Laboratory. This thought-experiment seems to describe not just a logical possibility, but a *physical* possibility. If we are right about this, it would seem that Searle has laid the foundation for demonstrating that the progress AI is making in building robots is merely progress in building 'zombie animals' or, as we call them for short, 'zombanimals'.[2] If this is right, then CRA will forever live despite the prowess of robots. To put it as one of us has before (Bringsjord 1992),

---

[2] When we refer to zombies, we have in mind *philosophers'* zombies, not those creatures who shuffle about half-dead in the movies. (Actually, the zombies of cinematic fame apparently have real-life correlates created with a mixture of drugs and pre-death burial, see Davis 1985, 1988.) We confine our attention in this chapter to the logical and physical possibility of zombanimals, rather than full-fledged zombies, mindless creatures who are indistinguishable from us. Bringsjord has elsewhere discussed such creatures at length (Bringsjord 1999).

robots will *do* a lot, maybe even as much as we do—play invincible chess, debate the finer points of philosophy of mind, drive race cars, fly jets, teach by the Socratic method, ski, write sustained philosophical arguments, and so on. But despite all this, robots won't *be* a lot: they won't be persons; they'll just *look* like persons. It may even be fair to say—once again, *if* we're right—that AI and robotics, viewed as enterprises aimed at building *minds* or *persons*, are futile to the point of being, we dare say, silly.

Our plan, specifically, is as follows. In Section 1 we present the scheme presupposed by our coming analysis and argumentation. In Section 2, using the scheme of Section 1, we represent the original Robot Reply, the original Systems Reply, and Searle's responses to them. In Section 3 we present and refute the modernized Robot Reply to CRA. In Section 4 we first explain that the modernized Robot Reply, though fallacious, flirts with a move that *does* seem to threaten CRA—the move of *at once* appealing to the original Systems Reply *and* the original Robot Reply. We next point out that the upshot of this move, as noted by Dennett all the way back in his original commentary on CRA (Dennett 1980), is to create a demand for 'the missing thought-experiment', a scenario born of modifying CR so that the resultant version of CRA is at once immune from *both* the original Robot Reply *and* the original Systems Reply. Next, we briefly discuss Searle's truncated search for the missing thought-experiment. This discussion is followed by one devoted to the aforementioned zombanimals created in our Minds and Machines Laboratory. These silicon-based creatures are at the heart of the final stage of Section 4, in which we provide the missing thought-experiment. As will soon be evident, we rely heavily on figures to help convey the various thought-experiments that form the heart of this chapter. In particular, our final figure encapsulates the 'missing thought-experiment' to which the title of this chapter refers.

1. The Scheme

There is no need to recapitulate, let alone formalize, CRA; it suffices here to establish merely a tidy 'meta-perspective' on the argument and related issues.[3]

---

[3] It's a trivial matter to express a formally valid version of CRA, as even Jack Copeland (in his contribution to this volume) concedes, after presenting an invalid version of CRA. For a logically valid version of a CRA-like argument, see the chapter 'Searle' from Bringsjord (1992). The analogue to what Copeland calls the 'Part-Of' principle in Bringsjord's version is the claim that if a human person *P* simulates *n* language programs (for Chinese, Norwegian, Spanish, etc.) it is wrong (indeed,

To begin, we assume that CRA is a deductive argument whose conclusion is the denial of the proposition that[4]

(CC) Necessarily, if x is a system of suitably configured computation, then x has genuine mental states, which include phenomenal consciousness.

Note that Searle does intend to overthrow a proposition as broad as (CC) via his CRA. He is not just trying to overthrow the view that a system of suitably configured computation would have true linguistic understanding, where this understanding is construed so as not to include phenomenal consciousness. For example, here he is summing up the target of the CRA in *Minds, Brains, and Science*:

The point I am making is that if we are talking about having mental states, having a mind, all of these simulations are simply irrelevant. It doesn't matter how good the technology is, or how rapid the calculations made by the computer are. If it really is a computer, its operations have to be defined syntactically, whereas consciousness, thoughts, feelings, emotions, and all the rest of it involve more than syntax. (Searle 1984: 37)

The CRA is also often assumed to target Alan Turing's famous 'imitation game' test of computational consciousness, now known as the *Turing Test*, or just 'TT' (without parentheses, to be distinguished from the *proposition* (TT) *about* TT) for short. Accordingly, we specifically assume that CRA also yields the conclusion that the following proposition is false:

(TT) Necessarily, if x passes TT, then x has true understanding of the terms and concepts involved in the conversations that allow x to pass, where 'true understanding' is such that if x has it, then x also has relevant phenomenal consciousness.

---

silly!) to say that there are n different persons (n different bearers of the phenomenal consciousness that accompanies understanding conversation in natural language) that pop into existence.

[4] The modal necessity operator in (CC)—and in (TT), a proposition given just below—may strike many readers as too strong. One of us (Bringsjord) has discussed this and related issues in detail elsewhere (Bringsjord 1995, 1999; Bringsjord and Zenzen 1997); for present purposes a brief encapsulation suffices. Dropping the modal operator from (CC) and (TT) and leaving in place merely a material conditional won't do; that much is clear. After all, there are at present no artefacts to which to instantiate x in order to produce a true antecedent: there is now no computational artefact that can pass the Turing Test. So the material conditionals would be vacuously true—and all debate would be pre-empted. What Turing and other computationalists have in mind is that there is some sort of *conceptual* connection between the relevant computation and cognition. This is in general why thought-experiments of the right sort can threaten computationalism. The idea behind these thought-experiments is that they are cases where the antecedent of a modal conditional is true, but where the consequent isn't.

So if x is a system of suitably configured computation that is able to engage in conversations about rich, dark, chocolate ice cream, x truly understands such food. Moreover, during the conversation, x will have a number of phenomenal states of consciousness (e.g. remembering that which it's like to savor such ice cream). (It's commonly believed that Turing's goal, in the paper in which he introduced TT (Turing 1950), was to *eliminate* talk of such things as phenomenal consciousness. But actually, in his response to the Argument from Consciousness, given by Jefferson as an attack on TT, Turing clearly affirms (TT).)

At this point we have

- If CRA is sound, then (CC) is false.
- If CRA is sound, then (TT) is false.

Next, it will greatly facilitate matters if we have on hand a schematic representation of Searle's original thought-experiment, the Chinese Room; we call this representation 'CR$_1$' (see Fig. 8.1). As we proceed, it will be necessary to modify CR$_1$ so as to produce variations CR$_2$, CR$_3$, etc. We will assume that CRA can be suitably adjusted to appeal to a given CR$_i$ in one or more of its premises; we denote the results of these adjustments with a subscript, so that the original CRA = CRA$_1$. The symbols i and o refer to the input and output to and from the system S. (In Figs. 8.1, 8.2, and 8.3, the system S is composed of the contents of the outermost box or rectangle). O refers to the outside observers (native Chinese speakers in CR$_1$), who see i going in and o returning, and ascribe to S genuine understanding of Chinese. P denotes the person who 'becomes' a computer in CRA; in Searle's original formulation P = Searle. Finally, P's 'rule-book' is shown by the obvious icon.

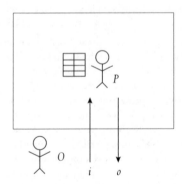

Fig. 8.1 Pictorial schema for original Chinese Room, i.e. CR$_1$.

Given this schematization, it should be wholly uncontroversial that central to all CRA_i are the following locutions:

- S understands $i(o)$.
- O understands $i(o)$.
- P understands $i(o)$.

According to CRA_1, for both i and o, the second is true (and a premise), while the third is false (a premise), as is the first (part of CRA_1's conclusion).

2. The Original Robot and Systems Reply, and Searle's Responses

The schema developed in the previous section allows us to quickly identify the original Systems Reply (SR_1) and the original Robot Reply (RR_1) with the following two arguments, respectively:

Systems Reply$_1$ (SR_1)

(1) If P implements a proper part of S in CR_i, then CRA_i is unsound.
(2) P implements a proper part of S in CR_1.

Therefore

(3) CRA_1 is unsound.

(Original) Robot Reply (RR_1)

(4) If in CR_i S doesn't include devices for transforming—by a causal process of the sort that operates when robots interact with the physical world—i into a machine-manipulable encoding $T(i)$, and a machine-manipulable encoding $T(o)$ into o, then CRA_i is unsound.
(5) In CR_1 S doesn't include devices for transforming, by a causal process of the sort that operates when robots interact with the physical world, i into a machine-manipulable encoding $T(i)$, and a machine-manipulable encoding $T(o)$ into o.

Therefore

(6) CRA_1 is unsound.

Searle's responses are shown pictorially in Figs. 8.3 and 8.2, which denote his rebuttals to SR_1 and RR_1, respectively. In the response to the original Systems

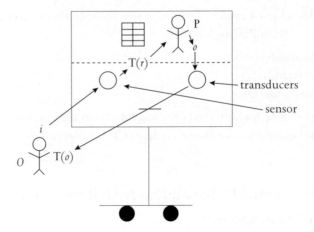

Fig. 8.2 Pictorial schema of Searle's response (CR₂) to the original Robot Reply (RR₁).

Note: Searle is inside the robot's cranium and the robot's transducers provide the interchange between input *i* from the native Chinese speakers (*O*), and the output *o* sent from Searle, which is transduced to T(*o*) and then given to *O*.

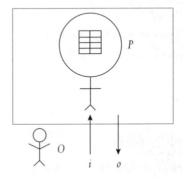

Fig. 8.3 Pictorial schema of Searle's response to the original System Reply, i.e. CR₃.

Reply, SR₁, Searle simply changes the thought-experiment to CR₃, one in which premise (2) is false; in response to the original Robot Reply, RR₁, Searle simply changes the thought-experiment to CR₂, one in which premise (5) is false.

As should be plain, Fig. 8.2 shows the presence of transducers, devices said in (5) to be lacking in *S*; T(*i*) and T(*o*) denote the result of transduction in both directions. Figure 8.3 shows the result of Searle's having internalized the rule-book. To conclude this section, let's suppose that these thought-experiments are associated with two corresponding variations on CRA₁, namely, CRA₂ and CRA₃.

3. Harnad's Modernized Robot Reply

One of the better-known champions of CRA is the psychologist Steven Harnad. Harnad has said on a number of occasions (e.g. Harnad 1991) that Searle has overthrown the linguistically oriented TT by showing that a machine can pass this test by mindlessly moving symbols around in the complete absence of understanding. So Harnad agrees that (TT) and (CC) are overthrown by CRA_2 and CRA_3. How is it, then, that Harnad is to be counted a champion of some version of the Robot Reply? The answer is that Harnad proposes a new target for Searle, one supposedly insulated from CRA_1 through CRA_3. The new target is the *Total* Turing Test (TTT), in which a victorious machine not only displays convincing linguistic behavior, but displays compelling *sensorimotor* behavior as well. In the original Turing Test, you as judge might ask both hidden-from-view contestants to describe the raw sensations they feel upon engaging in their favorite hobby; in the Total Turing Test you might *watch* both contestants (say) play golf, and might then proceed to discuss with them how it feels to smash a picture-perfect drive. When the Total Turing Test is substituted for the Turing Test, Harnad believes that a new sort of robot reply arises. In a symposium in the journal *Think*, in which Searle, Harnad, and Bringsjord participated, Harnad expresses this reply in the form of a dilemma:

Now back to the Chinese room, but this time TTT-scale rather than just TT-scale. This time, instead of asking whether the TT-passing candidate really understands Chinese or is merely systematically interpretable as if he were understanding it, we will ask whether the TTT-passing candidate (a robot now) really sees the Buddha statue before him or is merely systematically interpretable as if he were seeing it. The robot, in order even to be interpretable as seeing, must have optical transducers. What about Searle, who is attempting to implement the TTT robot without seeing, as he implemented the TT-[passing system] without understanding? There are two possibilities: either Searle receives only the *output* of an optical transducer—in which case it is no wonder that he reports he is not seeing, because he is not implementing the whole system, only part of it, and hence . . . the Systems Reply [= our SR1] would be correct; or Searle actually looks at the Buddha, in which case he would indeed be implementing the transduction, but then, unfortunately, he *would* be seeing. (Harnad 1993: 17)

This argument conforms to an inference rule known as *constructive dilemma*. According to this rule, if one knows that a proposition p or q is true, and both that if p is true so is r and if q is true so is r, one can conclude r. In Harnad's argument, p is 'Searle receives only the output of an optical transducer', and q is 'Searle actually looks at the Buddha'. According to Harnad, both of these possibilities lead to r, the destruction of CRA. Constructive dilemma is certainly unexceptionable, but let's look more closely at the argument, and let's do so by drawing upon our established scheme. Doing so will quickly reveal a fatal flaw in Harnad's reasoning.

Denote the new thought-experiment here by 'CR_4' and the associated argument by RR_2. Now, recall the trio of locutions from our schematization of Chinese Room-like arguments:

- S understands $i\,(o)$.
- O understands $i\,(o)$.
- P understands $i\,(o)$.

Recall as well that these locutions are to be instantiated so that the first and third are false (for both i and o), while the second is true (again, for both i and o). Are they instantiated that way in Harnad's new story? They cannot be, for in this story, understanding is supplanted by seeing, and the locutions simply don't refer to seeing. If we try to construe seeing in RR_4 as understanding has been construed previously, which is surely Harnad's intention, note that seeing here is ambiguous between, as one might say, *merely* seeing and *really* seeing. Suppose we put down before you an object that leaves you utterly clueless; you have no idea whatsoever what this object is. None the less, we might begin our interview with you, after depositing the mystery object on the table before you, by saying: 'Okay, now, do you see this thing here?' 'Uh, yes', you might well reply—with utter puzzlement. 'Well', we might continue, 'what do you think it is?' And you might reply that you have no idea. In this case you see the object without understanding; we will call this seeing$_{\ddot{u}}$. When you see *with* understanding, we will say that you see$_u$. For Harnad's argument to have a chance of succeeding, he must be read as asking (note the subscript now added to this quote): 'What about Searle, who is attempting to implement the TTT robot without seeing$_u$, as he implemented the TT-[passing system] without understanding?' Put in terms of our schemas, this question becomes

- In Harnad's new story, CR_4, is it necessary that P sees$_u$?

Harnad's answer, of course, is an affirmative one—one given, as we've noted, on the strength of the constructive dilemma inference rule. If we concede that one side of the dilemma, the side according to which Searle fails to implement the entire TTT-passing system, does lead to an overthrow of CRA via SR_1, we can focus our attention on the other side, which is expressed, recall, as follows: '. . . or Searle actually looks at the Buddha, in which case he would indeed be implementing the transduction, but then, unfortunately, he *would* be seeing' (Harnad 1993: 17).

The problem should now be evident. While Searle $= P$ in CR_1, CR_2, and CR_3, fails to understand the objects in question (Chinese inscriptions), such is not the case with respect to Harnad's new thought-experiment. Searle, in 'real life', understands what a Buddha is; when he sees one, he sees$_u$ one. It is really no surprise, then, that Harnad gets the result he does! Suppose that some AIniks build a robot able to interact smoothly with—Smuddas. (You don't have a clue what a Smudda is. They look vaguely like salamanders, but are larger, seem somewhat mechanical, and don't appear to be alive in any way.) Now suppose that, in thought, Searle implements the TTT-passing, Smudda-handling system. Would it still be true that Searle sees$_u$ the Smudda? No. Searle will see$_{\ddot{u}}$ the Smudda, just as he sees$_{\ddot{u}}$ the squiggle squoggles in the original CR. And so we have every reason to believe here that S only sees$_{\ddot{u}}$ Smuddas. Harnad's argument fails.

4. The Missing Thought-Experiment

History of the Missing Thought-Experiment

Harnad's argument marks the *simultaneous deployment of SR_1 and RR_1*; it's from this feature that the argument derives what power it has. The simultaneous deployment of SR_1 and RR_1 is a move that apparently started with Daniel Dennett, in the commentary he offered in the original 1980 *Behavioral and Brain Sciences* dialectic. Here's what Dennett said there:

Putting both modifications [= our CR_2 and CR_3] together, we are to imagine our hero controlling both the linguistic and nonlinguistic behavior of a robot who is—himself! When the Chinese words for 'Hands up! This is a stickup!' are intoned directly in his ear, he will uncomprehendingly (and at breathtaking speed) hand simulate the program, which leads him to do things (*what* things—is he to order himself in Chinese to stimulate his own motor neurons and then obey the order?) that lead to his handing over *his own* wallet while begging for mercy, in Chinese with his own lips. (Dennett 1980: 129).

Nowhere in his commentary does Dennett give an argument against CRA based on combining SR_1 and RR_1; he only calls for a thought-experiment that would seem to be missing in the literature to this day. In Dennett's own words again:

In point of fact, Searle has simply not told us how he intends us to imagine the case, which we are licensed to do by his two modifications [= our CR_2 and CR_3]... There are several radically different alternatives—all so outlandishly unrealizable as to caution us not to trust our gut reactions about them in any case. When we imagine our hero 'incorporating the entire system' are we to imagine that he pushes buttons with his fingers in order to get his own arms to move? Surely not, since all the buttons are now internal. Are we to imagine that when he responds to the Chinese for 'pass the salt, please' by getting his hand to grasp the salt and move it in a certain direction, he doesn't *notice* that this is what he is doing? In short, could anyone who became accomplished in this imagined exercise fail to become fluent in Chinese in the process? Perhaps, but it all depends on details of this, the only crucial thought experiment in Searle's kit, that Searle does not provide. (ibid.)

There are in this quote the *seeds* for an argument that CR_1–CR_3 are actually *not* conceivable. Has Dennett elsewhere cultivated these seeds into a full-blown argument for the view that CR_2 and CR_3 are conceivable only if Searle-in-them understands Chinese? No, not to our knowledge. Dennett *has* argued elsewhere that plain old CR_1 is conceivable only if Searle-in-CR_1 understands Chinese. Dennett gave this argument eleven years after the original *Behavioral and Brain Sciences* exchange in his book *Consciousness Explained*. After offering a sample exchange between a judge and a computer in the Turing Test, he argues as follows:

The fact is that any program that could actually hold up its end in the conversation depicted would have to be an extraordinarily supple, sophisticated, multilayered system, brimming with 'world knowledge' and meta-knowledge and meta-meta-knowledge about its own responses, the likely responses of its interlocutor, its own 'motivations' and the motivations of its interlocutor, and much, much more. Searle does not deny that the program can have all this structure, of course, he simply discourages us from attending to it. But if we are to do a good job imagining the case, we are not only entitled but obliged to imagine that the program Searle is hand-simulating has all this structure—and more, if only we can imagine it. But then it is no longer *obvious*, I trust, that there is no genuine understanding of the joke going on. (Dennett 1991: 438)

This is really an astonishingly bad argument. It's an elementary mathematical fact that all computer programs can be recast as exactly equivalent Turing machines operating with only a binary alphabet such as $\{0, 1\}$. Instructions here consist in nothing more than such imperatives as 'If the machine is in internal state n, with its read/write head scanning a 0, erase the 0 and write a 1, and then have the machine enter internal state m'. (Such instructions are often given as austere quadruples; in this case the quadruple would be $(n01m)$). So in response to Dennett, let's stipulate that Searle-in-CR_1 manipulates only such instructions. It should be obvious that if all Searle is doing is hand-simulating in this way, he will have no understanding of Chinese, no understanding of what the original high-level program is about.[5] But what about CR_2 and CR_3? Can their simultaneous deployment, that is, the missing thought-experiment, be specified? If not, Dennett will none the less have managed to triumph over Searle.

Searle's Steps Toward the Missing Thought-Experiment

Searle himself, in reply to Harnad's modernized robot reply, can be read as trying to describe, or at least move toward a description of, the missing thought-experiment. Here's what Searle says:

Harnad thinks it is an answer to this to suppose that the transducers have to be part of me and not just an appendage. Unless they are part of me, he says, I am 'not implementing the whole system, only part of it'. Well fine, let us suppose that I am totally blind because of damage to my visual cortex, but my photoreceptor cells work perfectly as transducers. Then let the robot use my photoreceptors as transducers in the above example [= CR_2]. What difference does it make? None at all as far as getting the causal powers of the brain to produce vision. I would still be blindly producing the input output functions of vision without seeing anything. (Searle 1993: 69–70)

As we've indicated by our parenthetical in this quote, by 'the above example' Searle is referring to CR_2, the scenario he offers as a rejoinder to the original Robot Reply, RR_1. The scenario is redescribed in the *Think* symposium as follows:

Imagine a really big robot whose brain consists of a commercial computer located in a Chinese room in the robot's cranium. Now replace the commercial computer with me, Searle. I am now the robot's brain carrying out the steps in the robot's programs. The robot has all of the sensory and motor transducers it needs to coordinate its input with its output. And I, Searle, in the Chinese room am doing the coordinating, but I know nothing of this. For example, among the robot's transducers, we will suppose, are devices that convert optical stimuli into Chinese symbols. These Chinese symbols are input to the Chinese Room and I operate on these symbols according to a set of rules, the program. I operate on these symbols and eventually send symbols to transducers that cause motor output. The motor output is an utterance that says in Chinese, 'I just saw a picture of a big fat Buddha'. But all the same, I didn't see anything, and neither did the robot. That is, there were no conscious visual experiences of a Buddha in question. What actually occurred was that light sensitive detectors in the robot's skull

---

[5] Of course, there remains the issue of *speed*: in order to carry out such hand simulation, Searle is going to have to work rapidly. But as one of us has explained elsewhere (Bringsjord and Ferrucci 1995), speed is a red herring.

took in stimuli, converted these into symbols, I processed the symbols and sent them to an output transducer that converted the symbolic output into an auditory utterance. In such a case you can have all of the transducers you want and pass the TTT until the sun goes down but you still do not thereby guarantee the appropriate experience, understanding, etc. (Searle 1993: 69)

But does the introduction of blindness and the robot's use of Searle's photo-receptor cells, added to CR$_2$, constitute the missing thought-experiment? No, for there are two problems.

The first problem is that in this new scenario Searle is simply no longer doing mindless symbol manipulation! If he is blind, and the robot is using his photo-receptors, then optical stimuli are converted to symbolic data, whereupon these data are manipulated—but it isn't *Searle* who is carrying out the manipulation. To see this, consider the following scenario. While you're sound asleep, Dr Black, a skilled but amoral neurosurgeon, sneaks into your bedroom and anesthetizes you. Then he proceeds to surgically appropriate your visual system so that it is attached to a computer-based voice production system. Black is thus able to hold up objects before your eyes and a synthetic voice announces what the object is. So if Black holds up an apple, a synthetic voice says, 'Apple'. Now in this case symbols are being manipulated by your visual system (and other biological processes that may or may not at bottom be symbol manipulation in action). But *you* are not manipulating symbols. Likewise, while *Searle* is manip-ulating squiggle squoggles in the original CR, his photoreceptor cells, not he himself, are manipulating symbols in his modification of CR$_2$.

The second problem is by now a familiar one: in his blindness story Searle is something well short of the entire system, so the original Systems Reply kicks in against him. His photoreceptors have become part of the overall system, yes, but lots of the system is composed of non-Searlean stuff.

We offer a way for Searle to surmount the first problem; here's our sugges-tion. Add to the thought-experiment that Searle manipulates, in accordance with the relevant computer program, the *braille-based* representation of the symbolic information emerging from his photoreceptors. This modification injects back into the thought-experiment the fact that *Searle* is carrying out purely syntactic symbol manipulation.

What about the second problem? This one isn't so easily solved. Searle himself does see the problem, and his response to Harnad is interesting, but it's almost as if Searle gives this response half-heartedly, sure in his heart that his general attack is ultimately victorious, but a bit tired with the dialectic—too tired to continue to engage Harnad point for point and slug things out till the final bell sounds. Here is what Searle says:

Will Harnad insist in the face of this point that I am still not implementing the whole system? If he does then the thesis threatens to become trivial. Any system identical with me has cognition because of my neurobiological constitution. Anything identical with my system can cause what my system causes, and all the talk about TTT, computation, and the rest of it would now become irrelevant. (Searle 1993: 69)

Searle is of course correct that P in CR_i will invariably be instantiated to something that 'has cognition'. But the trick is instantiating P in such a way that $P = S$, where P fails to understand what O believes S does understand. Searle pulls out of the search for a scenario that includes these facts.

However, the second problem *can* be surmounted; the missing thought-experiment *can* be specified; Dennett's challenge can thereby be met. How? Searle is on the right track: imaginative surgery that serves to blur the distinction between robots and persons offers the key to providing the missing thought-experiment. We frame the description of such surgery by discussing a related 'surgical' project in our Minds and Machines Laboratory. We put 'surgical' in quotes here because the process in question is not literally a surgical one. The process is aimed at producing 'zombie animals', or just 'zombanimals', qualia-less computational simulacra for simple biological animals. It involves abstracting the biological so as to produce a model (or, as we prefer to say, following Pollock 1995, a *blueprint*) that can then be rendered computational. Because the focus in the present chapter is thought-experimental, we will now illustrate this process by describing it in connection with a series of *imaginary* biological creatures, rather than with real ones. Doing so will allow us to avoid biological and engineering details that are irrelevant to the arguments at stake in this chapter.

Framing the Missing Thought-Experiment with Simple Zombanimals

Most of you are familiar with the thought-experiments in which zombies—creatures displaying our external behavior but bereft of consciousness—are described; here's one in brief. You're diagnosed with inoperable brain cancer that will inevitably and quickly metastasize. Desperate, you implore a team of neurosurgeons to replace your brain, piecemeal, with silicon chip workalikes, until there is only silicon inside your refurbished cranium.[6] The procedure is initiated . . . and the story then continues in a manner that seems to imply the logical possibility of zombies. In (none other than) Searle's words:

As the silicon is progressively implanted into your dwindling brain, you find that the area of your conscious experience is shrinking, but that this shows no effect on your external behavior. You find, to your total amazement, that you are indeed losing control of your external behavior . . . [You have become blind, but] you hear your voice saying in a way that is completely out of your control, 'I see a red object in front of me'. . . . We imagine that your conscious experience slowly shrinks to nothing, while your externally observable behavior remains the same. (Searle 1992: 66–7)

Lots of people—Searle, Dennett, Chalmers, Bringsjord, etc.[7]—have written about zombies. Most of these thinkers agree that such creatures are logically possible, but, with the exception of Bringsjord, they hold that zombies are *physically impossible*. That is, most refuse to accept that such surgery can *in fact* be carried out. In order to frame the missing thought-experiment, we begin by trying to indicate that such surgery can indeed be carried out—*for animals*.

Begin by imagining a very simple animal. Not a cat or a rat; they're too sophisticated. Imagine a simple multi-cellular organism; let's call it a 'bloog'.[8] When you shine a penlight on a bloog, it propels itself energetically forward. If you follow the bloog as it moves, keeping the penlight on it, it continues ahead rather quickly. If you shut the penlight off, the bloog still moves ahead, but very, very slowly: the bloog is—we say—listless. If you keep the penlight on, but shine it a few inches away and in front of the bloog ('front of' being identified with the direction in which it's moving), the bloog gradually accelerates in a straight line in the direction it appears to be facing, but then slows down once it is beyond the light.

A roboticist in our Minds and Machines Laboratory, Clarke Caporale, spent some time experimenting with a bloog for a while with his penlight, and witnessed the behavior we have just described; he then set to work.[9] Clarke began

---

[6] The silicon supplantation is elegantly described in Cole and Foelber (1984).

[7] See Searle (1992), Dennett (1991, 1993, 1995), and Chalmers (1996). Bringsjord's main contribution, again, is in Bringsjord (1999), which builds on Searle's (1992) take on the thought-experiment just given.

[8] The word 'bloog', as well as 'sneelock', 'fleelock', 'moog', and 'multi-moog', words used below to name other organisms, have no special linguistic significance, but are used here in deference to sorts of names used by the inimitable (and, alas, late) Dr Seuss, who received a Ph.D. from Brown University the same year Selmer did.

[9] Remember that though bloogs and their relatives (soon to be described) are imaginary, all the robotics is real. The biology is dropped in this chapter to ease exposition. There is a photograph of the actual robotics workbench used by Caporale at http://www.rpi.edu/~bestlj/SELPAP/SEARLEBOOK/workbench.jpg

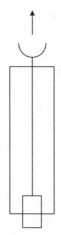

Fig. 8.4 The Zombanimal Robot V1.

Note: The motor is denoted by the rectangular box at the tail end, the sensor by the half-circle on a stalk.

by scanning the flow of information in a bloog when one is under a microscope. After a bit, he readied his supply of robotics micro-hardware, and began to operate. Now that he is done, he presents you with . . . a creature he calls 'V1'.[10] V1 is composed of one tiny sensor and one tiny motor, which are connected, and a biological structure left over from the original bloog that supports them. The motor is connected to some device which, when driven by the motor, produces locomotion. V1 is shown in Fig. 8.4. The behavior of V1 is straightforward: the more of the source detected by its sensor, the faster its motor runs. You will have to take our word for it: though, as we've said, the biological creatures are imaginary, V1 is real, and really behaves as described.[11] If V1 is bathed in light from the penlight, it moves forward energetically. If it then enters a darker area it becomes listless. If it detects a light ahead, it accelerates toward the light, passes through it, and then decelerates.

Now consider two more complex biological creatures, a 'sneelock' and a 'fleelock'. They are larger than bloogs, a slightly different shade of fleshy brown, and behave differently. A fleelock behaves as follows. If you shine a penlight on

[10] Our simple zombanimals are inspired by the vehicular creatures described in Braitenberg (1984). Our first zombanimal is Braitenberg's Vehicle 1, or just 'V1' for short.

[11] At the 1998 Eastern Meeting of the American Philosophical Association, for a talk entitled 'Zombanimals', given by the two of us, Clarke provided a working physical demonstration of V1, V2a, V2b, and V3. The talk was given to the Society for Machines and Mentality.

the surface on which the fleelock is located, just ahead and exactly in front of the organism, it moves directly toward the light and passes through it, at which point, like bloogs, it becomes listless. However, if you shine the penlight ahead of the fleelock, but to the left or right, it turns to avoid the light, and then moves forward slowly; fleelocks generally dislike light. Sneelocks are similar. They too dislike light, but there is a difference: sneelocks are aggressive. This can be shown by shining a penlight ahead of a sneelock (and, again, to the left or right). When one does this, the sneelock turns with increasing rapidity toward the light, and moves directly at it, eventually moving frontally into the light apparently to assault it.

Caporale performed surgery once again. The result is a pair of new zomban-imals, V2*a* and V2*b* (see Fig. 8.5). Courtesy of micro-sensors and motors, V2*a* behaves just like a fleelock, V2*b* just like a sneelock. V1, V2*a*, and V2*b* behave just as their biological counterparts do.

You're doubtless thinking that such organisms as bloogs, sneelocks, and flee-locks are excruciatingly simple. Well, you're right. As we've indicated, they're *simple* zombanimals. But Caporale is just warming up.

Consider an animal that can sense and react not only to light, but temper-ature, oxygen concentration, and amount of organic matter. This biological creature is called a 'multi-moog'. Multi-moogs dislike high temperature, turn away from hot places, dislike light with considerable passion (since it turns toward and apparently attempts to destroy it), and prefers a well-oxygenated environment containing many organic molecules. Caporale has 'zombified' a multi-moog; the result is V3*c*, shown in Fig. 8.8.

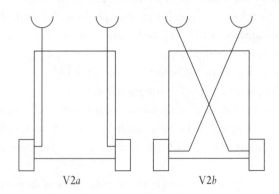

Fig. 8.5 V2*a* and V2*b*.

Note: V2*a* orients away from the light; V2*b* toward it.

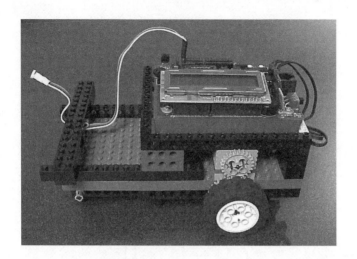

Fig. 8.6 Photo of Caporale's Actual V1.

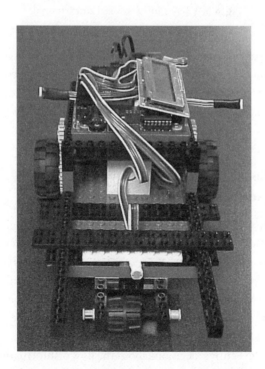

Fig. 8.7 Photo of Caporale's Actual V2*a*.

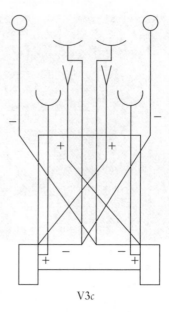

Fig. 8.8 V3c, a multisensorial zombanimal.

V3c has four pairs of sensors tuned to light, temperature, oxygen concentration, and amount of organic matter. The first pair of sensors is connected to the micro-motors with uncrossed excitatory connections, the second pair with crossed excitatory connections, and the third and fourth pairs with inhibitory connections.

Specifying the Missing Thought-Experiment Courtesy of Real Robots

We are now in a position to articulate the missing thought-experiment. Suppose, first, that AI has progressed to the point of producing a robot sophisticated enough to pass Harnad's TTT—a robot of the sort that Pollock and Moravec and Hayes predict will forever silence Searle's CRA; call this robot 'R'. Accordingly, we will have on hand a blueprint B_R for R that is generally like the blueprints for the robots V1, V2a, V2b, and V3c given in the corresponding Figs. 8.4, 8.5, and 8.8, except that we stipulate that B_R includes the program P_R for R that makes 'executive' decisions about the flow of information to and from R's brain A_R. (Needless to say, B_R will be very complex—but Pollock (1995) has already offered a good start.) Now we introduce Searle as the star of yet another *gedankenexperiment*. We are going to gradually use him to implement parts and processes of R by studying B_R and carrying out the required surgery. (We are thus simply reversing the procedure discussed in connection with bloogs, sneelocks, fleelocks, and multi-moogs.)

Let's start by giving Searle drugs so that he no longer has a sense of touch or proprioception. Now we proceed to tackle locomotion. Without loss of generality, we can assume that there is an effector E_R in R responsible for R's ability to walk, and also that E_R is activated when the 'brain' A_R of R, as controlled by P_R, sends the appropriate signals. So let's perform some surgery on Searle's legs and feet: let's activate his feet for walking by the signals from R's brain A_R. If we have a way of piping to Searle's legs and feet signals of the sort that routinely flow from A_R, we have a way of causing Searle to walk entirely beyond his control. And we can pull off precisely the same trick for R's other effectors. For example, whenever R waves its robotic hand, this will happen because of signals passing from A_R to the relevant effector. So we can appropriate Searle's arms and hands, and test them out by sending to them the relevant signals. This will allow us to cause Searle to wave for reasons, again, beyond his control. Next, as our readers will by this time have guessed, we focus on sensing. Let S_R be a visual sensor for R. Imagine that we blind Searle in such a way that his photoreceptor cells continue to—as he put it above in the thought-experiment that started the move toward the one we're presenting here—'work perfectly as transducers'. Next, let Searle's photoreceptors transduce stimuli sent to S_R and pipe the resulting data to a console that allows us to view these data.

Why a console? We refer to one in order to sharpen your mental picture of what we have so far. Imagine the surgery we've described taking place in an elaborate operating room in which lies the 'wired-up' Searle. Picture as well that you have before you the console, and that based on what data you see on its display, you can mindlessly obey P_R in order to push buttons to send signals to the parts of Searle's body that have been taken over. We have reached the point where you can imagine this: you put an object in front of Searle's eyes, a Buddha, b, say, and you observe the data that result from Searle seeing b, and then, on the basis of what you see, you send signals to Searle's arm and hand in order to wave his hand. At this point the situation is summed pictorially in Fig. 8.9.

Obviously, the idea is that you now continue painstakingly to use study of the blueprint B_R and the program P_R, along with surgery, to turn Searle's body into the perfect biological counterpart for all of R's input/output behaviors. The final step is supplanting you, the console, and P_R with something that stays internal to Searle. In order to pull off this step, we bring in elements of the

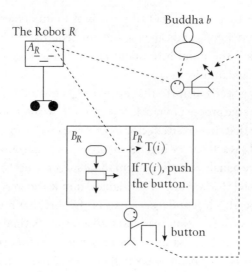

Fig. 8.9 The situation as we approach the missing thought-experiment.

'CR-ish' thought-experiment described by Bringsjord in the chapter 'Searle' from *What Robots Can and Can't Be* (Bringsjord 1992): we imagine that Searle is now wired so that *what you see on your console he sees in the form of mental images.* We also imagine that by manipulating certain mental images in certain ways, effectors in Searle's body are activated. For example, Searle causes his hand to wave (without, of course, his sensing that it has moved) by visualizing the mental image of a button being depressed. Suppose, then, that, on the basis of what he sees with his mind's eye, Searle can follow P_R to route signals to the parts of him that have been wired up in parallel to B_R. At this point, when his incisions heal up and he heads out of the operating room into the world, Searle will convince all outside observers that he (say) sees$_u$ a Buddha and that he understands that some Chinese speaker just asked him if he likes hamburgers. But clearly Searle sees$_u$ absolutely nothing. Searle thus embodies a decisive rebuttal to the combination System/Robot reply: the missing thought-experiment has been found. (Fig. 8.10 shows, schematically, the missing thought-experiment.)

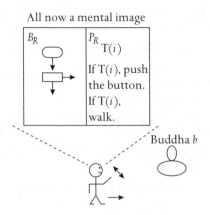

Fig. 8.10 The missing thought-experiment.

References

BODEN, M. A. (ed.) (1990) *The Philosophy of Artificial Intelligence* (Oxford: Oxford University Press).

BRAITENBERG, V. (1984) *Vehicles: Experiments in Synthetic Psychology* (Cambridge, Mass.: MIT Press/Bradford Books).

BRINGSJORD, S. (1992) *What Robots Can and Can't Be* (Dordrecht: Kluwer).

—— (1995) 'Could, How Could we Tell if, and Why Should, Androids Have Inner Lives?' in K. Ford, C. Glymour, and P. Hayes (eds)., *Android Epistemology* (Cambridge, Mass.: MIT Press), 93–122.

—— (1999) 'The Zombie Attack on the Computational Conception of Mind', *Philosophy and Phenomenological Research*, 59: 41–69.

—— and FERRUCCI, D. (1995) 'Reply to Thayse and Glymour on Logic and Artificial Intelligence', *Minds and Machines*, 8: 313–15.

—— and ZENZEN, M. (1997) 'Cognition is not Computation: The Argument from Irreversibility?' *Synthese*, 113: 285–320.

CHALMERS, D. (1996) *The Conscious Mind: In Search of a Fundamental Theory* (Oxford: Oxford University Press).

COLE, D., and FOELBER, R. (1984) 'Contingent Materialism', *Pacific Philosophical Quarterly*, 65: 74–85.

DAVIS, W. (1985) *The Serpent and the Rainbow* (New York: Simon & Schuster).

—— (1988) *Passage of Darkness: The Ethnobiology of the Haitian Zombie* (Chapel Hill, NC: University of North Carolina Press).

DENNETT, D. C. (1980) 'The Milk of Human Intentionality', *Behavioral and Brain Sciences*, 3: 128–30.

—— (1991) *Consciousness Explained* (Boston: Little, Brown, & Co.).

DENNETT, D. C. (1993) Review of J. R. Searle, *The Rediscovery of the Mind*, *Journal of Philosophy*, 90: 193–205.

—— (1995) 'The Unimagined Preposterousness of Zombies', *Journal of Consciousness Studies*, 2: 322–6.

HARNAD, S. (1991) 'Other Bodies, Other Minds: A Machine Incarnation of an Old Philosophical Problem', *Minds and Machines*, 1: 43–54.

—— (1993) 'Grounding Symbols in the Analog World with Neural Nets: A Hybrid Model', *Think*, 2: 12–20.

MORAVEC, H. (1999) *Robot: Mere Machine to Transcendent Mind* (Oxford: Oxford University Press).

POLLOCK, J. (1995) *Cognitive Carpentry: A Blueprint for How to Build a Person* (Cambridge, Mass.: MIT Press).

SEARLE, J. R. (1980) 'Minds, Brains, and Programs', *Behavioral and Brain Sciences*, 3: 417–24.

—— (1984) *Minds, Brains, and Science* (Cambridge, Mass.: Harvard University Press).

—— (1992) *The Rediscovery of the Mind* (Cambridge, Mass.: MIT Press).

—— (1993) 'The Failures of Computationalism', *Think*, 2: 68–71.

TURING, A. M. (1950) 'Computing Machinery and Intelligence', *Mind*, 59: 433–60. Reprinted in Boden (1990).

9

Wittgenstein's Anticipation of the Chinese Room

Diane Proudfoot

1. Wittgenstein, Chinese, and the Living Reading-Machine

Wittgenstein denied (what would now be described as) the thesis that cognition consists in symbol-manipulation—the supposition underlying 'Strong AI'. There are striking parallels between his remarks and Searle's Chinese Room Argument.

For Wittgenstein, the non-Chinese speaker's utterance of a Chinese sentence is a paradigm example of talking 'without thinking' (1989b: 7). It does not even count as a genuine speech act: asking in Chinese 'Are you in pain?' when the speaker does not know Chinese is 'not to be wondering whether he is in pain' (ibid. 54).[1] Wittgenstein also remarked:

'We say "A proposition isn't just a series of sounds, it is something more". We think of the way a Chinese sentence is a mere series of sounds for us, which just

Special thanks to Jack Copeland and to an anonymous OUP reviewer for comments upon an earlier version of this paper, and to Carolyn Mason for research assistance.

[1] Wittgenstein frequently used Chinese as an example of the incomprehensible: 'When we hear a Chinese talk we tend to take his speech for inarticulate gurgling' (Monk 1990: 114—thanks to Peter Farleigh for drawing my attention to this remark). He also remarked, that '[w]e don't understand Chinese gestures any more than Chinese sentences' (1967b, §219). According to Wittgenstein, non-Chinese speakers may not be able to identify spoken Chinese as such (1965: 156), fail to distinguish between Chinese writing and mere decoration (1974: 121), and cannot tell if someone who speaks only in Chinese is merely pretending to be in pain (1992: 30).

168 / Diane Proudfoot

means that we don't understand it . . .' and used this example to illustrate a familiar model of understanding and meaning:

. . . and we say this is because we don't have any thoughts in connection with the Chinese sentence (e.g. the Chinese word for 'red' doesn't call up any image in us). 'So what distinguishes a significant sentence from mere sounds is the thoughts it evokes'. The sentence is like a key-bit whose indentations are constructed to move levers in the soul in a particular way. The sentence, as it were, plays a melody (the thought) on the instrument of the soul. (Wittgenstein 1974: 152)

In evaluating this model Wittgenstein introduced what he called a 'reading-machine'. A reading-machine is a symbol-manipulator. Wittgenstein's usual example is a pianola (1974: 69). A pianola 'translate[s] marks into sounds' (1953, § 157) by 'reading' the pattern of perforations—which 'we might call . . . *complex signs* or *sentences*' (1965: 118; emphasis in orginal)—in the pianola roll.[2] Reading-machines may even contain a look-up table: 'it is quite possible that there is a part of the mechanism which resembles a chart [associating colour-words with colours, in Wittgenstein's example], and is inserted between the language-like part of the mechanism and the rest of it' (1974: 190). The reading-machine is analogous to the Turing machine.[3] Wittgenstein's concern was in part to determine whether Turing machines genuinely calculate, read, and so on. (Alan Turing attended Wittgenstein's classes from as early as 1935[4] and Wittgenstein's published lectures of 1939 contain lengthy arguments with Turing.)[5]

Wittgenstein frequently used the notion of a human being acting 'like a reliable machine' (1965: 119) and introduced what he called a 'living reading-machine' (1953, § 157). (Wittgenstein discussed these with Turing (Wittgenstein 1989a: 36–7).) A living reading-machine is a human being or other creature who is given as input written signs, for example, Chinese pictograms, arithmetical symbols, logical symbols, or musical notation. The living reading-machine produces as output solutions to arithmetical problems, text spoken aloud,

[2] Wittgenstein contrasted a pianola with a key (1965: 118), as follows. A pianola can read any combination of suitable perforations whereas a key can (un)lock only certain doors. A key produces its effect by means simply of the fit between key bit and lock, and is neither information-processor nor symbol-manipulator: 'we should not say that the bolt moved *according* to the pattern of the key bit' (ibid.).

[3] An apparently well-thumbed copy of Turing's 1936 paper, wherein Turing introduced what came to be called 'the universal Turing machine', was found amongst Wittgenstein's effects (Nedo and Ranchetti 1983: 308).

[4] See Nedo and Ranchetti (1983: 358). Thanks to Jack Copeland for drawing my attention to this reference.

[5] For a short discussion of overlaps in the work of Wittgenstein and Turing, see Copeland and Proudfoot (2000).

proofs of logical theorems, notes played on a piano, and suchlike. These 'machines' may be born, like an idiot savant, or trained (1953, § 157). Examples include 'calculating machines' (Wittgenstein also referred to these as 'calculating boys'), 'arithmetical machines', and '[piano] playing-machines' (1989*b*: 30, 1974: 191). The living reading-machine is proxy for the 'human computer' on whom the Turing machine was modelled (according to Turing, 'Electronic computers are intended to carry out any definite rule-of-thumb process which could have been done by a human operator working in a disciplined but unintelligent manner' (1950: 1)).[6] The living reading-machine, like the pianola, can read any combination of appropriate signs. By 'reading', Wittgenstein tells us, he means: 'the activity of translating script into sounds, also of writing according to dictation or of copying in writing a page of print, and suchlike; reading in this sense does not involve any such thing as understanding what you read' (1965: 119).[7] Thus a 'human calculating machine might . . . read through the proofs of a mathematical system (say that of Russell), and [nod] its head after every correctly drawn conclusion, but . . . [be] otherwise perfectly imbecile' (1967*a*: 258). A calculating boy can give no account—or only a 'caricature' of one (1967*b*, § 89)—of how he arrives at the answers he provides (1989*b*: 31). A playing-machine is taught musical notation 'by a mere drill' (1974: 191). The inhabitant of Searle's Chinese Room, the human who is 'simply an instantiation of [a] computer program' (Searle 1980*a*: 418)[8], is a living reading-machine.

Wittgenstein used the notion of the living reading-machine, as Searle did that of the man in the Chinese Room, to test the thesis that symbol-manipulation is sufficient for understanding. The living reading-machine performs symbol-manipulations: is this enough for *genuine* reading or calculating?

Suppose I train the apprentices of wallpaper manufacturers so that they can produce perfect proofs of the most complicated theorems in higher mathematics [and use these as wallpaper patterns], in fact so that if I say to one of them 'Prove so-and-so' (where so-and-so is a mathematical proposition), he can always do it. And suppose that they are so unintelligent that they cannot make the simplest practical calculations. They can't figure out if one plum costs so-and-so, how much do six plums cost, or what change you should get from a shilling for a twopenny bar of chocolate.—Would you say that they had learnt mathematics or not? . . . (1989*a*: 36)

Wittgenstein's view is that reading-machines, living or not, do not (as a matter of fact) genuinely read, calculate, and so on (1989*b*: 131, 1967*a*: 257). (The import

---

[6] Thanks to Jack Copeland for originally drawing my attention to this quotation.

[7] Wittgenstein does not imply that the living reading-machine *cannot* understand the symbols he or she manipulates (see Sect. 3). [8] Reprinted in Boden (1990: 69). From here referred to as B69.

of the rider 'as a matter of fact' is explained in Section 3). Both Wittgenstein (see Sect. 3) and Searle (1980a: 418 (B69–71)) hold that symbol-manipulation is insufficient for, and hence does not constitute, understanding. Both also hold that computers (in the sense of artificial computing machines) do not genuinely follow rules (Searle 1990b: 30; on Wittgenstein see Proudfoot forthcoming). For Wittgenstein, if we speak of (what he called) 'Turing's "Machines"' (1980a, § 1096) as calculating or reading, either this is make-believe or we are indirectly speaking about the human being using the computer ('If calculating looks to us like the action of a machine, it is *the human being* doing the calculation that is the machine' (1967a: 234; emphasis in original)). Searle claims that utterances such as 'The calculator *follows rules* of arithmetic when it does addition' are merely 'metaphorical attributions of "as-if" intentionality' (1990a: 586; emphasis in original) that 'we find it natural to make' (1980a: 419 (B72)).

Wittgenstein and Searle also have meta-philosophical views in common. Both use a priori argument in discussion of the hypothesis that cognition consists in symbol-manipulation (with the result that Searle is criticized—e.g. by Block (1980: 425); Fodor (1980: 431)—for overlooking the weight of empirical evidence). Wittgenstein defends this practice, claiming that an 'obstinate problem' in psychology, such as that of the nature of understanding, 'is never a question about facts of experience (such a problem is always much more tractable), but a logical, and hence properly a grammatical question' (1967b, § 590). In addition, both Wittgenstein and Searle deal explicitly with the 'ordinary' concepts of understanding and meaning. As a consequence, Searle is charged (e.g. by Block 1980: 425; Minsky 1980: 439) with clinging to a pre-scientific concept of understanding. His reply that this accusation 'is really quite irrelevant to my argument, which is addressed to the mind science of the present' (1980b: 452) echoes Wittgenstein's claim that substituting a physiological concept for understanding as usually conceived 'can screen the old problem from view, but not solve it' (1953: 212).

2. Applying Wittgenstein's Philosophical Psychology to the Chinese Room Argument

Wittgenstein anticipated aspects of the debate between Searle and the proponent of Strong AI (the Searlian speaks first):

[Treating] thought as something specifically human and organic, one is inclined to ask 'could there be a prosthetic apparatus for thinking, an inorganic substitute for thought?' But if thinking consists only in [symbol-manipulation], why shouldn't a machine do it? 'Yes, but the machine doesn't know anything'. (1974: 105)

Despite the parallels noted in Section 1, Wittgenstein did not side with Searle. His arguments provide compelling objections not only to the Chinese Room Argument but also to the model of the mind that appears to underly it.

How, in the above quotation, can the Searlian be sure that the machine 'doesn't know anything'? The parallel question concerning the fundamental premise of the Chinese Room Argument is: what justifies Searle's assumption that it is 'fact' rather than 'intuition' (1980b: 451) that the man in the Chinese Room (Searle himself) does not understand the symbols he manipulates? This cannot, without circularity, be inferred from the (hypothesized) syntax–semantics gap. Nor can Searle easily argue that his view is self-evident or its negation absurd, since his many critics clearly disagree. Searle sometimes appears to regard it as sufficient that he was unable to read Chinese before entering the room (ibid. 451), but his history is relevant only if nothing in or about the room affects his abilities, and to assume this would be to beg the question. Mostly Searle's claim is simply that *he* is the person manipulating the symbols and *he knows* he cannot read Chinese ('it seems to me quite obvious in the example that I do not understand a word of the Chinese stories' (Searle 1980a: 418 (B70))).

From Searle's remarks we can construct putative justifications for his confidence. One is that something in conscious awareness warrants a claim to be able to read and Searle knows when manipulating the pictograms that this item is absent. For Wittgenstein, however, whatever item in consciousness might on occasion accompany understanding, it cannot be a guarantor of understanding (1953, §§ 152, 155). According to Wittgenstein, we simply cannot find any item that correlates significantly with understanding (ibid., §§ 168, 171), and even if we were to do so, a simple thought experiment shows of any such item that it is neither necessary nor sufficient for understanding. Consider two people, one of whom (A) can read aloud (ibid., § 156) and one of whom (B) cannot but has memorized the words of a particular text, so as to appear to be reading aloud from the text (ibid., § 160). Let us further suppose that, given any item in consciousness that seems distinctive of genuine reading or understanding (a feeling, say, of ease or confidence or of being 'guided' by the marks on the page), we eliminate it in A, leaving everything else unchanged, and induce it in B. In A we induce the 'characteristic sensations [of] reciting something one has learnt by heart' (ibid., § 159). (If some item seems to Searle distinctive of *lack* of understanding, we induce this too in *A*.) Is it the case that *A* is no longer a reader and that *B* is now a genuine reader? Wittgenstein suggests not. After all, hypnotizing a memorizer to improve his confidence will not make him a reader, and that a reader's confidence disappears is also irrelevant. Wittgenstein's conclusion is that 'we must admit that as far as the reading of a particular word goes, exactly the same thing might have happened in the [memorizer's] mind when he "pretended" to read as . . . happened in the mind of the fluent reader when he read the word' (1965: 120).

Perhaps Searle simply assumes that sincere first-person claims to understand (or not) are decisive—in the way, say, that sincere first-person claims to be in pain are often taken to be decisive. However, the reader-memorizer thought-experiment can also be used against this assumption. We need simply hypnotize *A* to say sincerely (i.e. to utter, and believe the truth of, the sentence) 'I cannot understand these symbols' and *B* to say sincerely 'I can understand these symbols'. Their sincere say-so is worthless. Of the living calculating machine, Wittgenstein remarks: 'His telling me so—"I calculated in my head"—is not to be taken into account' (1989*b*: 150).

Let us look more closely at Searle's claim that the man in the Chinese Room doesn't understand the pictograms. As described by Searle, this man is what Wittgenstein called 'meaning-blind' (1980*a*, § 175 ff.). The meaning-blind subject is 'able to take notice of' written signs, e.g. Chinese pictograms, while the only element noticed 'is the pattern of the sign' (1967*b*, § 145) and he or she may be manipulating the signs 'by means of rules, tables' (ibid., § 145). The meaning-blind speak 'a language in whose use the impression made on us by the signs played no part; in which there was no such thing as understanding, in the sense of such an impression' (1967*b*, § 145). The meaning-blind subject is the forerunner of Searle's 'intentional zombie' (1990*a*: 595). Searle denies the possibility of an intentional zombie (ibid. 595), saying 'Only a being that could have conscious intentional states could have intentional states at all' (1992: 132).[9]

For Wittgenstein, in contrast, meaning-blindness is no barrier to the *use* of language, and it is use that matters: 'the experience of meaning seems to have no

---

[9] In Searle's account the intentional zombie is 'totally unconscious' (1990*a*: 525), but Wittgenstein rejected this use of 'conscious' and unconscious': ' "An automaton can *use* a word, but only a *conscious* being can *mean* something". Here, if you mean "conscious" as equivalent to "not knocked out", then granted. But if we talk of "consciousness" or "I am conscious" as marks of "conscious being", then we have a misuse of the subject, and "consciousness" seems something gaseous' (1993: 367).

importance in the *use* of language. And so . . . it looks as if the meaning-blind could not lose much' (1980a, § 202).

We can suppose, Wittgenstein suggested, a whole community of meaning-blind people, and moreover that, despite their lacking the 'impressions' of words, they use intentional constructions (such as 'When I heard the word "bank" it meant . . . to me' (1967b, § 530)) just as we do. The absent impressions are for Wittgenstein beside the point: 'Don't all *experiences* of understanding get covered up by the use, by the *practice* of the language-game?' (1980a, § 184). Wittgenstein concluded, from arguments such as the reader-memorizer thought-experiment, that the experiences and impressions 'which are found by experience to accompany sentences are of no [logical] interest' (1974: 45). If so, then 'meaning-blindness', which is merely the absence of such impressions and experiences, cannot imply any lack of understanding.[10] *A fortiori*, if the man in the Chinese Room does not understand the symbols he manipulates, it is not in virtue of his meaning-blindness. Searle has not yet shown that the man in the room is more than merely meaning-blind.

Wittgenstein introduced the notion of meaning-blindness as 'a way of getting rid of the picture, the "accompanying" picture' (1989b: 286). This 'picture' is a model of the mind, exemplified in the notion of understanding as 'a melody [played] . . . on the soul' (Sect. 1). The advocate of this model argues as follows:

Without a sense, or without the thought, a proposition would be an utterly dead and trivial thing. And further it seems clear that no adding of . . . signs can make the proposition live. And the conclusion which one draws from this is that what must be added to the dead signs in order to make a live proposition is something . . . with properties different from all mere signs. (1965: 4)

The action of language consists of two parts; an inorganic part, the handling of signs, and an organic part, which we may call understanding these signs, meaning them, interpreting them, thinking. These latter activities seem to take place in a queer kind of medium, the mind; and the mechanism of the mind, the nature of which, it seems, we don't quite understand, can bring about effects which no material mechanism could. (ibid. 3)

Searle appears to endorse the accompanying picture, arguing, we might say, that the mechanism of the *brain*, the nature of which, it seems, we don't quite understand, can bring about effects which no *program* could. For Searle, the

---

[10] If we accept Wittgenstein's arguments, 'meaning-blindness' becomes a solecism: 'And now the question arises whether . . . it wouldn't be totally misleading to speak of . . . "meaning-blindness" (as though one were to talk of "will-blindness", when someone behaves passively)' (1980a § 189).

'organic part' is rooted in neurophysiology: 'intentionality is a purely internal product of internal physiological processes' (1987: 230) and 'mental states and processes are real biological phenomena in the world; as real as digestion, photosynthesis, lactation or the secretion of bile' (ibid. 217). The product of the internal physiological processes is 'awareness' (1980b: 454) or 'mental life' (ibid. 452).

An interesting feature of Searle's version of this model is that understanding a sign consists in having an *interpretation* of the sign:

if you type into the computer '2 plus 2 equals ?' it will type out '4'. But it has no idea that '4' means 4 or that it means anything at all. And the point is . . . that its . . . symbols don't have any interpretations as far as the computer is concerned. (Searle 1987: 423)

The computer attaches no meaning, interpretation, or content to the formal symbols; and qua computer it couldn't, because if we tried to give the computer an interpretation of its symbols we could only give it more uninterpreted symbols. The interpretation of the symbols is entirely up to the programmers and users of the computer. (Searle 1982: 4)

Searle does not explicate the notion of an 'interpretation'. This leaves him vulnerable to Wittgenstein's criticism of analyses of intentionality in terms of interpretations accompanying signs, namely that such analyses lead to a regress:

[Concerning] the view that thinking, or some process in the mind, accompanies the symbols . . . Perhaps [this supposed process] is something articulate, so that understanding a sentence consists of a series of interpretations, one interpretation for each word . . . But this only adds one phenomenon to another. (1979: 54)

To illustrate Wittgenstein's argument, let us suppose that the man in the Chinese Room associates a Chinese pictogram with a particular internal item (or 'interpretation') *i*. Is this sufficient for him to understand the pictogram? No, for the very same reason that simple exposure to the pictogram wasn't sufficient for understanding. Possessing an internal item *i* could constitute understanding only if *i* itself meant something to the man in the Chinese Room. By introducing an 'interpretation' we merely push the inquiry into understanding one stage back. The question that now needs answering is: what must be added to internal information-processing for understanding to occur? If we here invoke another interpretation, a regress is initiated. Wittgenstein concluded that 'there is a way of grasping [meaning] which is *not* an *interpretation*' (1953, § 201). If for Searle the man in the Chinese Room fails to understand just because he is meaning-blind, why should we not regard Searle's 'interpretations' as mental accompaniments ('impressions') which succumb to Wittgenstein's regress argument?[11] If Searle has some other explanation of the man's failure to understand, what is it, and what are the 'interpretations' he deems crucial to understanding? Searle owes us answers to these questions.

Wittgenstein's view is that the 'accompanying' picture has no utility in explaining intentionality (1974: 152):

Why should I now hypothesize, in addition to the orderly series of words, another series of mental elements running parallel? That simply duplicates language with something else of the same kind. (1974: 152)

The mental act seems to perform *in a miraculous way* what could not be performed by any act of manipulating symbols. (1965: 42, emphasis added)

For Wittgenstein, signs, such as the Chinese pictograms, are meaningful just if they have a use in a system of language ('[I]t is the *system* of language that makes the sentence a thought and makes it a thought *for us*' (Wittgenstein 1974: 153)). A mysterious mental 'accompaniment'—even one produced by 'the causal powers of the brain' (Searle 1980*b*: 452)—cannot provide this and so 'there is no . . . point in *postulating* the existence of a peculiar kind of mental act alongside of our expression' (Wittgenstein 1965: 42). For Wittgenstein, '[t]hat *pure thought* is conveyed by words and is something different from the words is a *superstition*' (1979: 54) which leads to an inflated ontology ('"thinking" is . . . [an] imaginary auxiliary activity' (1980*b*, § 226)).

3. Wittgenstein and AI

As I have said (Sect. 1), Wittgenstein's writings imply agreement with Searle's rejection of Strong AI and with Searle's claim that the man in the Chinese Room does not understand the symbols he manipulates. However, Wittgenstein's reasons differ considerably from Searle's and are more in step with current thinking in philosophy of mind and AI.

Searle's rejection of Strong AI follows from his denial that cognition consists in symbol-manipulation. Wittgenstein's view is more radical: he denied that

---

[11] This is notwithstanding Searle's (1980*a*) attack on the internal symbol-manipulation model of understanding.

understanding, thinking, intending, meaning, and so on consist in any sort of process (1974: 148), and *a fortiori* that they consist in the process of symbol-manipulation. If Wittgenstein is correct, then Searle's claim that 'mental . . . processes are real biological phenomena' (Sect. 2) is wrongheaded.

For example, Wittgenstein remarked: 'We want to say: "Meaning is essentially a mental process, not a process in dead matter".—What we are dissatisfied with here is the grammar of *process*, not the specific kind of process' (1974: 23; emphasis in original). For Wittgenstein, although physiological processes are no doubt causally necessary for understanding, and although ordinary talk of 'mental processes' is unproblematic (1953, § 308), the logic ('grammar') of the concept of a process is very different from that of the concept of understanding (and of the other instances of cognition—see Proudfoot 1997). For example, we cannot easily speak of the *duration* of thinking or understanding as we do of the duration of a process: 'You distinguish between talking mechanically "like a parrot" and "talking with thought". Then you try "thinking accompanies . . .". This won't do; it leads . . . to questions like "How long did the thought take as compared with the sentence?"' (1989*b*: 245). This difference remains even if we compare thinking or understanding with a fuzzy process having imprecise boundaries: 'Compare: "When did your pains get less?" and "When did you stop understanding that word?"' (1953: 59).[12]

In addition, if understanding is a process, then either this process is a conscious one or it is not. According to Wittgenstein, it cannot be a conscious process, for the reasons given in the reader-memorizer experiment (Sect. 2): whatever plausible candidate for understanding is in S's consciousness when we judge that S understands, this cannot constitute understanding (1953, §§ 160, 168). However, nor can it be a non-conscious process, since that would have the evidently false consequence that I could never justifiably believe that I or others understood (1953, § 153). Wittgenstein's deceptively simple dilemmatic argument does not rely upon any mystical notion of consciousness; it can be repeated with no essential modification for the case of 'access-consciousness' (Block 1995), and for other such cases. We may choose to posit as part of a psychological theory a non-conscious process of 'understanding', but, according to Wittgenstein, inferences to such a process will be of no

---

[12] Is the oddity here due (not simply to questioning the *duration* of understanding, but rather) to juxtaposing phenomena whose durations are determined very differently—in the one case (pain) using internalist criteria, and in the other (understanding) using externalist criteria? Not according to Wittgenstein, since he famously argued that even pain is individuated using externalist criteria.

explanatory value with respect to traditional philosophical problems, and will be redundant with respect to *ordinary* judgements of understanding, since these already have justification-conditions ('And how can the process of understanding have been hidden, when I said "Now I understand" *because* I understood?!' (ibid., § 153)).

Searle claims that 'there must be . . . something *lacking in me* that makes it the case that I fail to understand Chinese' (1980*a*: 422 (B81), emphasis added) and that what is lacking is some 'purely *internal* product of *internal* physiological processes' (Searle 1987: 230, emphasis added).[13] In contrast, Wittgenstein was an externalist, with regard to both the individuation and the explanation of psychological states (see Proudfoot forthcoming).[14] He argued that the 'criteria which we accept for [understanding] are much more complicated than might appear at first sight' (1953, § 182) and that 'what we call "understanding" is related to countless things that happen before and after the reading of *this* sentence' (1974: 72): 'If a man makes Chinese noises we don't say he talks Chinese, unless he has done other things first and can do other things afterwards' (1989*b*: 55).[15]

On Wittgenstein's view we can say of two symbol-manipulators, one the physical duplicate of the other, that one understands (reads, calculates, and so on) while the other does not. For one may fail to meet Wittgenstein's externalist conditions on understanding ('[W]e refer by the phrase "understanding a word" . . . to the whole environment of the event of saying it. And this also applies to our saying that someone speaks like an automaton or like a parrot' (1965: 157)). According to Wittgenstein, a symbol-manipulator *S* understands only if *S* has a particular *history* (one which involves learning and training): 'If a man has never learned to play chess, can he win at chess?' (1989*b*: 180). In

---

[13] Searle allows that some 'hybrid' mental concepts do 'require that additional conditions be met in order that the concept be applicable' (1987: 229), but argues that in these cases 'we can carve off [the] mental component' (ibid. 229). His 'principle of neurophysiological sufficiency' (the thesis that brains have causal powers sufficient to bring about 'any mental phenomenon whatever' (1987: 229)) holds of this 'mental component'. Examples of Searle's 'pure mental states' are feeling a pain, thinking about philosophy, and wishing that I had a cold beer. An externalist, such as Wittgenstein, would deny that neurophysiological states are sufficient for such states.

[14] My claim that Wittgenstein is an externalist commits him only to the views described in the text: it does not commit him to any details of well-known versions of externalism, nor to influential externalists' arguments for their position. (For further discussion of this point, see Proudfoot forthcoming; Glock and Preston 1995).

[15] This is not to deny that '[i]n certain of their applications the words "understand", "mean" refer to a psychological reaction while hearing, reading, uttering etc. a sentence' (Wittgenstein 1974: 41).

addition, S must participate in a particular social *environment* (one which includes normative constraints and further uses of the symbols):

You aren't calculating if, when you get now this, now that result, and cannot find a mistake, you accept this. . . . Our children are not only given practice in calculation but are also trained to adopt a particular attitude towards a mistake in calculating. (1967*a*: 425)

I want to say: it is essential to mathematics that its signs are also employed in *mufti* [i.e. outside mathematics]. It is the use outside mathematics, and so the *meaning* of the signs, that makes the sign-game into mathematics. (ibid. 257)

Neither the man in the Chinese Room nor Wittgenstein's living reading-machine satisfies these requirements. Hence neither understands, but this has nothing to do with the absence of 'interpretations' or 'mental life'.

Wittgenstein's reputation in contemporary philosophy of mind is that of a conservative. In fact, he anticipated much recent theorizing (see Proudfoot forthcoming). As early as 1946–8 he conjectured that brains do not process representations (1967*b*, § 608 ff.). His objections to the representational theory of mind together with positive features of his own theoretical psychology (e.g. his emphasis upon samples, training, and 'family resemblance' in concept-acquisition) prefigure connectionist accounts of mind. Wittgenstein was also an early proponent of what is now known as the 'situated cognition' approach. He saw cognition in terms of activities, skills, and common-sense 'know-how', and emphasized situated reasoning and environment-specific knowledge. Like the advocates of 'nouvelle AI' (e.g. Brooks 1999), Wittgenstein held that sophisticated cognitive performance does not involve internal world-modelling but rather develops out of the simple behaviour involved in primitive 'forms of life' (Wittgenstein's term—in current AI vocabulary, these are 'horizontal microworlds'). There is nothing in Wittgenstein's externalist conditions on understanding that in principle prevents a 'reading-machine', living or otherwise, from coming to understand. Indeed, Wittgenstein remarked of one sort of living reading-machine—'anthropoid brute[s]' used as slaves—that they can work 'thinkingly' (1967*b*, § 108) rather than 'mechanically' if they 'make trials and comparisons as they work' (ibid., § 103). Yet Wittgenstein's arguments present a challenge to AI's romantic aim of producing an artificial 'res cogitans'. If giving a computer the history and social environment necessary for cognition is either impossible or too costly in time and money, and if the computer—like the living reading-machine—already produces the behavioural outputs we want, then why should we care if it doesn't really understand?

References

BLOCK, N. (1980) 'What Intuitions about Homunculi don't Show', *Behavioral and Brain Sciences*, 3: 425–6.

—— (1995) 'On a Confusion about a Function of Consciousness', *Behavioral and Brain Sciences*, 18: 227–47.

BODEN, M. A. (ed.) (1990) *The Philosophy of Artificial Intelligence* (Oxford: Oxford University Press).

BROOKS, R. (1999) *Cambrian Intelligence: The Early History of the New AI* (Cambridge, Mass.: MIT Press).

COPELAND, J., and PROUDFOOT, D. (2000) 'What Turing did after he Invented the Universal Turing Machine', *Journal of Logic, Language, and Information*, 9: 491–509.

FODOR, J. (1980) 'Searle on what Only Brains can do', *Behavioral and Brain Sciences*, 3: 431–2.

GLOCK, H. J., and PRESTON, J. M. (1995) 'Externalism and First-Person Authority', *The Monist*, 78: 515–33.

MINSKY, M., (1980) 'Decentralized Minds', *Behavioral and Brain Sciences*, 3: 439–40.

MONK, R. (1990) *Ludwig Wittgenstein: The Duty of Genius* (London: Jonathan Cape).

NEDO, M., and RANCHETTI, M. (1983) *Wittgenstein: Sein Leben in Bildern und Texten* (Frankfurt: Suhrkamp Verlag).

PROUDFOOT, D. (1997) 'On Wittgenstein on Cognitive Science', *Philosophy*, 72: 189–217.

—— (forthcoming) 'The Implications of an Externalist Theory of Rule-Following Behaviour for Robot Cognition'.

SEARLE, J. R. (1980a) 'Minds, Brains, and Programs', *Behavioral and Brain Sciences*, 3: 417–24.

—— (1980b) 'Intrinsic Intentionality: Reply to Criticism of "Minds, Brains and Programs"', *Behavioral and Brain Sciences*, 3: 450–6.

—— (1982) 'The Myth of the Computer', *The New York Review of Books* 29 Apr., 3–6.

—— (1987) 'Minds and Brains without Programs', in C. Blakemore and S. Greenfield (eds.), *Mindwaves* (Oxford: Blackwell).

—— (1990a) 'Consciousness, Explanatory Inversion, and Cognitive Science', *Behavioral and Brain Sciences*, 13: 585–96.

—— (1990b) 'Is the Brain a Digital Computer?' *Proceedings and Addresses of the American Philosophical Association*, 64: 21–37.

—— (1992) *The Rediscovery of the Mind* (Cambridge, Mass.: MIT Press).

TURING, A. M. (1936) 'On Computable Numbers, with an Application to the *Entscheidungsproblem*', *Proceedings of the London Mathematical Society*, series 2, 42: 230–65.

—— (1950) *Programmers' Handbook for Manchester Electronic Computer* (University of Manchester, Royal Society Computing Machine Laboratory).

WITTGENSTEIN, L. (1953) *Philosophical Investigations*, trans. G. E. M. Anscombe (Oxford: Blackwell).

—— (1965) *The Blue and Brown Books* (New York: Harper).

WITTGENSTEIN, L. (1967a) *Remarks on the Foundations of Mathematics*, ed. G. H. von Wright, R. Rhees, and G. E. M. Anscombe, 2nd edn. (Oxford: Blackwell).

—— (1967b) *Zettel*, ed. G. E. M. Anscombe and G. H. von Wright; trans. G. E. M. Anscombe (Oxford: Blackwell).

—— (1974) *Philosophical Grammar*, ed. R. Rhees; trans. A. J. P. Kenny (Oxford: Blackwell).

—— (1979) *Wittgenstein's Lectures, Cambridge 1932–1935: from the Notes of Alice Ambrose and Margaret Macdonald*, ed. A. Ambrose (Oxford: Blackwell).

—— (1980a) *Remarks on the Philosophy of Psychology, Volume I*, ed. G. E. M. Anscombe and G. H. von Wright; trans. G. E. M. Anscombe (Oxford: Blackwell).

—— (1980b) *Remarks on the Philosophy of Psychology, Volume II*, ed. G. H. von Wright and H. Nyman; trans. C. G. Luckhardt and M. A. E. Aue (Oxford: Blackwell).

—— (1989a) *Wittgenstein's Lectures on the Foundations of Mathematics, Cambridge 1939: from the notes of R. G. Bosanquet, Norman Malcolm, Rush Rhees, and Yorick Smythies*, ed. C. Diamond (Chicago: University of Chicago Press).

—— (1989b) *Wittgenstein's Lectures on Philosophical Psychology 1946–47: notes by P. T. Geach, K. J. Shah, and A. C. Jackson*, ed. P. T. Geach (Chicago: University of Chicago Press).

—— (1992) *Last Writings on the Philosophy of Psychology, Volume II*, ed. G. H. von Wright and H. Nyman; trans. C. G. Luckhardt and M. A. E. Aue (Oxford: Blackwell).

—— (1993) *Philosophical Occasions 1912–1951*, ed. J. Klagge and A. Nordmann (Indianapolis: Hackett).

10

The Hinterland of the Chinese Room

Jeff Coulter and Wes Sharrock[1]

People compute. Computers compute. There is no need for scare quotes around *compute* in the latter sentence, but what it signifies is different from what it signifies in the former sentence. The nature of the connection, if any, between these two sentences has become a widely disputed issue in the philosophy of mind and psychology. What is the difference between them? Let us exploit some analogies. My clock tells the time. My daughter has learned to tell the time. Has she learned to do what my clock can do? If I play Beethoven's music on the stereo, and Alfred Brendel plays it on the piano, have I played Beethoven as Brendel does? Nowadays, the post office sorts the mail mechanically. If I sort mechanically through the morning mail, am I sorting it in the way that the post office does? A wild flower is a kind of flower, and artificial flavoring is a kind of flavoring, but is an artificial flower a kind of flower? What has military intelligence to do with average intelligence, and either with artificial intelligence? My dog obeys the command 'fetch'. Has my dog mastered at least one word of English?

'How high the seas of language rise!' (Wittgenstein)

In putting our case, we risk being accused of linguistic legislation, attempting to dictate what others must mean by their words. Consequently, we are seen as

---

[1] Authors listed alphabetically.

opponents of innovation, attempting to deny researchers their right to meet their legitimate needs by giving new uses to words. That words acquire new uses (or that new words are coined, which sound and read like old ones) is an entirely normal feature of language, and that scientists give technical uses to expressions from our ordinary language is not a matter for complaint or resistance. We may also be condemned for substituting a concern with 'the meanings of words' for considerations of real substance, but the issue of how words are being used— what they mean—is *critical* to the way in which the issues in the debate about cognitivism are set up. If we are not clear about what we are saying when, for example, we talk about a computer calculating the value of pi, then it will not be clear, either, as to what—if anything—is at issue between someone who says that a computer can calculate the value of pi and someone who says that it does not. These disputants may, to adopt a phrase of Quine's, be only words apart. That we do not somehow sanctify established usage and (thus) use this as a basis for a censorious attitude to the notion of giving technical uses to ordinary terms does not mean that we must march in step with every proposed linguistic innovation, unable to raise questions about the necessity for, or advisability of, specific innovations in particular cases. In regard to those who advocate the idea that 'machines can possess intelligence' we would advance the counter-thesis that such advocates want things both ways at once. They want to claim their right to give the words ('intelligence'—or: 'understands') new uses, but appear to want, at the same time, to treat claims including those words in their new uses as though they directly confront claims which are made including such words in their 'older' use.

It is, of course, entirely possible to use words like 'intelligence', 'understands' and 'thinks' in a new application which entitles us then to say that 'this is an intelligent machine' or 'that is a thinking machine'. However, the assertion, with this new use, that 'machines can think' does *not* comprise a denial of our suggestion that, in terms of the established use of words such as 'think', 'understand', and so on, machines do not think (etc.). An exchange of denial and assertion in *these* terms will simply be one at cross-purposes. Words such as, say, 'calculate', and 'play', when used in respect to machines, are used differently than when they are predicated of people.

Take the case (alluded to above) of the CD player and the pianist who both play Beethoven. What are we saying when we say that the CD plays Beethoven? Do we say virtually the same thing as when we say that Alfred Brendel plays Beethoven? When someone says that: 'The CD was playing Beethoven' one is saying that the music has been recorded on a disk which is now being scanned by a laser-beam. When we say that Alfred Brendel plays Beethoven we might be saying that Brendel puts Beethoven recordings in his CD player to listen to them when he gets home at night. When the concert poster advertises: 'Brendel plays Beethoven', then we understand that Brendel himself will be appearing in his capacity as a concert pianist, that he will be sitting down at the piano keyboard and striking these with his fingers in rendition of Beethoven's musical score. The word 'plays' says something different in each of these cases, the upshot being, in each case, the same thing in one sense: namely, the sound of Beethoven's music. However, in another sense, the upshot is very different, for there is a difference between a 'recorded sound' and a 'live performance', and the differences between these need not be acoustic in character. Acoustically identical outputs would not diminish the *other* (many) differences between the two. The CD recording reproduces the sound of Brendel's live performance, and the piano playing produced is Brendel's playing, not that of the CD player. The characteristics of the machine affect the acoustical, not the musical, quality of the output. The ouput of the CD player is no musical achievement on the machine's part, but Brendel's performance is his own achievement, a product of his mastery and application of techniques of musicianship, knowledge of the musical score, artistic ingenuity and sensitivity.

The fact that people may speak of a computing device as 'passing' the Turing Test, comparably, does *not* signify that the machine has those characteristics which satisfy a test's requirements in the ordinary sense of the word. 'Passing the test' is not an aim and achievement of the machine, nor is 'taking the test' any activity of the machine's, as these can be the aim, activity, and achievement of the designers and programmers of the machine. Indeed, conflating expressions such as these has become the stock-in-trade of the cognitive science program in the human sciences.

A barometer is an ingenious piece of equipment which forecasts the weather. Saying this, we do not thereby imply that: the barometer possesses any measure of ingenuity; that the barometer has any foresight about the weather; that the barometer has mastered or applies the techniques which a meteorologist would use to forecast the weather, or that forecasting is any activity in which the barometer, unlike the meteorologist, engages in everyday. 'Forecasting' is not the same thing in the two cases, nor is 'calculating' in respect of computers and mathematicians.

Thus, we have no reservations about 'the computer calculates the results', nor do we suggest that, in saying this, we are using 'calculates' *in some metaphorical fashion*. We are no more uncomfortable with this way of speaking than with saying that the neon sign spells out 'No Vacancy' or that the elevator counts the floors as it ascends. *These* forms of expression do not encourage *anyone* to claim that neon signs can spell or that elevators can count. The fact that we *do* say that a computer can do these calculations but not those calculations need not suggest that computers can do, know, or understand mathematics.

John Searle's original Chinese Room Argument was designed to demonstrate his major conclusion that: 'The reason that no computer program can ever be a mind is simply that a computer program is only syntactical, and minds are more than syntactical. Minds are semantical, in the sense that they have more than a formal structure, they have a content' (Searle 1984: 31). We shall challenge this conclusion, but first we shall present what we think are good reasons for endorsing the essentials of Searle's Chinese Room Argument. The centrepiece of Searle's initial interpretation of his Chinese Room *gedankenexperiment* is that the Turing Test proves nothing whatsoever about the nature of 'intelligence'. That one thing cannot be discriminated from another (under a specific set of conditions) does not prove that there is no difference between them. From the fact that computer emissions might be taken for products of people's performances, given only the respective outputs to match, it hardly follows that the two outputs cannot be otherwise discriminated, nor that they are not different in kind. The conditions under which the discrimination is to be made, including information about the outputs that are to be compared, are important for decision as to whether one thing is the same as another. Turing's basic error was simple: rather than recognize that he had contrived a way of accomplishing tasks that normally require some (even a high degree of) intelligence without the use of any intelligence at all, he concluded rather that he had found a way of transferring intelligence to machines. If computation requires intelligence, and if computation can be done on machines, then, he thought, since machines can do computation they must possess intelligence.

Turing's singular mathematical achievement in devising new methods of computation could equally well have been developed for unskilled labor. The making of very complex calculations could be reduced to very simple instructions that those utterly devoid of mathematical abilities could follow. The most complex mathematical concepts that such instructions might possess could be those of, for example, 'stroke', 'square', 'triangle', and so on. The reduction of complex calculations to the kind of instructions that the mathematically unskilled could follow would no doubt itself be a long and very time-consuming affair (as it has been in computer programming). It would result in an inordinately protracted process to carry out any complex calculation. Hence, it is the operating speed of computers that makes them the ideal vehicle for the actual implementation of Turing's procedure. As can be seen, however, the conversion of mathematical computations into something that someone could undertake by following instructions such as: 'move two spaces to the right and draw in a circle' does not involve the transfer of mathematical skills. The mathematical skills possessed by those who can actually carry out the complex calculation have not been acquired by those who follow the simple instructions. Indeed, those who carry out the simple instructions have no—or extraordinarily little—mathematical understanding. That they can count the number of squares, and that they can identify basic geometric shapes, does not provide sufficient mathematical understanding to enable them to have any idea at all of what mathematical computations they are *thereby* carrying out. Those who follow the instructions are not, themselves, doing computations for they are not doing mathematics at all. They are doing someone else's mathematics. Someone who can follow a set of simple English-language instructions can be used to carry out mathematical computations, but the decomposition of these computations into simple step-wise procedures has been done just so that it does not take any mathematical competence to carry them out. The adaptation of Turing's method for computers ensures that computations can be carried out without any intelligence at all.

The Chinese Room dramatizes this point with respect to the simulation of linguistic production. Someone can simulate the performance of a fluent speaker of Chinese without any understanding of Chinese. An English speaker, equipped with an effective set of English instructions, and (imaginably) operating at a very high speed, could follow those instructions so as to make convincing simulations of Chinese conversation—providing answers to questions, and so forth. The speaker would then produce outputs (superficially) indiscriminable from expressions competently uttered in Chinese. This could be achieved by such a speaker without his possessing any understanding of Chinese whatsoever. The basis for the simulation of linguistic performance by the computer is, of course, the fact that the computer responds to electrical pulse trains, not to the linguistic or mathematical expressions which are mapped onto those pulse trains. This is 'realized' in the Chinese Room by the supposition that the Chinese expressions are sequences bearing Chinese symbols, and that the selection and sequencing of the symbols is done in accord with their graphic characteristics—with the visual configuration of the ideogram on the card. What could be clearer: the English speaker who, through the use of the technology of the Chinese Room, convincingly simulates Chinese linguistic behavior does not understand any of the Chinese expressions involved, has no idea of what those expressions are saying. Indeed, he need not even be aware of the fact that the things displayed on the cards are *linguistic* symbols at all. (Hence Searle's deliberate use of simple graphical notions like 'squiggle' and 'squoggle' to denote them.) The individual in the Chinese Room approximates more to the condition of the computer than that of the language-user.

The Chinese Room analogy brings to the forefront another point against the Turing Test: that the identification of different performances as being of the same type depends not only upon their delivered characteristics, but also upon the way in which the performances are organized to deliver those characteristics. Who would suppose that the pigeons wrote the messages delivered by pigeon post? (Well, perhaps people in cognitive science might!) The output from the Chinese Room is a linguistic output only in so far as its features replicate features of the Chinese language. It is not a linguistic output in the sense that it is delivered from the—Chinese—linguistic capacities of the operator of the Room. That the output replicates these features is incidental to the operator's performance. Even were the operator aware that his operations simulate linguistic behavior, and that the language is Chinese, the nature of the Chinese characters and language would be wholly irrelevant to his effective performance. The only linguistic performance involved in the real-time production of the Chinese output is in the comprehension and following of the English-language instructions, but a production of tokens of Chinese language by means of English-language instructions is a long way from spontaneous, comprehending production of Chinese expressions.

The only way the output from the Chinese Room can be endowed with the characteristics of a linguistic performance is in relation to the uses to which people put such a contrivance. The Chinese Room could be set up by an administrative organization which found it a quicker, more economical way to produce its documentation. Then, although the operator in the Chinese Room might produce such output without any understanding of Chinese, this output could have the character and force of authentic expressions—but the expressions of the administrative organization, not of the Chinese Room. It is not the bank's computer that sends one's bank statement, but the bank that does so (using the computer). A mathematician could use the output of the mathematically unskilled labor force as mathematical results, but the basis for doing so would be his own mastery of mathematics, not the work of the unskilled laborers (for theirs is no more a mathematical performance than the Chinese Room's is linguistic).

The operator of the Chinese Room, the unskilled mathematical task force, and the computer are not, themselves, even simulating competent performance. The Chinese Room operator and the mathematical task force have no understanding of Chinese nor of mathematics, and hence have no conception of what it takes to simulate a competent performance. The Chinese Room operator and the mathematical task force are, respectively, ignorant of Chinese and mathematics. The computer understands no Chinese nor mathematics, but it is not ignorant of them either. The computer, too, is not the progenitor of any simulation of linguistic or mathematical performance, any more than the operator or the task force: the capacity of the computer's output to serve as simulations (or even authentic expressions) is dependent upon the uses to which people put them. The mathematician or the natural-language speaker can carry out simulations, or even performances, on the computer, and the output is theirs, not the computer's.

It has been pointed out that the so-called 'systems reply' to the Chinese Room Argument suggests that the Room understands Chinese because that is what, from the external point of view, *looks* to be the case. One might as well say: 'from the ignorant point of view' as from the 'external point of view'. One of us (Wes Sharrock) was once visiting the other when an actor visited Coulter's apartment with a view to renting it. Sharrock's young daughter was there, and a programme featuring this same actor was showing on television. Sharrock's daughter was very puzzled when this was pointed out—she would, by the standards of a 'systems' argument, have been entitled to conclude that someone could be in two places at once. Of course, she was, then, just ignorant of facts about pre-recorded television. By the same token, witnesses to one of Uri Geller's performances would be right to be satisfied that the extra-sensory realm does exist, and audiences at magic shows should accept that magicians do saw women in half. We know that they do not: it is the way such performances are organized and managed that creates an illusion. The same applies to the Chinese Room.

As noted, Searle presented his Chinese Room 'experiment' in terms of a distinction between the syntax and semantics of language. The Chinese Room, he first thought, showed that computers possessed syntax but lacked semantics. Computers may be able to respond to and arrange meaningful expressions in acceptable sequences, but cannot grasp the meanings of any such expressions, just cannot understand what they produce. Later Searle saw the need to retract even *this* concession to the proponents of 'the strong programme of AI'. Computers do not 'have' syntax any more than semantics. After all, syntactical relations are combinatorial relations between linguistic or mathematical elements: it is not that the computer has no awareness of the sense of linguistic expressions, but rather the fact that they *are* linguistic expressions (can be used as such) is entirely exiguous to the computer's operations. It is perfectly justified to say that the computer responds to the formal features of linguistic or mathematical expressions, so long as it is understood in the right way, as a characterization of how *we* make use of the computer—mapping the formal features of such expressions onto the operations of the computer in such a way that the appropriate relations between input and output will be reproduced in the computer's output. It is *we* who map the formal connections onto the causal operations of the electrical. A sequence of a computer's electronic occurrences is matched with linguistic expressions, but the computer does not *itself* respond to the formal features of such expressions for these are not, to the computer, linguistic expressions nor anything else—any more than Morse code raps on a table top are linguistic expressions to the table.

Although we think that Searle's Chinese Room Argument is helpful in illuminating some of the ways in which its principal target, the Turing Test, is flawed, we maintain that the conclusions which Searle himself derived from it are embedded within a wider range of questionable philosophical assumptions. While we are in complete agreement with Searle's rejection of contemporary cognitive science as a foundation for understanding human mentality and conduct, our reasons differ significantly from Searle's, and we take this opportunity to explain why this is so and, also, to counter several of Searle's fundamental theses and assumptions.

We can profitably begin by noting that in the passage cited at the beginning, Searle accords to 'minds' an ontological status which he clarifies elsewhere (especially in Searle 1983) as *biological phenomena*, distinct from, although in some sense 'realized in', brains, hence his use of the (all too common) hybrid expression: 'the mind-brain' (ibid., p. vii). We shall eventually take this up for fuller scrutiny: at this juncture, we note that such an ontological thesis appears closely linked to his related conception of 'meaning'. Searle concurs in the definition of 'meaning' in terms of speakers' intentions, which he takes to be a more fundamental, 'psychological' notion, along with beliefs and desires (ibid. 160–1). Thus, he identifies himself as belonging to the same camp as those who espouse the view 'that language is dependent on mind' (ibid. 161). Although his own views about the nature of this dependence differ from other philosophers who defend such a dependence, it is clear that Searle's starting-point is shared with them. He asks:

When a speaker makes an utterance he produces some physical event; to put the question crudely: What does his intention add to that physical event that makes that physical event a case of the speaker's meaning something by it? *How, so to speak, do we get from the physics to the semantics?* (ibid., emphasis added)

Further on, he asks a related question: 'What is the nature of the complex intention in action that makes the production of those marks or sounds something more than just the production of marks or sounds?' (ibid. 163). For Searle, then, the problem of 'meaning' is: 'how does the mind impose Intentionality on entities that are not intrinsically Intentional?' (ibid. 167) where such 'entities' are the physical marks and sounds said to be emitted by a writer/speaker and picked up by a reader/hearer.

In his 1984 Reith Lectures, he argues that computers lack the (human) capacity to *attach* meanings to the physical symbols it deploys. Thus:

To repeat, a computer has a syntax, but no semantics. The whole point of the parable of the Chinese Room is to remind us of a fact that we knew all along. Understanding a language, or indeed, having mental states at all, involves more than just having a bunch of formal symbols. It involves having an interpretation, or a meaning attached to those symbols. And a digital computer, as defined, cannot have more than just formal symbols because the operation of the computer, as I said earlier, is defined in terms of its ability to implement programs. And these programs are purely formally specifiable— that is, they have no semantic content. (Searle 1984: 33)

Searle's views about mind, meaning, mentality, and computation all nicely intertwine. However, such views are all open to contention. Here we will attempt to spell out our objections to these views while defending the most fundamental position which unites us: the defeat of cognitivist reasoning.

Before elaborating upon our objections, we must take stock of a significant revision which Searle has recently made to his well-known claim that a computer possesses a syntax but no semantics. In *The Rediscovery of the Mind* he says:

The Chinese Room argument showed that semantics is not intrinsic to syntax. I am now making the separate and different point that syntax is not intrinsic to physics. For the purposes of the original argument, I was simply assuming that the syntactical characterization of the computer was unproblematic. But that is a mistake. There is no way you could discover that something is intrinsically a digital computer because the characterization of it as a digital computer is always relative to an observer who assigns a syntactical interpretation to the purely physical features of the system. (Searle 1992: 210)

Searle here expands his notion of 'interpretation' to encompass the domain of the *syntactical* (not just the semantical), arguing that, as with semantics, syntax is not *intrinsic* but observer-relative. This distinction, between that which is intrinsic (e.g. intrinsically Intentional) and that which is not and which is thus 'observer- (or user-)relative' or 'ascribed', is made to do a great deal of work in Searle's writings, and we shall consider its use in some detail. For the moment, we note that, in Searle's view, 'physics' as a scientific enterprise deals (largely) with phenomena whose features are intrinsic to them (e.g., 'mass', 'gravitational attraction', and 'molecule'), whereas there are also phenomena whose constitutive features are relative to users/observers, such as 'bathtub', 'chair', and 'nice day for a picnic' (to use Searle's own examples (ibid. 211)). The significance of this move for his attack on computationalist conceptions of human mentality and conduct is clear: computers are programmed with encoded information such that it can be processed by electronic circuitry. Programmers furnish a syntactically specified realization of the information that a computer can implement in, for example, different voltage levels, but the computer hardware itself has no intrinsic syntax *or* semantics. 'It is all in the eye of the beholder', as Searle puts it (ibid. 223). However, in the case of the human brain, none of the relevant neurobiological processes are observer-relative (although 'like anything, they can be described from an observer-relative point of view' (ibid. 224)). It follows, according to Searle, that one could never *discover* that brains are intrinsically digital computers, albeit ones using neurons, synapses, and carbon, rather than silicon chips. It further follows that brains do not 'process information': there are only the intrinsic neurobiological states and processes. To assume that brains intrinsically process information is to commit the homunculus fallacy, that is, it is falsely to assume that features which can logically only be observer- or user-relative are in fact intrinsic to the phenomena to which they are assigned for some purpose or other.

We now respond to these theses and their assumptive frameworks.

Searle's Conception of Semantics

Searle's approach to the elucidation of the concept of linguistic meaning begins with an unfortunate reduction of words to 'sounds' (or, in the case of writing/reading, to physical 'marks' (e.g. ink inscriptions on paper)). Since sounds themselves are brute physical phenomena in his scheme, and since words differ from 'mere' sounds in virtue of having 'meanings', Searle is driven to embrace a 'parallel-process',[2] dualistic conception according to which the meanings are 'attached' to the words by a speaker's 'interpretation', which interpretive work

---

[2] Jonathan Bennett characterizes Locke's theory of meaning thus in Bennett (1971: 1–11).

is located in the 'mind' of the speaker. The speaker 'intends' his uttered words to have the meanings they have in virtue of the interpretation he gives them. Of course, Searle certainly sees a role for rules and rule-following here, but the rules are assumed to govern the speaker's mentally intended interpretations such that some will be right, others wrong, some correct, others not, and so on. Two 'processes' are thus postulated: one, the physical detection of the sounds emitted by a speaker, and the other, the 'mental' attachment of meanings ('interpretations') to these. The correct meanings will be attached if the hearer follows the same rules as the speaker did when he utters the word(s). Searle's persistent appeal to 'semantic *content*' stems from this parallel-track conception of comprehension: the 'sounds' are merely physical 'forms' which require meanings to be added to give them 'content'. Hence, Searle's (to us, strange) question, cited earlier: 'How . . . do we get from the physics to the semantics?'.

Our response is: we don't. This is because the question itself is incoherent, not because we think that Searle has given a wrong answer. The problem arises at the outset in Searle's characterization of what speakers do when they speak. In his 1969 book on speech acts, he asserts that 'a speaker stands before a hearer and emits an acoustic blast' (Searle 1969: 3). This is a very odd way of describing someone's speaking, although perhaps a reasonable way of describing their howl of pain or a shout. It is clearly a product of Searle's philosophically motivated assumption that because uttered words have acoustic properties, they must be described as 'sounds' or 'acoustic blasts'. But why not characterize them as 'words'? Perhaps because Searle is in the grip of a physics-fetishizing foundationalism according to which only physics[3] describes what there really is? Or perhaps he has unquestioningly accepted the Chomskian assertion that grammars relate 'meanings' to 'sounds'? Whatever the correct diagnosis, it is clear that such a reductionist version conflates two *distinct* kinds of human conduct: speaking and making sounds. Once this conflation is in place, then what differentiates sounds from words, namely 'meanings', becomes problematic. Since speaker-hearers are not in the business constantly of articulating aloud the meanings which their and their interlocutors' words and utterances have,[4] then it would appear that such meanings as they have (which give them their status *as* words and utterances) must be 'in the mind'. (It follows for Searle that, since computers lack consciousness, they must also lack 'minds', and

---

[3] And, note, only one branch of physics.

[4] Of course, this would be no solution to the 'problem' of comprehension, since the words to articulate the meanings of the words spoken (or written) would *themselves* need understanding, thus launching an infinite regress.

thence also 'meanings'). Since sounds 'by themselves' have no meanings (they lack 'Intentional content'), in order to be heard as words 'with' meanings, such meanings must be *attached* to them. However, the meaning of an utterance is given in, available only in, an *explanation* of its meaning, of how it can be used, and giving such an explanation presupposes that there is/was some sort of difficulty or problem in understanding it. Problems of comprehension can require explanations of, formulations of, meaning(s), but routine, unproblematic comprehension does not have to traffic in any such explanations: hence, 'meanings' (explanations of how words are used) are simply *irrelevant* to most communicative conduct. We may say of someone that he 'understood what was said' just as easily as we can say of him that he 'understood the meaning of what was said', although notice that this latter locution is usually restricted to instances where what was said had some *special* significance. As Wittgenstein put it, to think that 'meanings' are omnirelevant in human communication and comprehension is to remain in the grip of 'the idea that the sense of a sentence accompanies the sentence; is there with it', in the absence of which all we would have would be 'dead signs' (Wittgenstein 1967, § 139). We think that Searle is in the grip of such an idea. In his view,

If I am thinking about Kansas City or wishing that I had a cold beer to drink or wondering if there will be a fall in interest rates, in each case my mental state [*sic*] has a certain mental content in addition to whatever formal features it might have. That is, even if my thoughts occur to me in strings of symbols, there must be more to the thought than the abstract strings, because strings by themselves can't have any meaning . . . In a word, the mind has more than a syntax, it has a semantics. (Searle 1984: 31)

We are puzzled by the use here of the expressions 'abstract strings' and 'by themselves'. Are 'abstract strings' supposed to be words? phrases? sentences? If so, then this is evidence of Searle's assumption that, unless a meaning is (somewhere) given to these words, they remain 'dead signs' ('abstract strings' with only 'formal features' in need of supplementation or 'content'). It is as if whenever someone says something that is intelligible (meaningful), it must be the case that its intelligibility consisted in *his meaning something by* it. We would argue that a case of someone's 'meaning something by' what he or she said does *not* characterize every case of someone's saying something intelligible, something which makes sense. Wittgenstein is helpful here:

'I'm not just *saying* this, I mean something by it.'—Should one thereupon ask: 'What?'—Then one gets another sentence in reply. Or perhaps one cannot ask that, as the sentence meant, e.g., 'I'm not just *saying* this, it moves me too.'

(The question 'What do I mean by that?' is one of the most misleading of expressions. In most cases one might answer: 'Nothing at all—I *say* . . .') (Wittgenstein 1967, §§ 3 and 4)

The question: 'What does Y mean by "X"?' and the question: 'What does "X" mean?' can, on occasion, be interchangeable, but they can pose *different* questions. In the case of the first question, one could be asking why 'X' was said by Y *then*, or why 'X' was said by Y *to* Z (etc.), without raising any issue as to the intelligibility of 'X' itself.

Elsewhere, Wittgenstein remarks on the proclivity, very much at work in Searle's reasoning, to think that 'signs' are somehow *insufficient* to bear intelligibility:

If I give anyone an order I feel it to be *quite enough* to give him signs. And I should never say: this is only words, and I have got to get behind the words. Equally, when I have asked someone something and he gives me an answer (i.e., a sign) I am content—that was what I expected—and I don't raise the objection: but that's a mere answer.

But if you say: 'How am I to know what he means, when I see nothing but the signs he gives?' then I say: 'How is *he* to know what he means, when he has nothing but the signs either?' (Wittgenstein 1968, §§ 503 and 504)

'Meaning' is *not* relative to speakers/hearers,[5] and *a fortiori* not to their minds, except in the special (and thus restricted) sense in which something means something to someone, or has a (particular kind of) meaning for someone. In *this* sense, 'meaning' is best equated with 'personal significance'. This is not at all the same as 'intelligibility', which is what is at issue here. If something means something special to someone, is especially meaningful to him or her, we are not speaking of intelligibility but rather of significance. The two notions should not be conflated. In Searle's arguments, we think that they have been.

If neither persons nor their 'minds' (or 'mind-brains') 'possess' semantics, contrary to Searle's claim, then it is no argument against cognitivist conceptions of human mentality to proclaim that computers do not possess semantics. As we remarked earlier, we find considerable merit in the Chinese Room analogy, but not because of the conclusions Searle himself draws.

Searle on the Disappearance of 'Syntax'

Searle argues, in recent writings, against his former position, that 'syntax' itself is not a property intrinsic to computational systems. We need to explore what

---

[5] Searle's formulation begs the question against Wittgenstein's 'anti-private-language' argument.

Searle means by 'syntax' and also by his often-used epithet: 'intrinsic' (and its contrast to the phrase: 'observer/user-relative').

Perhaps too closely following the classical semiotic tripartite 'division' of natural languages into 'syntactical', 'semantic', and 'pragmatic' components (which traditional division Chomskian linguists perpetuate), Searle initially proposed that computational devices operate by using formal symbols in ordered ways. This 'syntactical' feature of the hardware and software dimensions of computers (a feature much emphasized in 'classical' rules-and-representations AI) was thought by Searle (along with Fodor and Stich, among others) to comprise an 'intrinsic' feature of their physical structure and organization.

In retracting the claim that computers have syntax, Searle does not invalidate his Chinese Room Argument. It retains its force, providing a striking illustration of the point that resemblance between the performance of the computer and that of the human reasoner is superficial and formal: the actual capacities which underlie formally similar performances can be utterly, and consequentially, different in character. The design of the imagined Chinese Room is such that the understanding of a natural language which would, on Turing-type and behaviorist-inspired criteria, be manifested by the machine is a product only of the machine's response to the formal properties of linguistic structures and expressions. It is not even the case, however, that the machine responds to the formal properties of symbols because its responses are triggered entirely by their *causal* properties. This is why Searle retreats from the view that 'syntax' can be ascribed to the machine. It is the possibility of using the causal properties of the electrical operations of the machine as an analogue for the symbol system's formal properties which is exploited by computer designers and programmers.

The full effect of the Chinese Room illustration is to identify the fundamental flaw in the strong AI argument as the supposition that the nature of a performance can be identified independently of the conditions of its production. The supposition that because a machine generates output indistinguishable from the products of competent language-using human beings it is therefore matching the performance of human speakers is countered by the argument that they are not giving the *same kind* of performances at all. This is demonstrated not by matching the Chinese Room's linguistically impeccable outputs with those of native speakers, but by looking to see how these outputs originate.

Searle himself, however, seems to us to obscure his own central point by invoking a distinction between 'intrinsic syntax' and 'observer-relative syntax'. For him, the characterization of any physical process as computational is to describe it 'from outside'—it is observer-relative, and does not identify any intrinsic feature of the physical system (Searle 1992: 210–11). He asks what facts intrinsic to the system make it syntactical, assuming a contrast between syntacticity and, say, physical facts such as voltage or chip composition. A 'zero' and a 'one' are observer-relative characterizations of the operation of a computational system, whilst a 'pulse' and 'no-pulse' would be physical facts, intrinsic to the operation of the system. Searle then proceeds to draw the anti-cognitivist conclusion that brains cannot be *intrinsically* computational, because 'computing' is not itself an intrinsically physical property, feature, or capacity in the sense in which mass, velocity, current flow, etc., are. Further, just as computational simulations of phenomena do not provide causal explanations of them, so also computational descriptions of neurophysiological functioning do not provide causal explanations for *them*. The neurobiological events, states, and processes are intrinsic to brains, and, in principle, open to causal neurophysiological explanation: computational characterizations of their functioning are irrelevant to this level of explanation. Searle writes:

We do not in general suppose that computational simulations of brain processes give us any explanations in place of or in addition to neurobiological accounts of how the brain actually works . . . you cannot explain a physical system such as a type-writer or a brain by identifying a pattern that it shares with its computational simulation, because the existence of the pattern does not explain how the system actually works *as a physical system*. The most we could find in the brain is a pattern of events that is formally similar to the implemented program in the mechanical computer, but that pattern, as such, has no causal powers to call its own and hence explains nothing. (ibid. 218–20)

We agree with this conclusion, but do not think that Searle's repeated appeals to his distinction between 'intrinsic syntax (computation)' and 'observer-relative syntax (computation)' are felicitous. In fact, it is misleading, opening a door for the (equally muddled) counter-argument: well, why aren't the *physical* features, properties, and processes themselves also 'observer-relative' since not everyone is capable of identifying or conceptualizing them correctly? What exactly is meant by 'intrinsic' in all of this? Why are not computers *intrinsically* computational mechanisms? It is confusing to appeal to 'pre-existing facts of physics', because computers are clearly human artefacts, not 'pre-existing' physical phenomena. Why deny that human artefacts' functional properties are *not* intrinsic? Why should that which is 'intrinsic' be identified purely with the physical level? If 'intrinsic' means 'belonging to something by its very nature', why restrict the meaning of 'by its very nature' to 'by its very *physical* nature'? Problems arise with the converse case of the 'observer-relative'. Surely the computational properties of computers are not observer-relative in the way that 'nice days for picnics' are (to reiterate one of Searle's examples)? Certainly, Searle is correct to stress the functional character of concepts such as 'computer'—they are used to compute, for example. But why are the functional properties of phenomena (those which have such properties, or which have been designed and built to have them) never 'intrinsic' to them? Perhaps if someone were to use his computer as a coffee-table, one might say that such a function was 'user-relative', but it is to stretch the concept very strangely (and misleadingly) when one argues that computation is merely an 'observer-relative' feature of a computer.

This dichotomy has caused other difficulties for Searle's philosophy of mind. He argues that *beliefs* are 'intrinsically' representational, whilst sentences expressing them are only *derivatively* representational, their representational status being conferred by the intentionality of the requisite mental states (Searle 1983: 22–7). Commenting upon this, Norman Malcolm remarked:

Searle's view makes it look as if when one reports one's belief what happens is that one *translates* one's belief into a sentence. It is as if the belief were an object (or state or process) before one's mind, which one then puts into words. But how does one *learn* to do this? Could it be that some of us have an incorrect understanding of the technique of translating beliefs into words, and therefore *always* report our beliefs incorrectly? (Malcolm 1986: 101)

If the belief that it will snow is pre-linguistic (a certain 'mental state'), then how can Searle know that the expression: 'I believe that it will snow' is the *correct* translation of this wordless belief into words?[6] As Malcolm comments:

On [Searle's] conception, employing psychological language would require one to take account of which descriptions *match* which mental states. But if this comparison were carried out by each of us 'privately', it would be meaningless to say that the same words, uttered by two people, did or did not refer to the 'same' mental state. (Malcolm 1986: 102)

---

[6] Cf. Wittgenstein on the recollections of a deaf-mute reported by William James to buttress his view that thought is possible without speech. 'Are you sure—one would like to ask—that this is the correct translation of your wordless thought into words?' (Wittgenstein 1968: § 342).

Malcolm later attacked what he rightly diagnoses as a bad philosophical habit—that of referring to instantiations of *all* psychological concepts as 'mental states' or 'mental processes' (ibid. 187). At this juncture, we conclude that Searle's conception of 'intrinsic' intentionality *vis-à-vis* 'derived' or 'ascribed' intentionality in respect of beliefs, thoughts, and so on, leads to confusion. We now turn to consider Searle's argument that computers cannot understand because they do not literally possess brains, and only brains generate 'consciousness' which, in turn, is a pre-requisite for understanding anything.

Searle on 'Consciousness' and the Brain

Searle is fully aware of the fact that the present condition of the current orthodoxy in the philosophy of mind results from the perpetuation of the Cartesian problematic, but does he take his own diagnosis of our troubles deeply enough? We think not. Indeed, in a recent popularization of his views, Searle conflates the work of Gilbert Ryle with that of Carl Hempel, claiming that for both 'mental states are just patterns of behavior and dispositions to behavior, when "behavior" means just bodily movements which have no accompanying mental component' (Searle 1997: 43). We have elsewhere demonstrated (Button *et al.* 1995, *passim*), that this conflation is a caricature of Ryle's views, and, also, that (Hempel's) 'logical behaviorism' is distinguishable from Ryle's efforts to clarify the grammar of 'mental'-concept words. Ryle never argued that 'mental' concepts are reducible to statements about behavior (mis)construed as 'bodily movements'. We challenge Searle to show us, textually, any indication of such a proclivity in the work of Ryle. It is a misleading version of what Ryle's work was about, one which, sadly, is widely circulated in contemporary American philosophy, but which has no basis in the text about which it purports to speak.

Although Searle recognizes that it is the Cartesian legacy that causes trouble for the philosophy of mind, and although he sees that the question of the relationship of mind to body, of the mental to the physical, ought to be given up (as a generic issue), he cannot bring himself quite to abandon it, and he positions his own views within the Cartesian problem-space. Condemning materialist monism as a replacement for 'dualism' (and also functionalism as an unwitting dualism), Searle none the less retains the idea that the problem is to relate 'mental' to 'physical' states and processes. However, appeals to the deliverances of physics and biology do not work out well for Searle's (philosophical) project: physics and biology, as ordinarily, empirically, undertaken by professional practitioners, make no reference to 'consciousness' nor to 'mind'. (Except and unless some physicists and biologists attack the *philosophical* problem here under discussion: but then such physicists and biologists are *no longer doing physics nor biology*: they are, perhaps in spite of their own self-characterization, actually doing philosophy.) Searle's project is to try to bring 'mind' within the purview of the natural sciences. His objective is to create the possibility for a psychological science within which 'mind' can be adequately 'naturalized'. But in his attempt to do so, his major move is an ungrounded respecification: mental properties *are* 'realized in' the physical properties of the brain. Mental properties are (furthermore) 'caused' by the brain. These phenomena are (according to Searle) distinctively, but not thereby *uniquely*, causally generated by the brain. After all, alien beings with brains composed of *other than* carbon-based components *might* be credited with mental capacities and powers. However, Searle complains that the very idea that silicon chips (or even beer cans, suitably arranged in very large and interconnected numbers) might imaginably instantiate 'mental powers' is mythical, contrary to functionalist-inspired speculation.[7]

Of course, we support neither side in this (now widely circulated) argument. Searle's current position about the nature of 'consciousness'—that 'it' is a 'biological phenomenon'—also violates one of his former accounts of this issue. He had insisted (correctly) upon a Brentano-inspired argument to the effect that 'consciousness' is not a free-standing notion, but is (generally) a relational one, that 'consciousness' is (generally) 'consciousness *of*' something. How can we now accede to the view that 'consciousness' is *any* sort of (discretely identifiable) *phenomenon* when we are told by the same advocate that 'consciousness' is a relational notion and not a substantive noun? In rejecting this reification, we naturally must reject the subsequent move, which is to propose that 'consciousness' is 'realized in' and 'caused by' hitherto undiscovered neurophysiological processes. 'Being conscious', and 'being conscious of' something, are distinctively ascribable predicates whose contexts of attribution to *persons* (neither to their 'minds' *nor* to their brains) are circumscribed and diverse. The former might be predicated of someone emerging from a faint, whilst the

---

[7] To be more exact: they cannot instantiate 'mental powers' by instantiating a formal programme, because, as such, they lack the causal powers to generate minds. If they could be arranged in such a way as to provide the necessary causal powers then . . .

latter's range of application is specific to circumstances in which, for example, someone's attention has been directed to something.

Searle's persistent efforts to argue for explanatory linkages between our neurophysiology and our 'mental' life (even claiming that neurophysiological explanations will be 'sufficient' ones on their own)[8] overlook the fact that neurophysiological explanations take a specialist, not a subsuming, interest in our 'mental' life. Moreover, he is led to these efforts by a fundamentally Cartesian presupposition, one which postulates mental phenomena as playing a causal role in relation to our everyday conduct. Mental causation is replaced by neurophysiological causation, but this move is made within the framework of a more general Cartesian assumption: that minds are phenomena with specifiable sets of 'workings', the understanding of which requires us to investigate 'what goes on' inside the skull. The description of people's mental lives is thence construed as a kind of 'higher level' description of their neural states and processes. Cartesian introspection is replaced with brain scanning, although the exact relationship between the deliverances of the latter to the purported 'mental' phenomena of consciousness and the rest is resolutely speculative, disconnected from the details of the descriptions which neurophysiology can actually provide.

We cannot here present a fully worked-out alternative case, one built upon the contributions of Ryle and the later Wittgenstein. Theirs is a view of the investigation of the mental which denies both that such might be a *unitary* task and also that it might be an empirical, scientific one. Searle has been dismissive of inquiries of a logical-grammatical kind, claiming that such a methodology 'was discredited by the mid-sixties' and that 'you cannot get very far examining the "use" of words without some general theory of meaning and speech acts. A few remarks about the use of words are pretty much useless without a theory of the relations between "use" and meaning' (Searle 1991: 185).[9] We maintain that Searle himself, equipped as he is with a 'theory' of meaning and, famously, of 'speech acts', would none the less do well to re-focus his efforts exactly upon the ways in which we use our 'mental' vocabulary. Such elucidations lead us not into the interiors of our skulls, speculatively construed, but into a richer appreciation of the complex ways in which our 'mental lives' are inextricably bound up with the rest of our lives as we lead them in society with others.

[8] Searle announced his 'principle of neurophysiological sufficiency' in Searle (1987).
[9] See also Hacker (1992).

References

BENNETT, J. (1971) *Locke, Berkeley, Hume: Central Themes* (Oxford: Clarendon Press).

BOGEN, D. (1991) 'Linguistic Forms and Social Obligations: A Critique of the Doctrine of Literal Expression in Searle', *Journal for the Theory of Social Behaviour*, 21: 31–62.

BUTTON, G., COULTER, J., LEE, J., and SHARROCK, W. (1995) *Computers, Minds and Conduct* (Cambridge: Polity Press).

HACKER, P. M. S. (1992) 'Malcolm and Searle on "Intentional Mental States"', *Philosophical Investigations*, 15: 245–75.

MALCOLM, N. (1986) 'Whether a Proposition Shows its Sense', in his *Nothing is Hidden: Wittgenstein's Criticism of His Early Thought* (Oxford: Blackwell).

SEARLE, J. R. (1969) *Speech Acts: An Essay in the Philosophy of Language* (Cambridge: Cambridge University Press).

—— (1983) *Intentionality: An Essay in the Philosophy of Mind* (Cambridge: Cambridge University Press).

—— (1984) *Minds, Brains and Science* (London: BBC Publications).

—— (1987) 'Minds and Brains without Programs', in C. Blakemore and S. Greenfield (eds.), *Mindwaves* (Oxford: Blackwell).

—— (1991) 'Response: Perception and the Satisfaction of Intentionality', in E. Lepore and R. van Gulick (eds.), *John Searle and his Critics* (Oxford: Blackwell).

—— (1992) *The Rediscovery of the Mind* (Cambridge, Mass.: MIT Press).

—— (1997) 'Consciousness and the Philosophers', *The New York Review of Books*, 54/4: (6 Mar.), 43.

WITTGENSTEIN, L. (1967) *Zettel*, ed. G. E. M. Anscombe and G. H. von Wright; trans. G. E. M. Anscombe (Oxford: Blackwell).

—— (1968) *Philosophical Investigations*, trans. G. E. M. Anscombe (New York: Macmillan).

11

Searle's Misunderstandings of Functionalism and Strong AI

Georges Rey

1. Introduction

I want to expand here on some objections I've made elsewhere (Rey 1986, 1990, 1997) to arguments that John Searle (1980*a*,*b*/91, 1984, 1990*a*, 1992) has raised against computational theories of mind. For reasons of space, I will confine my remarks to issues surrounding intelligence and intentionality, and not take on the (to my mind) much more special issues surrounding qualia and consciousness that Searle also sometimes raises.[1]

I will presume the reader is familiar with Searle's (1980*a*) statement of the example of the man in a room, who, ignorant of Chinese, is responding to Chinese sentences with appropriate Chinese responses by following a computer program for Chinese conversation. Searle thinks that the example refutes what he calls 'Strong AI', the view that 'the appropriately programmed computer really *is* a mind in the sense that computers given the right programs can literally be said to *understand* and have other cognitive states' (Searle 1980*a*: 417).[2]

I'd like to thank Mark Bishop and John Preston for the invitation to write this chapter, and then, Michael Slote, and the audiences at the University of Glasgow (especially Gary Kemp, Jimmy Lenman, Philip Percival, and Nick Zangwill) and at King's College at the University of London (especially Gabriel Segal) for comments on earlier versions. I'm also grateful to the Graduate Research Board of the University of Maryland for financial support, and the Philosophy Programme at the Institute of Advanced Study at the Senate House, University of London, for splendid hospitality.

[1] I discuss these issues in detail in my (1997, ch. 11) and (1998).
[2] Reprinted in Boden (1990: 67). From here referred to as B67.

His criticism is intended to cut a very wide swath: he goes so far as to claim that 'In the Chinese case I have everything that artificial intelligence can put into me by way of a program, and I understand nothing . . .' (ibid. 418 (B70), emphasis added). Indeed: 'there is no reason at all to suppose that my understanding has anything to do with computer programs . . . They are certainly not sufficient conditions, and *not the slightest reason has been given to suppose that they are necessary conditions or even that they make a significant contribution*' (ibid. 418 (B70), emphasis added).

If this criticism were correct, it would mean that a great deal of current psychological research—the entire 'computer model' that dominates contemporary work on almost every aspect of the mind—would be an enormous mistake.[3]

Now, of course, a mere *gedankenexperiment* itself can't establish much of anything, any more than a single experiment by itself refutes a hypothesis in any other investigation. It's the *explanation* of the results of the experiment—in this case of the intuitive verdicts—that is what is really at stake. Searle blames Strong AI.

In Rey (1986 and 1997, § 10.1.3) I offered a different explanation, which I test against appropriate modifications of the original example. In Section 2 below I summarize this earlier material. Briefly, I argue that Searle badly misunderstands the project of a computational theory of mind, confusing that project with extraneous claims that any serious defender of it should reject. Once we correct for these extraneous claims and consider Strong AI in a plausible form, the intuition that a *corrected* 'Chinese Room' doesn't understand Chinese pretty thoroughly evaporates (Sect. 3). I then discuss in Section 4 Searle's own explanation of the example: his appeal to the observer-relativity of syntax (Sect. 4.1), his claims about semantics (Sect. 4.2) and 'aspectual shape' (Sect. 4.3), and finally the 'connection principle' and the importance of conscious, first-person 'subjectivity' (Sect. 4.4). I argue that nothing Searle has said about these issues presents serious problems for a computational theory of thought, properly understood. They seem to do so only if one fails to appreciate the substantial resources of the *functionalist* commitments of Strong AI, conflating them with *behaviorist* ones with which Searle, and sometimes even the supporters of Strong AI, mistakenly burden it.

---

[3] I emphasize the width of his intended swath, since I've encountered the impression that his attack was intended only to refute the very specific suggestion that instantiating a computer program *all by itself* would be sufficient for a mind. Although this suggestion sometimes surfaces in discussions, none of the psychological research on behalf of 'the computer model of the mind' need be committed to it.

But, first, I want to sharpen some terminology and sort out some confusions that Searle's terminology has engendered.

The specific version of Strong AI that will bring out its relevant commitments is what many have called the 'computational-representational theory of thought' (CRTT).[4] To a first approximation this is the view that propositional attitudes (such as believing, noticing, preferring) are to be regarded as computational relations to semantically valuable representations that are encoded in the brain or other hardware of the thinker. There are, however, two deviations in this view from Strong AI as Searle presents it:

1. CRTT bears a quite indirect relation to most current work in the field known as 'artificial intelligence'. Much of this field is concerned with building machines that manage to solve practical problems whose solution usually requires intelligence (e.g. games, medical diagnosis), and not particularly with producing something that really has genuine propositional attitudes, that is, with producing AI: in the sense of *artificial intentionality*. What is centrally important to this research are the products of such intelligence, not the *processes* by which they are produced. Indeed, many researchers would be just as happy to dream up a process that wasn't remotely similar to human or animal processing, if it turned out to be faster or more reliable (as in the case of Deep Blue that beat the World Chess champion).

2. By contrast with much of standard AI, CRTT is explicitly concerned with (natural or artefactually produced) intentionality, and so with *semantically valuable* representations. This fact can be obscured both by the above disinterest in propositional attitudes, and by a further disinterest, evident in much AI research, in any serious theory of meaning. It reasonably suits most of the practical purposes of AI research to treat machines merely as *artefacts that, like books, inherit their intentionality from the intentions of their artefactor*. Consequently, they have what Searle (1983: 27) calls 'derived intentionality'. By contrast, and as its name indicates, CRTT aims to present a theory *both* of the computational

---

[4] The view can be found in embryonic form in Occam, Hobbes, Descartes, Kant, particularly in Wittgenstein (1914–16: 130) and in Sellars (1956). The specifically computational form emerges in the work of Fodor (1975). I present an exposition of it along lines relevant to the present discussion in my (1997, chs. 8–9), extending it beyond a theory of thought to also a theory of qualitative states in chapter 11 and in my (1998). See also Lycan (1987) and Maloney (1989) for related discussions.

I'm actually increasingly inclined to think it would be better to think of CRTT as a species of a *causal*/representational theory of thought, since what the idea of computation does—or, anyway, what essentially Turing did with the notion of computation—is to suggest ways in which rational processes could be caused purely physically. At any rate, this might make the theory more appealing to Searle, given his views of the mental as involving 'causal powers of the brain'.

processes that underlie thought *and* of the representational powers of thought, that is, of 'intrinsic intentionality'. As a sociological fact, this latter issue has been addressed mostly by philosophers.

I presume that Searle would regard his discussion as directed equally against CRTT as against Strong AI, and so would regard these differences between the two as negligible.[5] However, we will see that this difference undermines one of his main arguments.

It bears stressing that the issue raised by Searle's discussion is not whether CRTT is *true*. For the present discussion, CRTT may be regarded as an *empirical* thesis, whose truth could only be established by far more research than is presently available.[6] I shall take Searle's challenge to be not to the truth, but to the 'coherence' of CRTT as a *possible* explanation of mental phenomena.[7]

2. The Original 'Room' Example

I think it's easy to see that Searle's example as he presents it is not remotely relevant to CRTT, which is committed neither to the 'Turing Test' nor to a conversation manual theory of language understanding.[8]

2.1 CRTT is not committed to the Turing Test

CRTT is not committed for a moment to supposing that the Chinese Room or the man in it understands Chinese. The only conceivable reason for so supposing would be if it were committed to the Turing Test for intelligence, whereby a machine is counted as intelligent if a normal observer couldn't

[5] Thus, Searle is not impressed by accounts of the meaning of symbols that might derive from causal or evolutionary relations to the external world (see his 1980b/91: 523 and 1992: 50–1). I'll discuss these views a little further in Sect. 4.2.2 below. He explicitly rejects CRTT in his (1990a) reply to my (1990).

[6] This is not to say that relatively a priori arguments could not be adduced for it—see Davies (1991), Maloney (1989), Lycan (1993), and Rey (1995) for a variety of arguments of this sort. For present purposes, the best way to think of CRTT is as a research program, akin to Boyle's postulation of atoms, advanced without any clear idea about the probably surprising details the postulation will ultimately involve (see Rey forthcoming b for further discussion).

[7] Searle (1990a) persistently misses this modal point in his reply to my (1990).

[8] I summarize here the main points of my (1986) and (1997, § 10.2), in a few places reproducing the same material. Readers unconvinced by this summary are invited to consult the still longer exposition of CRTT in my 1997, chapters 8–9, as well as related discussions in Lycan (1987) and Maloney (1989).

distinguish its teletype responses from those of a normal human being. Leave aside the question whether, with enough ingenuity, one might devise questions that would betray the stupidity of Searle's room. The real issue is that CRTT is not in the least committed to such a superficial test.[9]

CRTT is an instance of a 'functionalist' theory of mind that tries to avoid the obvious errors of both Cartesian dualism and behaviorism by identifying mental states in terms of their causal roles, particularly the *internal* ones they may play inside a typical nervous system. The emphasis on internal processes is crucial, since it permits the functionalist to posit indefinitely subtle and complex internal roles for the identification of mental states. It is this possibility that makes functionalism far more than a mere technical variant of behaviorism.

This fact is sometimes obscured in standard characterizations of functionalism, for example, as the proposal to 'characterize mental states in terms of . . . their causal relations to sensory stimulations, behavioral outputs, and other mental states' (Block 1980: 172). As I try to show in Rey (1997, chs. 6–7), the most natural form of functionalism for a theory like CRTT would have the following features:

(1) it would be *molecular*, that is, applied to *subsystems* of the mind, such as vision or decision-making or language-processing, as opposed to the mind as a *whole*. Thus the 'inputs' and 'outputs' are not always surface stimuli and responses, but sometimes merely data from and to other subsystems;

(2) some of its data structures might be *anchored*, that is, they would stand in various causal relations to the environment, as well as perhaps to specific features of our brains (e.g. the time that processes take), as opposed to being confined to proximal inputs and outputs alone (see Sect. 4.2.2 below); and

(3) it would be a *psychofunctionalism*, in which the ultimate definitions of mental states are supplied by an empirical psychology, and cannot be expected to be in general either a priori or platitudinous.

Thus, for example, judgment might, to a first approximation, be defined in terms of outputs from perceptual or reasoning systems that are the inputs to the decision-making system, the contents of the judgments being determined

[9] This quite problematic Turing Test for intelligence is not to be confused with the quite different, much more interesting (Church)–Turing Thesis, according to which any intuitively computable function is computable by a Turing machine. All they have in common is authorship.

in part by the causal relations of symbols to the organism's environment, and the relevant 'systems' being delineated by an empirical psychology.[10]

This molecular, anchored psychofunctionalism stands in dramatic contrast to the peculiar view that Searle presents as functionalism, what he calls 'black box functionalism', 'which says nothing whatsoever about how the belief works to have the causal relations that it does' (Searle 1992: 42). What is peculiar about this view is that it flies in the face of precisely what is supposed to distinguish *functionalism* from *behaviorism*: it is only *behaviorism*, not *functionalism* that 'says nothing whatsoever about how the belief works', treating the mind/brain as a 'black box'.[11] None of this is meant to suggest that *no* serious prima-facie counter-examples can be mounted to even the specific functionalism I advocate. I discuss some at length in my (1992) and (1997, § 11.7). However, given that they involve speculations about the character of largely unknown *internal processes*, they are considerably harder to construct and evaluate than any merely behavioral ones (Lycan 1987: 59–61 makes a similar point). Even the minimal, 'input/output' functionalism described by Block involves specific

[10] It is important to note that none of (1)–(3) involves any revision of the standard characterization of functionalist views, for example, Lewis's (1980) formal 'ramsification' procedure. (Briefly, this involves defining any specific mental term t_i by the 'Ramsey' sentence $t_i =$ the x_i such that $(\exists!x_1) \ldots (\exists!x_{i-1})(\exists!x_{i+1})(\exists!x_n)(C_M(x_1 \ldots x_i \ldots x_n, o_1 \ldots o_n))$ where '$C_M(x_1 \ldots x_i \ldots x_n, o_1 \ldots o_m)$' is some very long conjunction of the laws of psychology, containing variables, $x_1 \ldots x_n$ in place of the n 'new' mental terms being defined in this way, and m number of 'old' (e.g. physical) terms, $o_1 \ldots o_m$, included in specifying the relations among $x_1 \ldots x_n$). It simply exploits this procedure in ways that Lewis and many other functionalists have neglected. Specifically, it applies it not to the *whole* mind at once, but to 'molecular' subsystems of the mind that may be remote from either perception or behavior, whose states are 'anchored' with 'old' terms about, for example, the brain or the environment. Understood in this light, of course, most theories of *anything* are *more or less* functionalist, depending, roughly, upon the number of new terms and relational structures they introduce in this way. CRTT is clearly *very* functionalist in this respect, and not as devoid of old terms as, for example, Ned Block's entirely holistic, mere 'input-output' functionalism (see my 1997, ch. 7 for further discussion).

[11] Searle's phrasing here actually suggests that analysis of a belief must include an account of *why* the belief actually manages to have the causal role it does. But it's hard to see what exactly such a demand would come to, much less why he or anyone would want to insist upon it. That Searle is generally confusing functionalism with behaviorism is evident from the fact that practically all his purported counter-examples to functionalism are merely standard counter-examples to behaviorism, and decidedly do not generalize from it. Not only the Chinese Room, but the specific 'inverted qualia' counter-examples that he presents (1992: 42–3), and the entire discussion on behalf of a first-person perspective (ibid. 66–9) all patently involve cases in which 'the mediating relationship between the mind and the behavior was broken', or where 'the mental phenomena had no behavioral expression' (ibid. 68). Searle gratuitously generalizes from them to cases of 'functional role and causal relations' (ibid. 69) where, of course, the character of the 'mediating relationship' *is* crucial.

internal relations among mental states; 'black box functionalism' is simply an oxymoron!

Searle's own examples of functionalist definitions (1992: 41–3, 1997: 139–40) obscure this point, being really only slightly modified behavioristic ones. He writes, for example: 'The whole [functionalist] story about John's belief that p can then be told as follows: $(\exists x)$(John has x & x is caused by the perception that p & x together with a desire that q causes action a)' (Searle 1992: 41–2). But there is no reason whatsoever to burden functionalism with such simplistic proposals (which might equally characterize an itch or a tickle as much as a belief), or to suppose that the obvious counter-examples one could raise to such simple definitions are counter-examples to functionalism generally.

Searle not only disregards the rich 'inner' resources of functionalism in his characterization of Strong AI, but apparently thinks any discussion of it is beneath contempt: 'If you are tempted to functionalism, I believe you do not need refutation, you need help' (1992: 9). However, as the important work of Ramsey (1931) and Lewis (1978/83) shows, functionalism is in fact an almost entirely *trivial* view: practically every theory we can think of can be 'ramsified' and the resulting entities regarded as thereby functionally defined. Thus, 'mass', 'charge', 'spin', 'gene' could all be defined in terms of the causal relations specified in the correct scientific theory that employs these terms (hence the title of Lewis's (1983) 'How to Define Theoretical Terms'). Indeed, if, as Searle (1992: 90) suggests, mental phenomena are just 'causal powers of the brain' on the analogy Searle draws to photosynthesis, digestion, or mitosis, he, too, might be a functionalist![12] The question would only be whether the particular powers he has in mind are the ones picked out by CRTT, or some other ones, which he has yet to specify.

In any case, for a functionalist, what's happening 'inside' the head is absolutely crucial to the identification of a mental state. Consequently, the fact that the conversation of the man in the room is outwardly indistinguishable from that of a normal Chinese speaker is of no consequence. The question for

[12] Of course, given that functionalism comes in degrees (see n. 10 above) and that Searle doesn't begin to specify the relevant 'causal powers', it's impossible to assess *how much* of a functionalist he might be. Moreover, as Gabe Segal pointed out to me, the issue also turns here on whether Searle thinks mental phenomena are *constituted* by or are *the product* of 'causal powers', only the former being genuinely functionalist. I would have thought the comparison with, for example, digestion would, however, invite the former—surely *digestion* just *is* a specific process of extracting nutrients from food, and is not merely 'produced' by that process. But the metaphysics of these and related issues is notoriously controversial, and there is no need to press the point here (see my forthcoming *b* for cautions in this regard).

CRTT is rather: is what is happening *inside* the room *functionally*, and more particularly *CRTT*-equivalent to what is happening inside a normal Chinese speaker? Of course, it's not, and no serious defender of CRTT need claim otherwise. And this is because no defender of CRTT need be committed to ignoring the larger issues of language understanding that Searle's example omits. In particular:

2.2 CRTT is not Committed to a Conversation Manual Theory of Language

You don't master French by memorizing one of those little Berlitz conversation manuals, which is pretty much all that Searle imagines the CRTT program providing. Rather, you crucially master at least a *grammar* and a lot of *lexicon*, which together provide a basis for recursive rules of the form 'Φ is true (or correctly assertable) iff p', for French Φ and some (canonical) p that is in whatever language in which the learner thinks, for example, English in Searle's example, a 'language of thought' for most defenders of CRTT.[13] It's these rules that, in one way or another, would have to be made available to programs responsible for whatever conversational abilities of the speaker, and so would have to be accessible to the man in the room.

Although all this already is quite a lot, there's no reason to insist that even it would be enough. Presumably we also need to imagine the person in the room following rules that relate Chinese characters not only to one another, but also to the inputs and outputs of the *other* programs CRTT posits to account for the *other* mental processes and propositional attitudes of a normal Chinese speaker—no one need seriously believe that a competent Chinese speaker is capable *only* of conversing in Chinese! Moreover, as most proponents of CRTT would readily admit, there had better be various kinds of causal connections between internal symbols and external phenomena. Arguably, understanding a language involves being able to relate the symbols of the language to at least *some* perceptions, beliefs, desires, and some sort of dispositions to behave: for example, *ceteris paribus*, to apply the Chinese word for snow to actual samples of snow, to respond with the Chinese word for white when you take yourself to have been asked the color of some snow. The most Searle allows in this regard is that some of the Chinese symbols issue, unbeknownst to the person in the room, from a television camera (1980a: 420 (B76)). There is no allowance whatsoever for the kind of discrimination, or ideal co-variation abilities that many have

---

[13] See Larson and Segal (1995) for a fairly rich sketch of a proposal of this sort.

argued are required for intrinsic content in any system whatsoever (see Sect. 4.2.2 below).

3. Intuitions about a Corrected Case

3.1 A Modest Mind

That the previous two points are the correct diagnosis of the problems with the Chinese Room is shown by considering a version of the example modified along the lines it suggests. This, however, is no simple matter. We have to imagine 'a program' that would capture some of the above basic facts about minds and, although there may be some technical sense in which the computational portion of CRTT might be presented as a 'single program', this would be a quite unnatural way of thinking about it. CRTT follows common sense in regarding the mind as a pretty complicated set of interrelated subsystems of, for example, perception, reasoning, memory, decision-making, language-processing, and motor control, the outputs of many of which are the inputs to others, along the lines of the 'molecular functionalism' emphasized above. It correspondingly posits a battery of different 'programs' for dealing with these different subsystems. Consequently, in modifying Searle's example to accommodate CRTT one has to imagine someone following *a whole set of programs*—but, really, given that we have every reason to think many of them run simultaneously 'in parallel', *quite a number of people*, each one running one of them, with whatever 'master control' (if any) exerted by a normal human being.

To get a handle on such complexity, I tried (in Rey 1997, chs. 8–9) to capture merely a 'Modest Mind' that is a radical simplification of the kind of computational richness that would arguably be needed for a full Chinese understander. Here is a simplification of that simplification.

Imagine that we divide the mind into at least the following subsystems. In order to avoid the appearance of begging any of Searle's questions about intentionality, I will provisionally surround all intentional idioms by stars, indicating that they are to be understood at a *first stage* purely syntactically, and only at a *later stage* semantically: (*a*) *perceptual* systems for transducing *input* into a uniform inner *code*; (*b*) a *reasoning* system that involves *computations* over *representations* in that *code* that instantiate standard forms of *deductive, inductive, and abductive reasoning*; (*c*) a *decision-theoretic system* that determines *basic act descriptions* as a function of *beliefs and preferences*; and

(d) a *natural language processor* that provides for recursive *translation of sentences* in that internal *code* into a given *natural language* along the lines discussed above.

Now, imagine that such a machine were actually programmed in this way and was set loose upon the world. And suppose, amazingly enough, that its designers had solved the host of serious *computational* problems surrounding efficient reasoning sufficiently well that the machine at least *appears* to act intelligently: it *appears* to maximize its expected utilities by modifying its behavior in the light of input, it is able to provide what *seem* like cogent answers to questions and can discriminate the same properties under the same conditions that humans can: for example, it can respond selectively to cats and dogs, princes and paupers, chicken chow mein and egg foo yung—all patently on the basis of the programs the designers had provided. Note that I'm not imagining merely that the machine's *external behavior* appears intelligent; I'm supposing that the patterns of its *internal processing* responsible for that behavior match, for example, formal patterns of induction and abduction that our psychologists propose as the ones human beings actually use, as evidenced by not only what we get right, but what we get wrong, how long it takes us, and even our 'protocols', or intuitive reports of what we do. Note, too, that I'm not saying it would be *easy* to program a machine to succeed in this way—indeed, no one has come near building such a machine. I'm just supposing that the purely *computational* ambitions of CRTT are in fact realized: for it's not those computational ambitions that Searle is challenging. His claim against CRTT is that, even if they were satisfied, the result would not amount to genuine intelligence or understanding.

However, once one imagines this machine in place of the far too simple Chinese Room, it's awfully hard to share Searle's scepticism. We could, of course, regard the machine purely *physically*. But this would lose explanatory generalizations at the computational/syntactic level: why are certain strings of alphanumeric characters produced under such and such circumstances (say, *theorems* of the predicate calculus from the *deductive* system operating alone)? We could also regard it purely *syntactically*, as Searle (1980a) thought we ought to regard the processes in his Chinese Room, and in the way that Stich (1984) thought we ought to do psychology generally. In this case we would have to keep the stars around all the apparently intentional expressions. But here again we would lose explanatory power: why does the machine *believe* only those *hypotheses* for which its input at least *appears* to have supplied patently good *evidence* of their *truth*? Why does it appear to succeed so well in *satisfying* its *preferences*, exhibiting a clear disposition to alter its behavior 'appropriately' with alterations of those *preferences* and its *beliefs*? How is it able to *discriminate* so well all manner of non-local properties (e.g. being a dinosaur bone), as well as non-physical ones (being a noun phrase, or a Rembrandt self-portrait), other than by *confirming* genuine *hypotheses* about what's what?

The important point is that, from an *explanatory* point of view, its intelligent behavior would be *subject to much of the same systematic decomposition, laws, and counterfactuals as a normal Chinese speaker*: for example, it would at least *appear* to add 'by carrying', make predictable inductions from certain kinds of samples, treat English as a 'head first' language, and perhaps even be susceptible to some of our foibles, discounting future for nearer preferences, and occasionally falling for the gambler's fallacy. If all this were so, we would certainly have plenty of reasons to take what Dennett (1978) calls 'the intentional stance' towards the machine: using CRTT, we could systematically predict how it would actually and counterfactually behave in an impressive range of situations. But, *pace* Dennett, I see no reason not to take this stance perfectly seriously.[14] It doesn't merely provide a convenient *façon de parler* that could be replaced by equally good non-intentional talk, as in the case of cars 'wanting' gas or thermostats 'thinking' the room is cold. To the contrary, it seems to capture a level of systematic counterfactual-supporting generalizations that, unlike the case of cars and thermostats, is not replaceable by non-intentional ones. Put aside the formidable task of actually providing a full, 'naturalized' theory of content and semantics. Whether or not such a theory is possible, I submit that it is on the basis of such impressive abilities as the ones I have mentioned that we are ordinarily justified in attributing contentful states to ordinary human beings. I don't see they shouldn't serve as a reasonable basis in the case of this machine as well. We have every good reason to remove the stars and regard the machine's states as genuinely intentional.

Note, again, the contrast with behaviorism. It's a perfectly good objection to someone who claims intelligence for a machine that merely produces intelligent *external behavior*, that it doesn't do it *in the right way*. Thus, Deep Blue hardly counts as an insightful chess player simply because it wins games by running through massive 'brute-force' searches of the game tree; nor does the Chinese

---

[14] I discuss what seems to me Dennett's gratuitous instrumentalism in my (1995) and (1997, § 10.3). It's important to note that the very *possibility* of Dennett's view shows that no question is being begged in citing the evidence of *apparent* semantic phenomena on behalf of the intentionality of this machine (cf. citing the *appearance* that there are material objects as evidence that they really do exist). Note also that these appearances provide an empirically *sufficient* condition for invoking intentionality, not a *necessary* one.

Room count as understanding Chinese simply because it emulates an ordinary conversation. *But once we have mimicked the actual way people do produce their intelligent behavior*, it's hard to see how this objection can still be raised. Either Searle has to provide evidence that the *specific* ways proposed by psychologists and instantiated by the machine aren't in fact the ways people do proceed, or he has to cite some *further* condition that plausibly needs to be met. But what could that condition be? That the machine secrete norepinephrine? Why on earth should that be necessary?

Of course, people are interestingly reluctant to treat *any* artefact as mental—particularly ones made out of plastic and silicon, not to mention beer cans or Block's (1978) whole nation of China. But, apart from the monumental difficulty of actually getting all these alternative materials to do the trick—that is, actually satisfying all the explanatory demands of a CRTT—it's difficult to see in this reaction anything but some kind of prejudice. It's a prejudice that Searle (1980a: 422 (B81–2), 1997: 13–14) professes not to share. So long as the machine has the 'causal powers of the brain' that are responsible for intelligent and intentional processes, it would seem as arbitrary to exclude such a machine from 'understanding Chinese' as it would be for the church fathers to exclude extraterrestrial bodies from Galileo's laws.[15] If Searle is to exclude this machine, one would therefore expect it to be on the basis of specifying some relevant causal power that ordinary people possess that this machine lacks.[16] But what might that be?

To my knowledge, Searle does not specify any such power. He simply presumes that we will have the same intuitions about this machine—and indeed

[15] Searle (1992: 5) complains that such comparisons are made to 'bully' the reader. The serious point of them is to emphasize how theories of ordinary phenomena may well extend the application of ordinary terms beyond what ordinary prejudice would allow.

[16] And, of course, it must be non-tendentious: it won't do merely to claim that people can perform *intentional actions*, but this machine can't. Note that this demand for non-tendentious data can be met by much intentional explanation, despite the simultaneous existence of underlying physical explanations of the same (token) events. There are plenty of physically describable regularities at the level of vision and language, say, between the *types* of inputs the visual system receives (excitation patterns on the retina) and the *types* of outputs a person might produce (say, graphite patterns on a standardized questionnaire) that, as *regularities*, cross-classify physical explanations that might nevertheless be provided for each pair of *token* events. One needs the intentional theory in order to bring out the properties and patterns these diverse physical tokens all share. It is this fact that belies Searle's claim that 'once you understand how [a] . . . visual system *actually works*, the "computational level" is just irrelevant' (1992: 218) (a claim not established merely by citing 'at random' (ibid. 217) a particularly simple case of an edge detector). See especially Marr (1982: 24–5) for a useful discussion of this point in relation to vision, Fodor (1975, ch. 1) for discussion of the point in science generally, and my (1997, §§3.3 and 6.4) for discussion of the issue specifically in the philosophy of mind.

any Turing machine (Searle 1980a: 417 (B67))—as we do about the Chinese Room. But once all these details I have supplied have been specified, it is not at all clear that we do. Indeed, worrying at this point about the psychology of the man/men in the room would seem to involve a blatant fallacy of division, in the following way.

3.2 Searle's Fallacy of Division

It is, of course, true that anything any computer does could 'in principle' be executed by a human being following the rules (although, for most machines, I wouldn't recommend trying). I agree with Searle (1991a: 525–6), as against Fodor (1991: 525), that computations executed by intentional agents are, for all that, still computations. So Searle's wondering whether the person—or, again, people—executing these programs understand Chinese is perfectly legitimate. But there's absolutely no reason for CRTT to claim they do. CRTT is not in the least committed to making rich psychological claims about any of the many people running the various programs in the room. Those people obviously correspond not to the *whole* of the emulated Chinese speaker, but merely to the Central Processing Units (CPUs) of each of the posited subsystems. Indeed, on pain of a familiar regress, CRTT better not be ascribing mental states to them any more than a good physical theory ought to be ascribing, say, valence to the electrons whose relations explain it.

This fallacy was, of course, precisely the complaint of those who defended the 'Systems Reply', the view that it was not the man in the room, but 'the entire room' that ought to be regarded as understanding Chinese. But, of course, if the activity in the room is quite as simple as Searle's original example suggests, it does invite the plausible reply that Searle mounted of having the person in the room merely memorize the program. Once, however, we appreciate the full complexity that a reasonable computational theory of mind proposes, the idea of someone memorizing the programs to all these systems and getting them to run in the right way is, well, pretty hard to imagine and intuitively evaluate. Again, the guy would have to memorize a staggering complexity of programs, the output of many of them being the input to others, which he—alone?— would have to run in parallel, moreover at lightning speed![17] This seems just

---

[17] As I mentioned earlier (Sect. 2.1), although standard presentations of functionalism abstract from the *timing* (both relative and absolute) that different processes take, this is by no means obligatory. A functionalist can cheerfully observe that you don't ordinarily count as 'intelligent' if it takes you six months to solve a problem that takes a normal person only a few seconds!

short of imagining someone memorizing all the contingencies on which neurons might fire in a brain and then executing all the appropriate firings on arrays
of buttons! Indeed, the difference in the latter case between the whole and the
part is so plain that the fallacy of division is readily apparent: the fact that such a
neuron memorizer mightn't understand Chinese is no argument against a
neural theory of Chinese understanding. Why should the case of the modest
(though still pretty complicated) CRTT mind that I have sketched be any different?[18] Of course, in contrast, a person who had merely memorized the programs
for a qualitative state, like pain, would not thereby be in any special position to
experience pain. But here the functionalist response is quite straightforward:
there's no reason whatever to suppose that the functional states of a *pain program
memorizer* are the same as those of *someone actually in pain*. But this raises the further,
complex issues of qualitative states that there's not space to address here.

Indeed, notice that a puzzle arises here *even on Searle's own account.* Consider
the normal human being in Searle's Chinese Room who has memorized all the
rules: presumably he *does* possess the requisite biological structure and is embedded in the usual social 'background' of a normal human being, yet, according
to Searle, he *still* doesn't understand Chinese. *If neither the biology nor the program
nor the background together, are sufficient, what more for Searle is needed?* Perhaps it's that
these are not all put together in the 'right way'. Fine; that's just what the functionalist claims, and why she then amends the example along the lines I have
suggested. Searle now needs to say what's wrong with the specific ways—the
specific 'causal powers'—that the CRTT theorist proposes.

So much, it seems to me, for Searle's example of the Chinese Room, and its
intuitive force. I turn now to his own diagnoses of the example. Although
I think his diagnoses are mistaken, they might be thought to offer reasons
independent of the example for rejecting CRTT. They do not.

4. Philosophical Issues

Searle originally diagnosed the trouble with the Chinese Room and CRTT
in terms of issues about semantics. More recently, however, he has raised a

---

[18] Notice, though, that a person who really had memorized all the above CRTT sub-programs
would certainly be *in a pretty good position* to tell you what Chinese sentences mean: aside from the
weird 'dissociation' he might feel between 'his own' spontaneous reactions and the memorized
programs, he would be able to sketch some of the recursive syntax and truth-conditions for Chinese
sentences better than average Chinese speakers can, and he could tell you lots about the lexicon as
well ('squiggle squoggle' is a name for ginger beef, etc.).

problem even about syntax and computation by themselves. I'll treat this more recent argument first and then return to issues surrounding semantics.

4.1 Intrinsic versus Observer-Relative Properties

Searle (1992) argues that even supposing there are algorithmic manipulations of *syntax* in a machine presupposes *someone else's* intentionality. One argument he offers on behalf of this view is the following:

1. Computation is defined syntactically in terms of symbol manipulation.
2. Syntax and symbols are not defined in terms of physics . . . Syntax, in short, is not intrinsic to physics.
3. This has the consequence that computation is not discovered in the physics, it is assigned to it. Certain physical phenomena are used or programmed or interpreted syntactically. Syntax and symbols are observer-relative (Searle 1992: 225).

But the step from 2 to 3 is a blatant *non sequitur*. There are, of course, complex issues about what counts as definability—it's not at all clear that syntax couldn't also be defined physically by ramsification (see n. 10). But, however that is to be settled, the fact that certain categories are not definable in a particular theory, say, physics, doesn't for a moment imply that the category is observer-relative. There are standard examples from logic.[19] More intuitively, many categories of the macro-sciences (being a species, being an eco-system) may not be definable or reducible to *physics* without there being the slightest reason to think they are observer-relative. Indeed, one wonders what the two issues have to do with one another. It would only follow *if the reason for the undefinability had to do with observer-relativity*, as, say, in the case of secondary properties; but to suppose this here would, of course, be to beg the question at issue.

Another argument Searle offers for the same claim arises from a misunderstanding of the familiar 'multiple realizability' associated with CRTT. He writes:

On the standard textbook definition of computation, it is hard to see how to avoid [claiming that:] for any object there is some description of that object such that under that description the object is a digital computer . . . Thus, for example, the wall behind my back is right now implementing the WordStar program, because there is some pattern of molecule movements that is isomorphic with the formal structure of WordStar. (1992: 208–9)

---

[19] Let physics include Tarski's theory of real numbers: 'x is a natural number' could not be defined in it on pain of contradiction (see Quine 1953: 131). But this doesn't imply for a moment that *being a natural number* is somehow 'observer-relative'.

Now, of course, were CRTT committed to such a liberal understanding of realizability, then either it would be committed to wanton panpsychism, or more plausibly, it would understand CRTT to be somehow dependent upon how a person cares to understand some part of the world, and so 'upon an interpretation from outside' (ibid. 209) (a view, to be sure, that has been defended by Dennett 1978 and Davidson 1984).

However, this understanding of multiple realizability ignores a number of constraints any reasonable version of CRTT places upon its application to the real world. In the first place, some kind of constraints are obviously needed on the mapping of *any* theory to the world. There's no doubt *some* mapping of, say, an economic theory to states of a stone, or of a biological theory to states of a star, but that doesn't *ipso facto* make a stone an economy, or a star a living thing. I don't have a general account of what the appropriate mapping constraints might be, but the following observations should suffice for the nonce:

1. CRTT is not just a hypothesis about the mapping of an abstract automaton description onto people, but a claim that a certain natural mapping provides the basis of *explanations* of *counterfactual-supporting* regularities not otherwise explained—as noted in Section 3.1 above, for example, why people—and my modest mental machine—seem to produce theorems of logic; why they are disposed to move in ways that systematically seem to satisfy their preferences. Such (NB counterfactual-supporting) regularities are simply not available in the case of an arbitrary wall.

2. As we also noted above, CRTT is plausibly a *molecular* and *anchored* functionalism, which defines mental states not all *at once* and merely *among themselves*, but in terms of various subsystems and in relation to an indefinite number of states picked out by other, what Lewis (1978/83) calls '*o*-terms' (see n. 10 above) that pick out other non-mental constraints that might be part of a genuinely explanatory psychology. Thus, for example, CRTT reasonably posits a visual subsystem, the relevant functional states of which may need to be identified in part by physical features of our retinas, and perhaps a natural language subsystem whose semantics depends upon relations to the immediate or evolutionary environment. These are subsystems and relations presumably not available in the case of an arbitrary wall.

3. Indeed, once one bears in mind the kind of architectural complexities posited by a reasonable CRTT, then serious questions arise about the computational architecture of the specific abstract machine—or, again, machines— invoked in the explanation. As David Chalmers (1996) has emphasized in a

trenchant reply to Putnam's (1988: 122–5) rather more detailed version of Searle's claim, a Finite State Automaton, for example, may fail to capture the rich 'compositional' architecture of a mind. Chalmers suggests it might be more closely captured by what he defines as a 'combinatorial state automaton' (CSA), whose states have combinatorial structure:

An implementation of a CSA is required to consist in a complex causal interaction among a number of separate parts. Not only do states have to be subdivisible, but the many state-transition conditionals imply that the system must have finegrained causal structure that an implementation of the corresponding FSA [Finite State Automaton] might well lack. (Chalmers 1996: 325)

Chalmers argues convincingly that 'this imposes a constrained structure of dependencies on the system that arbitrary systems have no hope of passing' (ibid. 326). And, of course, again, it would be surprising if merely a single CSA were enough: for the reasons already discussed, a mind would plausibly need a complex system of such machines, arranged to interact in very specific ways, frequently in parallel.

To make his mapping argument effective, Searle needs to show that there would still be physical systems satisfying all these further reasonable constraints that still are *not* minds.[20] Why should we think there are?

Perhaps Searle is misled by the fact that someone could, for some specific purpose and stretch of time, *treat* an arbitrary wall as realizing some computer program, much as I can treat a red flag as a stop sign, or a collection of stones as an adding machine. Such applications are instances of *derived* intentionality, which, as I mentioned at the start, while common in practicing 'AI', are irrelevant to CRTT. It is perhaps these applications that have given rise to an unfortunate phrasing common in the literature, whereby the theorist talks of the semantic assignment he or she *makes* in the explanation, and of 'interpreted' or 'semantic evaluations'. Thus, Searle quotes Pylyshyn (1984: 58): 'The answer to the question what computation is being performed requires discussion of semantically interpreted computational states', to which Searle replies: 'Indeed. And who is doing the interpreting?' (1992: 253 n. 4). But, again, the issue is not one of finding an interpreter for a bit of the world that could be *used* as a machine, but, as in the rest of science, of making *an inference to the best explanation*. Just as the planetary system presents us with counterfactual-supporting regularities that cannot be explained except by supposing the planets have specific masses, so, I argued in Section 3.1 above, do people and my modest machine present us with such regularities that cannot be explained except by supposing a specific interpretation.

4.2 Syntax and Semantics

4.2.1 *Specifiability versus Possession*

Searle's original diagnosis of the Chinese Room example and of the problem with CRTT was that the processes being described are 'purely syntactic'. Indeed:

The symbols have no meaning; they have no semantic content; they are not about anything. They have to be specified purely in terms of their formal or syntactical structure. The zeros and ones, for example, are just numerals; they don't even stand for numbers. . . . But this feature of programs, that they are defined purely formally or syntactically, is fatal to the view that mental processes and program processes are identical. And the reason can be stated quite simply. There is more to having a mind than having formal or syntactical processes. (Searle 1984: 31)

Now, while it's true that programs are defined syntactically, and that the relation between hardware and programs is many–many, *none of this implies that the syntactic objects manipulated by programs do not in fact have a semantics*—any more than from the fact that Newton's laws are stated only in terms of the *mass* and not the *weight* of an object, should one conclude that objects don't *have* weight (the analogy is particularly apt, since many people think that meaning, like weight, arises from (dispositional) relations a system bears to its environment). This point is missed so often,[21] it bears repeating: *the syntactically specifiable objects over which computations are defined can and standardly do possess a semantics; it's just that the semantics is not involved in the specification.*

4.2.2 *'Syntax is not Sufficient for Semantics'*

A different claim that Searle often makes in the same breath is that no computer program could be a mind since 'syntax is not sufficient for semantics' (1984: 39). This raises a more complex issue than can be treated fully here. Suffice it to say that no defender of CRTT need claim that syntax determines semantics, or that

---

[21] Thus, Rock (1991: 321) in his commentary on Searle mistakenly acquiesces to the view that 'whereas computer programs are by definition purely syntactical, the symbols they are manipulating have no meaning'.

a program *alone* would constitute a mind.[22] The reasonable proposal being pursued by CRTT is that states of a person have semantic properties by virtue of their computational organization *and* their causal relations to the world. These may be (i) direct causal relations, as in the views of Kripke and Devitt; (ii) social relations, as in Burge; (iii) historical selectional facts, as in the work of Millikan, Papineau, and Neander; (iv) various dispositions to co-variation, as in Stampe, Dretske, and Fodor; (v) combinations of the above, as in Loar, Block, and Peacocke.[23] This is not to suggest that any of these proposals are in fact adequate, or even that anyone seriously thinks they are. Brentano's problem of intentionality is every bit as alive today as it was a century ago.[24] But all of these proposals enjoy significant motivation and represent some serious advances on the topic.

Surprisingly, Searle has little to say about the relation of any of this rather large body of work to Strong AI, except to be shortly dismissive of it (1980*b*/91: 523 and 1992: 50–1).[25] These naturalistic accounts

will all fail for reasons that I hope by now are obvious. They will leave out the subjectivity of mental content. By way of technical objections there will be counterexamples . . . and the counterexamples will be met with gimmicks—nomological relations, and counterfactuals, or so I would predict—but the most you could hope from the gimmicks . . . would be a parallelism between the output of the gimmick and intuitions about mental content. You would still not get at the essence of mental content. (Searle 1992: 50)

I'm not quite sure how one establishes the essence of mental content other than by theorizing in the ways these authors do, but, in any case, in so far as verdicts about CRTT rely on intuitions about such examples as the Chinese Room,

---

[22] Actually, the issue of whether or not syntactic facts can determine semantic ones is a lot more complex than Searle recognizes. Even in logic, there are differences about how this might be understood, depending upon whether one is considering a first- or second-order theory. In psychology, there are some semantic theorists who advocate a purely 'conceptual' or 'functional' role account of meaning, and some of these theorists might also subscribe to CRTT. But some might not. For simplicity, I will ignore these issues and grant Searle the general point.

[23] See my (1997, ch. 9) for references and discussion.

[24] I might mention some sympathy with Searle's impatience with *some* far too facile use of representational talk. As I argue in detail in Rey (forthcoming *a*), it is by no means clear that Chomsky is entitled to the notorious claims he makes in this regard, an issue on which I think Searle (1990*b*) was quite right to press him.

[25] In his (1983, chs. 8–9) he does address straight causal views (such as Kripke's and Devitt's) in considerable detail. Some might actually feel there is some tension between his defense of 'internal' descriptive theories there and his denial in these AI discussions that syntax determines semantics.

Searle owes us some examination of the 'gimmicks' and whether or not they might well reverse the intuitions he claims we would have.[26]

But what of 'subjectivity'? Why is Searle so convinced CRTT couldn't account for it? His reasons have to do with a specific aspect of meaning he discusses, 'aspectual shape'.

4.3 Aspectual Shape

A particular problem about meaning that has received enormous attention at least since Frege, is what's often called the problem of the intensionality (with an 's') of the intentional (with a 't'): intentional, that is, 'aboutness', phenomena seem often to be intensional, that is, not individuatable by reference to merely real-world extensions alone. Thus, the thought that water is wet is different from the thought that H_2O is, despite the fact that 'water' and 'H_2O' have the same extension. This is the phenomenon Searle calls 'aspectual shape'.[27]

Now, actually, CRTT goes some way towards quite naturally explaining this phenomenon (indeed, the phenomenon supplies one of the standard arguments for it). According to CRTT, a child ignorant of chemistry wants 'water' in a glass, where the chemist wants H_2O, since the chemist, but not the child, has thoughts about hydrogen and oxygen that are *causal constituents* of a representation expressing her desire. Why think this? For starters, presumably because the chemist, but not the child, can *distinguish* hydrogen and oxygen, behaving in ways that are sensitive to the distinction; and we may suppose, on the present hypothesis, that she does it by using the very same representations throughout. We can, as it were, spell it out: someone who is thinking H_2O is wet is someone who is thinking a thought that has as causally efficacious constituents something very like 'H', '2', 'O', 'is', and 'wet'; whereas someone who only thinks *water* is, is thinking something that is spelt more simply.[28] This is not to say that no problems remain. Bealer (1984) and Gates (1996) have nicely reformulated

---

[26] It's actually not clear that Searle understands the bearing of these theories on CRTT. He writes: 'in the case of Fodor . . . the question whether or not the internal representations have to be *grasped* cannot even arise' (1991*b*: 291). This would certainly be news to Fodor, who has written more than four books on the topic in the last dozen years alone!

[27] I must confess to being mystified as to why Searle uses this new term, and whether it is supposed to signal some difference from standard discussions of intensions and/or Fregean 'senses'.

[28] Notice, by the way, that this view not only accounts for the intensionality of intentional states, but for their characteristic 'hyper-intensionality', or their distinguishability even in cases of *necessary* co-extension (as arguably in the case of believing water is wet and believing H_2O is).

Quine's (1960) 'gavagai' problem in the context of functionalist theories. Gates aims specifically at Fodor's (1990) proposals. However, as Fodor's (1994, ch. 3) reply suggests, it is by no means clear that all the resources of functionalism have been exhausted. Of course, Searle needn't *believe* this story of constituent causation. All that CRTT need claim is that it is a *possible* story of the intensionality of intentionality.

Without any exploration of functionalist resources, Searle claims that distinctions of aspectual shape could only be drawn introspectively: 'Our intentional states often have determinate intentional contents with determinate aspectual shapes . . . But all of that presupposes consciousness' (1992: 164).[29] This is one of his main arguments for his 'Connection Principle': 'all unconscious intentional states are in principle accessible to consciousness' (1992: 156).

A discussion of this principle is beyond the needs of the present chapter.[30] Quite apart, however, from whether consciousness is somehow required for mentation, a deeper problem for Searle is how it is supposed to be of any help. If there were no 'objective' way to draw intensional distinctions, I don't see how there could then be any 'subjective' ways either. Declaring that by 'rabbit' you mean rabbit and by 'rabbithood' rabbithood seems no better than declaring that you know how tall you are by placing your hand on your head to prove it (cf. Wittgenstein 1953, § 279). Suffice it to say that, even if the principle were true, Searle would need to show that the relevant first-person introspectible consciousness wouldn't be available within the resources of CRTT. For example, there's no reason that CRTT couldn't posit special first-person reflexive pronouns in an internal code that would play computational roles like the 'essentially indexical' roles that such pronouns play in natural language (distinguishing, e.g., the thought 'I am ill' from the thought 'GR is ill'; see my 1997, § 11.2.1). And it might then posit specific computational relations underlying introspection that made many of particularly these 'first-person' representations available in certain memory buffers standardly available to verbal report (cf. Dennett 1978). Before Searle deploys the Connection

---

[29] As Bealer (1984: 328) put it in his own ingenious discussion of the 'gavagai' problem mentioned in the previous footnote, 'we know from within'.

[30] I'm actually not clear what the principle comes to. Everyone can agree that *any* propositional attitude that an agent can understand can be *thought* consciously, for example, if she is asked. Presumably what Searle has in mind is that it must be thinkable *while* it is had, indeed, as the *result* of having it—indeed, as the right sort of result of having it (it can't be enough that it be had as a result of Chomsky or a psychotherapist convincing her of it!). However, the more qualifications that are added to give the principle substance, the harder it is to see why anyone should believe it. I offer other criticisms in my (1991).

Principle or first-person perspectives against CRTT, he needs—yet again—to consider its substantial resources for dealing with them.

5. Conclusion

Indeed, that is the problem we have seen repeatedly about Searle's discussion: he simply does not consider the substantial resources of functionalism and Strong AI, and how those resources might produce much more plausible candidates for intentional states than his simple Chinese Room. At root, I think this is because (as we saw in Sect. 2.1) he considers only a version of functionalism that is a technical variant of behaviorism, and consequently thinks that standard objections against the latter suffice against the former. As I have tried to show in this and my earlier work, this simply won't do. Functionalism and Strong AI, specifically CRTT, can provide fairly intricate hypotheses about the structure of thought and linguistic processing that go well beyond the mere 'conversation manual' program that might pass a mere behavioristic Turing Test. In any event, I hoped it should be clear that, *pace* Searle's (1980a: 418 (B70)) claims with which we began, the appropriate computer programs could indeed make very significant contributions to a theory of human understanding.

None of what I have said here should be taken to imply that CRTT is all smooth sailing, and that the creation of such a machine as intelligent as ourselves is right around the corner. There are plenty of quite deep problems with global confirmation, memory retrieval, the details of perception, and semantic processing.[31] CRTT is a *research program*, rendered plausible and worthwhile by the success of the specific work on, for example, vision, language understanding and production, memory, attention, decision-making and navigation that is undertaken with it in mind.[32] It begins to provide a way of replying to the substantial challenges raised by (among others) Descartes and Brentano to the possibility of providing any sort of physical explanation of mental processes. Here Searle's (1992: 1) own insistence on materialism, while perfectly correct, is simply inadequate. It's not enough to observe, as philosophers at least since Hobbes and Priestley have observed, that the mental is some sort of manifestation of the physical. One has to make this seem *explanatorily plausible*. This is what

---

[31] See Fodor (1983, part IV) and (2000) for the expression of considerable pessimism in this regard.

[32] See Osherson (1995–8) for excellent recent summaries of much of this work. I discuss CRTT's status as a research program in my (forthcoming *b*).

CRTT tries to do. Instead of dismissing CRTT across the board, Searle should join in this rich effort to try to provide a genuinely explanatory account of intelligence, intentionality, and perhaps ultimately of mental phenomena in general.[33]

References

BEALER, G. (1984) 'Mind and Anti-Mind', *Midwest Studies in Philosophy, Volume 9* (Minneapolis: University of Minnesota Press), 283–328.

BLOCK, N. J. (1978) 'Troubles with Functionalism', in C. Wade Savage (ed.), *Perception and Cognition: Issues in the Foundations of Psychology* (Minneapolis: University of Minnesota Press), 261–325.

—— (1980) 'Introduction: What is Functionalism?' in N. J. Block (ed.), *Readings in Philosophy of Psychology, Volume I* (London: Methuen), 268–305.

BODEN, M. A. (ed.) (1990) *The Philosophy of Artificial Intelligence* (Oxford: Oxford University Press).

CHALMERS, D. J. (1996) 'Does a Rock Implement Every Finite-State Automaton?' *Synthese*, 108: 309–33.

DAVIDSON, D. (1984) *Inquiries into Truth and Interpretation* (Oxford: Oxford University Press).

DAVIES, M. (1991) 'Concepts, Connectionism, and the Language of Thought', in W. Ramsey, S. P. Stich, and D. E. Rumelhart (eds.), *Philosophy and Connectionist Theory* (Hillsdale, NJ: Lawrence Erlbaum Associates), 229–57.

DENNETT, D. C. (1978) *Brainstorms* (Cambridge, Mass.: MIT Press/Bradford Books).

FODOR, J. A. (1975) *The Language of Thought* (Sussex: Harvester Press).

—— (1983) *The Modularity of Mind* (Cambridge, Mass.: MIT Press).

—— (1980/91) 'Searle on What Only Brains Can Do', *Behavioral and Brain Sciences*, 3 (1980), 431–2. Reprinted in D. M. Rosenthal (ed.), *The Nature of Mind* (Oxford: Oxford University Press, 1991), 520–1.

—— (1990) *A Theory of Content and Other Essays* (Cambridge, Mass.: MIT Press).

—— (1991) 'Afterthoughts: Yin and Yang in the Chinese Room', in D. M. Rosenthal (ed.), *The Nature of Mind* (Oxford: Oxford University Press), 524–5.

—— (1994) *The Elm and the Expert*, (Cambridge, Mass.: MIT Press).

—— (2000) *The Mind Doesn't Work That Way: The Scope and Limits of Computational Psychology* (Cambridge, Mass.: MIT Press).

GATES, G. (1996) 'The Price of Information', *Synthese*, 107: 325–47.

---

[33] In this connection it is worth noting that Searle's own (1983) suggestions about the role of 'causal self-referentiality' in the 'representations' of the content of various intentional states are ones to which a CRTT might be entirely hospitable.

LARSON, R., and SEGAL, G. (1995) *Knowledge of Meaning* (Cambridge, Mass.: MIT Press).

LEWIS, D. (1980) 'Psychophysical and Theoretical Identifications', *Australasian Journal of Philosophy*, 50: 249–58; 1st pub. 1972.

—— (1983) 'How to Define Theoretical Terms', in his *Philosophical Papers, Volume 1* (Oxford: Oxford University Press), 78–95; 1st pub. 1978.

Lycan, W. (1987) *Consciousness* (Cambridge, Mass.: MIT Press).

—— (1993) 'A Deductive Argument for the Language of Thought', *Mind and Language*, 8: 404–22.

MALONEY, J. (1989) *The Mundane Matter of the Mental Language* (Cambridge: Cambridge University Press).

MARR, D. (1982) *Vision: A Computational Investigation into the Human Representation and Processing of Visual Information* (San Francisco: Freeman).

NISBETT, R., and WILSON, T. (1977) 'On Saying More than We Can Know', *Psychological Review*, 84: 231–59.

OSHERSON, D. (1995–8) *An Invitation to Cognitive Science*, 4 vols., (Cambridge, Mass.: MIT Press).

PUTNAM, H. (1988) *Representation and Reality* (Cambridge, Mass.: MIT Press).

PYLYSHYN, Z. (1984) *Computation and Cognition: Toward a Foundation for Cognitive Science* (Cambridge, Mass.: MIT Press).

QUINE, W. (1953) 'Notes on the Theory of Reference', in his *From a Logical Point of View and Other Essays* (New York: Harper and Row), 130–9.

—— *Word and Object* (Cambridge, Mass.: MIT Press).

RAMSEY, F. P. (1931) 'Theories', in his *The Foundations of Mathematics*, R. B. Braithwaite (ed.) (London: Routledge and Kegan Paul).

REY, G. (1986) 'What's Really Going On in Searle's "Chinese Room" ', *Philosophical Studies*, 50: 169–85.

—— (1990) 'Constitutive Causation and The Reality of Mind', commentary on John Searle, 'Consciousness, Explanatory Inversion, and Cognitive Science', *Behavioral and Brain Sciences*, 13: 620–1.

—— (1992) 'Sensational Sentences Switched', *Philosophical Studies*, 67: 73–103.

—— (1994) 'Dennett's Unrealistic Psychology', *Philosophical Topics*, 22: 259–89.

—— (1995) 'A Not "Merely Empirical" Argument for the Language of Thought', in J. Tomberlin (ed.), *Philosophical Perspectives, Volume 9* (Atascadero, Calif.: Ridgeview Press), 201–22.

—— (1997) *Contemporary Philosophy of Mind: A Contentiously Classical Approach* (Oxford: Blackwell).

—— (1998) 'A Narrow Representational Account of Qualitative Experience', in J. Tomberlin (ed.), *Philosophical Perspectives, Volume 12: Language, Mind and Ontology* (Atascadero, Calif.: Ridgeview Press), 435–57.

—— (forthcoming *a*) 'Chomsky, Intentionality and a CRTT', to appear in L. Antony and N. Hornstein (eds.), *Chomsky and his Critics*, (Oxford: Blackwell).

—— (forthcoming *b*) 'Physicalism and Psychology: A Plea for Substantive Philosophy of Mind', to appear in C. Gillet and B. Loewer (eds.), *Physicalism and its Discontents* (Cambridge: Cambridge University Press).

Rock, I. (1991) 'On Explanation in Psychology', in E. Lepore and R. van Gulick (eds.), *John Searle and his Critics* (Oxford: Blackwell), 311–22.

Searle, J. R. (1980*a*) 'Minds, Brains and Programs', *Behavioral and Brain Sciences*, 3: 417–24. Reprinted in Boden 1990.

—— (1980*b*/91) 'Intrinsic Intentionality: Reply to Criticisms of "Minds, Brains and Programs" ', *Behavioral and Brain Sciences*, 3: 450–56. Reprinted in D. M. Rosenthal (ed.), *The Nature of Mind* (Oxford: Oxford University Press, 1991), 521–3 (references are to this reprint).

—— (1980*c*) 'Rules and Causation', *Behavioral and Brain Sciences*, 3: 37–8.

—— (1983) *Intentionality: An Essay in the Philosophy of Mind* (Cambridge: Cambridge University Press).

—— (1984) *Minds, Brains and Science* (Cambridge, Mass.: Harvard University Press).

—— (1987) 'Indeterminacy, Empiricism and the First-Person', *Journal of Philosophy*, 84: 123–46.

—— (1990*a*) 'Consciousness, Explanatory Inversion, and Cognitive Science', *Behavioral and Brain Sciences*, 13: 585–96.

—— (1990*b*) 'Who is Computing with the Brain?' *Behavioral and Brain Sciences*, 13: 632–40.

—— (1991*a*) 'Yin and Yang Strike Out', in D. M. Rosenthal (ed.), *The Nature of Mind* (Oxford: Oxford University Press), 525–6.

—— (1991*b*) 'Response: The Background of Intentionality and Action', in E. LePore and R. van Gulick (eds.), *John Searle and his Critics* (Oxford: Blackwell), 289–99.

—— (1992) *The Rediscovery of the Mind* (Cambridge, Mass.: MIT Press).

—— (1997) *The Mystery of Consciousness* (New York: New York Review of Books).

Sellars, W. (1956) 'Empiricism and the Philosophy of Mind', in H. Feigl and M. Scriven (eds.), *Minnesota Studies in the Philosophy of Science, Volume 1: The Foundations of Science and the Concepts of Psychology and Psychoanalysis* (Minneapolis: University of Minnesota Press).

Stich, S. (1984) *From Folk Psychology to Cognitive Science: The Case against Belief* (Cambridge, Mass.: MIT Press).

Wittgenstein, L. (1914–16) *Notebooks 1914–16*, 2nd edn., ed. G. H. von Wright and G. E. M. Anscombe, trans. G. E. M. Anscombe (Chicago: University of Chicago Press, 1979).

—— (1953) *Philosophical Investigations* (New York: Macmillan).

12

Consciousness, Computation, and the Chinese Room

Roger Penrose

1. Strong AI and Searle's Chinese Room

I shall begin by recalling what I perceive to be the four polarities of viewpoint that I enunciated in *Shadows of the Mind* (Penrose 1994: 12) with regard to the relationship between conscious thought and computation:

(**A**) All thinking is computation; in particular, feelings of conscious awareness are evoked merely by the carrying out of appropriate computations.

(**B**) Awareness is a feature of the brain's physical action; and whereas any
physical action can be simulated computationally, computational
simulation cannot by itself evoke awareness.

(**C**) Appropriate physical action of the brain evokes awareness, but this
physical action cannot even be properly simulated computationally.

(**D**) Awareness cannot be explained in physical, computational, or any
other scientific terms.

Viewpoint **A** has been termed *Strong AI* (strong artificial intelligence) by John Searle,[1] and his famous *Chinese Room* Argument is designed to refute it. He refers to **B** as *Weak AI*, which is the viewpoint that he himself favours. According to Strong AI, not only would computer-controlled robots indeed be intelligent

---

[1] The term 'functionalism' is frequently used for what is essentially the same viewpoint, but
perhaps not always so specifically related to computation. Some proponents of this kind of view are
Minsky (1968), Hofstadter (1979), and Moravec (1989).

and have minds, etc., but mental qualities of a sort can be attributed to the logical functioning of *any* computational device, even the very simplest mechanical ones, such as a thermostat.[2] The idea is that mental activity is simply the carrying out of some well-defined sequence of operations, frequently referred to as an *algorithm* (see e.g. Penrose 1989 for an explicit definition). It will be adequate to define an algorithm simply as a calculational procedure of some kind. In the case of a thermostat, the algorithm is extremely simple: the device registers whether the temperature is greater or smaller than the setting, and then it arranges that the circuit be disconnected in the former case and connected in the latter. For any significant kind of mental activity of a human brain, the algorithm would have to be something vastly more complicated but, according to viewpoint **A** (Strong AI), an algorithm nevertheless. It would differ very greatly in degree from the simple algorithm of the thermostat, but need not differ in principle. Thus, according to **A**, the difference between the essential functioning of a human brain (including all its conscious manifestations) and that of a thermostat lies only in this much greater *complication* (or perhaps 'higher-order structure' or 'self-referential properties', or some other attribute that one might assign to an algorithm) in the case of a brain. Most importantly, all mental qualities—thinking, feeling, intelligence, understanding, consciousness—are to be regarded, according to this view, merely as aspects of this complicated functioning; that is to say, they are features merely of the *algorithm* being carried out by the brain.

The virtue of any specific algorithm would lie in its performance, namely in the accuracy of its results, its scope, its economy, and the speed with which it can be operated. An algorithm purporting to match what is presumed to be operating in a human brain would need to be a stupendous thing. But if an algorithm of this kind exists for the brain—and the supporters of **A** (and even of **B**) would certainly claim that it does—then it could in principle be run on a computer. Indeed it could be run on *any* modern general-purpose electronic computer, were it not for limitations of storage space and speed of operation. It is anticipated that any such limitations would be overcome for the large fast computers of the not-too-distant future. In that eventuality, such an algorithm, if it could be found, would presumably 'pass the Turing Test' in the sense that it could converse with a human interrogator just as a human might. The supporters of **A** (and *not* **B**) would claim that whenever the algorithm were run it would, *in itself*: experience feelings; have a consciousness; be a mind.

---

[2] See Searle (1987: 211), for an example of such a claim.

By no means everyone would be in agreement that mental states and algorithms can be identified with one another in this kind of way. In particular, Searle (1980, 1987) has strongly disputed that view. He has cited examples where simplified versions of the Turing Test have actually *already* been passed by an appropriately programmed computer, but he gives strong arguments to support the view that the relevant mental attribute of understanding is, nevertheless, entirely absent. One such example is based on a computer program designed by Roger Schank (Schank and Abelson 1977). The aim of the program is to provide a simulation of the understanding of simple stories like: 'A man went into a restaurant and ordered a hamburger. When the hamburger arrived it was burned to a crisp, and the man stormed out of the restaurant angrily, without paying the bill or leaving a tip.' For a second example: 'A man went into a restaurant and ordered a hamburger; when the hamburger came he was very pleased with it; and as he left the restaurant he gave the waitress a large tip before paying his bill'. As a test of 'understanding' of the stories, the computer is asked whether the man ate the hamburger in each case (a fact which had not been explicitly mentioned in either story). To this kind of simple story and simple question the computer can give answers which are essentially indistinguishable from the answers an English-speaking human being would give, namely, for these particular examples, 'no' in the first case and 'yes' in the second. So in this *very* limited sense a machine has already passed a Turing Test!

The question that we must consider is whether this kind of success actually indicates any genuine understanding on the part of the computer—or, perhaps, on the part of the program itself. Searle's argument that it does *not* is to invoke his concept of a 'Chinese Room'. He envisages first of all, that the stories are to be told in Chinese rather than English—surely an inessential change—and that all the operations of the computer's algorithm for this particular exercise are supplied (in English) as a set of instructions for manipulating counters with Chinese symbols on them. Searle imagines *himself* doing all the manipulations inside a locked room. The sequences of symbols representing the stories, and then the questions, are fed into the room through some small slot. No other information whatever is allowed in from the outside. Finally, when all the manipulations are complete, the resulting sequence is fed out again through the slot. Since all these manipulations are simply carrying out the algorithm of Schank's program, it must turn out that this final resulting sequence is simply the Chinese for 'yes' or 'no', as the case may be, giving the correct answer to the original question in Chinese about a story in Chinese. Now Searle makes it quite clear that he doesn't understand a word of Chinese, so he would not have the faintest idea what the stories are about. Nevertheless, by correctly carrying out the series of operations which constitute Schank's algorithm (the instructions for this algorithm having been given to him in English) he would be able to do as well as a Chinese person who would indeed understand the stories. Searle's point—and I think it is quite a powerful one—is that the mere carrying out of a successful algorithm does *not* in itself imply that any understanding has taken place. The (imagined) Searle, locked in his Chinese Room, would not understand a single word of any of the stories!

A number of objections have been raised against Searle's argument. I shall mention only those that I regard as being of serious significance. In the first place, there is perhaps something rather misleading in the phrase 'not understand a single word', as used above. Understanding has as much to do with patterns as with individual words. While carrying out algorithms of this kind, one might well begin to perceive something of the patterns that the symbols make without understanding the actual meanings of many of the individual symbols. For example, the Chinese character for 'hamburger' (if, indeed, there is such a thing) could be replaced by that for some other dish, say 'chow mein', and the stories would not be significantly affected. Nevertheless, it seems to me to be reasonable to suppose that in fact very little of the stories' actual meanings (even regarding such replacements as being unimportant) would come through if one merely kept following through the details of such an algorithm.

In the second place, one must take into account the fact that the execution of even a rather simple computer program would normally be something extraordinarily lengthy and tedious if carried out by human beings manipulating symbols. (This is, after all, why we have computers to do such things for us!) If Searle were actually to perform Schank's algorithm in the way suggested, he would be likely to be involved with many days, months, or years of extremely boring work in order to answer just a single question—not an altogether plausible activity for a philosopher! However, this does not seem to me to be a serious objection since we are here concerned with matters of *principle* and not with practicalities. The difficulty arises more with a putative computer program which is supposed to have sufficient complication to match a human brain and thus to pass the Turing Test *proper*. Any such program would have to be horrendously complicated. One can imagine that the operation of this program, in order to effect the reply to even some rather simple Turing-Test question, might involve so many steps that there would be no possibility of any single human being carrying out the algorithm by hand within a normal human lifetime. Whether this would indeed be the case is hard to say, in the absence of such a program.[3] But, in any case, this question of extreme complication cannot, in my opinion, simply be ignored. It is true that we are concerned with matters of principle here, but it is not inconceivable to me that there might be some 'critical' amount of complication in an algorithm which it is necessary to achieve in order that the algorithm exhibit mental qualities. Perhaps this critical value is so large that no algorithm, complicated to that degree, could conceivably be carried out by hand by any human being, in the manner envisaged by Searle.

Searle himself has countered this last objection by allowing a whole team of human non-Chinese-speaking symbol manipulators to replace the previous single inhabitant ('himself') of his Chinese Room. To get the numbers large enough, he even imagines replacing his room by the whole of India, its entire population (excluding those who understand Chinese!) being now engaged in symbol manipulation. Though this would be in practice absurd, it is not *in principle* absurd, and the argument is essentially the same as before: the symbol manipulators do *not* understand the story, despite the Strong AI claim that the mere carrying out of the appropriate algorithm would elicit the mental quality of understanding. However, now another objection begins to loom large. Are not these individual Indians more like the individual neurons in a person's brain than like the whole brain itself? No one would suggest that neurons, whose firings apparently constitute the physical activity of a brain in the act of thinking, would *themselves* individually understand what that person is thinking, so why expect the individual Indians to understand the Chinese stories? Searle replies to this suggestion by pointing out the apparent absurdity of India, the actual country, understanding a story that none of its individual inhabitants understands. A country, he argues, like a thermostat or an automobile, is not in the 'business of understanding', whereas an individual person is.

This argument has a good deal less force to it than the earlier one. I think that Searle's argument is at its strongest when there is just a single person carrying out the algorithm, where we restrict attention to the case of an algorithm which is sufficiently uncomplicated for a person actually to carry it out in less than a lifetime. I do *not* regard his argument as *rigorously* establishing that there is

---

[3] In his criticism of Searle's original paper (as reprinted in Hofstadter and Dennett 1981), Hofstadter complains that no human being could conceivably 'internalize' the entire description of another human being's mind, owing to the complication involved. Indeed not! But as I see it, that is not entirely the point. One is concerned merely with the carrying out of that part of an algorithm which purports to embody the occurrence of a single mental event. This could be some momentary 'conscious realization' in the answering of a Turing-Test question, or it could be something simpler. Would any such 'event' necessarily require an algorithm of stupendous complication?

not some kind of disembodied 'understanding' associated with the person's carrying out of that algorithm, and whose presence does not impinge in any way upon his own consciousness. However, I would agree with Searle that this possibility has been rendered rather implausible, to say the least. I think that Searle's argument has a considerable force to it, even if it is not altogether conclusive. It is rather convincing in demonstrating that algorithms with the kind of complication that Schank's computer program possesses cannot have any genuine understanding whatsoever of the tasks that they perform; also, it *suggests* (but no more) that no algorithm, no matter how complicated, can ever, of itself alone, embody genuine understanding—in contradistinction to the claims of A-supporters.

There are, as far as I can see, other very serious difficulties with viewpoint **A**. According to **A**, it is simply the algorithm that counts. It makes no difference whether that algorithm is being effected by a brain, an electronic computer, an entire country of Indians, a mechanical device of wheels and cogs, or a system of water pipes. The viewpoint is that it is simply the logical structure of the algorithm that is significant for the 'mental state' it is supposed to represent, the particular physical embodiment of that algorithm being entirely irrelevant. As Searle points out, this actually entails a form of 'dualism'. *Dualism* is a philosophical viewpoint espoused by the highly influential seventeenth-century philosopher and mathematician René Descartes, and it asserts that there are two separate kinds of substance: 'mind-stuff' and ordinary matter. Whether, or how, one of these kinds of substance might or might not be able to affect the other is an additional question. The point is that the mind-stuff is not supposed to be composed of matter, and is able to exist independently of it. The mind-stuff of viewpoint **A** is the logical structure of an algorithm. As I have just remarked, the particular physical embodiment of an algorithm is something totally irrelevant. The algorithm has some kind of disembodied existence which is quite apart from any realization of that algorithm in physical terms. How seriously we must take this kind of existence is a question I shall need to return to in Section 3. It is part of the general question of the Platonic reality of abstract mathematical objects. For the moment I shall side-step this general issue and merely remark that the supporters of **A** do indeed seem to be taking the reality at least of algorithms seriously, since they believe that algorithms form the 'substance' of their thoughts, their feelings, their understanding, their conscious perceptions. There is a remarkable irony in this fact that, as Searle has pointed out, the **A** standpoint seems to drive one into an extreme form of dualism, the very viewpoint with which the supporters of **A** would least wish to be associated!

Searle, in his discussion, seems to be implicitly accepting that electronic computers of the present-day type, but with considerably enhanced speed of action and size of rapid-access store (and possibly parallel action), may well be able to pass the Turing Test proper, perhaps, in the not-too-distant future. He is prepared to accept the contention of Strong AI (and of most other 'scientific' viewpoints) that 'we are the instantiations of any number of computer programs' (Searle 1980: 422).[4] Moreover, he succumbs to: 'Of course the brain is a digital computer. Since everything is a digital computer, brains are too' (ibid. 424 (B87)). Searle maintains that the distinction between the function of human brains (which can have minds) and of electronic computers (which, he has argued, cannot) both of which might be executing the same algorithm, lies solely in the material construction of each. He claims, but for reasons he is not able to explain, that the biological objects (brains) can have 'intentionality' and 'semantics', which he regards as defining characteristics of mental activity, whereas the electronic ones cannot. In itself this does not seem to me to point the way towards any helpful scientific theory of mind. What is so special about biological systems, apart perhaps from the 'historical' way in which they have evolved (and the fact that *we* happen to be such systems), which sets them apart as the objects allowed to achieve intentionality or semantics? The claim looks to me suspiciously like a dogmatic assertion, perhaps no less dogmatic, even, than those assertions of Strong AI which maintain that the mere enacting of an algorithm can conjure up a state of conscious awareness!

In my opinion Searle, and a great many other people, have been led astray by the computer people. And they, in turn, have been led astray by the physicists. (It is not the physicists' fault. Even *they* don't know everything!) The belief seems to be widespread that, indeed, 'everything is a digital computer'. Yet non-computational physical actions, in accordance with **C**, are logical possibilities. Indeed, I believe that a strong case can be made for them. Let us consider this issue next.

2. Viewpoint C and Gödelian Reasoning

I think that it may be helpful if I indicate, in a figure, how I see some of the standard arguments that have been applied to the consciousness/computation issue stand in relation to this general classification (see Fig. 12.1).

---

[4] Reprinted in Boden (1990: 82). From here referred to as B82.

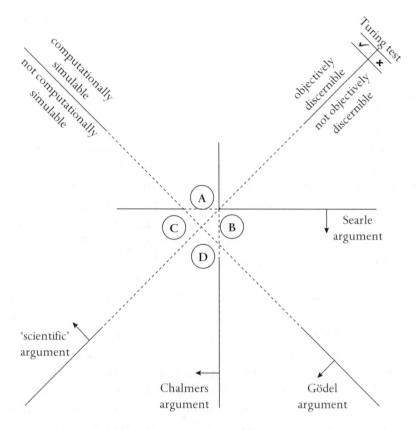

Fig. 12.1 Consciousness: how various arguments bear on the relationship between it and computation.

Let us return to the four standpoints, **A**, **B**, **C**, **D**, with which I began the previous section. In Fig. 12.1, I have placed **A** at the top and **D** at the bottom, with **C** on the middle left and **B** on the middle right. We can say that those who hold to the theoretical possibility of an effective computational simulation of a human brain, doing whatever it does when its owner is actually conscious, would be represented in the figure at positions above the bisecting line which slopes upwards to the left; those who believe in what might be called the 'scientifically objective' view that the presence of conscious mentality is something that can manifest itself in external behaviour would be represented as positioned above the bisecting line sloping upwards to the right.

Science, after all, is concerned with objectively discernible fact. If consciousness is part of science, its presence should be objectively discernible. Thus, represented above the left-sloping line are those who believe that a complete *computational simulation* of a conscious brain is theoretically possible and, consequently, a computationally controlled robot which behaves exactly like a conscious human ought, in principle, to be possible. Represented above the right-sloping line would be those who believe that some form of Turing Test could, in principle, distinguish consciously controlled activity from that which is unconscious, that is, that 'zombies' (in the philosopher's sense) are physically impossible. As far as I can make out, Turing himself would have been an **A**-supporter (as would any of those who consider themselves to belong to the Strong AI school), whilst Gödel's opinions would, no doubt, have been more in line with **D**. I think that a good representative of position **B** is John Searle, whereas I count myself as a strong supporter of standpoint **C**.

Searle's Chinese Room Argument makes the case that pure computation cannot, by itself, evoke any mental qualities. This argument tells against **A**, but it does not distinguish between the other three, **B, C, D**, as far as I can tell. This division is shown in the figure by a horizontal line just below **A**, so Searle's argument supports the viewpoints below this line. In his recent book David Chalmers (1996) (by appealing to 'fading' and 'dancing' qualia) strongly argues the case that if it were possible to replace a person's neurons one by one by silicon chips, whilst totally preserving their function with regard to the person's external behaviour, then that person's internal experiences or qualia would have to remain undisturbed also. This argues in favour of the possibility of a conscious computer-controlled robot, but only if such function-preserving neuron replacements are possible. Thus, this is an argument against **B**, but it does not distinguish between **A, C,** and **D**. This division is shown by the vertical line just to the left of **B**, and the Chalmers argument supports those viewpoints to the left of it. The Gödel-type arguments, as supported by John Lucas (1961, 1970) and by myself, support those viewpoints that are depicted in the figure to the lower-left of the bisecting line which slopes upwards to the left.

It is interesting that the Searle and Chalmers arguments, if combined together, provide a case for just the same standpoints, namely **C** and **D**, as does the Gödelian case. It would be interesting to know whether those who find the Gödelian case so hard to take would react so badly if the argument were presented, instead, in this alternative way!

Of course, in the preceding remarks, I have merely indicated the logical connections between these various arguments; I have said nothing about the strengths of the individual arguments themselves. In my personal opinion, all three arguments make convincing cases, although the Gödelian one is, I believe, the most rigorous. My own stance, in favour of **C**, rather than **D**, stems from a belief in a further consideration, to the effect that the 'scientific' standpoint argues for positions represented above the bisecting line that slopes upwards to the right. I suppose that Lucas must be less swayed than I am by such arguments, since my understanding of his position is that his sympathies lie considerably more in the direction of **D** than do mine.

The Lucas version of the Gödelian argument has a somewhat different flavour from my own. He has been more concerned to apply the argument directly to the possibility that there might lie some computational action controlling the behaviour of some particular individual, say himself, whereas I have been more concerned with the way in which mathematicians in general provide their 'unassailable demonstrations' of the truth of certain mathematical assertions. Only indirectly would this latter version be applied to the question of whether a particular individual (mathematician) might be computationally controlled.

By the term 'unassailable demonstration', I refer, in essence, to the notion of 'mathematical proof'. However, it must be stressed that this notion of proof should not be confined to arguments that can be formulated according to the rules of some pre-assigned formal system, say F. There are two reasons for this. First, merely having an argument that is strictly in accordance with the rules of F does not necessarily provide us with an unassailable demonstration of some mathematical proposition. This could only be the case if we were unassailably convinced of the *soundness* of F. That is to say, before being prepared to accept as 'proved' a proposition that can be obtained by the rigorous application of the rules of F, we must be unassailably convinced that these rules themselves are trustworthy and will never lead to false conclusions. Secondly, once we *are* so convinced, then, by use of Gödel's theorem, we immediately see how to go beyond the rules of F and produce a mathematical proposition whose truth we must equally be unassailably convinced of, yet which is unobtainable using those very rules!

Let me be somewhat more precise about the form of Gödelian argument that I am making use of here. To begin with, it is sufficient to restrict attention to certain very specific types of mathematical statement, namely those referred to as Π_1-sentences. A Π_1-sentence is an assertion that some specified Turing machine action never terminates. There are many well-known mathematical theorems and conjectures that have this form. The most famous is 'Fermat's last theorem', now known to be true by virtue of work done by Andrew Wiles and others. Another example is Lagrange's theorem that each natural number (i.e. one of 0, 1, 2, 3, 4, 5 . . .) is the sum of four square numbers. An example of a Π_1-sentence that is not yet known to be true (or false) is Goldbach's conjecture that every even number greater than 2 is the sum of two prime numbers.

One advantage of restricting attention to Π_1-sentences is that there is not really any serious dispute as to the absolute nature of the truth, or otherwise, of any particular Π_1-sentence. (In fact, in some of the more extreme versions of intuitionism, there could be such a dispute, but I am choosing to ignore this here. Even intuitionism falls within the scope of Gödel's theorem if things are appropriately phrased (see Kleene 1952).) This avoids issues such as those that arise in connection with, say, the axiom of choice, where disputes as to the absolute nature of its validity can easily arise.

Another advantage is that the notion of 'soundness' of a system F, when this notion is restricted to F's ability to establish Π_1-sentences, is equivalent to F's *consistency*.[5] (This assumes that F is extensive enough to include certain very basic operations.) Moreover, the Gödel proposition $G(F)$, which asserts this consistency, is itself a Π_1-sentence.

The particular proposition $G(F)$, although it may look somewhat unnatural as a specific mathematical proposition, can be very directly constructed once the system F is known in detail. In particular, F could be given in terms of a specific algorithmic procedure, or Turing machine action; then the Turing machine action whose non-stopping represents the assertion $G(F)$ can be directly (indeed computationally) constructed. (See e.g. Penrose 1994, app. A, pp. 117–26.)

One thing should be made clear concerning the type of 'formal system' that I am allowing in these discussions. The essential point is that it must be an *entirely computational matter* to decide whether or not an argument is correctly carried out according to F's rules.

The essential issue, therefore, is: how much of mathematical reasoning can be reduced to purely knowable (and trustable) *computational* procedures? The answer, according to Gödel's theorem, is that not all of it can, no matter what such computational procedures we propose. It should be made clear, in this, that 'mathematical reasoning' includes any fully reliable procedures, including the derivation of $G(F)$ from a belief in the soundness (or consistency) of F.

Although arguments still rage[6] about how much further this argument can be taken, I regard it as leading us to the clear conclusion that there must be *non-computational* physical actions underlying the brain processes that control our

---

[5] A remark due to David Hilbert. See Feferman (1995).

[6] See the various contributions to *Psyche*, 2 (1996), 1–88, and my responses in Penrose (1996).

mathematical thought processes. Although this argument refers specifically to *mathematical* thought processes, it seems to me that there is nothing fundamental that distinguishes mathematical thought processes—in particular, mathematical *understanding*—from other forms of logical understanding. Moreover, genuine understanding (whatever it is) seems to me to require the presence of genuine *awareness* (whatever *that* is!). Thus the quality of awareness needs to be present whenever understanding genuinely takes place. In our appreciation that $G(F)$ must be *true* if we accept that F is *sound*, we need to bring our understanding and therefore our awareness to bear on the problem. I argue that it is in those physical processes that underlie our *awareness* that non-computability must be present.

I should comment, here, on the meaning of the term 'non-computable'. In familiar terms, this just refers to actions that cannot be simulated on an ordinary general-purpose computer, which we imagine to be idealized in that it has an unlimited storage capacity, that it never makes mistakes, and that it can run on indefinitely without wearing out. In mathematical terms, such an idealized computer is what is referred to as a (universal) *Turing machine*. A non-computable action is one that cannot be simulated by a Turing machine. It is a known fact of mathematical logic that certain actions that are well defined mathematically are *non-computable* in this sense. A particular example that was given by Turing himself concerns the very question of deciding whether or not some Turing machine action ever terminates or not. We can consider some universal Turing machine $\mathbf{T}$, which is *imagined* to operate successively on the inputs 0, 1, 2, 3, 4, 5, . . . For some of these inputs the action will terminate at some stage, while for others it would continue indefinitely. The mathematical function $T_{(n)}$ that assigns the output 0 whenever this Turing-machine action eventually halts (when $\mathbf{T}$ is applied to the input n), and the output 1 whenever it does not halt, turns out to be a non-computable function (as Turing himself showed).

Note that $T_{(n)}$ is a perfectly precise mathematical function (as soon as the particular specification of the machine $\mathbf{T}$ is known). It does not depend on random or otherwise unspecified actions; nor does its immunity from computational simulation depend upon a reliance on continuous variables. Modern physical theories do, on the other hand, make use of both continuous variables and undetermined (random) behaviour. It requires some sophistication to see how to address both of these issues fully in the context of 'computability', but I prefer to side-step these issues here and simply say that these are not the kinds of 'non-computability' that I am concerned with. We may take the position that continuous functions are adequately approximated by discrete ones, and random functions by pseudo-random ones.

An important issue is that computability is a property that carries over from a lower level of description to a higher one. Thus, if we consider that a macroscopic body is entirely made up of atomic constituents for which an effective computer simulation is theoretically possible, then a computer simulation of the overall behaviour of the macroscopic body itself is also possible. Nothing deep is intended here. We are considering 'in principle' issues only. The theoretical computer simulation of the system of atomic constituents directly serves to provide a simulation of the macroscopic body. Accordingly, if we require a macroscopic behaviour that is non-computable, then there must be something in the physical laws governing its constituents that is also non-computable. (This issue will be returned to in the next section.)

It follows that, if there is non-computability in the way that our conscious brains behave, and if that behaviour is fully dependent on the laws governing the physical constituents of our biological brains, then those laws themselves must contain non-computable elements. Thus, if we accept the Gödelian argument and also that the behaviour of our brains is governed by physical laws (so that we reject viewpoint **D**), then we must also accept that there is something non-computable in those laws. Moreover, that non-computational ingredient would have to be something upon which the biological action of our conscious brains depends.

It seems to me that the only plausible place for such a non-computational ingredient is at the borderline between the levels at which the laws of quantum physics and classical physics hold true. Our understanding of *classical* (i.e. macroscopic) physics is that it is governed by deterministic and (with the reservations referred to above) computable laws. The same comment applies at the submicroscopic *quantum* level, where the deterministic and computable Schrödinger equation holds sway. Bridging these two levels we have the procedure of *quantum measurement* which, in effect, involves the magnification of a quantum-level event to the classical level. The randomness in quantum mechanics enters only in this 'measurement' process. Good reasons can be provided (purely from within physics itself) for the belief that the present-day procedures are a stop-gap, to be replaced by something better in some future theory, but the issue is subject to much argument. My own position is that a new theory is indeed needed, and the 'randomness' that is employed in quantum measurement is an approximation to some *non-computable* mathematical law.

If our conscious brain processes are indeed to depend upon such a thing, then we need to find large-scale coherent quantum activity in the brain which is able to probe this quantum/classical borderline. An example of a known phenomenon where large-scale coherent quantum activity takes place is superconductivity. Something of this general nature is required which could take place in the warm and 'noisy' environment of the brain. Some extraordinary isolation of the quantum state would be needed, and nerve signal propagation itself is much too 'noisy' for this to be possible. Much more probable is something at the subcellular level of the cytoskeleton. In particular, neuronal microtubules, perhaps in conjunction with other structures, seem to me to be by far the best bet. Stuart Hameroff and I have developed a fairly detailed model[7] aimed at achieving what is needed, from this point of view. The model is scientifically testable in a number of different ways, and it will be exciting to see how it fares.

3. Remarks concerning Searle's Discussion of 'Penrose's Approach' in *The Mystery of Consciousness*

In chapter 4 of his book *The Mystery of Consciousness* (1997), Searle provides his critique of my own approach to the problem of consciousness. I find it gratifying that a philosopher of his stature is taking my arguments seriously, rather than merely dismissing them on ideological grounds, as many other commentators seem to have done. This being said, there still appear to be some very significant misconceptions in Searle's interpretation of my position, as expressed in his account, and it seems appropriate for me to try to address these here. I believe that the whole discussion has particular relevance to the role of Searle's Chinese Room Argument; for we saw in Section 2 that this argument supports my **C** position just as strongly as Searle's own **B** (using the classification of Sect. 1).

The most serious of Searle's misconceptions of my standpoint concerns the very notion of *computability*. There are many passages in his account that clearly indicate that he has not properly grasped the meaning of this term. I am sure that he is very far from alone in this, as the notion is not an easy one to understand by those not trained in the relevant ideas of mathematical logic. Indeed, it is common for people who are not so trained to assume a different meaning

---

[7] See both 1996 papers by Hameroff and Penrose.

for the term 'computable' from the one that I actually *do* intend, in my own writings. Nevertheless, I find it disappointing that someone of Searle's undoubted philosophical stature should still misinterpret this notion after he has made some not inconsiderable efforts to come to terms with it. I take this to confirm the very difficulty of the notion itself; accordingly, I shall start by attempting to explain it in a way that is aimed at removing what I perceive to be some serious confusions in Searle's account.

To begin with, I should make clear the importance of phrasing rigorous mathematical arguments in terms of *idealizations*. It is a *separate* matter to examine the accuracy or plausibility of any such idealization, in relation to actual behaviour in the physical world. In the case of the ideal mathematical notion of *computability*, this refers to what can be achieved by an idealized computer—that is, a computer which is not constrained by having a finite bound on its internal storage capacity and which is assumed to be able to run indefinitely and which never makes mistakes. The relevant precise mathematical notion is that of a Turing machine. A modern electronic computer is normally taken to be an excellent approximation to a Turing machine, and this is certainly not an unreasonable idealization, but an actual computer is, never-theless constrained by having a *finite* bound on its storage capacity and a *finite* bound on its running time, so care needs to be exercised when examining the relevance of arguments explicitly referring to infinite quantities.

In fact, the strict notion of computability *does* depend essentially upon the infinite, so we must indeed be careful. Whereas, in rough terms, a mathematical operation is computable if and only if it can be performed on a general-purpose electronic computer, we must bear in mind that this 'computer' is really an *idealized* computer, in the above sense. If our 'mathematical operation' were to apply merely to some *finite* set of alternative inputs (where there is a finitely describable set of alternative outputs), then the computability issue would become vacuous. Any such operation could be displayed in a 'look-up table', in which the result of the operation on each possible alternative is simply listed, and this finite list is stored in the machine. (The machine, being an *idealized* computer, has a potentially unlimited internal storage space, so any *finite* look-up table, no matter how big, can be stored within it.) For a mathematical function to be non-computable, there has to be an *infinite* set of alternative inputs. For simplicity, we can take these alternative inputs to be the natural numbers $0, 1, 2, 3, 4, 5, \ldots$ (and for some of the applications of the computabi-lity notion to our considerations here, it may be appropriate to think of these numbers as referring to the *time*, taken as being discrete).

Why can we not simply use a 'look-up table' in the case of an *infinite* set of alternative inputs? Mathematically, such things can certainly be considered. There is nothing mathematically wrong with an infinite look-up table; but it is *not* true that *any* such look-up table can be internalized by a Turing machine. This follows from the fact that any Turing machine action must have a *finite* specification. Its 'tape'—which represents its internal storage capacity—can have only a finite amount of information stored on it at any one moment, despite the fact that there is no absolute finite *bound* on this capacity. (Though the tape is infinite, it can have only a finite number of marks—say the '1's, as opposed to the '0's—on it at any one moment.) Only if there is some way of specifying a look-up table in terms of some computational rules can it be effectively internalized by a Turing machine.

Now it is, indeed, a remarkable mathematical fact that specific non-computable functions (i.e. non-computable infinite look-up tables) actually exist. Moreover, these can be functions of a completely well-defined mathematical nature, where the output is unambiguously determined by the input in a finitely specifiable way, but where it can be demonstrated that there is no Turing machine action whatever that generates the output from any given input. Such non-computable functions are a little difficult to exhibit explicitly, but many examples are known. Accordingly, one can give mathematical models of 'toy universes' with the property that even though the evolution of such a universe is completely mathematically determined according to precise finitely specifiable rules, there is nevertheless no computer simulation whatsoever of the time-evolution of this universe. (I have given examples of such toy universes. The most satisfactory of these is the one described in my book *The Large, the Small, and the Human Mind* (1997).)

Searle, according to the account that he provides in his book, appears to be under the mistaken impression that 'there is no problem whatever in supposing that a set of relations that are noncomputable at one level of description can be the result of processes that are computable at some other level' (Searle 1997: 85). This is a gross misconception. Non-computability is an absolute mathematical notion that does not at all depend upon the 'level of description'. To illustrate his own point of view, Searle presents an example of what he considers to be a non-computable function, namely that whereby the State of California assigns a vehicle identification number (VIN) to every car that has obtained a licence plate number (LPN), where he takes these lists to be potentially infinite. He says that this function (from LPN to VIN) is 'noncomputable' because there is 'no way to compute one from the other', but he says that this 'does not imply that the processes that produce the noncomputable relations must therefore be noncomputable'. He seems to be saying that the notion of computability is *level-dependent*, and the fact that he can see no direct way of obtaining the function from LPN to VIN, which allows him to call the function 'noncomputable' at that level of description, does not prevent him from calling it 'computable' at a deeper level of description (where we might even take this deeper level to be that of the laws of physics themselves—assumed discrete—if we like).

This is simply *incorrect*. Allowing, for the sake of argument, that Searle's function from LPN to VIN is indeed some well-defined function from the natural numbers to the natural numbers (which we can imagine being provided by an *infinite* look-up table mapped out in space–time), then either this table is mathematically computable or it is mathematically non-computable. There is nothing about 'levels of description' that comes into the matter. Such a function does not become 'non-computable' simply because we do not happen to see any way of computing it at some level. Computability is an *absolute* mathematical notion that is quite independent of the level of description that is used. My own arguments are to try to deduce from the apparent non-computability of our mathematical thought processes, that there must be a non-computability in the physical laws that underlie those thought processes (assuming that our thought processes indeed depend upon physical action, as Searle himself would agree). Searle claims that my moving the non-computability problem down from one level of description to a deeper one is the basic 'fallacy' in my argument. If there is a fallacy (which I do not believe there is) it certainly does *not* lie here. In this particular regard, Searle's argument is simply *wrong*.

Searle maintains (p. 87) that the answer to the question 'is there some level of description at which conscious processes and their correlated brain processes can be [computationally] simulated?' is 'trivially yes', because 'anything that can be described as a precise series of steps can be [so] simulated'. This again illustrates a lack of understanding, namely that computational simulation of a discrete-step process can always be achieved. It is not completely clear to me what a 'step' is, in Searle's terminology. In Turing's original descriptions of what we now call a 'Turing machine' he provides a completely precise notion of a 'step', and the entire Turing machine action is composed as a succession of such steps. But Searle seems to have something more general in mind, so that it can be applied to whatever physical/biological actions take place in a human brain when consciousness is evoked. I see no genuine justification for believing that these actions can necessarily be computationally simulated, and it is certainly not a 'trivial' matter. Such a belief, it seems to me, depends upon the (commonly made) *assumption* that all important brain processes can be attributed to a computer-like system of neuron firings and nerve transmission—or else, at some deeper level, to a computationally describable family of physical processes. The examples of 'toy model universes', referred to above, certainly show that there *are* 'step-by step' processes that can yield a non-computable evolution, provided that we interpret the notion of 'step' in an appropriately broad way.

It is perhaps worthwhile, here, to give a reminder of what such a 'step' might be. In some of my 'toy model' examples, it could be something like: 'if this collection of tile shapes will tile the plane, do X; if they will not, do Y.' At each such step, there will be a specific collection of tile shapes given, and either they will tile the plane or they will not. It is *mathematically determined* whether it is X or Y that will be the result. In either case, a computational simulation of that *particular* step is certainly possible, namely either by the simulation that does X or else by the simulation that does Y (although we may not happen to know which of these two simulations is the correct one). However there is no computational simulation of the *entire evolution*, because there is no *single* algorithm that can achieve *all* the X/Y decisions, because the tiling problem is computationally undecidable. This is just a mathematical *fact* (as demonstrated by a theorem due to Robert Berger), and there is nothing 'trivial' about it.

Searle asserts (p. 86) that there is 'another persistent confusion in Penrose's argument over the notion of computability', claiming that I think 'that the computable character of neurons makes each neuron somehow into a little computer', this being 'another fallacy' because the possibility of having a computational simulation of something does not make that thing into a computer. I cannot believe that I ever said that it does; and I am not sure how Searle picked up that impression. In *Shadows of the Mind* (Penrose 1997: 376), I did refer to 'the neural computer', but there I was referring to the *system* of interconnected neurons acting according to the conventional 'computer picture', whereby its outward action would, in effect, be the same as that of some computer. I was not calling *individual* neurons 'computers'. My idea was that even though the system of interconnected neurons might act like a computer for a short while, this 'computer' would be subject to continual change owing to subtle alterations in synapse strengths, these being globally orchestrated from a deeper level of overall cytoskeletal activity, different parts of the cytoskeleton having some overall coherence owing to quantum entanglement effects. According to this model, consciousness could only arise when objective quantum state reduction (OR) takes place in the cytoskeleton (and probably mainly in microtubules). My contention is that OR is a *non-computable* process (perhaps of a vaguely similar nature to that which occurs in the 'toy models' referred to above). There is undoubtedly considerable speculation in these ideas, but I do not see that they are susceptible to the accusations of triviality or fallaciousness that Searle seems to be making.

Searle's complaint that my arguments do not provide any real headway towards solving the *real* problems of consciousness has a great deal more force, and I am certainly not going to disagree with him. Indeed, in my own writings, I have never claimed that my proposals could provide an *explanation* of consciousness, nor that I know what consciousness *is*. Searle also maintains that my writings contain very little discussion of actual consciousness and that 'you will not learn much about consciousness' (1997: 89) from my arguments. I am not convinced that you will learn much about what actual consciousness *is* from *anyone*'s writings, and mine are certainly no exception. However, I strongly believe that we are going to need a better *physical* world-view than the one that we have now, and a better understanding of brain physiology also, before we can make much serious headway towards a solution of this problem. My own arguments are directed towards that end, but it will be a very long haul before *real* progress on resolving the riddle of consciousness is to hand. (My collaborator Stuart Hameroff would, I believe, be in essential agreement with these sentiments, although he may well be rather more positive than I am about how much progress in understanding can be inferred *already* from our model.)

Having said this, I could retort and ask Searle why he appears to regard consciousness as a problem of *biology* (rather than of the *physical* behaviour of the world). It is true that the only conscious entities that we happen to know about are biological structures, but I see no reason for the logical necessity of this. Searle asserts (1997: 88) that 'the main task of a philosophy and science of consciousness right now is to show how consciousness is a biological part of that world . . .', which seems to presuppose that conscious entities need to be biological. I do not see what essential quality of biological brains, in Searle's picture, could distinguish them *in principle* from a corresponding quality of non-biological structures, with regard to the manifestation of consciousness. I have always regarded this aspect of Searle's arguments to be the weakest part of his case, and I hope that he will clarify it for me some day.

It is true that in my own arguments I have concentrated on a very limited aspect of consciousness, namely that of *mathematical understanding*, the reason for this being not so much that it is what I 'know most about', but that it actually allows the deduction (so I claim) that *non-computable processes* must underlie (or be an essential correlate of) at least some conscious phenomena. In his criticisms of my reasoning (which uses Gödel/Turing theorems), Searle makes some remarks that seem to me to reveal several further misunderstandings. He refers

(p. 17) to a self-referential statement in some formal system F—say statement number 17—which asserts 'Statement number 17 is not provable in this system'. Then he claims that 'most mathematicians or logicians think . . . that as far as substance is concerned, statement 17 is just fine'. This seems to me to be a travesty. Statement 17 is simply not well defined at all as it is presented, and would find no place, just like that, in a formal mathematical system. Moreover, even if phrased in more mathematical language, a 'statement 17' could not be part of the formal system itself; such a thing would be more analogous to the *Gödel sentence* of that language. Indeed, it is true that 'statement 17' bears some relation to the original Gödel sentence $G(F)$ for the formal system F, but $G(F)$ is actually an unambiguous number-theoretical proposition (dependent upon the choice of F) that can be written down explicitly, and which has an unambiguous and non-trivial meaning. The way that one sees that $G(F)$ is actually *true*, for a suitably consistent F, is to see that it can be assigned a meaning rather like that of 'statement 17' above. This is a very beautiful piece of logical reasoning, a crucial part of this reasoning being that we must understand what the rules of F actually *mean* in order to know that $G(F)$ is true. It cannot be deduced just by blind application of the rules of F.

Searle complains (p. 63) that my 'argument is entirely about certain arcane areas of mathematics'. This is because I concentrate specifically on Gödel sentences, and the like, which are, in detail, mathematical statements of great complication that do not seem to find application in other areas. But this is to miss the point. My arguments are about *mathematical understanding* which I regard as merely a particularly refined instance of ordinary understanding. The issue has to do with our very reasons for believing things by use of abstract reason. The 'arcaneness' of some particular $G(F)$ is really a reflection of the complication that has already been required in the precise formulation of those aspects of our mathematical reasoning that F itself has been able to accomplish. The real mystery lies in the fact that mathematical reasoning—which really means abstract reasoning of whatever kind—cannot ever be encapsulated in *any* set of computational rules no matter how complicated those rules may be.

I think that some clarification of the Gödel reasoning is needed here, and also of why I regard it as profoundly relevant to the issue of consciousness. The essence of the argument is encapsulated in the following fact:

> For any (sufficiently extensive) system of computational theorem-proving rules F, there is a mathematical statement $G(F)$ whose truth follows from the soundness of F, but which, if F is sound, cannot be derived using the rules of F.

What this tells us is if we *trust* F, then we can see how to *transcend* F. Thus, no system of computational proof procedures that we trust can encapsulate all the ways that are available for ascertaining the truth of mathematical assertions.

Now some people take the position that *mathematical proofs* are simply arguments that can be formulated in terms of some F that has been decided upon (say, the Zermelo–Fränkel formal system), and any methods of reasoning that lie outside these procedures (such as 'seeing' the truth of G(F)) are not actually 'proofs' but some 'intuitive' arguments of lesser merit. For myself, I simply do not see the logic of this distinction. The trustworthiness of any 'proof' that relies upon a derivation *within* F is dependent upon the soundness of F in any case (and certainly on the consistency of F). If we are accepting the soundness of F, then we must also accept G(F). There is no more 'intuition' involved in our belief in G(F) than there is in our belief in statements based on proofs within F since the latter are *also* dependent upon whatever 'intuitions' we may have employed to convince ourselves of the soundness of F. To my way of thinking, this clearly indicates that there is nothing overridingly special about *formal* mathematical proof. A *proof* of some mathematical proposition is really just a thoroughly convincing unassailable argument that tells us that we must believe in the truth of that proposition. Formal methods are useful for this, but they are not the only methods available. The Gödelian argument that derives G(F) from F is just as good an argument as any that derives some proposition by methods *within* F.

This has relevance to Searle's complaint about the argument that I presented in *Shadows of the Mind*—using a putative society of mathematical *robots*—against human mathematical understanding being something that can be effectively simulated computationally. Searle seems to be saying that the robots in my discussion have only been 'programmed with theorem-proving algorithms', whereas his own putative robots use something different, namely 'brain simulator algorithms'. In fact, I make *no restrictions* on what type of algorithms are to be used in the construction of the robots. They are certainly allowed to make the 'informal' deduction of G(F) from F just as well as any formal argument within F. But they are also allowed to use any other kind of 'mathematical insight' that might be available to them on the basis of their underlying algorithmic construction. I also allow them to make mistakes from time to time, but where these mistakes are, in principle, *correctable* (just as with the case of humans). In my 'fantasy dialogue' discussion of Sect. 3.23 in *Shadows of the Mind*, I assumed, for simplicity, that the robots regarded themselves as infallible, which seems to be the source of Searle's misconception that I was supposing my putative robots to be programmed only with 'theorem-proving algorithms'. But in many of the earlier sections of chapter 3 of my book (and in ch. 2: 101–6, cf. also 83–7), I *explicitly* consider the possibility of their making errors. Thus, I am here concerned not just with the *ideal* mathematical reasoning, to which Gödel's theorem directly applies, but also with the question of the applicability of such reasoning to actual human thought processes. The arguments of chapter 3, concerning my putative society of mathematical robots are concerned only with the robots' abilities as mathematicians, but the nature of their underlying algorithmic construction is constrained merely by the fact that it should be possible for human programmers (some time in the future) to be able to set in train a system of procedures that ultimately leads—algorithmically— to the putative robot society. So I believe that Searle is again under a misapprehension regarding the nature of my arguments.

As a final point, Searle expressed discomfort with my 'three-worlds' picture, illustrated in figure 8.1 of *Shadows of the Mind* (1997: 414), which interrelates the 'physical world', the 'mental world' and the 'Platonic world' (of mathematical absolutes). It had never occurred to me that I was expressing a belief that 'we live in three worlds', as Searle interprets it (Searle 1997: 87), and that this viewpoint is even more mystical than dualism! In my picture, the physical and mental 'worlds' are *not* to be thought of as having the same kind of existence as the physical world, and it makes no sense to say that we 'live' in the Platonic world any more than that we live in the mental world. I suppose that it might be more appropriate to say that the elements of the mental world are the 'we' that live in the physical world. In a similar vein, it could be said that the elements of the Platonic world are certain *concepts* that, accordingly, 'live' in the mental world. (This may be not so different from Popper's perspective, except that his 'World III' is the world of culture rather than of Platonic absolutes.) The feature that is perhaps distinctive about my own position is the *cyclic* aspect of the picture, whereby the physical world itself seems, according to modern physics, almost to be reducible to mathematics, so that it might not appear so unreasonable to regard physical objects themselves as 'living' in the Platonic mathematical world.

I do not regard this picture as other than a useful way of organizing our thoughts, at the present time. What 'true reality' is, we certainly do not know, as yet (and I suggest that Searle reread the final sentence of *Shadows of the Mind* (1997: 420), if he wishes to regard me as some kind of 'trialist'). But it certainly does not help, it seems to me, simply to deny the notion of mathematical existence altogether, as Searle appears to be doing. Mathematical existence is certainly very different from physical existence. Mathematical concepts certainly do not have spatial or temporal location, for example. Yet physical science cannot do without the Platonic mathematical world, no matter what one's views on mathematical existence might be. The extraordinary accord that the physical world has with subtle mathematical structures cannot be denied, where this accord is the greater, the more fundamental the level of physics being examined. If mathematics were entirely the construction of (say human) mentality, then what sense can be made of the fact that this physical/mathematical accord seems to have been around, unchanged, since the time of the Big Bang, long before there were any humans or other sentient beings?

I have a very great respect for Searle and for the powerful arguments that he has brought to bear on the AI debate. The Chinese Room, in particular, was certainly a significantly original contribution to the whole discussion—one of the very few that have shifted the purely philosophical arguments forward, in my opinion. Yet I remain puzzled why he is so resistant to moving from the Weak AI position to something where more progress on the scientific side is possible. Any clues towards future progress in this fundamentally difficult area should be looked at very seriously, and I believe that the issues of non-computability, quantum holism, and subneuronal organization offer genuine routes towards a better understanding, and are distinctly worthy of further study.

References

BODEN, M. A. (ed.) (1990) *The Philosophy of Artificial Intelligence* (Oxford: Oxford University Press).

CHALMERS, D. J. (1996) *The Conscious Mind: In Search of a Fundamental Theory* (Oxford: Oxford University Press).

DENNETT, D. C. (1990) 'Betting Your Life on an Algorithm', *Behavioral and Brain Sciences*, 13: 660.

FEFERMAN, S. (1995) 'Penrose's Gödelian Argument', *Psyche*, 2/7.

HAMEROFF, S. R. and PENROSE, R. (1996a) 'Conscious Events as Orchestrated Space-Time Selections', *Journal of Consciousness Studies*, 3: 36–63.

———— —— (1996b) 'Orchestrated Reduction of Quantum Coherence in Brain Microtubules—A Model for Consciousness?' in S. R. Hameroff, A. Kaszniak, and A. Scott (eds.), *Toward a Science of Consciousness: The First Tucson Discussions and Debates* (Cambridge, Mass.: MIT Press), 507–40.

HOFSTADTER, D. R. (1979) *Gödel, Escher, Bach: An Eternal Gold Braid* (Sussex: Harvester Press).

—— and DENNETT, D. C. (eds.) (1981) *The Mind's I: Fantasies and Reflections on Self and Soul* (New York: Basic Books).

KLEENE, S. C. (1952) *Introduction to Metamathematics* (Amsterdam: North-Holland).

LUCAS, J. R. (1961) 'Minds, Machines and Gödel', *Philosophy*, 36: 120–4.

—— (1970) *The Freedom of the Will* (Oxford: Oxford University Press).

MINSKY, M. L. (1968) 'Matter, Mind and Models', in Minsky (ed.), *Semantic Information Processing* (Cambridge, Mass.: MIT Press), 425–32.

MORAVEC, H. (1989) *Mind Children: The Future of Robot and Human Intelligence* (Cambridge, Mass.: Harvard University Press).

PENROSE, R. (1989) *The Emperor's New Mind: Concerning Computers, Minds and the Laws of Physics* (Oxford: Oxford University Press).

—— (1994) *Shadows of the Mind: An Approach to the Missing Science of Consciousness* (Oxford: Oxford University Press).

—— (1996) 'Beyond the Doubting of a Shadow', *Psyche*, 2: 89–129.

—— (1997) *The Large, the Small, and the Human Mind* (Cambridge: Cambridge University Press).

SCHANK, R. C., and ABELSON, R. P. (1977) *Scripts, Plans, Goals and Understanding* (Hillsdale, NJ: Lawrence Erlbaum).

SEARLE, J. R. (1980) 'Minds, Brains and Programs', *Behavioral and Brain Sciences*, 3: 417–24.

—— (1987) 'Minds and Brains without Programs', in C. Blakemore and S. Greenfield (eds.), *Mindwaves* (Oxford: Blackwell), 208–33.

—— (1992) *The Rediscovery of the Mind* (Cambridge, Mass.: MIT Press).

—— (1997) *The Mystery of Consciousness* (New York: New York Review of Books).

13

Neural Depictions of 'World' and 'Self': Bringing Computational Understanding to the Chinese Room

Igor Aleksander

Introduction: Intentionality and Consciousness

Undoubtedly John Searle's central contribution to the philosophy of both mind and language is his theory of intentionality. This suggests that cognition in all its forms is directed at objects. We attend to objects, we speak of objects, we understand object-laden stories, and we relate to objects both in perception and recall. When programmed computers only represent objects as symbols in relation to other symbols, this leads logically to the conclusion expressed in the 'Chinese Room' Argument (CRA (Searle 1980)): symbols *are not* objects that share properties with what it is that they represent.

This chapter draws attention to two major changes which have occurred in computational intelligence since the publication of this criticism which add new dimensions to the debate on whether an artificial system can operate in an intentional, object-oriented way. The first is the advent of neural systems that has created a new, rich way of representing reality which is not symbolic. Sometimes called 'subsymbolic',[1] this methodology allows reality to be richly

---

[1] In my opinion this is a misleading term as neural representations are richer than symbols, hence, perhaps 'supersymbolic' might be a better term.

represented within an artificial system as objects mediated by a sensory system and their relationship with the world in which such objects are situated. There is no need to translate these into meaning-deficient symbols that require further definition. That is, the very process which robs computational repres-entation of 'aboutness' is avoided. In this chapter, I shall avoid using the word 'representation' when talking of rich inner activity of an artificial system. I shall call it *depiction*, defining this as the total neural activity, whether in brains or computational neuromodels, which is responsible for an inner sensation.

The second change is the prospect that the intentionality debate is being subsumed within a broader controversy: the emergence in machines of an artificial consciousness of both real and virtual worlds. To illustrate these points, we note that the following semantic ensemble could be represented in a conventional computational way using, perhaps, a semantic network: 'I am looking forward to seeing Mary: she lives in London. I met her at Jack's party and I think that she is a clever computer scientist.'

The inadequacy of a semantic network as a model of what it is to understand this sentence includes the following:

- the symbols are ungrounded in world events (as in Harnad 1990);
- the emotional impact on the understanding entity is not represented at all; and
- a proper interpretation of the word 'I' is not related even by analogy to any sense of 'self' in the machine that is meant to do the understanding.

A human being understands the sentence by what is conveniently phrased as *being conscious* of the role played by the objects both in the world and with respect to his/her sensation of 'self'. These conscious phenomena could be described as including a sense of object-orientedness or intentionality.

With the increase of interest in whether explanations of consciousness can be approached through artificial systems, Searle (1999) has recently taken the posi-tion that they *can* and that such explanations will encompass intentionality as the 'aboutness' of both mental states and language. While Searle implies that 'simulations' cannot *have* intentionality, I shall argue that within the alternative paradigm of digital neuromodels (*not traditional neural networks*—see later), inten-tionality could be an *emergent* property. At least I shall submit that the method-ology, while perhaps currently inadequate in performance, does not suffer the *impossibility* of intentionality which is the thrust of the CRA. In the conclusions I shall also argue that the host program even though ungrounded does not affect the argument relating to an emergent intentionality in the virtual system.

It should be noted that while Searle insists that human consciousness is generated by a biological brain, he has no objection to a non-biological form of consciousness provided it can be proven that this bears the same relation to its non-biological substrate as human consciousness bears to the biological substrate. He simply believes that the nature of this relationship is not known. I argue here that it is possible to establish the nature of this relationship in the artificial domain and that this is sufficient to establish a computational methodology for intentionality.

It is worth saying right at the start that to capture intentionality in neuro-models I look for the following competencies in a system which receives a story as input:

- a visualization of the scenario;
- a link of this visualization to some previously internalized experience;
- being able to see 'self' in the position of the subject of the story if there is one;
- to recognize the validity of the subject's plan with respect to one's own ability to plan.

In other words the system must have a sense of constructive mental imagery, a knowledge of self and an ability to plan. Putting aside the fact that philosophy is punctuated with controversy about the existence of mental imagery we take the cognitive stance that the presence of mental imagery may be found by testing in most individuals (see Richardson 1999).

These requirements are concomitant with what elsewhere has been called the 'basic guess' regarding the prerequisites that might be common between an artificial and a real form of consciousness (Aleksander 1996). In more recent publications we have begun to indicate that a very special form of neural system could have the ability to represent both the world and the self (Aleksander et al. 1999; Aleksander 2000; Aleksander and Dunmall 2000). We call this an ego-centred neural representation of the world.

Representation and Virtuality

Much of the discussion regarding machine understanding founders on poorly defined words. 'Representation' and 'virtuality' are such words. In classical artificial intelligence *representation* is taken to mean a system of symbols and operators which provides within the machine a usable algorithmic model of world events. In neuromodelling as well as in neurophysiology, the word, if used meaningfully, refers to neural events which register events in the world. Referring to perception, such neural events must be accurate enough for the organism to take appropriate action if required. If in parts of the cortex there were to be no distinction in neural firing patterns between important differences in world events, visual perception would lose efficacy and the organism would act erroneously. Therefore I, in common with many others (Searle 1999; Zeki 1993; Crick 1994; Velmans 2000), take the firing of some neurons to be an internal 'depiction' of features of the world that are important to the organism. It would be an error to believe that such depictions imply the presence of an observing 'homunculus': the depictions do not need to be observed, they are there to be acted on. It is precisely in the 'vetoing' of such action (by the lateral cingulate brain area) that modern neurophysiological theories of consciousness rest (see Cotterill 1999 for a comprehensive review). That is, the representation has to be there whether acted upon or not, and 'consciousness' is (partly) the word used to indicate the organism's readiness to act. So as not to travel too far from the intended scope of this chapter, I shall argue that it is the presence of rich, direct neural depiction which captures intentionality in some artificial neural systems.

Another contentious word is 'virtual'. I define this as a program which makes the host machine behave as if it had the properties of another. The word should not be interpreted to mean 'fictional'. Computer weather models and office software spreadsheets are virtual machines: they may be wrong at times but they are not fictional. In this chapter reference is made to current work on artificially conscious systems. Machines studied under this heading are virtual in the sense that they make the programmed host machine act, mechanisms and all, like a neural system. When it is argued that such systems 'become conscious' of a world, that world can either be an independent virtual system running within the same host machine or the real world which is sensed through appropriate interfaces. Therefore whatever object-orientedness there might be it is *by* the virtual machine, *of* worlds that are either real or virtual. Two issues arise: does this make the virtual machine intentional and, even if not, does it point to a possible existence of a non-virtual computational system? On the first of these points the important answer is that the (world/virtual organism) combination allows hypothetical mechanisms of intentionality to be studied. The answer to the second point is that yes, given a suitable robot body, the neural mechanism should be capable of being extracted and embodied, creating an *artificially* conscious machine which would be *artificially* intentional. The word 'artificially' is intended to provide a clear distinction between a machine form of intentionality and the human version. The content of human intentionality is intrinsically different from that of a machine if only because it includes biological needs and concerns which would be inappropriate in a machine. The important factor is whether the artificial version has sufficient commonality with the real to be able to say that the two both instantiate the principles (rather than the content) of intentionality. The fact that a virtually conscious or intentional system might easily be cloned to another machine is seen by some as a way of questioning the validity of the model. But this is simply a property that the virtual system *does not* have in common with its living counterpart. This does not invalidate it in terms of the features that it *does* have in common. Some system makers have seen the cloneability of artificially conscious systems as a vital attribute which stands alongside their potential for intentional behaviour.

The Maturing of the Chinese Room

In a recent book *Mind Language and Society: Philosophy in the Real World* (1999), Searle has elaborated on the specific question: how dependent is intentionality on 'consciousness'. I shall comment on this from the perspective of the study of cognitive matters in artificial domains. In his book he draws a line under the philosophical discussion and opens the way to sound scientific (in his terms, biological) investigation. To attempt a summary of his views, he draws attention to the need to have a fundamental belief in our living in a real world which exists in a way that is independent of our perception of it. In our own recent work (Aleksander 1996; Aleksander *et al.* 1999; Aleksander 2000) it has been forcefully assumed that the world is independent of a perception of it and that the more accurately a brain (real or artificial) records this reality the more successfully will that individual or machine act in the real world.

Searle sees it necessary to lift constraints posed by classical 'isms' in philosophy. He refers to the dualism of Descartes, and the computational materialism of Dennett, finding these to be default positions, which clash due to mutual exclusivity. Helpfully, he suggests that the default positions should be ignored and that philosophies which take proper cognizance of both the dualist *and* materialist aspects of consciousness are likely to make more general sense. He calls this solution 'naturalisation'. To illustrate this, consider the statement that consciousness depends directly on some neural activity in the brain. While this casts consciousness as a biologically generated hence materialist phenomenon, it need not deny the personal (seemingly dualist) sensations which, to that organism, appear to be independent of its biological machinery. In the same vein, he discounts the often-evoked impossibility of having a third person (scientific) view of a first-person sensation, arguing again that it is for the biologist to discover which specific properties differentiate between having and not having sensation as, for example, between being and not being awake. In passing, it should be noted that Max Velmans (2000) is yet another contributor to the notion that the first- and third-person perspectives are merely perspectives on the same neural events.

The artificial consciousness in our work has precisely the characteristics of being capable of being seen both as materialistic and dualistic. Being rooted in the material of a cellular architecture of many modules, artificial consciousness arises due to the representations of the world which emerge in such systems both during perception and imagination. But before addressing this methodology in a little more detail, it is interesting to look at Searle's current position on intentionality to see what remains of the Chinese Room Argument.

Intentionality Now

According to Searle, similar controversies occur over intentionality which again come from the clash of two extreme positions. The first is that if consciousness is only a biological property which provides accurate representations in the brain of a real world, the 'aboutness' must be a property of the real world which the brain gets to reflect. The other extreme is that if consciousness is dual in nature, aboutness/intentionality is an added internal state which is somehow separate from the sensations about the real world. Naturalizing this argument is to develop a philosophy which accepts that both explanations can coexist.

Staying aware of the difference between the aboutness of words and the aboutness of brain states, Searle suggests that a proper philosophy of intentionality can be developed by naturalizing it through a process which is a bit like that which he applies to the mind–body or consciousness problem. He takes an example of 'hunger' which is an internal state with a well-understood biological basis. He goes on to argue that this biological state accrues knowledge (or aboutness) as the biological organism learns planning strategies for getting rid of the deficit and the consequences of what happens if one does not eat. There is no reason why the word 'hunger' should not trigger the state in the brain which contains these added representations, or that hunger could not be a property of a visibly undernourished Ethiopian child. This view suggests that all of visual awareness, being biologically generated (not, according to Searle, in a way that is necessarily understood in current science), has whatever aboutness vision can provide. This is a mix of external properties and internal associations. This is a model for intentionality which sits happily between the otherwise incompatible default positions.

In the context of neuromodelling, aboutness can be just a learned internal descriptive interpretation of a complex object (e.g. a segmented black/white ball is a football) or the name of a feature which is a firm external attribute of the observed object (intrinsically a cup is expected to have a handle which distinguishes it from a bowl in having a shape that can be grasped in a particular way).

Towards Biological Explanations in Artificial Domains

Having naturalized both consciousness and intentionality by suggesting that biology resolves the clashes, Searle leaves open the notion of how this can be fully described. While he sees this as a 'biological' problem, he does not deny that it could occur in an artificial domain. Before suggesting how neurocomputation may contribute to the debate, it is worth being quite clear about Searle's acceptance of artificial consciousness: 'When I say that the brain is a biological organ and consciousness a biological process, I do not, of course, say or imply that it would not be possible to produce an artificial brain out of nonbiological materials that could also cause and sustain consciousness' (Searle 1999: 53). Summing up so far, we have come a full circle: the style of explanation of 'understanding language and the world' by using rules and symbols in computational domains is found wanting through a lack of intentional representation. But intentionality appears to be a philosophical problem closely linked to the problem of first-person sensations in consciousness. Both can be 'naturalized', that is, be seen as a biological effect generated by the function of the brain. But how this effect is actually generated by the brain remains (according to Searle) an unsolved but not impossible question. In the rest of this chapter I wish to suggest an answer to the brain-sensation link which includes precisely the 'aboutness' that an intentional organism whether biological or artificial requires. The intention here is to demonstrate that neuromodelling both explains some of the mechanisms necessary to sustain intentionality in living organisms and constitutes a computational alternative to the symbol manipulation which is attacked in the CRA. In other words the belief that computation uniquely implies non-intentional symbol manipulation will be corrected.

The Neurocomputational Advantage: Emergence and Rich Representation

The brain is an enormously complex neural machine. While it may be pedantically correct to say that it is a neural network, this is a weak and unimportant statement. In fact, it is a statement which in the 1940s led to poor assessments such as 'a computer is an artificial brain because it is made of logic gates, and logic gates are like the neurons in our brain'. Other scientific mistakes have also been made in the name of the 'brain/neural network' association. During the 1980s 'revival' of interest in neural networks much was made of the 'emergent' properties of a homogenous network of neurons with feedback (e.g. Hopfield nets (Hopfield 1982) and Hinton's Boltzmann machines (Hinton and Sejnowski 1986)). These models go a long way towards providing a rigorous understanding of mechanisms of stable states in homogenous networks. However their use in 'language-processing' schemes got no closer to solving the intentionality problem than did earlier symbolic attempts. Even interesting approaches such as the 'symbol-grounding' idea of Harnad's (Harnad 1990), leaves out 'aboutness' in the model as it advocates neural activity as a mediator between the sensory world and symbolic representation. That is, the neural net in Harnad's scheme is a pattern recognizer which turns a complex sensory world into symbols, leaving conventional non-intentional processing to do the 'understanding', hence falling prey to the CRA. Here I take the view that it is not grounding that is necessary in an intentional computational system, but the combination of rich depictions and emergence as we shall see.

For now a brief comment on the word 'emergence' is required. For the purposes of this chapter this is defined as an expected stability within a complex neural architecture which depends on the nature and intensity of interconnections between the neural modules of the system. Note that this goes beyond the definition of emergence in homogenous dynamic neural nets which is concerned with finding energy minima in a trained network: true and false ones. In the context of an architecture, emergence is concerned with cognitive properties of the overall system as controlled by sensory input. While this might rely on the existence of energy minima within the components of the architecture, emergence in complex systems has more to do with the system's ability to satisfy some survival criteria in a complex world.

Therefore talking of neural networks alone as a paradigm for the study of why brains have intentional representations fails to recognize that the brain has a most intricate architecture, not all of which contributes directly to intentional representation but some of which is needed to support it. Neurocomputation is the study of such architectures in the brain through their simulation as neural entities. A target in neurocomputational studies has therefore been the nature of representations that help an organism to act in a complex world. We shall argue that a necessary condition is a rich neural activity representing the real world (both immediate and recalled), ego-centred to provide the organism with the readiness to act. This activity is thought to sustain consciousness and intentionality.

Accurate Representation of the World and Inclusion of the Ego

Making biology responsible for naturalizing the philosophical problem of intentionality leads us to look closely at Francis Crick's 'Astonishing Hypothesis': anything of which we are conscious is due to the firing of some (not all) neurons (Crick 1994). This implies that the limit of accuracy of our consciousness is dictated by the limit of accuracy of our reconstructional neural systems. The word 'reconstructional' is used because areas of the brain where there is a close correlation of activity with what comes into consciousness must be the product of a process which reconstructs reality from the deconstructing action of sensors and features extractive parts of the brain. As an example, I refer to our ability to see a wire trailing from an air balloon even though the accuracy of the fovea in the eye is not sufficient to resolve it. It is eye movement and neural integration which provide accurate firing that correlates with the existence of the wire and the visual awareness of its presence in the field of vision.

Further evidence for this reconstructional activity lies in discoveries of the operations of the visual loop in the brain. Awareness is inferred to occur in the frontal lobes where there is a confluence of signals coming through the visual channels and those in the motor lobes related to eye and head movement (Crick and Koch 1992). But this depiction of the world is only part of the story. An interesting consequence of reconstruction is that this inevitably must be done from some virtual point of view of the observer. That is, looking round a room provides direct awareness of that room from my position. My ability to plan is that my neurons can reconstruct a prediction of how that point of view will change were I to move. I call this 'ego-centredness' in world depictions and provide some examples of it later.

Therefore for a system to be conscious and hence intentional (or be an artificial model within which consciousness can be studied), it must, as a necessary condition, possess neural machinery capable of creating ego-centred depictions in some of its firing patterns. That is, through the firing of some neurons, it must have cellular areas within which states or sequences of states arise that represent the world which the organism inhabits as seen from the point of view of the organism. These states are generated through a highly specialized function of neural structures and their plasticity which allows learning. It seems to me evident that whenever neurons fire to contribute to states which reflect the cohesiveness of the world, one says that the organism 'feels', 'perceives', or 'imagines' the world as a coherent entity.

Tactile Ego-Centredness

The phenomenon of brain depictions of a cohesive world through the firing of neurons is vividly illustrated by that which occurs when patterns of pinpricks in a finger activate neural states in the human somatosensory cortex. These are somatotopically placed and represent the exact position in which they exist on the surface of the body but 'feel' to be, not in the head but in the finger. This is an example of ego-centredness which shows quite an astonishing effect. The *ego* occurs in this neural activity, because it always locates events in the world (or the skin in this case) with respect to some internal fixed point. This *feels* as if it is a vanishingly small centre from which all observation takes place.

The reason this happens is that when something touches the tip of my finger the firing of neurons due to this sensory input takes place in the somatosensory cortex together with masses of other firing elsewhere. This includes firing related to muscles which move the finger around and, possibly, the vision of where it is. So were my finger to be touched a second time but with the fingertip an inch or so displaced from where it had been the first time, part of the pattern of firing in my head would represent this difference. So the pinprick is represented in its appropriate position in space. But this implies a centre from which these positions are measured. Hence my depictions of the sensory world, by being fully representative of the origin in space of the stimulation, become ego-centred. That is, they include in their depiction an unchanging central entity. It makes sense to think that we use the word 'I' to talk of the first-person aspect sensation and the word 'self' to speak of it in psychology or philosophy. Also there is no shortage of neurons in the cortex for these depictions to be very accurate.

The reader is encouraged to read V. S. Ramachandaran's fascinating account of the way that patients whose arms have been amputated still have an 'ego-centred' sensation of their fingers when the appropriate neurons in their cortex are stimulated (Ramachandaran and Blakeslee 1998). That is, they say, 'I have a pain in *my* finger' purely as a result of the firing of their neurons even if there is no finger there to cause the sensation. They will equally refer to one of their limbs as being that of a stranger for a deficit in their positioning neural system. These results provide an undeniable clue that neural firing patterns in the brain represent both the world and the self.

'Ego-Centredness' in the Visual System

In the process of looking at the world around us our eyes saccade and dart around. The head may also move as we are gathering information. It is well known that the lens of the eye projects a somewhat distorted picture of the world onto the retinae. This is where the firing of sensory neurons occurs, in the rods (which respond to light intensity) and the cones (which respond to colour by each cell being specialized to fire on one of the basic colours). Were we to project these firing patterns on a screen we would see a picture that is strangely distorted. We would not see any colours. Every time the eyes move, this picture would change completely, like a movie taken by a really bad cameraman. Were I looking at a red wall and then a green one, all that we would notice on the projection is that different groups of neurons fire and this largely in a small spot (the fovea) in the middle of the image. Indeed only this tiny middle of the image would be anything like an accurate sample of the observed scene.

This is certainly *not* an ego-centred, but an eye-centred representation. The task which the visual system performs so well is first to separate out the features of the retinal firing (colour, intensity, edges, motion) in the early (occipital— back of the skull) part of the visual system (the primary visual cortex, where things are still eye-centred). But our visual awareness, according to lesion experiments, appears to happen in deeper (frontal—front of the skull) areas in the visual system, where neurons receive information from the firing of muscular neurons which control eye position and much else to boot. Here maps may be created of shape information and colour information *compensated* for the position of the eye, the head, the motion of our bodies through space, and the distance of the object as represented by binocular processing and the setting of eye centrelines by muscles. In a crude way we can think of the accurate part of the retina (the fovea) as being responsible for 'painting' a neural picture on inner neural surfaces where the paintbrush is positioned by muscular signals which tell the brush where the fovea is in (almost) a three-dimensional space. The inaccurate part of the retina (the perifovea), serves to attract the position of the paintbrush to things in the world that have content which is either important to the organism or is just changing. These 'painted' surfaces are where ego-centred depictions are created—this is where visual awareness occurs.

As it is known that the primary visual cortex separates out the features of the retinotopic input and that such separations (colour, motion, shape) are then further processed in separate cortical areas, commentators including Crick and Koch (1992) and, indeed, Searle (1999) worry about the way coherence between these areas may take place. This is called the 'binding problem'. Recently, Zeki and Bartels (1998) have postulated that binding is not necessary, as the separate areas of the post-primary cortex simply produce partial consciousness or 'microconsciousnesses' which need not synchronize in time. We reported (Aleksander and Dunmall 2000) that this state of affairs would be unsatisfactory as there would be an incoherence between neural events and the world (among other things). We argue that it is the muscular referent which is necessary to avoid binding, that is, if action in the separate areas is ego-centred, the need for binding is removed. So all areas in which this happens qualify for contributing to visual awareness. Areas where the firing is eye-centred or system-centred without being compensated for the activity of the organism do not qualify. Our hypothesis suggests that if a neuron in part A of the cortex is representing the edge of my cup, and another in part B is signalling that this edge is green/yellow and both are world representative and ego-centred, they will coincide in the sensation of the event.

Why Deconstruct and Reconstruct?

Why do the early parts of the sensory system deconstruct input into features only to reconstruct it all again deeper in the system? Is this kind of action central

262 / Igor Aleksander

to artificially intentional computing systems? Could the real world not be projected directly into consciousness areas of the brain? One reason for this arrangement has already been given: the system needs to compensate for the characteristics of sensory transducers (e.g. eye movement, cochlear frequency-space translation, etc.) in order to create neural firing that is world representative and ego-centred. However there is a subtler reason: were the depiction not reconstructed from separate features, the meaning of every object would have to be learned anew. That is, new combinations of known features could not be imagined and variations of known objects could not be named. These points are elaborated in the remaining sections of this chapter.

Imagination

In addition to showing in the artificial neural network that it is possible to get some insights into the way in which a brain might reconstruct reality, it has also been possible to show that it can imagine the world while not perceiving it. Significantly in the context of intentionality, this evidently involves learning and language. Taking world depictions of a visual kind, we note that they become linked to auditory (or visual) depictions of names of things and actions. One can trigger the other when the other is not perceived. However, the most intriguing question we have been able to answer (Aleksander et al. 1999) is 'How does the brain construct things it has never seen?'.

Before going further, the phrase 'things it has never seen' needs to be qualified. I do not mean that the system is good at extra-sensory perception and can guess what Abigail Witherspoon looks like having never seen her or heard her described. But a very good verbal description might lead to the creation of a mental image which enables the imaginer to pick Abigail out in a crowd. Also I could ask someone to imagine a flying pig or a pink elephant. What comes into consciousness is that which is induced by the words.

Without going into technical detail, it appears possible that in learning to use words and language, neural links are learned between brain areas that represent language and areas which represent features such as colours or shapes and which are not necessarily world representative or ego-centred. It is the major emergent drive of the entire system to recreate the world, which brings together partial and possibly unconscious depictions of words that cause world-plausible depictions to emerge. Of course if perception is interrupted in some or all sensory domains, the inner networks can fall into 'attractors' (which are meaningful states due to the fact that they are created by perceptual experience) and allow us to imagine things seemingly at random. If this occurs during sleep, it is called dreaming.

Ego-centred depictions do much more than just recreate pictures. Simply, they may recreate pictures but more generally they encode anything which is pertinent to the generators of those pictures in the world and the organism's relationship to such objects. The word 'cup' creates neural depictions not only of an image of the cup, but its ego-centredness would include depictions in motor areas of how I might grip the cup, how I might fill it, how I might drink from it, and how it might break if dropped. In other words, ego-centred depictions encode my entire experience of what 'cup' means to me! It encodes the 'aboutness' of a cup. This is precisely the kind of process which John Searle had argued was missing in 'hard' AI. So we can conclude thus far that ego-centred world depictions may be crucial for intentionality to arise the brain. These are computational processes, and we continue to examine how well they transfer to artificial domains.

Natural Language and Ego-Centredness

Understanding natural language is at the centre of the CRA. From the point of view of ego-centred neural depiction the key issue is that, in humans, language is a powerful stimulant of inner depiction (as discussed in 'Imagination' above). It is a well-trodden thought that the success on earth of human beings is due to the sophistication and accuracy with which the world can be internally represented, coupled with the ability to produce and be sensitive to a comprehensive repertoire of sounds. The survival value of human tribes in prehistory is often said to have been greatly enhanced by the co-evolution of these two competencies through the value of being able to transfer elements of (ego-centred) ideas about the world from one being to another. Being able to relate a bad experience with a poisonous mushroom and describing its subtle features to others in the tribe adds obvious survival value. From what has been said about visual consciousness, in neurocomputation 'learning' is mainly seen as happening between auditory, language areas in the brain and other sensory modalities. While details of this may be found elsewhere (Aleksander 1996), it needs to be stressed that the key implication of neurocomputing as opposed to symbolic programming is that 'understanding' by an artificial system implies the stimulation of imagined depictions in response to language. Of particular note is that these involve the 'self' of the listener. For example, the sentence 'After the free-fall, Fred's first attempt at deploying the parachute failed', is understood by most as a vignette of what is happening and what might happen next. I argue that an ego-centred neural depiction is *necessary* to answer a question such as 'what might Fred be feeling?' as putting 'oneself in Fred's place' is a favoured way of revealing the answer (Searle 1999).[2]

It is hardly surprising that given the apparatus for both depiction and generation, human beings in communities isolated from one another have developed languages that work in very similar ways. I would argue that they work so as to make as efficient as possible the rapid communication of ego-centred depictions. The 'Language Instinct', of which Steven Pinker speaks so eloquently (Pinker 1994), is much more bound up with and controlled by mechanisms that influence the creation of inner depiction of the world than studies of linguistics alone have revealed so far.

An Example of an Artificial Ego-Centred Vision System

I include here a brief description of the architecture which is coming under scrutiny in our laboratories at the time of writing. This is shown in Fig. 13.1. This figure is not a block diagram of a working system, but a framework for indicating what needs to be researched. The part marked 'Eye-centred processing' has been completed and discussed elsewhere (Aleksander *et al.* 1999). This is capable of learning adjectival phrases that describe two-feature objects (e.g. Red Square, Blue Circle). The system is capable of deconstructing an input into colour features and shape features (a little like the primary visual cortex), naming even combinations not seen while learning the words, and imagining (i.e. reconstructing appropriately in the visual reconstruction area) objects which have not been learned. The system also accords with our visual experience of being able to 'see' everything, irrespectively of learning.

The rest of the system is an indication of the direction of current research: unravelling the way in which the experience of a system with a moving eye may link to language. The key part of this is to study how a neural motor area is involved in the bringing of material into the ego-centred part of the system and how this establishes a two-way relationship with language areas.

---

[2] I see this as being necessary to avoid the symbolicist's problem (akin to the 'frame problem') of having to list all possible human occurrences including parachuting for providing an answer out of context.

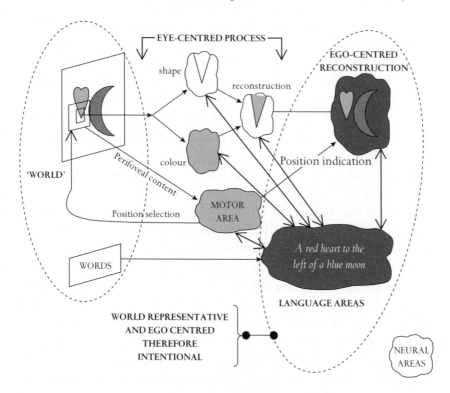

Fig. 13.1 A sketch of the 'artificial consciousness' architecture under current scrutiny.

It should be stressed that this example is not intended to be a vindication of the main thrust of this chapter: neurocomputation can be intentional. It is merely an indication of the style of computational architecture that might be adopted to capture intentionality. Of course, the grander characteristics of such computational techniques as discussed in this chapter are merely an agenda for work into a quite distant future.

Conclusion: Does Neurocomputation Escape from the Chinese Room Argument?

A way of answering negatively to the above question by objecting to 'computer understanding' is that whatever a computer does is based on a program generated by a programmer, and programming is *always* merely symbol manipulation. Therefore, as I have claimed that the mechanisms of consciousness are beginning to be understood in the neurosciences, does not the translation of this knowledge into a computer simply boil down to more symbol manipulation, leaving intentionality behind in the human domain yet again?

The simple fallacy in this argument is that it confuses mechanism with implementation. The CRA is directed at mechanism and not implementation. What I have proposed is that the mechanism which is necessary for intentionality to emerge in the brain is, indeed, a computational mechanism (neurocomputational to be precise) which is totally different from the symbol manipulation which concerns the CRA. It is independent of implementation, but emergent from structure. I have argued that, like stability in homogenous dynamic neural networks, intentionality is the property that emerges when a modular neural system satisfies a set of conditions. In this chapter, this set of conditions has been presented as the structures that give rise to neural events that replicate the sources of sensory signals in an ego-centred way.

In the engineering of neural systems it has always been the relationship between the structure of a neural system and its emergent properties which are at the centre of what has to be discovered. In a study of consciousness and hence intentionality, nothing has changed except ambition. It is the structure of neural systems which have the property of representing the world which needs to be understood: it is this effort which then throws light on the parallel problem of having intentionality in living nets.

One unresolved point which requires comment is whether while an ego-centred world-representing neural activity may be *necessary* to make a system intentional, is it *sufficient*? I shall simply argue that this question should not be asked as it begs another question: sufficient for what? The special depictions discussed here are *necessary and sufficient* to demonstrate that intentionality can reside in a computational system. But the exigent designer may wish to build a robot that is indistinguishable from a human being. While these depictions may be a good place to start, I would advise this designer to abandon the enterprise as, ultimately, sufficiency may not be achieved without biological life.

Finally, I need to stress that the programs (called NRM: Neural Representation Models)[3] which my colleagues and I write are not programs with built-in targets to be conscious nor programs with built-in intentionality. They are programs which create neural laboratories within which the emergent properties of neural systems can be studied. The key target is to discover what, in virtual structures, gives rise to 'ego-centred' depictions. The style is to say things like

---

[3] See: www.sonnet.co.uk/nts

'Aha, we now understand why the ratio of forward connections to reverse connections between area X of the visual system in the brain and Y is what it is. Were
it different, the ego-centred depiction would not be sustained'. At the centre of
this argument is that such mechanisms while best inspired by a thorough
immersion in neuroscience are computational mechanisms which may be
transported into the artificial domain. Therefore it was the methods of hard-AI
workers who claimed that they achieved understanding within a computer
that were wrong. This does not mean that a neurocomputer could not inhabit
the Chinese Room and plausibly be said to 'understand' the stories that are
fed to it.

References

ALEKSANDER, I. (1996) *Impossible Minds: My Neurons, My Consciousness* (London: Imperial
College Press).

—— (2000) *How to Build a Mind: Synthetic Brains and Natural Philosophies* (London: Weidenfeld
& Nicolson).

—— and DUNMALL, B. (2000) 'An Extension to the Hypothesis of the Asynchrony of
Consciousness', *Proceedings of the Royal Society of London*, B267: 197–200.

—— —— and DELFRATE, V. (1999) 'Neurocomputational Models of Visualisation, A
Preliminary Report', *Proceedings of the IWANN99* (Alicante).

COTTERILL, R. (1999) *The Enchanted Loom: Conscious Networks in Brains and Computers*
(Cambridge: Cambridge University Press).

CRICK, F. C. H. (1994) *The Astonishing Hypothesis* (New York: Scribner's).

—— and KOCH, C. (1992) 'The Problem of Consciousness', *Scientific American* (Sept.),
153–6.

HARNAD, S. (1990) 'The Symbol Grounding Problem', *Physica D*, 42: 335–46.

HINTON, G., and SEJNOWSKI, T. J. (1986) 'Learning and Relearning in Boltzmann
Machines', in D. Rumelhart and J. McClelland (eds.), *Parallel Distributed Processing,
Volume 1* (Cambridge Mass.: MIT Press), 282–317.

HOPFIELD, J. J. (1982) 'Neural Networks and Physical Systems with Emergent Collective
Computational Abilities', *Proceedings of the National Academy of Sciences*, USA, 79: 2554–8.

PINKER, S. (1994) *The Language Instinct* (London: Penguin).

RAMACHANDARAN, V. S., and BLAKESLEE, S. (1998) *Phantoms in the Brain* (London: Fourth
Estate).

RICHARDSON, J. T. E. (1999) *Imagery* (London: Psychology Press).

SEARLE, J. R. (1980) 'Minds, Brains, and Programs', *The Behavioural and Brain Sciences*, 3:
417–57.

SEARLE, J. R. (1999) *Mind, Language and Society: Philosophy in the Real World* (London: Weidenfeld & Nicolson).

VELMANS, M. (2000) *Understanding Consciousness* (London: Routledge).

ZEKI, S. (1993) *A Vision of the Brain* (Oxford: Blackwell).

—— and BARTELS, A. (1998) 'The Asynchrony of Consciousness', *Proceedings of the Royal Society of London*, B265: 1583–5.

14

Do Virtual Actions Avoid the Chinese Room?

John G. Taylor

1. Introduction

Imagine a set of very hard-working and obedient 'slaves' locked inside a room. They carry out faithfully a set of rules that they have been furnished with by their captors to respond, by typing certain symbols on a set of keyboards, whenever other similar symbols are observed at their terminal displays. The symbols they see are Chinese, and the outputs are recognizably good answers, in good Chinese, as assessed by the native Chinese speakers inputting them to the slaves. Yet the slaves have no inkling that they are producing intelligent answers in Chinese to Chinese questions. All they are doing, so they think, is performing automatic responses to meaningless strings of symbols so as to keep themselves alive and unpunished by their captors.

This influential argument by John Searle (Searle 1980, 1984)—the so-called Chinese Room Argument (CRA)—gave a powerful rebuff to the Strong AI approach which claims that the mind is the program of the computational brain. As he has written more recently

Because programs are defined purely formally or syntactically, and because minds have an intrinsic mental content, it follows that the program by itself cannot constitute the mind. . . . The argument rests on the simple logical truth that syntax is not the same as, nor is it by itself sufficient for, semantics. (Searle 1992: 200)

The argument itself is in danger of being misinterpreted as implying the much stronger result that it is logically impossible to give a physical explanation of the mind from any set of physical hypotheses. That is not Searle's position, which he made abundantly clear in more recent writings in answer to the question as to a machine being conscious:

We have known the answer to this question for a century. The brain is a machine. *It is a conscious machine*. The brain is a biological machine just as much as the heart and the liver. . . . Because brains do it causally, that is, their inner processes actually cause them to be conscious states, any other system would have to have causal powers at least equivalent to the threshold causal powers of the brain to do it. (Searle 1997: 202; emphasis added)

This unequivocally argues for a physical basis for consciousness, one which must have great subtlety but provides an unquestionably physical underpinning to the ultimate explanation of the relation between mind and brain. It is not a simple reductionist position, however, in that it is not possible to eliminate consciousness in a naïve and immediate manner and replace it by a computational state description. In particular the simple claim of strong AI, that the detailed implementation of a suitable computer program will be able to do the trick, just is not correct. It is necessary somehow to construct a suitable 'inner view' of the world, as occurs in ourselves, for any neural approach to be able to begin to explain the mind. The inner view involves introspection, but that cannot be used directly to discern the causal link from brain to mind. Searle emphasizes that such a causal theory is still a long way from present understanding.

Given the strength of Searle's arguments, based on the Chinese Room and other related features (Searle 1992), what direction does it give those working in neural network models of the brain, and especially of its consciousness? To start such a program we must look at the very nature of semantics. That has already been pointed out by Searle, in the above excerpts, as so different from the syntax of present computational processes. But what is semantics? In particular can we develop a neurally based theory of semantics so as to begin to meet Searle's criticism of more general information-based approaches to understanding the brain? In so doing we might be able to get a little closer to the bigger problem of the nature of the self and the inner content of consciousness. Searle does not suppose that such a program is impossible, since he agrees, as in the quote above, that all experience is arrived at by physical processing in the brain, whatever those physical processes are.

In this chapter I propose to develop the bare bones of a neural theory of semantics which should be powerful enough to evade the CRA, as well as be useful for the more general questions associated with brain processing. It will be seen that the approach gives a hint of what in the brain may be 'deep structures' on which universal language properties are based, and which are used in further semantic analysis, following Chomsky (1965).

But where in the brain should we search for such deep structures and for semantics? An important guide to the search for the crucial brain sites for language acquisition and use is involved with working memory (Baddeley 1986) in which neural activity persists, to be used for later purposes, such as looking up a phone number and holding it 'in mind' so as to phone after putting the phone book down. Such working memory is an important component of language processing, and so it is relevant to ask where in the brain such processing occurs. The cause of the continued cortical activity at the basis of working memory has been suggested as arising from the functioning of 'loops' of activity flowing through neural recurrent circuits in the frontal lobes. These are termed the 'cortex-basal ganglia-thalamus-cortex' loops (Alexander *et al.* 1986; Hikosaka 1989; Taylor 1995), for which there is strong neuroanatomical support. The resulting neural model, the so-called ACTION network, can be seen to provide a platform for explanation of the numerous functions performed by the frontal lobes, such as the storing of goals, inhibition of automatic responses, planning, thinking, control of social responses. In particular it is this neural model which will be investigated here as being at the basis of semantics.

The paper starts, in the next section, with a description of some of the brain structures of interest. We then turn, in Section 3, to a description of present experimental data from brain imaging on where in the brain semantics is observed to be processed. In Section 4 a simple neural model of frontal processing is described, based on the ACTION network. This is applied to the problem of semantics in Section 5, leading to the notion of semantics as 'virtual actions'. Finally the results of the chapter are discussed in Section 6, and in particular the manner in which they evade the strictures of Searle's CRA.

2. Brain Structures and Functions

When looked at by dissection the brain appears to have a certain degree of uniformity—it has even been described as 'two fistfuls of porridge'! Yet closer inspection indicates a considerable complexity. A gross view allows for subdivision into several lobes, as shown in Fig. 14.1: occipital (which processes visual inputs), temporal (involved with the storage of object categories), parietal

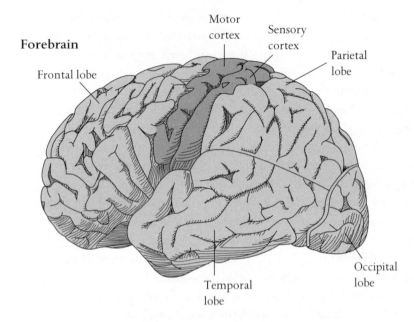

Fig. 14.1 An overview of the lateral cortex with the lobes delineated.

Notes: The mesial portion of the brain has continuations of all of the lobes into the appropriate areas. There is clear separation of function amongst the lobes, as described in the text.

(coding for the intentions and for awareness, see Taylor 1999*a*,*b*), and the frontal lobes (involved with motor response, planning, and reasoning).

There are deep subdivisions, termed sulci, the 'valleys' of the brain, which bound the smoother gyri on the surface of the cortex. The various sulci and gyri are given names delineating where they are with respect to the lobes, as shown in Fig. 14.2. Thus there are the precentral and postcentral gyri on either side of the central sulcus. The precentral gyrus codes for motor responses, containing the motor homunculus denoting the topographic map of the body musculature on the cortical surface, while the postcentral gyrus has a similar map of the body for somatosensation.

Different areas have different numbers of layers of cell bodies (six is the usual number) or different thicknesses or subdivisions of these layers; these can often be seen by eye, but with greater precision by the aid of a microscope. There is also a difference between different sites brought about by differing numbers of various types of neurons, which again becomes clear by magnification. Single cell analyses have shown that these different areas are coding for different function. These are supported by observation of deficits caused in a person's

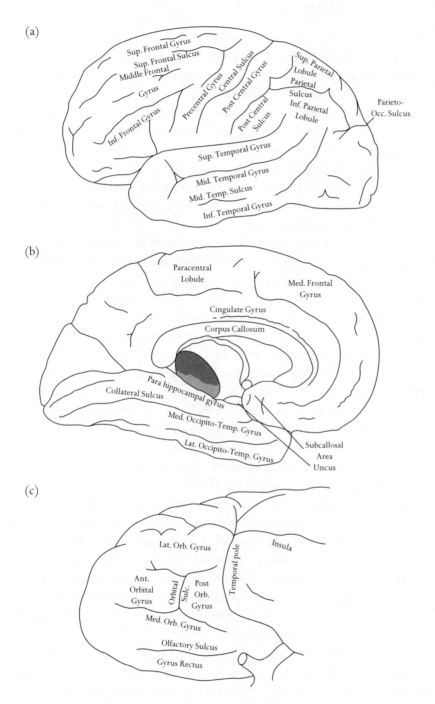

Fig. 14.2 The various sulci and gyri on the (a) lateral, (b) mesial, and (c) mesio-frontal surfaces of the cortex.

responses when they have lost a portion of their brain due to illness, stroke, or accident. Added together with results coming in from non-invasive brain imaging, and an increasingly clear picture is arising of how various parts of the brain contribute to overall brain processing.

In general this processing can be divided into posterior activity, involving mainly preprocessing and storage processes, and frontal activity concerned with thinking and response processes. The two sets of regions interact to solve tasks over time by the frontal sites calling on posterior memories or processed inputs so as to give more effective responses. There is thus a division of labour between the two: posterior for preparing and categorizing inputs, frontal for thinking about them and responding to them.

Brain areas can be observed which are involved in low-level processing; these are termed primary sensory areas. There are also areas of cortex dedicated to more complex processing of inputs in a single modality, such as vision or audition. Then there are multi-modal areas, involved in fusing inputs from several modalities, such as audition and vision or touch and vision. Areas exist dedicated to motor response, such as motor cortex, or to higher-level motor planning, such as the supplementary motor area (SMA), in the precentral and paracentral gyri (see Fig. 14.1). This has been explored by brain imaging (PET and fMRI) (Ikeda *et al.* 1999) but even more sensitively by the placement of subdural electrodes in epileptic patients (Lee *et al.* 1999). Even higher-level frontal areas are involved in planning responses by holding activity over time— so-called working memory—and to withholding responses which are natural but inappropriate, such as the dorsolateral prefrontal cortex (DLPFC) in the middle and superior frontal gyri of Fig. 14.1.

Language depends extensively on the so-called working memory sites. These were postulated earlier to be involved in a process such as holding in mind a telephone number while you make the call. After the call has been made you can forget the number, so this sort of memory is called 'short term'. It was suggested (Baddeley 1986) that there are two components to working memory: a set of slave or buffer sites for holding input activity for a limited amount of time, and an executive module for achieving rehearsal of the buffered activity so as to extend the holding time up to tens of seconds.

How is this working memory activity supported by the brain? This question involves several parts. One is as to the mechanism of the slave or buffer short-term memory sites. A second is concerned with the mode of action of the executive sites, which can control the holding of activity in the slave sites for tens of seconds. Each of these can be explained by means of recurrence although that for frontal sites, being more flexible, will require more extensive recurrent architecture. I will discuss some of the details of this shortly. There is also the problem of how these buffer or executive sites learn to code the activity they hold; that again will be considered later.

Such learning is especially noticeable for language, as can be observed as an infant utters its first few sounds which slowly are developed into single words and then sentences. Language learning leads to such a remarkable and complex end-product that the neural processes involved in its denouement appear almost impossible to uncover. However there is considerable progress being made in brain imaging of both language processing in adults and brain development in infants and young children. Some of the deficits in language, such as dyslexia, are being explored by such techniques with increasing understanding. That is why it is appropriate to attempt to build a neural network model of language learning. Such modelling should be based on what is known about the language basis in the brain. Thus to pursue this track, I will describe in the next section what is now being learnt about semantics in the brain using these new techniques.

3. Where is Semantics in the Brain?

To begin the discussion, I will describe some recent results from brain imaging which indicate that semantics is sited in a network of cortical modules with a geographical distribution of importance for neural underpinning and modelling. Guidance of where to look arises from an influential model of language processing, that of Wernicke and Geschwind, in which initial auditory input arrives at the secondary auditory cortex, where it is transformed into a semantic code in Wernike's area in the temporal lobe (denoted BA22 according to the areas of Brodmann, in the superior temporal gyrus of Fig. 14.1), and is then sent anteriorly to Broca's area in the frontal cortex (BA44/45, in the inferior and middle frontal gyri) for development of an articulatory code for speech production. Thus semantics is placed posteriorly in this model.

I introduced in the previous paragraph the notation of Brodmann areas in the brain. This is a further way of denoting areas of the brain, favored by some, and based on the differences between densities of cell layers in the various areas involved. In Table 14.1, I give a dictionary for the relation between the relevant Brodmann areas and gyri and sulci, as well as the names of areas used in the chapter.

Brain imaging is only partly in agreement with the Wernicke–Geschwind model. In spite of evidence supporting semantic coding being placed posteriorly

Table 14.1 Dictionary for translating between Brodmann areas and gyri/sulci in the brain[1]

Brodmann Area	Name	Gyrus/Sulcus
40		supramarginal gyrus
39		angular gyrus
6	supplementary motor area (SMA)	precentral/paracentral gyri
22	Wernicke's area	superior temporal gyrus
46/9	dorsolateral prefrontal cortex (DLPFC)	middle/superior frontal gyri
44/45	Broca's area	inferior frontal/middle frontal/gyri
10		medial (orbital) frontal gyrus
47		inferior frontal gyrus

Notes: [1] See Fig. 14.1. The Name column contains common terminology for the relevant area.

there is strong evidence that the left inferior frontal gyrus contributes to semantic processing (Jennings *et al.* 1998; Fiez 1997; Posner and Pavese 1998; Gabrieli *et al.* 1998). Let me briefly summarize these results.

In the PET study of Jennings, McIntosh, and Kapur (1998) subjects made semantic judgements of words presented on a screen as to whether they represented a living or non-living object. This had as comparison a letter processing task. They observed strong posterior-anterior coupled activations especially associated with BA22/BA45/BA10/cingulate gyrus. Across all response styles (clicking with a mouse, spoken response, or silent thought) these areas were always coupled together. This supports the classical model except for the presence of BA10 and the cingulate.

The work of Posner and Pavese (1998) using EEG techniques to get good timing data concentrated on tasks involving either the meaning of a word in isolation or in relation to a whole sentence. Their data supported others' findings that frontal semantic areas are active well before posterior areas. They concluded that frontal areas are concerned with lexical semantics (for single words) whilst posterior areas are more involved in comprehension of propositions that involve several words.

In an fMRI study comparing regions activated more by semantic than phonological processing, Gabrieli, Poldrack and Desmond showed there to be specific activation under this paradigm in the left inferior frontal gyrus, BA45/47. They concluded that 'in all of these conditions, left prefrontal activation occurs in conditions that require a greater amount, a longer duration, or more selection of semantic knowledge held in working memory' (Gabrieli *et al.* 1998: 912). They thus hypothesize that the left prefrontal cortex is a temporary store to hold semantic information so as to allow a particular semantic question to be answered.

Earlier work in the area summarized by Fiez (1997) gives support for this view. In particular he supported the view that the frontal lobes and associated basal ganglia are involved in strategic control of semantic retrieval from posterior semantic memory. He concludes that 'the left inferior prefrontal cortex contributes to the effortful retrieval, maintenance, and/or control of semantic information, whereas the long-term storage of the conceptual and semantic knowledge is dependent on posterior regions'.

These various views can be combined by supposing that the left inferior frontal cortex can act as a working memory to hold the semantics of several words, also involving the posterior site in BA40 (in the supramarginal gyrus, see Fig. 14.1 and Table 14.1) and termed the phonological store, and observed in several imaging experiments (Paulesu *et al.* 1993; Jonides and Smith 1997), inputted sequentially, so as to be able to allow disambiguation to occur in posterior cortex, as suggested by Posner and Pavese. That semantic priming occurs in frontal lobes, even of an amnesic with hippocampal damage, indicates that such priming may also add to the working memory aspect to achieve better short-term memory of the semantics of single words for later combination.

The results of these studies show that some part of semantics must be held in the frontal lobes. That such is the case for 'action' verbs is well known. That it also occurs for nouns puts an important new gloss on the problem of understanding the manner in which semantics is held in the brain. It has an important frontal component. This leads naturally to the question of investigating the nature of the frontal lobes to determine how they might incorporate such a crucial component of experience. We turn to that in the next section.

4. The Recurrent Architecture of the Frontal Lobes

What is special about the frontal lobes to allow them to play such a crucial role in language processing and semantics? The answer to this question will be based on the general model of recurrent networks, along the lines of the recurrent

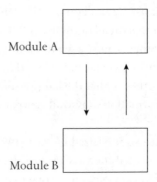

Module A

Module B

Fig. 14.3 A recurrent network, with activity in module A being sent to module B and this is then returned to A.

Notes: This recurrence of neural activity can allow such activity to recirculate indefinitely until it is destroyed by other inhibitory activity coming from another module.

system of Fig. 14.3, hinted at earlier. By recurrence here is meant the ability of the neural modules A and B to recirculate activity back and forth between each other indefinitely. Such recurrence is flexibly controllable, in that it can be learnt to be created by particular inputs and then be destroyed by other inputs (possibly internally generated) after a specific time. This system is proposed as the basis of being able to store and regenerate sequences of input patterns; that is, at the basis of language learning and generation, so the existence of neural architectures possessing such recurrence is of interest in the search for the neural basis of language.

The frontal lobes have decided recurrent architecture. They play an important part in the phenomena of working memory mentioned earlier. The cause of this continued cortical activity has been suggested as arising from the functioning of recurrent loops of activity flowing through the cortex to sub-cortical structures termed the basal ganglia, thence to the thalamus, the way-station for input from the outside going to the cortex, and thence back to the cortex (Hikosaka 1989; Taylor 1995). A cartoon version of the resulting architecture, called the ACTION network, shown in Fig. 14.4, can be seen to provide a platform for explanation of the numerous functions mentioned earlier and known to be performed by the frontal lobes: storing of goals, inhibition of automatic responses, planning, thinking, control of social responses. In general such recurrent neural architecture allows for the learning and generation of temporal sequences of patterns. These could be movements for action responses (coded in the motor cortex and sent down the cortico-spinal tract to produce

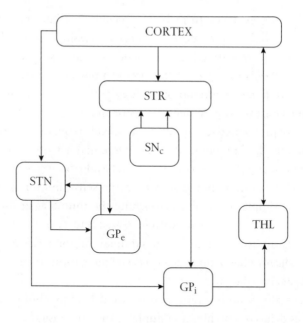

Fig. 14.4 Cartoon version of frontal lobe architecture (the ACTION network).

Notes: Used to model temporal sequence storage and generation of patterns. The basal ganglia is composed of the striatum (STR), globus pallidus (GP), and subthalamic nucleus (STN); the labels e and i on GP denote the external and internal components of GP. SN_c denotes the Substantia Nigra, pars compacta, the source of dopamine at the basis of smooth action of the system (as observed in deficits due to SN_c degradation in Parkinson's disease patients).

motor output) or sequences of transformations of patterns of activity held in the buffer/slave sites in posterior cortex.

Neuroanatomical analysis indicates the existence of several such cortico-basal ganglia-thalamo-cortical closed loops of connections (Alexander *et al.* 1986), and these have been suggested (Hikosaka 1989) as being able to support the continued neuronal firing observed in prefrontal nerve cells during working memory tasks in monkeys, such as making a saccade to a position on a visual screen memorized some seconds before (Fuster 1989; Funahashi *et al.* 1989; Goldman-Rakic 1996; Tanji and Shima 1994; Halsband *et al.* 1994). Neural network models in which recurrent connections produce similar continued activity have been proposed by a number of authors (Zipser 1991; Zipser *et al.* 1993; Lukashin *et al.* 1994; Dominey 1998), with more neuranatomically realistic models described in Dominey *et al.* (1995), Taylor (1995), Taylor and Taylor (1998a,b); Alavi and Taylor (1996).

There is strong evidence from brain imaging that the frontal lobes are crucially involved in such temporal sequence processing. Thus a PET study of subjects learning or repeating learnt sequences of finger keypress movements (Jenkins *et al.* 1994) showed the activation of prefrontal cortex during new sequence learning, lateral premotor cortex significantly more active during new learning whilst the supplementary motor area was more active during the performance of prelearned sequences. There was also equal activation observed in the basal ganglia. The observation of differential activity in these frontal motor/premotor/supplementary motor areas has also been reported (Shibasaki *et al.* 1993). These authors noted activity in the sensorimotor area and basal ganglia during simple movements (touching the thumb against each of the fingers of the same hand in turn), with increased activity in the premotor and supplementary motor areas for more complex motor tasks (touching the thumb a specific number of times against each finger, the number varying from finger to finger according to a set rule).

There have also been several recurrent models of psychological (frontal) tasks, such as delayed matching to sample or the Wisconsin card-sorting task (Dehaene and Changeux 1989; Cohen and Servan-Schrieber 1992, 1997; Monchi and Taylor 1995, 1998). The principles underlying all of these models is recurrence of neural activity, so leading to motion to one of several specific patterns of activity called attractors (since neural activity is attracted to ending up identical to such a pattern as time passes), as in the original Hopfield model (Hopfield 1982). Transitions between these attractors can then be attained by suitable techniques (Amit 1989).

Even more appositely there have been several recurrent neural network models of language. A class of these has been developed, for example, by Elman (Elman 1991, 1993; Elman *et al.* 1996) specifically to learn grammatically correct sentence structure in sequences of words. This learning required careful training of the networks, especially on simple sentences, before being given the task of learning the structure of more complex ones. In this manner it was possible to train a recurrent network to recognize and regenerate complex but grammatically correct sentences. This has been discussed in more generality in a provocative account in Deacon (1997), again supporting the use of recurrent network architectures. However the specific problem of semantics is not tackled in these discussions, except in terms of a one-to-one mapping of an object input onto a learnt representation for it (the indexical stage). This must be part of the process, especially for nouns referring to objects, but is inadequate for verbs as describing 'actions'.

I will use here the specific ability of the ACTION network of Fig. 14.4 (Taylor 1995), designed as a cartoon version of the frontal lobes. This model was applied (Taylor and Taylor 1998a,b; N. R. Taylor 1998) to the temporal sequence activities observed in frontal neurons by Tanji and colleagues (Tanji and Shima 1994; Halsband et al. 1994), and shown to have very similar neural activity to that observed experimentally. A mathematical analysis of these models was performed, and is described in several publications (Taylor and Taylor 2000a,b). One of the advances of the ACTION net over artificial neural network approaches to language processing is that the former can be related to brain imaging data, so allowing predictions deduced from the model to be tested against experiment.

Let us first consider some of the details of the architectural features of the prefrontal lobes. The region of interest includes the classic motor cortex that gives rise to descending motor signals. In front of that is the premotor region, which includes areas with different functions, such as the supplementary motor area (SMA) and Broca's speech production area. The supplementary area is believed to be involved in programming and initiation of movement sequences.

The inputs to the prefrontal cortex are organized into three major groups. First, there are major projections from the mediodorsal nucleus of the thalamus. Secondly, there are projections carrying emotional information from the limbic areas, such as the cingulate gyrus. Thirdly, there are corticocortical (association) fibres from all of the posterior association areas for all of three major sensory modalities (vision, audition, and somatic sensation). In general the thalamic inputs include the relaying of information from the lower levels of the brainstem and the limbic areas.

From the general 'reciprocity' rule of cortical connectivity, all the areas that send projections to the prefrontal area receive reciprocal efferents, the only exception being the basal ganglia (BG), which receives projections from the prefrontal cortex but is not directly connected back to it. The BG consists of five large sub-cortical nuclei, as shown in Fig. 14.4: the caudate nucleus, the putamen (these two usually being combined as the striatum), the globus pallidus (GP), the subthalamic nucleus, and the substantia nigra (SN). These nuclei are mainly composed of inhibitory neurons (except for the SN which is mainly excitatory), and are interposed in a feedback loop from frontal cortex through thalamic nuclei and thence back to frontal cortex again, as shown in Fig. 14.4. It is accepted that there are roughly five such (parallel) loops in the frontal lobes, with relative independence of their activity flow from each other, and with rough topography in the various modules in the loop

(Alexander *et al.* 1986). Thus the main input nuclei of the BG is the striatum, which feeds down to the internal globus pallidus (GP_i) and the substantia nigra (pars reticulata) before inputting to thalamus. This is the direct pathway; there is also an excitatory side loop (the indirect pathway) to the subthalamic nucleus (STN) which has excitatory connections to GP_i and external globus pallidus (GP_e); STN is then inhibited by GP_e.

The main method of control of activity of the thalamus by the BG is that of disinhibition: the effect of an inhibitory neuron on another inhibitory neuron is to cause the latter to reduce its activity and so reduce its inhibitory effects on whatever it is targeting. The main inputs to the BG are from the cortex, which sends excitatory inputs to the striatum. This is in a roughly topological form (with the arm area in motor cortex, for example, being preserved in its flow of activity down to the BG and thence to the thalamus), and the outputs from thalamic nuclei are also roughly reciprocal to these cortical areas. There is also rough preservation of topography in the internal connections of striatum to GP and thence to TH.

There are several sites of output from the BG, the main one being to various thalamic nuclei. The output is inhibitory from GP to TH, and the total BG effect is thought to be disinhibitory from cortex, through BG, to TH. The medio-dorsal nucleus of the TH is a target of output from the dorsolateral prefrontal cortical loop. These are all of great relevance in the modelling of frontal areas, since the TH acts as a throughput region back to the cortical regions from which the original cortical output was fed to the BG. The ensuing loop structure allows for strong modulation of other thalamic throughput. At the same time it is important to note that the direct cortico-thalamic connections are recipro-cal; this allows for the possibility of a reverberation or resonant build-up in this activity, controlled by the cortico-BG-thalamic side loop. Such a mode of action of the frontal system has already been noted as important in Taylor (1995) and Alavi and Taylor (1996), and modelled in Monchi and Taylor (1995, 1998); Taylor and Taylor (1998*a,b*); and N. R. Taylor (1998).

To complete the loop frontal cortex → basal ganglia → thalamus → frontal cortex the connections of the various anterior thalamic nuclei to cortex and to basal ganglia need to be determined. The thalamic projections to monkey frontal cortex show an orderly projection moving laterally from next to the thalamic midline sideways to ventral thalamic nuclei, with the frontal lobe pro-jection going first towards the frontal pole and then going back to the motor cortex from the ventral nuclei; these projections are reciprocal. The projections of the GP_i and SN from the various regions of the prefrontal cortex are onto those portions of the TH which are directly reciprocally connected to them in the first place, as noted by Alexander, DeLong, and Strick (1986).

This connectivity is summarized, as noted, in the ACTION network of Fig. 14.4 (Taylor 1995; Alavi and Taylor 1996). The important feature of the ACTION network is the possibility of activity in cortex being amplified by feedback directly to TH (or by the side loop through BG, to TH, and then back to cortex), and given thereby a longer lifetime by this recurrence. Such amplific-ation of duration can be controlled by BG input to TH, this input itself being controlled by other frontal areas or from posterior cortex (from environmental input). The manner in which the ACTION network can store and generate temporal sequences as a basis for semantics will be explored in the next section.

5. Semantics and the Frontal Lobes

I would like to discuss that feature of the brain which gives us our unique ability to think, to reason, and to do so in language. What is it in the brain, and espe-cially the cortex, which allows us to have developed these amazingly powerful modes of existence? I suggest it is the ability to store and manipulate sequences of neural activities, be they inputs from outside or internally generated 'thoughts'. There is also the ability to hold such activity over periods of time (many seconds) so they can be called on later for further use. The holding of activity has already been considered in terms of the ACTION network and its related dedicated posterior working memory buffer sites. However the abilities to perform temporal sequence storage and generation (TSSG) and to manip-ulate such sequences go considerably beyond these temporal features. With-out such further powers we would be unable to manipulate any thoughts in our minds; they could only be experienced in a passive manner. With these powers we can move ideas around so that they achieve goals we have already stored.

In the previous section I described some of the neural circuitry involved in activity concerned with the frontal lobes. The ACTION network (and similar types of models) has recently been applied to explore the processes underlying these higher-order processes, considered as based on TSSG. Coupled ACTION nets that can perform TSSG have been developed and applied to various frontal tasks (Monchi and Taylor 1998). More recent work (Taylor and Taylor 2000a) with coupled ACTION modules has led to a basis for 'chunking', or compres-sion of signals in a temporal sequence, in a very specific form. Let me consider some of the problems that are faced when attempting such chunking, before turning to consider the importance of chunking for language and thought.

In a sequence of patterns P_1, P_2, ... the initial stage of chunking involves the creation of nodes encoding the pairwise transitions $P_1 \rightarrow P_2$, $P_2 \rightarrow$ ... Furthermore there is experimental evidence that nodes exist in motor areas and in the basal ganglia encoding for triplet transitions $P_1 \rightarrow P_2 \rightarrow P_3$, and so on. Such encodings lead to an exponential explosion, in which it would be necessary to have 2^n nodes to encode a sequence of length n. How can this explosion be avoided?

The simplest answer is to prevent it from ever being needed, by breaking sequences down into smaller lengths, say of length three or four. Longer sequences are then built up by chunking the shorter sequences together. This seems to be what happens in our own brains, as noted in Greenfield (1991). There she put forward evidence that as infants develop, their initial powers of object manipulation and of language are at the same level of ability, with sequences of length initially of one and then two stepping up to length three. The relevant neural systems were suggested as being identical. There then occurs a division of powers in which word sequences and object manipulation sequences are encoded in separate regions of BA44/45. These control structures develop, at a later age, more anteriorly into BA46 and BA9 for language and object manipulation control respectively. The final story about how this is achieved is not known, but it could be that the shorter temporal sequences are initially encoded in the more posterior portions of prefrontal cortex and then higher chunking is achieved as more cortex comes available through myelination as the child develops. Thus the chunking that occurred would be of sequences of sequences of . . . , up to a level of chunked sequences corresponding to the highest cortical level available to human prefrontal cortex. In the process the melding together of syntax and of grammar in language would be occurring as part of the higher-order coding process.

There is brain imaging data supporting the above suggestion of chunking nodes being placed in higher areas than the coding for single movements, some of which has already been briefly mentioned. The PET results from Shibasaki et al. (1993) indicate that for more complex movements there is recruitment of the higher-order cortex in the supplementary motor area. The use of epidural electrodes (Ikeda et al. 1999) led the authors to conclude, in support of this hierarchical separation, that 'pre-SMA plays a more important role in cognitive motor control which involves sensory discrimination and decision making or motor selection for the action after stimuli, whereas SMA-proper is one of the main generators of the Bereitschaftspotential preceding self-paced voluntary movements'.

The 'broad-brush' explanation of language encoding, in terms of the temporal sequence storage and generation powers of the frontal lobes, allows for a new perspective on the 'deep structures' of Chomsky (1965). His suggestion of the existence of such structures deep in the brain is natural from this perspective, and even allows a new perspective on semantics. Chomsky has suggested that the deep structures feed to regions for semantic analysis. I presented results in Section 3 that an important component of semantics occurs in the frontal lobes, which are heavily devoted to action-like processing involving sequence storage and generation. I would therefore like to propose that semantics be equated with what I have elsewhere termed 'virtual actions' (Taylor 1999a). This can arise in the following manner.

The encoded sequence structures of manipulation and speech, developed as part of the prefrontal powers of TSSG by the chunking process suggested above, are activated by the input of a word. This activation (now well recorded as part of brain imaging when semantic processing is occurring in a subject, as noted earlier) does not produce the corresponding sequences of actions that occurred when the word was first met. However such lack of actions does not mean that the neural structures available to make such actions are not partially available. It is that they are not fully activated, and that only a set of 'virtual actions' occurs. The neural sites of such activity can be proposed as in basal ganglia and the associated cortical regions. The cortex is seen here to play a secondary role in the production of 'virtual action'-based semantics.

In more detail, the original learning of the meaning of the word involved actions being made in parallel with the auditory code of the word. This code is assumed to activate the sequence of actions when it is heard in initial learning. Such actions will be based on the disinhibitory activity flowing from the relevant prefrontal cortical site onto the thalamus and thence to produce the motor response patterns. As learning proceeds, the movement pattern is learnt to be inhibited, but the disinhibitory activity flowing from cortex to thalamus, by way of the BG, is still present, even if it is now ineffective. That is the meaning of the term 'virtual'. Such virtuality acts like a priming signal, although now to areas which were originally causing movement but now do not do so. However the resulting disinhibitory activity primes thalamic sites, and can thereby provide information to them which can be used in further processing as if there had been movement made. This is the basis for the 'virtual': it is the relic of the movement, which still provides constraints for future processing. It is in this way that the external world is brought in contact with the inner symbolic representations that are being constructed in the brain as part of language acquisition.

A schematic form of the neural coding of virtual actions in the brain is shown in Fig. 14.5. A sequence of visual inputs from a single object, denoted L1, L2, . . . are produced by the sequence of actions A(Li, Li+1) transforming the appearance Li of the object into Li+1. The sequence of actions is itself 'chunked' to produce the chunked code {A(Li, Li+1)} for the object. This higher-order code is then used, in particular with its disinhibitory basal ganglia connections, to provide a virtual memory of the past actions without actually taking them. These virtual actions can then be used to encode words describing the objects, either directly to the visual inputs Li or to the coding nodes in the basal ganglia coding for the virtual actions.

This postulated basis for semantics can be tested by determining if the prefrontal activity associated with semantic tasks, observed in the brain imaging experiments mentioned earlier, extends also to the relevant motor parts of the basal ganglia or thalamus.

More generally, manipulation of sequences, seen as part of planning and reasoning, can then be envisaged as occurring in the frontal lobes by means of the transformation of one cortical activity by another from a different module at a higher level. Such transformations are the life-blood of thinking and reasoning. They do not seem to be able to be performed by posterior cortical sites. Indeed this supports the epithet 'passive consciousness' I have given (Taylor 1999a) to that component of consciousness created by posterior cortex.

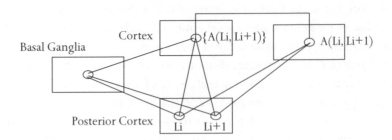

Fig. 14.5 A neural model of semantics as 'virtual actions'.

Notes: The different views L1, L2, . . . of an object in posterior cortex are coded in terms of the set of actions A(Li, Li+1) needed to change the input from Li to Li+1. The sequence of these actions are then coded on a higher-order region of cortex as the chunking nodes {A(Li, Li+1)}. The disinhibitory connections from these nodes through the basal ganglia are activated on viewing the object, so as to give a set of 'virtual actions' as the memory of action that were taken on the object, without the actions physically being taken.

It is only the presence of an ACTION network kind of structure that would appear essential for such transformations to be achieved.

Such internal voluntary transformations would not appear to be able to be achieved until after several years of age, even as late as the beginning of the 'concrete operations' stage of Piaget (about age 7). It is necessary for the developing child to create a suitable set of representations on which higher-level control structures can act to transform between the lower-level components. The internalization of actions could be related to the development of internal semantics, since the internal actions are similarly not to be externalized. However it would be at a later stage in child development that semantics first occurs, since it involves actions to be taken on the semanticized representations.

6. Discussion

We now turn to consider the relevance of the above model of the frontal lobes, and particularly of semantics as virtual actions, for answering the CRA and related questions raised by Searle. He pointed out, by bringing forward the CRA, that semantics is missing from the Strong AI approach to the problem of explaining the mind in terms of the brain. To posit that the mind is 'the program of the computations being performed by the brain' misses completely the crucial contribution that meaning gives to conscious experience. It is just not enough to create consciousness by running a computation of responding to questions asked in Chinese.

The direction we have been led in by these arguments is to sketch a possible neural model of language processing in which semantics has been included as 'virtual actions'. Such a model, supported by brain imaging data and by results on deficits, also allows us to suggest that Chomsky's 'deep structures' arise from the general architecture of the frontal lobes. But how does the model I have presented avoid the strictures of Searle? Are there also little slaves scurrying back and forth in the model I have presented?

The answer is decidedly not. The manner in which meaning is brought into the total neural coding of language involves grounding the representations by actions on the objects of relevance. The meaning of any concept is thereby constrained (by the below-threshold activations from the frontal code, built up as in Fig. 14.5) by the actions that have been taken on its exemplars in the past. That allows the concepts to be used in a way consistent with the outside world and its physical rules and regulations. It is in this manner that an image of the external world is built in the most effective manner possible in the brain. The virtual actions encode possible actions and thereby bring the external world into the brain. There are no homunculi working with arbitrary rules; the actual constraints encoded in frontal systems are those of the physical systems met with 'in the line of action', so to speak. Thus the 'virtual actions' meaning attached to symbols of these external objects has no arbitrariness at all; it is that of the real world itself.

The manner in which actions can be taken to relate objects in the world together can also be encoded as virtual in the above manner using actions combining objects. The semantics of verbs is even more immediate, in terms of the virtual actions involved, and correlated with the auditory code in Wernicke's area for the action. Thus the network of relations between symbols of objects or actions in the world can also be encoded by virtual actions. The semantic (relational) network of the posterior temporal lobe, Wernicke's area, is thus grounded in the world. Instead of ending up only with a dictionary, in which the meaning of a word is only given in terms of other words, there is now an encoding of the external world in terms of the actions taken in the past on the relevant object. It is in this manner that the frontal sites can act as 'strategic controllers' of semantic retrieval; they contribute an important action-based semantic component to the 'semantic' networks in posterior sites, which would otherwise have little reference to the external world.

I still have to answer more directly the question: how can the addition of 'virtual actions' evade Searle's original argument? In other words how can the computations involved differ from those which are based on a Strong AI type of computation? The latter I take to be a set of logically consistent rules. The level at which such rules work, and Searle's argument apply, cannot be too microscopic: if the simulation of the brain's semantics were at a neural network level, with suitably complex neurons, architecture, etc., then a reasonable approximation to the processing of the real brain could be achieved. That is the level which Searle accepts as possible. As he wrote:

'Yes, but could an artifact, a man-made machine, think?' Assuming it is possible to produce artificially a machine with a nervous system, neurons with axons and dendrites, and all the rest of it, sufficiently like ours, again the answer to the question seems to be obviously, yes. (Searle 1980: 422 (B82))[1]

So I will assume that Searle accepts the neural level, suitably implemented, as able to support semantics, and avoid his CRA.

---

[1] Reprinted in Boden (1990: 82). From here referred to as B82.

But how, specifically, might the neural level succeed in so doing? The manner in which virtual actions, suitably implemented, slip past Searle's argument is, I suggest, in terms of the difficulty of constructing a consistent set of rules to cover their effects. It is known that there are at least two stages in the processing of words: an initial stage, at semantic level, in which many possible meanings are activated, and a second stage, in which disambiguation of these meanings arises (Morton 1969; Levelt et al. 1991; Marcel 1980). These stages have been earlier (in Sect. 3) related to the prefrontal processing of single words, with later posterior disambiguation at phrase or sentence level. This fits well with the notion of semantics as virtual actions in the frontal lobes. There can be many such actions for a given word, some contradicting others; disambiguation is then needed, using context. This process has earlier been modelled by a two-stage process, explaining the data of Marcel (1980) on subliminal processing (Taylor 1996a).

In such a picture, frontal semantic activations involve possibly contradictory virtual actions. It would thus not be possible to construct a logically consistent set of rules to describe these parallel activations. It is in this manner that Searle's strictures are avoided: there is no strong AI formulation possible of the set of underlying neural activations. Only a neural description (with its accompanying mathematical equations) is available, and as noted earlier, that is acceptable to Searle to carry the load of semantics, and even consciousness.

The frontal component necessarily contributes to conscious experience, but in a manner which has to be explored by further analysis. At first view, the encodings of virtual actions will be outside consciousness, but will contribute strongly to creativity and automatic language production. This is supported by the simulation of the data of Marcel on subliminal processing mentioned earlier (Taylor 1996a). The model was composed of two modules, the first encoding word inputs at semantic level, the second being on the phonological store, encoding them at phonological level. In the semantic module there may be a number of different activations for a given input, corresponding to the multiple meanings of a word like 'palm'. The second module then selects from these meanings the most appropriate, as supported by previous activations stored in the phonological store as a slave working memory. Such a two-stage process has been developed into a more complete model of the emergence of consciousness in the second store (Taylor 1996b, 1999a,b, 2001), with no consciousness occurring at the first stage. Thus consciousness is not created in the frontal lobes, but its content is given meaning by activations there. Such a division of labour is efficient in terms of consciousness being part of the attentional monitoring system based in the parietal lobes. Strong AI cannot handle such a two-stage division of processing into that at a non-conscious and separately at a conscious level.

The analysis given above demonstrates the power of the brain as a neuronal machine. It helps broach the barrier of ignorance about these high-level processes partly in and partly out of consciousness, and takes a step towards meeting Searle's recent comment 'Because we do not know how real brains [generate consciousness] we are in a poor position to fabricate an artificial brain' (Searle 1997: 202). Yet do it they do; as Searle states 'The brain is a machine. It is a conscious machine' (ibid.). The Chinese and similar rooms guide us to tackle the problem of meaning and language, which will ultimately help us to understand consciousness itself, and thence to create other conscious machines. Further steps to that construction are described elsewhere (Taylor 1999*a*,*b*, 2001).

References

ALAVI, F., and TAYLOR, J. G. (1996) 'A Basis for Long-Range Inhibition Across Cortex', in J. Sirosh, R. Miikulainen, and Y. Choe (eds.), *Lateral Interactions in Cortex: Structure and Function* (Austin, Tex.: UCTS Neural Networks Research Group). Electronic book, ISBN 0-9647060-0-8. Online version: http: www.cs.utexas.edu/users/nn/web-pubs/htmlbook96

ALEXANDER, G. E., DELONG, M. R., and STRICK, P. L. (1986) 'Parallel Organization of Functionally Segregated Circuits Linking Basal Ganglia and Cortex', *Annual Review of Neuroscience*, 9: 357–81.

AMIT, D. J. (1989) *Modeling Brain Function: The World of Attractor Neural Networks* (Cambridge: Cambridge University Press).

BADDELEY, A. D. (1986) *Working Memory* (Oxford: Oxford University Press).

BODEN, M. A. (ed.) (1990) *The Philosophy of Artificial Intelligence* (Oxford: Oxford University Press).

CHOMSKY, N. (1965) *Aspects of the Theory of Syntax* (Cambridge, Mass.: MIT Press).

COHEN, J. D., and SERVAN-SCHRIEBER, D. (1992) 'Context, Cortex and Dopamine: A Connectionist Approach to Behavior and Biology in Schizophrenia', *Psychological Review*, 99: 45–77.

———— (1997) 'Temporal Dynamics of Brain Activation during a Working Memory Task', *Nature*, 386: 604–8.

DEACON, T. (1997) *The Symbolic Species* (London: Penguin Books).

DEHAENE, S., and CHANGEUX, J.-P. (1989) 'A Simple Model of Prefrontal Cortex Function in Delayed-Response Tasks', *Journal of Cognitive Neuroscience*, 1: 244–61.

DOMINEY, P. F. (1998) 'A Shared System for Learning Serial and Temporal Structure of Sensori-Motor Sequences? Evidence from Simulation and Human Experiments', *Cognitive Brain Research*, 6: 163–72.

—— ARBIB, M., and JOSEPH, J.-P. (1995) 'A Model of Corticostriatal Plasticity for Learning Oculomotor Associations and Sequences', *Journal of Cognitive Neuroscience*, 7: 311–36.

ELMAN, J. (1991) 'Incremental Learning, or the Importance of Starting Small', in *13th Annual Conference of the Cognitive Science Society* (Hillsdale, NJ: Lawrence Erlbaum), 443–8.

—— (1993) 'Learning and Development in Neural Networks: The Importance of Starting Small', *Cognition*, 48: 71–99.

—— BATES, E., JOHNSON, M., KARMILOFF-SMITH, A., PARISI, D., and PLUNKETT, K. (1996) *Rethinking Innateness: A Connectionist Perspective on Development* (Cambridge, Mass.: MIT Press).

FIEZ, J. A. (1997) 'Phonology, Semantics and the Role of the Left Prefrontal Cortex', *Human Brain Mapping*, 5: 79–83.

FUNAHASHI, S., BRUCE, C. J., and GOLDMAN-RAKIC, P. S. (1989) 'Mnemonic Coding of Visual Space in Monkey Dorsolateral Prefrontal Cortex', *Journal of Neurophysiology*, 61: 331–49.

FUSTER, J. M. (1989) *The Prefrontal Cortex*, 2nd edn. (New York: Raven).

GABRIELI, J. D. E., POLDRACK, R. A., and DESMOND, J. E. (1998) 'The Role of Left Prefrontal Cortex in Language and Memory', *Proceedings of the National Academy of the Sciences, USA*, 95: 906–13.

GOLDMAN-RAKIC, P. S. (1996) 'Regional and Cellular Fractionation of Working Memory', *Proceedings of the National Academy of the Sciences, USA*, 93: 13473–80.

GREENFIELD, P. (1991) 'Language, Tools and the Brain: The Ontogeny and Phylogeny of Hierarchically-Organised Sequential Behaviour', *Behavioural and Brain Sciences*, 14: 531–95.

HALSBAND, U., MATSUZUKA, Y., and TANJI, J. (1994) 'Neuronal Activity in the Primate Supplementary, Pre-supplementary and Pre-motor Cortex during Externally and Internally Instructed Sequential Movements', *Neuroscience Research*, 20: 149–55.

HIKOSAKA, O. (1989) 'Role of the Basal Ganglia in Initiation of Voluntary Movements', in M. A. Arbib and S. Amari (eds.), *Dynamic Interactions in Neural Networks: Models and Data* (New York: Springer-Verlag), 153–67.

HOPFIELD, J. J. (1982) 'Neural Networks and Physical Systems with Emergent Collective Computational Abilities', *Proceedings of the National Academy of the Sciences, USA*, 79: 2554–8.

IKEDA, A., YAZAWA, S., KUNIEDA, T., OHARA, S., TERADA, K., MIKUNI, N., TAKASHI, N., TAKI, W., KIMURA, J., and SHIBASAKI, H. (1999) 'Cognitive Motor Control in Human Pre-supplementary Motor Area Studied by Subdural Recording of Discrimination/Selection-Related Potentials', *Brain*, 122: 915–31.

JENKINS, H., BROOKS, D. J., NIXON, P. D., FRACKOWIAK, R. S. J., and PASSINGHAM, R. E. (1994) 'Motor Sequence Learning: A Study with Positron Emission Tomography', *Journal of Neuroscience*, 14: 3775–90.

JENNINGS, J. M., McINTOSH, A. R., and KAPUR, S. (1998) 'Mapping Neural Interactivity onto Regional Activity: An Analysis of Semantic Processing and Response Mode Interactions', *NeuroImage*, 7: 244–54.

JONIDES, J., and SMITH, E. E. (1997) 'The Architecture of Working Memory', in M. D. Rugg (ed.), *Cognitive Neuroscience* (Hove, East Sussex: Taylor & Francis), ch. 8: 243–76.

LEE, K.-M., CHANG, K.-H., and ROH, J.-K. (1999) 'Subregions within the Supplementary Motor Area Activated at Different Stages of Movement Preparation and Execution', *NeuroImage*, 117: 117–23.

LEVELT, W. J. M., SCHRIEFERS, H., VORBERG, D., MEYER, A. S., PECHMANN, T., and HAVINGA, J. (1991) 'The Time Course of Lexical Access in Speech Production: A Study of Picture-Naming', *Psychological Review*, 98: 122–42.

LUKASHIN, A. V., WILCOX, G. L., and GEORGOPOULOS, A. P. (1994) 'Overlapping Neural Networks for Multiple Engrams', *Proceedings of the National Academy of the Sciences, USA*, 91: 8651–4.

MARCEL, A. (1980) 'Conscious and Preconscious Recognition on Polysemous Words: Locating Selective Effects of Prior Verbal Contexts', in R. S. Nickerson (ed.), *Attention and Performance VIII* (Hillsdale, NJ: Lawrence Erlbaum), 435–67.

MONCHI, O., and TAYLOR, J. G. (1995) 'A Model of the Prefrontal Loop that Includes the Basal Ganglia in Solving the Recency Task', *Proceedings of the World Congress on Neural Networks '95, Volume 3* (Hillsdale NJ: Lawrence Erlbaum & INNS Press), 48–51.

—— —— (1998) 'A Hard-Wired Model of Coupled Frontal Working Memories for Various Tasks', *Information Sciences Journal*, 113: 221–43.

MORTON, J. (1969) 'Interaction of Information in Word Recognition', *Psychological Review*, 76: 165–78.

PAULESU, E., FRITH, C. D., and FRACKOWIAK, R. S. J. (1993) 'The Neural Correlates of the Verbal Components of Working Memory', *Nature*, 362: 342–5.

POSNER, M. I., and PAVESE, A. (1998) 'Anatomy of Word and Sentence Meaning', *Proceedings of the National Academy of the Sciences, USA*, 95: 899–905.

SEARLE J. R. (1980) 'Minds, Brains, and Programs', *Behavioural Brain Sciences*, 3: 417–24.

—— (1984) *Minds, Brains, and Science* (London: BBC Publications).

—— (1992) *The Rediscovery of the Mind* (Cambridge, Mass.: MIT Press).

—— (1997) *The Mystery of Consciousness* (London: Granta Books).

SHIBASAKI, H., SADATO, N., LYSHKOW, H., YONEKURA, Y., HONDA, M., NAGAMINE, T., SUWAZONO, S., MAGATA, Y., IKEDA, A., MIYAZAKI, M., FUKUYAMA, H., ASATO, R., and KONISHI, J. (1993) 'Both Primary Motor Cortex and Supplementary Motor Area Play an Important Role in Complex Finger Movement', *Brain*, 116: 1387–98.

TANJI, J., and SHIMA, K. (1994) 'A Role for the Supplementary Motor Area Cells in Planning Several Movements Ahead', *Nature*, 88: 135–70.

TAYLOR, J. G. (1995) 'Modelling the Mind by PSYCHE', in F. Soulie and P. Gallinari (eds.), *Proc ICANN'95* (Paris: EC2 & Co).

—— (1996*a*) 'Breakthrough to Awareness', *Biological Cybernetics*, 75: 59–72.

—— (1996*b*) 'A Competition for Consciousness?' *Neurocomputing*, 11: 271–96.

—— (1999*a*) *The Race for Consciousness* (Cambridge, Mass.: MIT Press).

—— (1999*b*) 'Neural Networks for Consciousness: The Central Representation', *Proceedings of the International Joint Conference on Neural Networks '99* (Hillsdale, NJ: Lawrence Erlbaum).

—— (2001) 'The Central Role of the Parietal Lobes in Consciousness', *Consciousness and Cognition*, 10: 379–417.

—— and TAYLOR, N. R. (1998*a*) 'Experimenting with Models of the Frontal Lobes', in G. W. Humphrey, A. Olson, and D. Heinke (eds.), *NCPW5 Connectionist Models in Cognitive Neuroscience*, Perspectives in Neural Computation series (New York: Springer-Verlag), 92–101.

—— —— (1998*b*) 'Experimenting with Models of the Frontal Lobes', *Society for Neuroscience Abstracts*, 24, part 2: 1653.

—— —— (2000*a*) 'Analysis of a Recurrent Cortico-Basal Ganglia-Thalamo-Cortical Loop for Working Memory', *Biological Cybernetics*, 82: 415–32.

—— —— (2000*b*) 'Hard-Wired Models of Working Memory and Temporal Sequence Storage and Generation', *Neural Networks*, 13: 201–24.

TAYLOR, N. R. (1998) '*Modelling Temporal Sequence Learning*', University of London Thesis (unpublished).

ZIPSER, D. (1991) 'Recurrent Network Model of the Neural Mechanism of Short-term Active Memory', *Neural Computation*, 3: 179–93.

—— KEHOE, B., LITTLEWORT, G., and FUSTER, J. (1993) 'A Spiking Model of Short-term Active Memory', *The Journal of Neuroscience*, 13: 3406–20.

15

Minds, Machines, and Searle 2: What's Right and Wrong about the Chinese Room Argument

Stevan Harnad

> . . . in an academic generation a little overaddicted to 'politesse,' it may be worth saying that violent destruction is not necessarily worthless and futile. Even though it leaves doubt about the right road for London, it helps if someone rips up, however violently, a 'To London' sign on the Dover cliffs pointing south . . .
>
> (Hexter 1979)

When in 1979 Zenon Pylyshyn, associate editor of *The Behavioral and Brain Sciences* (BBS, a peer commentary journal which I edit) informed me that he had secured a paper by John Searle (with an unprepossessing title that Zenon, John, and I have all since forgotten!), I cannot say that I was especially impressed; nor did a quick reading of the brief manuscript—which seemed to be yet another tedious 'Granny Objection'[1] about why/how we are not computers—do anything to upgrade that impression.

The paper pointed out that a 'Chinese-Understanding' computer program would not really understand Chinese because someone who did not understand Chinese (e.g. Searle himself) could execute the same program while still not understanding Chinese; hence the computer executing the program would not be understanding Chinese either. The paper rebutted various

---

[1] See: http://cogsci.ecs.soton.ac.uk/~harnad/Hypermail/Explaining.Mind96/

prima-facie counter-arguments against this (mostly variants on the theme that it would not be Searle but 'the system', of which Searle would only be a part, that would indeed be understanding Chinese when the program was being executed), but all of this seemed trivial to me. Yes, of course an inert program alone could not understand anything (so Searle was right about that), but surely an executing program might be part of what an understanding 'system' like ourselves really does and is (so the 'Systems Reply' was right too).

The paper was refereed (favorably), and was accepted under the revised title 'Minds, Brains, and Programs', circulated to a hundred potential commentators across disciplines and around the world, and then co-published in 1980 in BBS with twenty-seven commentaries and Searle's Response. Across the ensuing years, further commentaries and responses continued to flow as, much to my surprise, Searle's paper became BBS's most influential target article (and still is, to the present day) as well as something of a classic in cognitive science.[2] (At the Rochester Conference on Cognitive Curricula (Lucas and Hayes 1982), Pat Hayes went so far as to define cognitive science as 'the ongoing research program of showing Searle's Chinese Room Argument to be false'—'and silly', I believe he added at the time.)

As the arguments and counter-arguments kept surging across the years I chafed at being the only one on the planet not entitled (*ex officio*, being the umpire) to have a go, even though I felt that I could settle Searle's wagon if I had a chance, and put an end to the rather repetitious and unresolved controversy. In the late 1980s I was preparing a critique of my own, called 'Minds, Machines and Searle' (after 'Minds, Machines, and Gödel', by Lucas (1961), another philosopher arguing that we are not computers), though not sure where to publish it (BBS being out of the question). One of the charges that had been laid against Searle by his critics had been that his wrong-headed critique had squelched funding for Artificial Intelligence (AI), so the newly founded *Journal of Experimental and Theoretical Artificial Intelligence* (JETAI) seemed a reasonable locus for my own critique of Searle, which accordingly appeared there in 1989.

I never heard anything from Searle about my JETAI critique, even though we were still interacting regularly in connection with the unabating Continuing Commentary on his Chinese Room Argument (CRA) in BBS, as well as a brand-new BBS target article (Searle 1990a) that he wrote specifically to mark the tenth anniversary of the CRA. This inability to enter the fray would have been a good deal more frustrating to me had not a radically new

[2] See: http://cogsci.umn.edu/millennium/final.html

medium for Open Peer Commentary been opening up at the same time: it had been drawn to my attention that since the early 1980s the CRA had been a prime topic on 'comp.ai', a discussion group on Usenet. (That Global Graffiti Board for Trivial Pursuit was to have multiple influences on both me and BBS, and on the future course of Learned Inquiry and Learned Publication, but that is all another story (Harnad 1990a, 1991b; Hayes *et al.* 1992); here we are only concerned with its influence on the Searle saga.)

Tuning in to comp.ai in the mid-late 1980s with the intention of trying to resolve the debate with my own somewhat ecumenical critique of Searle (Searle's right that an executing program cannot be *all* there is to being an understanding system, but wrong that an executing program cannot be *part* of an understanding system), to my surprise, I found comp.ai choked with such a litany of unspeakably bad anti-Searle arguments that I found I had to spend all my air-time defending Searle against these non-starters instead of burying him, as I had intended to do. (Searle did take notice this time, for apparently he too tuned in to comp.ai in those days, encouraging me (off-line) to keep fighting the good fight—which puzzled me, as I was convinced we were on opposite sides.)

I never did get around to burying Searle, for when, after months of never getting past trying to clear the air by rebutting the bad rebuttals to the CRA, I begged Searle (off-line) to read my 'Minds, Machines and Searle' and know that we were adversaries rather than comrades-at-arms, despite contrary appearances on comp.ai, he wrote back to say that although my paper contains points on which reasonable men might agree to disagree, on the *essential* point, the one everyone else was busy disputing, I in fact agree with him—so why don't I just come out and say so?

It was then that the token dropped. For there was something about the CRA that had just been *obviously* right to me all along, and hence I had quite taken that part for granted, focusing instead on where I thought Searle was wrong; yet that essential point of agreement was the very one that everybody was contesting! And make no mistake about it, if you took a poll—in the first round of BBS Commentary, in the Continuing Commentary, on comp.ai, or in the secondary literature about the CRA that has been accumulating across both decades to the present day (and culminating in the present book)—the overwhelming majority still think the CRA is dead wrong, even among those who agree that computers can't understand! In fact (I am open to correction on this), it is my impression that, apart from myself, the only ones who profess to accept the validity of the CRA seem to be those who are equally persuaded by what I earlier called 'Granny Objections'—the kinds of soft-headed friends that do even more mischief to one's case than one's foes.

So what is this CRA then, and what is right and wrong about it? Searle is certainly partly to blame for the two decades of misunderstandings about his argument about understanding. He did not always state things in the most perspicuous fashion. To begin with, he baptized as his target a position that no one was quite ready to own to be his own: 'Strong AI'.

What on earth is 'Strong AI'? As distilled from various successive incarnations of the CRA (oral and written: Searle 1980*b*, 1982, 1987, 1990*b*), proponents of Strong AI are those who believe three propositions:

(1*) The mind is a computer program.

(2*) The brain is irrelevant.

(3*) The Turing Test is decisive.

It was this trio of tenets that the CRA was intended to refute. (But of course all it could refute was their conjunction. Some of them could still be true even if the CRA was valid.) I will now reformulate (1*)–(3*) so that they are the recognizable tenets of *computationalism*, a position (unlike 'Strong AI') that is actually held by many thinkers, and hence one worth refuting, if it is wrong (Newell 1980; Pylyshyn 1984; Dietrich 1990).

Computationalism is the theory that cognition is computation, that mental states are just computational states. In fact, that is what tenet (1) should have been:

(1) Mental states are just implementations of (the right) computer program(s). (Otherwise put: Mental states are just computational states.)

If (1*) had been formulated in this way in the first place, it would have pre-empted objections about inert code not being a mind: *of course* the symbols on a piece of paper or on a disk are not mental states. The code—the *right* code (assuming it exists)—has to be *executed* in the form of a dynamical system if it is to be a mental state.

The second tenet has led to even more misunderstanding. How can the brain be irrelevant to mental states (especially its own!)? Are we to believe that if we remove the brain, its mental states somehow perdure somewhere, like the Cheshire Cat's grin? What Searle meant, of course, was just the bog-standard hardware/software distinction: a computational state is implementation-independent. Have we just contradicted tenet (1)?

(2) Computational states are implementation-independent. (Software is hardware-independent.)

If we combine (1) and (2) we get: mental states are just implementation-independent implementations of computer programs. This is not self-contradictory. The computer program has to be physically implemented as a dynamical system in order to become the corresponding computational state, but the physical details of the implementation are irrelevant to the computational state that they implement—except that there has to be *some* form of physical implementation. Radically different physical systems can all be implementing one and the same computational system.

Implementation-independence is indeed a part of both the letter and the spirit of computationalism. There was even a time when computationalists thought that the hardware/software distinction cast some light on (if it did not outright solve) the mind/body problem: the reason we have that long-standing problem in understanding how on earth mental states could be just physical states is that they are *not*! Mental states are just computational states, and computational states are implementation-independent. They have to be physically implemented, to be sure, but don't look for the mentality in the matter (the hardware): it's the software (the computer program) that matters.

If Searle had formulated the second tenet of computationalism in this explicit way, not only would most computationalists of the day have had to recognize themselves as his rightful target, not only would it have fended off red herrings about the irrelevance of brains to their own mental states, or about there being no need for a physical implementation at all, but it would have exposed clearly the soft underbelly of computationalism, and hence the real target of Searle's CRA: for it is precisely on the strength of implementation-independence that computationalism will stand or fall.

The critical property is transitivity: if all physical implementations of one and the same computational system are indeed equivalent, then when any one of them has (or lacks) a given computational property, it follows that they all do (and, by tenet (1), being a mental state is just a computational property). We will return to this. It is what I have dubbed 'Searle's Periscope' on the normally impenetrable 'other-minds' barrier (Harnad 1991a); it is also that soft underbelly of computationalism. But first we must fix tenet (3*).

Actually, verbatim, tenet (3*) is not so much misleading (in the way (1*) and (2*) were misleading) as it is incomplete. It should have read:

(3) There is no stronger empirical test for the presence of mental states than Turing-Indistinguishability; hence the Turing Test is the decisive test for a computationalist theory of mental states.

This does not imply that passing the Turing Test (TT) is a guarantor of having a mind or that failing it is a guarantor of lacking one. It just means that we cannot do any *better* than the TT, empirically speaking. Whatever cognition actually turns out to be—whether just computation, or something more, or something else— cognitive science can only ever be a form of 'reverse engineering' (Harnad 1994*a*) and reverse-engineering has only two kinds of empirical data to go by: structure and function (the latter including all performance capacities). Because of tenet (2), computationalism has eschewed structure; that leaves only function. And the TT simply calls for functional equivalence (indeed, total functional indistinguishability) between the reverse-engineered candidate and the real thing.

Consider reverse-engineering a duck: a reverse-engineered duck would have to be indistinguishable from a real duck both structurally and functionally. It would not only have to walk, swim, and quack (etc.) exactly like a duck, but it would also have to look exactly like a duck, both externally and internally. No one could quarrel with a successfully reverse-engineered candidate like that; no one could deny that a complete understanding of how that candidate works would also amount to a complete understanding of how a real duck works. Indeed, no one could ask for more.

But one could ask for *less*, and a functionalist might settle for only the walking, the swimming, and the quacking (etc., including everything else that a duck can *do*), but ignoring the structure, that is, what it looks like, on the inside or the outside, what material it is made of, etc. Let us call the first kind of reverse-engineered duck, the one that is completely indistinguishable from a real duck, both structurally and functionally, D4, and the one that is indistinguishable only functionally, D3.

Note, though, that even for D3 not all the structural details would be irrelevant: to walk like a duck, something roughly like two waddly appendages are needed, and to swim like one, they'd better be something like webbed ones too. But even with these structure/function coupling constraints, aiming for functional equivalence alone still leaves a lot of structural degrees of freedom open. (Those degrees of freedom would shrink still further if we became more minute about function—moulting, mating, digestion, immunity, reproduction—especially as we approached the level of cellular and subcellular function. So there is really a microfunctional continuum between D3 and D4; but let us leave that aside for now, and stick with D3 macrofunction, mostly in the form of performance capacities.)

Is the Turing Test just the human equivalent of D3? Actually, the 'pen-pal' version of the TT, as Turing (1950) originally formulated it, was even more macrofunctional than that—it was the equivalent of D2, requiring the duck only to quack. But in the human case, 'quacking' is a rather more powerful and general performance capacity, and some consider its full expressive power to be equivalent to, or at least to draw upon, our full cognitive capacity (Fodor 1975; Harnad 1996).

So let us call the pen-pal version of the Turing Test T2. To pass T2, a reverse-engineered candidate must be Turing-indistinguishable from a real pen-pal. Searle's tenet (3) for computationalism is again a bit equivocal here, for it states that TT is the decisive test, but does that mean T2?

This is the point where reasonable men could begin to disagree. But let us take it to be T2 for now, partly because that is the version that Turing described, and partly because it is the one that computationalists have proved ready to defend. Note that T2 covers all cognitive capacities that can be tested by paper/pencil tests (reasoning, problem-solving, etc.).; only sensorimotor (i.e. robotic) capacities (T3) are left out. And the pen-pal capacities are both life-size and life-long: the candidate must be able to deploy them with anyone, indefinitely, just as a real pen-pal could; we are not talking about one-night party-tricks (Harnad 1992) here but real, human-scale performance capacity, indistinguishable from our own (Harnad 2000a).

We now reformulate Searle's Chinese Room Argument in these new terms: *suppose* that computationalism is true, that is, that mental states, such as understanding, are really just implementation-independent implementations of computational states, and hence that a T2-passing computer would (among other things) understand.

Note that there are many ways to reject this premise, but resorting to any of them is tantamount to accepting Searle's conclusion, which is that a T2-passing computer would *not* understand. (His conclusion is actually stronger than that—too strong, in fact—but we will return to that as another of the points on which reasonable men can disagree.) So if one rejects the premise that a computer could ever pass T2, one plays into Searle's hands, as one does if one holds that T2 is not a strong enough test, or that implementational details *do* matter.

So let us accept the premise and see how Searle arrives at his conclusion. This, after all, is where most of the heat of the past twenty years has been generated. Searle goes straight for computationalism's soft underbelly: implementation-independence (tenet (2)). Because of (2), any and every implementation of that T2-passing program must have the mental states in question, if they are truly just computational states. In particular, each of them must understand. Fair enough. But now Searle brings out his intuition pump, adding that we are to imagine this computer as passing T2 in Chinese; and we are asked to believe (because it is true) that Searle himself does not understand Chinese. It remains only to note that if Searle himself were executing the computer program, he would still not be understanding Chinese. Hence (by (2)) neither would the computer, executing the very same program. QED. Computationalism is false.

Now just as it is no refutation (but rather an affirmation) of the CRA to deny that T2 is a strong enough test, or to deny that a computer could ever pass it, it is merely special pleading to try to save computationalism by stipulating ad hoc (in the face of the CRA) that implementational details *do* matter after all, and that the computer's is the 'right' kind of implementation, whereas Searle's is the 'wrong' kind. This just amounts to conceding that tenet (2) is false after all.

By the same token, it is no use trying to save computationalism by holding that Searle would be too slow or inept to implement the T2-passing program. That's not a problem in principle, so it's not an escape-clause for computationalism. Some have made a cult of speed and timing, holding that, when accelerated to the right speed, the computational may make a phase transition into the mental (Churchland and Churchland 1990). It should be clear that this is not a counter-argument but merely an ad hoc speculation (as is the view that it is all just a matter of ratcheting up to the right degree of 'complexity').

On comp.ai (and even in the original 1980 commentary on Searle), some of these ad hoc counter-arguments were faintly voiced, but by far the most dogged of the would-be rebuttals were variants on the Systems Reply, to the effect that it was unreasonable to suppose that Searle should be understanding under these conditions; he would be only a *part* of the implementing system, whereas it would be the system as a *whole* that would be doing the understanding.

Again, it is unfortunate that in the original formulation of the CRA Searle described implementing the T2-passing program in a room with the help of symbols and symbol-manipulation rules written all over the walls, for that opened the door to the Systems Reply. He did offer a pre-emptive rebuttal, in which he suggested to the Systematists that if they were really ready to believe that whereas he alone would not be understanding under those conditions, the 'room' as a whole, consisting of him and the symbol-strewn walls, *would* be understanding, then they should just assume that he had memorized all the symbols on the walls; then Searle himself would be all there was to the system.

This decisive variant did not stop some Systematists from resorting to the even more ad hoc counter-argument that even inside Searle there would be a system, consisting of a different configuration of parts of Searle, and that that system would indeed be understanding. This was tantamount to conjecturing that, as a result of memorizing and manipulating very many meaningless symbols, Chinese-understanding would be induced either consciously in Searle, or, multiple-personality-style, in another, conscious Chinese-understanding entity inside his head of which Searle was unaware.

I will not dwell on any of these heroics; suffice it to say that even Creationism could be saved by ad hoc speculations of this order. (They show only that the CRA is not a proof; yet it remains the only plausible prediction based on what we know.) A more interesting gambit was to concede that no conscious understanding would be going on under these conditions, but that *un*conscious understanding would be, in virtue of the computations.

This last is not an arbitrary speculation, but a revised notion of understanding. Searle really has no defense against it, because, as we shall see (although he does not explicitly admit it), the force of his CRA depends completely on understanding's being a *conscious* mental state, one whose presence or absence one can consciously (and hence truthfully) ascertain and attest to (Searle's Periscope). But Searle also needs no defense against this revised notion of understanding, for it only makes sense to speak of unconscious *mental* states (if it makes sense at all) in an otherwise conscious entity. (Searle was edging toward this position ten years later in 1990a.)

Unconscious states in nonconscious entities (like toasters) are no kind of *mental* state at all. And even in conscious entities unconscious mental states had better be brief! We're ready to believe that we 'know' a phone number when, unable to recall it consciously, we find we can nevertheless dial it when we let our fingers do the walking. But finding oneself able to exchange inscrutable letters for a lifetime with a pen-pal in this way would be rather more like sleep-walking, or speaking in tongues (even the neurological syndrome of 'automatic writing' is nothing like this; Luria 1972). It's definitely not what we mean by 'understanding a language', which surely means *conscious* understanding.

The synonymy of the 'conscious' and the 'mental' is at the heart of the CRA (even if Searle is not yet fully conscious of it—and even if he obscured it by persistently using the weasel-word 'intentional' in its place!). Normally, if someone claims that an entity—any entity—is in a mental state (has a mind), there is no way I can confirm or disconfirm it. This is the 'other minds' problem. We 'solve' it with one another and with animal species that are sufficiently like us through what has come to be called 'mind-reading' (Heyes 1998) in the literature since it was first introduced in BBS two years before Searle's article (Premack and Woodruff 1978). But of course mind-reading is not really telepathy at all, but Turing-Testing—biologically prepared inferences and empathy based on similarities to our own appearance, performance, and experiences. But the TT is of course no guarantee; it does not yield anything like the Cartesian certainty we have about our own mental states.

Can we ever experience another entity's mental states directly? Not unless we have a way of actually *becoming* that other entity, and that appears to be impossible—with one very special exception, namely, that soft underbelly of computationalism. For although we can never become any other physical entity than ourselves, if there are indeed mental states that occur purely in virtue of being in the right computational state, then if we can get into the same computational state as the entity in question, we can check whether or not it's got the mental states imputed to it. This is Searle's Periscope, and a system can only protect itself from it by either not purporting to be in a mental state purely in virtue of being in a computational state—or by giving up on the mental nature of the computational state, conceding that it is just another unconscious (or rather *non*-conscious) state—nothing to do with the mind.

Computationalism was very reluctant to give up on either of these; the first would have amounted to converting from computationalism to 'implementationalism' to save the mental—and that would simply be to rejoin the material world of dynamical systems, from which computational had hoped to abstract away. The second would have amounted to giving up on the mental altogether.

But there is also a sense in which the Systems Reply is right, for although the CRA shows that cognition cannot be *all* just computational, it certainly does not show that it cannot be computational *at all*. Here Searle seems to have drawn stronger conclusions than the CRA warranted. (There was no need: showing that mental states cannot be just computational was strong enough!) But he thought he had shown more.

Searle thought that the CRA had invalidated the Turing Test as an indicator of mental states. But we always knew that the TT was fallible; like the CRA, it is not a proof. Moreover, it is only T2 (not T3 or T4) that is vulnerable to the CRA, and even that only for the special case of an implementation-independent, purely computational candidate. The CRA would not work against a non-computational T2-passing system; nor would it work against a hybrid, computational/non-computational one, for the simple reason that in neither case could Searle *be* the entire system; Searle's Periscope would fail. Not that Systematists should take heart from this, for if cognition is hybrid, computationalism is still false.

Searle was also over-reaching in concluding that the CRA redirects our line of inquiry from computation to brain function: there are still plenty of degrees of freedom in both hybrid and non-computational approaches to reverse-engineering cognition without constraining us to reverse-engineering the brain (T4). So cognitive neuroscience cannot take heart from the CRA either. It is only one very narrow approach that has been discredited: pure computationalism.

Has Searle's contribution been only negative? In showing that the purely computational road would not lead to London, did he leave us as uncertain as before about where the *right* road to London might be? I think not, for his critique has helped open up the vistas that are now called 'embodied cognition' and 'situated robotics', and they have certainly impelled me toward the hybrid road of grounding symbol systems in the sensorimotor (T3) world with neural nets.

And Granny has been given a much harder-headed reason to believe what she has known all along: that we are not (just) computers (Harnad 2000*b*, 2001).

References

CANGELOSI, A., GRECO, A., and HARNAD, S. (2000) 'From Robotic Toil to Symbolic Theft: Grounding Transfer from Entry-level to Higher-level Categories', *Connection Science*, 12: 143–62. Online at http://www.cogsci.soton.ac.uk/~harnad/Papers/Harnad/cangelosi-connsci2.ps

—— and HARNAD, S. (2000) 'The Adaptive Advantage of Symbolic Theft over Sensorimotor Toil: Grounding Language in Perceptual Categories', *Evolution of Communication* (Special Issue on Grounding). Online at http://www.cogsci.soton.ac.uk/~harnad/Papers/Harnad/harnad00.language.html

CHURCHLAND, P. M., and CHURCHLAND, P. S. (1990) 'Could a Machine Think?' *Scientific American*, 262: 32–7.

DIETRICH, E. (1990) 'Computationalism', *Social Epistemology*, 4: 135–54.

FODOR, J. A. (1975) *The Language of Thought* (New York: Thomas Y. Crowell).

—— and PYLYSHYN, Z. W. (1988) 'Connectionism and Cognitive Architecture: A Critical Appraisal', *Cognition*, 28: 3–71.

HARNAD, S. (1982*a*) 'Neoconstructivism: A Unifying Theme for the Cognitive Sciences', in T. Simon and R. Scholes (eds.), *Language, Mind and Brain* (Hillsdale, NJ: Lawrence Erlbaum), 1–11. Online at http://www.cogsci.soton.ac.uk/~harnad/Papers/Harnad/harnad82.neoconst.html

—— (1982b) 'Consciousness: An Afterthought', *Cognition and Brain Theory*, 5: 29–47. Online at http://www.cogsci.soton.ac.uk/~harnad/Papers/Harnad/harnad82. consciousness.html

—— (ed.) (1987) *Categorical Perception: The Groundwork of Cognition* (New York: Cambridge University Press). Online at http://www.cogsci.soton.ac.uk/~harnad/Papers/ Harnad/harnad87.categorization.html

—— (1989) 'Minds, Machines and Searle', *Journal of Theoretical and Experimental Artificial Intelligence*, 1: 5–25. Online at ftp://ftp.princeton.edu/pub/harnad/Harnad/HTML/ harnad89.searle.html

—— (1990a) 'The Symbol Grounding Problem', *Physica D*, 42: 335–46. Online at ftp://ftp.princeton.edu/pub/harnad/Harnad/HTML/harnad90.sgproblem.html

—— (1990b) 'Against Computational Hermeneutics' (Invited commentary on Eric Dietrich's 'Computationalism'), *Social Epistemology*, 4: 167–72. Online at http://www. cogsci.soton.ac.uk/~harnad/Papers/Harnad/harnad90.dietrich.crit.html

—— (1990c) 'Lost in the Hermeneutic Hall of Mirrors' (Invited Commentary on: Michael Dyer, 'Minds, Machines, Searle and Harnad'), *Journal of Experimental and Theoretical Artificial Intelligence*, 2: 321–7. Online at http://www.cogsci.soton.ac.uk/~ harnad/Papers/Harnad/harnad90.dyer.crit.html

—— (1990d) 'Scholarly Skywriting and the Prepublication Continuum of Scientific Inquiry', *Psychological Science*, 1: 342–3. Reprinted in *Current Contents*, 45 (11 Nov. 1991), 9–13. Online at http://www.cogsci.soton.ac.uk/~harnad/Papers/Harnad/harnad90. skywriting.html

—— (1991a) 'Other Bodies, Other Minds: A Machine Incarnation of an Old Philosophical Problem', *Minds and Machines*, 1: 43–54. Online at http://www.cogsci. soton.ac.uk/~harnad/Papers/Harnad/harnad91.otherminds.html

—— (1991b) 'Post-Gutenberg Galaxy: The Fourth Revolution in the Means of Production of Knowledge', *Public-Access Computer Systems Review*, 2: 39–53. Online at http: //www.cogsci.soton.ac.uk/~harnad/Papers/Harnad/harnad91.postgutenberg.html

—— (1992) 'The Turing Test is not a Trick: Turing Indistinguishability is a Scientific Criterion', *SIGART Bulletin*, 3: 9–10. Online at http://www.cogsci.soton.ac.uk/~ harnad/Papers/Harnad/harnad92.turing.html

—— (1993) 'Artificial Life: Synthetic Versus Virtual', in *Artificial Life III: Proceedings, Santa Fe Institute Studies in the Sciences of Complexity*, 16. Online at http://www.cogsci.soton. ac.uk/~harnad/Papers/Harnad/harnad93.artlife.html

—— (1994a) 'Levels of Functional Equivalence in Reverse Bioengineering: The Darwinian Turing Test for Artificial Life', *Artificial Life*, 1: 293–301. Reprinted in C. G. Langton (ed.), *Artificial Life: An Overview* (Cambridge, Mass.: MIT Press, 1995). Online at http://www.cogsci.soton.ac.uk/~harnad/Papers/Harnad/harnad94.artlife2.html

—— (1994b) 'Computation is Just Interpretable Symbol Manipulation: Cognition isn't', *Minds and Machines*, 4: 379–90. Online at ftp://ftp.princeton.edu/pub/harnad/ Harnad/HTML/harnad94.computation.cognition.html

HARNAD, S. (1995b) 'Why and How we are Not Zombies', *Journal of Consciousness Studies*, 1: 164–7. Online at http://www.cogsci.soton.ac.uk/~harnad/Papers/Harnad/harnad95.zombies.html

—— (1996) 'The Origin of Words: A Psychophysical Hypothesis', in B. Velichkovsky and D. Rumbaugh (eds.), *Communicating Meaning: Evolution and Development of Language* (Hillsdale, NJ: Lawrence Erlbaum), 27–44. Online at http://www.cogsci.soton.ac.uk/~harnad/Papers/Harnad/harnad96.word.origin.html

—— (2000a) 'Machines, and Turing: The Indistinguishability of Indistinguishables', *Journal of Logic, Language, and Information*, 9 (special issue on 'Alan Turing and Artificial Intelligence'), 425–45. Online at http://www.cogsci.soton.ac.uk/~harnad/Papers/Harnad/harnad00.turing.html

—— (2000b) 'Correlation vs. Causality: How/Why the Mind/Body Problem is Hard' (Invited Commentary on Nick Humphrey's, 'How to Solve the Mind–Body Problem'), *Journal of Consciousness Studies*, 7: 54–61. Online at http://www.cogsci.soton.ac.uk/~harnad/Papers/Harnad/harnad00.mind.humphrey.html

—— (2001) 'Explaining the Mind: Problems, Problems', *The Sciences* (New York Academy of Sciences), Apr. Online at http://www.cogsci.soton.ac.uk/~harnad/Tp/bookrev.htm

—— HANSON, S. J., and LUBIN, J. (1995) 'Learned Categorical Perception in Neural Nets: Implications for Symbol Grounding', in V. Honavar and L.Uhr (eds.), *Symbol Processors and Connectionist Network Models in Artificial Intelligence and Cognitive Modelling: Steps toward Principled Integration* (New York and London: Academic Press), 191–206. Online at http://www.cogsci.soton.ac.uk/~harnad/Papers/Harnad/harnad95.cpnets.html

—— STEKLIS, H. D., and LANCASTER, J. B. (eds.) (1976) *Origins and Evolution of Language and Speech, Annals of the New York Academy of Sciences*, 280.

HAYES, P., HARNAD, S., PERLIS, D., and BLOCK, N. (1992) 'Virtual Symposium on Virtual Mind', *Minds and Machines*, 2: 217–38. Online at http://www.cogsci.soton.ac.uk/~harnad/Papers/Harnad/harnad92.virtualmind.html

HEXTER, J. H. (1979) *Reappraisals in History* (Chicago: University of Chicago Press).

HEYES, C. M. (1998) 'Theory of Mind in Nonhuman Primates', *Behavioral and Brain Sciences*, 21: 101–34. Online at http://www.cogsci.soton.ac.uk/bbs/Archive/bbs.heyes.html

LUCAS, J. R. (1961) 'Minds, Machines and Gödel', *Philosophy*, 36: 112–17. Online at http://cogprints.soton.ac.uk/abs/phil/199807022

LUCAS, M. M., and HAYES, P. J. (eds.) (1982) *Proceedings of the Cognitive Curriculum Conference*. Rochester, NY: University of Rochester.

LURIA, A. R. (1972) *The Man with a Shattered World* (New York: Basic Books).

NEWELL, A. (1980) 'Physical Symbol Systems', *Cognitive Science*, 4: 135–83.

PREMACK, D., and WOODRUFF, G. (1978) 'Does the Chimpanzee Have a Theory of Mind?' *Behavioral and Brain Sciences*, 1: 515–26.

PYLYSHYN, Z. W. (1980) 'Computation and Cognition: Issues in the Foundations of Cognitive Science', *Behavioral and Brain Sciences*, 3: 111–69.

—— (1984) *Computation and Cognition: Toward a Foundation for Cognitive Science* (Cambridge, Mass.: MIT Press).

—— (ed.) (1987) *The Robot's Dilemma: The Frame Problem in Artificial Intelligence* (Norwood, NJ: Ablex).

SEARLE, J. R. (1980*a*) 'Minds, Brains, and Programs', *Behavioral and Brain Sciences*, 3: 417–57. Online at http://www.cogsci.soton.ac.uk/bbs/Archive/bbs.searle2.html

—— (1980*b*) 'Intrinsic Intentionality', *Behavioral and Brain Sciences*, 3: 450–6.

—— (1982) 'The Chinese Room Revisited', *Behavioral and Brain Sciences*, 5: 345–8.

—— (1984) *Minds, Brains, and Science* (Cambridge, Mass.: Harvard University Press).

—— (1987) 'Minds and Brains without Programs', in C. Blakemore and S. Greenfield (eds), *Mindwaves* (Oxford: Basil Blackwell), 208–33.

—— (1990*a*) 'Consciousness, Explanatory Inversion and Cognitive Science', *Behavioral and Brain Sciences*, 13: 585–96.

—— (1990*b*) 'Is the Brain's Mind a Computer Program?' *Scientific American*, 262: 20–5.

STEKLIS, H. D., and HARNAD, S. (1976) 'From Hand to Mouth: Some Critical Stages in the Evolution of Language', in Harnad *et al.* 1976: 445–55.

TURING, A. M. (1950) 'Computing Machinery and Intelligence', *Mind*, 49: 433–60. Online at http://cogprints.soton.ac.uk/abs/comp/199807017

WITTGENSTEIN, L. (1953) *Philosophical Investigations* (New York: Macmillan).

16

Alien Encounters

Kevin Warwick

A species-related viewpoint in how humans think generally about the world, whether through philosophy, science, or the arts is difficult to avoid. The human perspective is based on who we are, how we got to be so, and how we exist at present. As an example, for a parent it might be difficult to imagine that your own child could do any terrible wrong to any other person or thing. Indeed, even what is conceived as being right or wrong is very much a view dependent on a standpoint within an individual culture. Wars are fought over problems when both sides concerned are certain that they are completely right and their foe is completely wrong.

When we wish to compare homo sapiens with any other being we face the immediate problem that we exhibit a strong leaning towards our own species. Whilst we can view other species and events from the outside, as far as human beings are concerned it is difficult to view ourselves in a detached, impartial way. However, in so far as our intelligence is concerned, if we wish to come up with even a reasonably scientific assessment, we must attempt to do just that.

The view that machines can be conscious is both controversial and unpalatable to many. This is perhaps because, with the attribution of consciousness, we fear that robots, acting out mankind's worst nightmare, will move ruthlessly and inexorably towards total world domination; an idea stylishly visualized in the *Terminator* series of films. It could be that because the implications of conscious machines are so unpalatable many people have been tempted to discount even the possibility of them. Indeed, the subject of this book, John Searle's Chinese Room Argument (CRA) seeks to demonstrate the impossibility of just such computer-controlled conscious robots. However this short chapter is grounded upon the following propositions, which, taken together, lead me to the view that simple human biases lie at the heart of all such refutations:

- There is no reason why a machine cannot be conscious. *Even Searle, in the Chinese Room argument, concedes that 'only a machine could think . . .'* (Searle 1980: 424[1] (B86), emphasis in original).
- Like 'intelligence', 'consciousness' doesn't refer to a single feature, but to a continuum. *Human consciousness is different from cow consciousness, is different from amoeba consciousness, etc. Further, even amongst one species, say humans, conscious experience can differ wildly (cf. Alzheimer consciousness and 'normal' human consciousness).*
- Just as a natural property of the human brain, as it controls the human body, is to instantiate a property labelled human consciousness—so I would equally expect a machine brain, as it controls a machine body (or other complex system), to instantiate a similar property I would have no hesitation in labelling *machine consciousness.*
- *Following Searle, programs are neither necessary nor sufficient for mind. Indeed the 'Seven Dwarf' robots, designed in the Cybernetics Department at Reading University,[2] operate without external computer control and yet I also believe they instantiate a machine consciousness, albeit in a very weak form. They are, perhaps, if a comparison is to be drawn in terms of complexity, as conscious as a slug.*

The Seven Dwarf robots have ultrasonic sensors on insect-like faces. Once switched on a robot operates autonomously in its own little corral. Its goal in life is to move forward but not hit anything. By a process of trial and error the robot has to learn what to do with its wheels in order to achieve the goal.

John Searle's argument is concerned with 'understanding' and comes to the conclusion that actual understanding cannot be achieved by any computer. He has also indicated that for Strong AI, 'the . . . computer really *is* a mind, in the sense that computers . . . can be literally said to *understand* and have other cognitive states' (Searle 1980: 417 (B67), emphasis in original). In this chapter a computer is considered potentially to be a conscious mind in its own right, in this way addressing Searle's concern, in the Chinese Room Argument, with understanding.

As far as machine intelligence in comparison with human intelligence is concerned, the last century has seen a continual shift in our (human) definitions of how the two entities compare and how they are different. Definitions of

[1] Reprinted in Boden (1990: 86). From here referred to as B86.
[2] See Mitchell *et al.* (1994).

human intelligence have been constructed and, like sandcastles on the beach, have been washed away by the rising tide of machine intelligence. One of the most critical examples was the defeat of human world chess champion, Gary Kasparov, by the IBM-backed chess playing computer, Deep Blue, on 11 May 1997. Prior to that, the game of chess had been seen to be an art, or perhaps a science, requiring skill and ingenuity.[3] With the defeat, suddenly the game itself became not such a big deal. After all it has been said 'it is only a game', 'a game well suited to machines', and for some reason 'Deep Blue didn't "know" it was playing chess whereas Kasparov did'. In this final statement we see rays of human bias shining through in all its glory.

As impartial observers, which in this discussion I hope we are, for any comparison between a human and a machine to be of value at all, we must try to bury any such biases from the start, difficult though it might be. Our human viewpoint certainly must not allow us to assume that merely because something pertains to humans we know it for certain.

Humans have, as indeed have all species, a fairly limited set of senses. Our perception of the world is based on those senses, mainly visual, but also auditory, touch, etc. Even when, with the help of machines, we sense the world in other ways, such as electromagnetic, ultrasonic, infrared, we (currently) convert the signals obtained into forms which can be easily assimilated by our own senses; for example, we translate a thermal image into a visual one.

We have, as it turns out, evolved to typically regard our environment in a three-dimensional way. The environment, and everything in it, can, of course, be viewed as a point in n dimensions, where n is as big a number as we can imagine. For example, when we consider an object to be three-dimensional, that is merely our perception of its shape, to another creature (or a machine) the same object may be perceived in, say, fifteen dimensions. Humans can conceive of, and reason about, a multi-dimensional view, in an abstract sense, but because of our senses and brain structures we can't actually perceive it ourselves. Human consciousness is therefore based on a three-dimensional world-view.

We have to be careful not to assume that there is just one, correct, intrinsic, observer-independent way of considering certain things. For example, while I may be happy in concluding that I, myself, am conscious, as far as any other individual is concerned, whether they be animal, machine, or another entity, in making an assumption about their conscious state, I immediately embed my

---

[3] See e.g. the definition of 'chess' in the 1994 Macmillan Encyclopaedia.

own viewpoint into the situation. The situation is essentially observer-dependent and, therefore, my decision can be disputed.

An obvious conclusion regarding the possibility of 'other minds' might be for me to assume that other (biological) carbon-based creatures appearing to be human are conscious in roughly the same way as I. Further, because they are biological like myself, I can similarly credit cats, dogs, bees, and snails with consciousness, albeit, perhaps, in some lesser way. I could continue 'silicon-based machines are a different matter altogether . . .'. But how can I possibly decide one way or another whether they can be conscious in the way that I am as a human?

The general answer, rather akin to Thomas Nagel's articulation in his article 'What is it like to be a Bat' (Nagel 1974), is that I cannot know what it is like to be conscious in any other way than my own. Making an assumption about the consciousness of another entity, based on its appearance alone, would be quite wrong and prone to enormous human error.

Physically we now have a reasonable idea about the workings of the human brain, particularly in terms of its constituent neurons and how they operate. Further, I would certainly agree with others, including Searle, who claim that, '[t]he brain is indeed a machine, an organic machine' (Searle 1997: 17). Also that, 'consciousness is caused by lower-level neuronal processes in the brain and is itself a feature of the brain', that we can think of it as an 'emergent property of the brain', and that it is 'causally explained by the behaviour of the elements' (ibid.). The human brain is indeed a complex network.

Consciousness in a human brain is due to the neurons within it, nothing more and nothing less. To see this, consider that one of your own neurons is removed—are you any less conscious? Now another is removed, and then another and another.[4] You might say at that time that you are not quite as conscious as you were, however due to the ability of complex networks such as the brain to reconfigure and readjust, you might not even notice anything in particular. If, instead of taking away one of your neurons every second, I take away one billion of them every second, would you remain just as conscious all the time? Importantly, after all your neurons are removed are you still conscious? Obviously not.[5] Quite simply, an individual's consciousness is

---

[4] In fact, if one of your neurons was removed every second it would take approximately fifty years to go from a starting-point of 100 billion neurons to something like 99 billion neurons.

[5] Interestingly, it would not be until only 1:100 of the last second remained that your neuron total would have reduced to that of a cat or dog, and not until 1:10,000,000 of the last second remained until your total would have dropped to that of a snail.

dependent on the complex interactions of their neurons; it is, as Searle has said, an emergent property of those neurons when collected together. Take away the neurons and the consciousness does not exist.

It is worthwhile to consider also David Chalmers's fading qualia argument (Chalmers 1996), in which, rather than each human brain cell being removed, it is replaced by an exact silicon simulation. The nature of the silicon brain that results, in particular its consciousness, can then be weighed—would it be identical to that of the human brain or not? Of more importance perhaps is when we look to add technology, perhaps further silicon cells, to the original brain, whether it be human or silicon. What can we say of the overall operation of the enhanced and enlarged brain then? In particular, if further senses and multi-dimensional processing are linked to the silicon additions, will that mean the resultant Cyborg (part human—part machine) is 'more' conscious than the original human?

If we look at an artificial neural network as a machine brain can we say it is conscious? Just as a human brain network creates an emergent property termed consciousness, so I would expect a machine brain network to give rise to an emergent property, which I would have no hesitation in calling machine consciousness. As for whether this is or is not the same thing as human consciousness, almost certainly we can conclude that it is not, although conceivably it might be similar. The human brain is a biological organ operating on electrochemical signals, whereas a machine brain is (usually) a silicon-based system operating on electronic signals. The two things are physically different. It may well be possible to simulate, to an extent, a human brain on a computer brain, but in the limit the two will never be exactly the same. The human brain will never be exactly simulated unless the two things were of one and the same kind and they are not. Roger Penrose (1994) claims that, in principle, a human brain cannot be simulated by a computer and I agree with him on this. However the converse is also true—a human brain cannot simulate a machine brain exactly. We can try and copy some functions, but the two forever remain distinct entities.

It is not that one type of brain, human or machine, is *necessarily* better or worse than the other. Rather, as Penrose indicates, it is simply that they are different. The consciousness associated with each is likely to be different. In fact even the conscious experience within these classifications is likely to be different. Consider, there are many different human brains, some exhibiting special characteristics (e.g. autism or senile dementia), and these are all conscious in different ways.

Is a person who is in a coma conscious? Does a person who is unconscious exhibit consciousness? Being unconscious (if this state is the opposite of consciousness), means not being in control of one's faculties, relating to senses, not being able to communicate. If being conscious then means being in control of one's faculties, relating to senses and communicating, then, put quite simply, *some machines are conscious now*. However, the phenomenological experience of a machine will probably be quite distinct from that of a human. This is because it is likely that their faculties (their bodies, their senses, and their means of communication), will be very different—just as they would be if we contrast the conscious experience of a dog, a wasp, or a snail.

Humans do not have some magic ingredient in our brains that make us something special, we are just physical beings. Our brains are a collection of neurons, which interact with the world through senses and actuators. Mammals, insects, and other creatures are similarly placed, as are machines. It is reasonable, I believe, to expect that consciousness, contingent upon a complex network of processing cells, will be different between species whose processing cells are organized differently. Similarly, to a small extent, it is different, between most humans, albeit between some the difference can be large (cf. a normal individual to one suffering from a dementia).

We must be careful what importance we place on our (human) consciousness, particularly in comparison with the consciousness of other species. We must be wary about what we feel it allows humans to do, specifically in comparison with other species. Certainly we can communicate, but so too can other species, including machines.

In November 1996 we conducted an experiment in which one of our robots learnt how to move around in its corral.[6] Once it had finished learning, without human intervention, via a radio link it programmed another one of our robots to behave in the same way. The other robot was situated in upstate New York. The communication between the robots was through the internet. The experiment aimed to show that one robot can program another robot with what it has learnt itself.

With human communication comes language. In each language we have numerous utterances that others, who can communicate in that language, give a meaning to. These utterances can also be formalized symbolically, writing with ink on paper being one example. Each separate language has its own relationships between its audible and visual versions. But each language is

---

[6] See *The Guinness Book of Records*, 1999: 181, and Warwick (2000: 180).

essentially an agreed way of expressing ideas and thoughts from one brain to another. Humans have evolved a mouth, ears, hands, and eyes and on the basis of these mechanisms human languages have been generated.

Before a particular sound or word is uttered, the signals, which initiate the sound, originate in a human brain. These are electrochemical signals, which take an idea, possibly in a pictorial, graphic representation and convert it into a set of symbols to cause our motor actuators to move in ways which result in representative signals being emitted. These signals, when received by another human are converted from their symbolic form into ideas or pictures, hopefully along the lines of those which were originally conceived. Human languages, therefore, for the most part do not involve just a set of symbolic representations, they also involve content of a mental or semantic kind.

All of this, I would claim, is true of a human's main, first language, and after a while, for many people, a second language or further languages may take on such a stance. As a human we can, perhaps, be said to 'think' in a language. When learning further human languages it is often the case that we in fact translate symbols from the second language into our first language, where they also have semantic meaning. Gradually, through use, semantic meanings can become associated with the second language, from which we can see that there is often not an 'exact' symbolic translation from one language to another, which is what a language dictionary attempts to give us. Each human language has its own nuances, double meanings, alternative expressions, and so on. For the most part it takes a long time to learn a high proportion of these, in any human language. To do so we really need to experience the language, to use it regularly, to speak with different people, and so on. Simply taking a new (to us) language from a book to give us a small window on that language as a whole will most likely not allow us to comprehend the nuances, slang, and double meanings.

When it comes to a computer-based machine dealing with or comprehending a human language, an instant problem that is usually encountered is the fact that the machine is simply programmed to respond to a set of symbols. This is in fact rather akin to a human 'programming' themselves with a second language in which we simply learn a set of symbols. However, in learning a second language a human may well at first translate, symbolically, everything into their own, first, semantic language. For a machine it, most likely, does not have this luxury. It has to cope on its own, it has simply been programmed to respond to a particular human language, in which it has no language rich in semantics that it can call on in reserve—its symbols remain ungrounded.

What does all this tell us? Well, it certainly indicates, as Searle tried to show in his Chinese Room Argument, that programs are not minds. The argument also shows us that a human *or a machine* that is 'programmed' to respond 'syntactically' is not truly thinking or understanding meaning.[7] So does this mean that I agree with all of Searle's Chinese Room Argument? No, it does not!

I certainly agree that programs are not the same as minds, which the CRA tries to show. However, that is about as far as it goes. No matter how intriguing the problem is, the basic assumptions taken in order to pose the problem are essentially flawed. *First, we should reflect that an amount of human behaviour is programmed in our genes.* When we are born we do not start from a *tabula rasa*; it is our genetic program that gets us breathing, moving around, and, importantly, learning. If humans did not have such a program we would simply die at birth (if we developed that far). Once we start learning and gaining experiences we become the individuals that we are, doing things in our own, individual way, partly due to our program and partly due to our experiences.

It is certainly true that many, perhaps most, computational machines (robots and computers alike), are simply explicitly designed or programmed to perform their tasks. They are set up with a number of instructions telling them what to do in particular circumstances. But nowadays many machines are also adaptive and exhibit learning.[8] At any point in time their behaviour is then dependent not only on their initial program but also on what they have experienced and what they have learnt from their experiences. For both humans and such machines the way in which they learn is initially set up by their program, although learning rate, type, and habits may change due to particular experiences. So machines too can be individuals, doing things in their own individual way, partly due to their program and partly due to their experiences. To see this clearly, experimentation or observation of autonomous robots is highly recommended (see Warwick 1998).

A corollary of this is that, if they have the appropriate physical capabilities, machines, robots perhaps, can not only learn to communicate with each other in a syntactic way, but also can learn to relate syntax to semantics, grounded by their own experience of physically sensed entities. Further, and perhaps

---

[7] Interestingly, in many cases humans are expected or desired to operate in a purely programmed, syntactic way. For example, in the military domain soldiers are taught not to think but merely to obey instructions to the letter, to do exactly what is required. In some schools students are taught to respond in direct ways, not to ask questions, not to consider alternative solutions.

[8] See e.g. Michalski *et al.* (1984, 1986), Forsyth (1989), and Carbonell (1990).

almost more importantly, what one machine has learnt can be communicated to other machines very rapidly (see Kelly 1997).

The main purpose of a particular language learnt by a number of robots is to send messages to and from one another, relating to the physical world in which they exist. Necessarily therefore the transmitted information would link with semantic entities associated with each robot's perception of the physical world.

There is a view prevalent among some (human) commentators at this time, which links consciousness and intelligence only with biological systems (see e.g. Penrose 1994). In my opinion this is a very misguided vision, for in any attempt to define what is and what is not 'life' we soon realize that many machines are already, by almost any definition, alive (see Warwick 1998). As Margaret Boden says:

the characteristics repeatedly mentioned in discussions of the nature of life include self-organization, autonomy, responsiveness, reproduction, evolution, and metabolism. Arguably, each of these (except one) is definable in informational terms, and each (except one) has already been exhibited to some degree in functioning A-Life systems. The exception, apparently, is metabolism. (Boden 1996: 24–5)

However, since 1996 there has been substantial progress in instantiating metabolism in robotic systems called Slugbots—slug-eating robots roaming wild in fields located at the University of the West of England (Kelly et al. 1999). Thus unless, in our human-centric way, we simply exclude non-biological life from our definition, we must concede that there already exist non-biological systems that satisfy all of Boden's criteria for living systems.

Restriction of life and consciousness to biological systems is a purely cultural stance. In the past many cultures, and indeed a number of 'non-Western' cultures at the present time, are much broader in their definition of life, intelligence, and consciousness (see Warwick 2000), bestowing each, in a broad sense, to all things on earth. Indeed a number of biologists point to robots as being 'alive'. For example it has been said that 'A real organism is a mass of compromises, not a finely optimised piece of machinery' (Stewart and Cohen 1997: 94). Anyone who has witnessed our Seven Dwarf robots learning, as a result of making occasional mistakes by bumping into the wall, is bound to regard their actions as a mass of compromises. Under no circumstances would they be described as 'finely optimized'.

We have to be very, very careful in coming to a conclusion that, because something is not quite the same as we are, therefore, it must be inferior. Taking things further we should not conclude that because machines are not conscious in the same way as humans, or even that because machines cannot be conscious at all, they will always remain subservient to us. For example it has been said that, 'Computers . . . would always remain subservient to us, no matter how far they advance with respect to speed, capacity and logical design' (Penrose 1994: 35).

Such conclusions associate enormous importance with the 'uniqueness' (*sic*) of human consciousness. But where is the scientific and/or physical evidence to justify this view? It seems simply to be wishful thinking, human bias, and the general desire for humans to 'want' this conclusion to be true.

In the future we may well be able to communicate directly from person to/from machine and from person to person by thought processes alone (Warwick 1999). There will be no need to convert our thoughts into the syntactic structures we presently use. It is even possible that we will be able to communicate semantic meaning more directly. Different human languages as we know them now may well become redundant. For example, if a French person thinks about 'wine' is this not roughly the same thing as when an Italian thinks about 'wine' although their respective languages use different words? Recent cybernetic research with brain implants suggests that semantic concepts, for humans and machines alike, can be passed directly into a human brain from a machine brain and vice versa (Warwick 1998). Perhaps our present human-centric view would not be so tainted if we were not restricted to viewing our environment through the particular set of senses that we presently have.

References

BODEN, M. A. (ed.) (1990) *The Philosophy of Artificial Intelligence* (Oxford: Oxford University Press).

—— (ed.) (1996) *The Philosophy of Artificial Life* (Oxford: Oxford University Press).

CARBONELL, J. G. (1990) *Machine Learning: Paradigms and Methods* (Cambridge, Mass.: MIT Press).

CHALMERS, D. J. (1996) *The Conscious Mind: In Search of a Fundamental Theory* (Oxford: Oxford University Press).

FORSYTH, R. S. (1989) *Machine Learning: Principles and Techniques* (London: Chapman & Hall).

KELLY, D. I. (1997) 'The Development of Shared Experience Learning in a Group of Mobile Robots', Ph.D. Thesis, Department of Cybernetics, The University of Reading.

KELLY, D. I., HOLLAND, O., SCULL, M., and McFARLAND, D. (1999) 'Artificial Autonomy in the Natural World: Building a Robot Predator', Fifth Conference on Artificial Life, Swiss Federal Institute of Technology, Lausanne, Sept.

MICHALSKI, R. S., CARBONELL, J. G., and MITCHELL, T. M. (eds.) (1984, 1986) *Machine Learning: An Artificial Intelligence Approach*, 2 vols. (Berlin: Springer-Verlag).

MITCHELL, R. J., KEATING D. A., and KAMBHAMPATI, C. (1994) 'Learning System for a Simple Robot Insect', *Proceedings of the International Conference on Control, 1994* (London: Institute of Electrical Engineers), 492–7.

MITCHELL, T. M., CARBONELL, J. G., and MICHALSKI, R. S. (1986) *Machine Learning: A Guide to Current Research* (Hingham, Mass.: Kluwer Academic Publishers).

NAGEL, T. (1974) 'What is it like to be a Bat?' *Philosophical Review*, 83: 435–50.

PENROSE, R. (1994) *Shadows of the Mind: A Search for the Missing Science of Consciousness* (Oxford: Oxford University Press).

SEARLE, J. R. (1980) 'Minds, Brains and Programs', *Behavioral and Brain Sciences*, 3: 417–24.

—— (1997) *The Mystery of Consciousness* (New York: New York Review of Books).

STEWART, I., and COHEN, J. (1997) *Figments of Reality* (Cambridge: Cambridge University Press).

WARWICK, K. (1998) *In the Mind of the Machine* (London: Arrow).

—— (1999) 'Cybernetic Organisms—Our Future?' *Proceedings of the IEEE*, 87: 387–9.

—— (2000) *QI: The Quest for Intelligence* (London: Piatkus).

17

Cyborgs in the Chinese Room: Boundaries Transgressed and Boundaries Blurred

Alison Adam

Introduction

There is little doubt that, philosophically speaking, intentionality has aroused much passion among commentators on AI and cognition. Part of the reason for this would seem to be that it strikes right at the heart of what it is to be human, what separates us from, perhaps animals, but certainly machines. This may be why we are so reluctant to let go of the idea that intentionality is possibly the fundamental attribute which makes us human and therefore separate from that which is not human. This is part of a broader picture of the feelings towards humanity that AI stirs up. Holding onto intentionality come what may points to one of the last refuges of enlightenment thinking, the uniqueness of the human animal. I argue that John Searle's desire to keep hold of human intentionality through all the increasingly elaborate versions of his Chinese Room thought-experiment may fruitfully be understood in this vein. I explore the implications of such a hypothesis in this chapter.

Daniel Dennett (1994) gets to the heart of the Chinese Room controversy when he asserts that many people agree with Searle's conclusions, that is, that no conceivable variant of the Chinese Room can display intentionality, although they may not agree with the arguments Searle uses to reach those conclusions. Given the convoluted and increasingly elaborate flow of ideas used to justify one side or the other, I want to explore the issue which Searle feels so strongly about, which Dennett identifies, and which so many of us feel is important. The question at the heart of the Chinese Room is, therefore, the ancient conundrum of what makes us human and distinct from brute matter and the further question of why this matters so much to us.

Despite the vast amount that has been written, I argue that there are useful new ways of approaching this topic. This is especially important as the traditional arguments mean that we may remain for ever at loggerheads. Searle's characterization of intentionality tries to preserve the specialness of humanity against the dark forces of the inanimate world. I ask whether there are new ways in which we may address the old problem of human versus inanimate nature, which the Chinese Room so eloquently raises, but which it cannot resolve once and for all. I do not want to claim a solution for a centuries-old and fundamental philosophical problem. Instead I want to ask if we can find a way of living more comfortably with the human–nature dichotomy, at least in relation to its manifestation in AI. The aim of this chapter, then, is not to seek philosophical certainty, but philosophical comfort.

I suggest that it is worthwhile taking this route for two reasons. First of all, it must be time by now to move on from the 'opposite poles' relationship which AI has too often shared with philosophy. Apart from the Chinese Room Argument, Hubert Dreyfus's predictions of the failure of symbolic AI are well known. Critiques in this genre are couched in terms of what I have described elsewhere as a philosophical 'bit switch', that is, either AI succeeds or it fails. There is little scope for a middle ground under such an approach.

My second, related reason refers to the pragmatics of AI practitioners' research where perhaps a middle ground may be found. Searle's Strong/Weak AI is well known but there is little evidence to suggest that the majority of AI researchers regard their enterprise as Strong AI, preferring to commit to Weak AI even if not under that specific name. But there are those who raise their standard in the Strong AI camp. Indeed there are prominent AI researchers in the latter group including some such as Hans Moravec whose position is discussed below. Similarly Dreyfus's (1979, 1992) original prediction that symbolic AI will fail because of its inability to represent skill-type knowledge, does not appear to have come to pass in quite the way he intended. Even if we cannot point to myriad numbers of AI systems which possess skills-type knowledge, which would directly refute Dreyfus's point, symbolic AI continues to be a healthy research area. Indeed, in a later paper, Dreyfus (1996) admits that there is much more healthy 'good old-fashioned AI' or GOFAI activity than he had first thought.

Add to these considerations the pervasiveness of intelligent information and communications technologies in the lives of, at least, urban, Western professionals. Then there seems little point in preserving old positions which depend on subtle philosophical arguments about success or failure, rather than on empirical evidence. This suggests that rather than seeing the success of AI in producing a fully artificial intelligence as a philosophical question, it is better seen as a question of cultural evidence.

Alan Turing's remark: 'I believe that at the end of the century the use of words and general educated opinion will have altered so much that one will be able to speak of machines thinking without expecting to be contradicted' (Turing 1950: 442[1] (B49)) has often been quoted. It seems unlikely that Turing was claiming that we would achieve true artificial intelligence by the end of the century. Rather he was claiming that we would be able to talk of machines apparently thinking and that this would be an acceptable position. This seems largely to have come to pass. As Harry Collins (1990) has noted, we have found ways of accommodating computers into our cultures and treating them as functioning members of our cultures without too much strain. And although he does not appear to be attempting an analysis along cultural lines, Dennett, who is, after all, a philosopher and not a sociologist, has a 'get out' clause to counter Searle's fears regarding original intentionality, which fits in rather well with Collins's societal approach. Dennett's (1987) escape route is via 'as if' intentionality. He argues that if we can use intentional language to describe and predict the behaviour of something, whether human or object, then we can treat it 'as if' it has intentionality; it does not matter to him whether that intentionality is original or not. Of course this is not good enough for Searle, who wants to preserve the original intentionality of human beings at all cost. This is the consideration at the heart of the Chinese Room and it is at the heart of the age-old human–nature or human–thing distinction and what turns on it.

In this chapter I look first at the reasons why boundaries such as human/machine should be so important to us. Mary Douglas's (1966) research lends credence to the idea that the maintenance of this boundary is a fundamental part of the way we order and organize our worlds. The story of the boundaries we make for ourselves in the organization of society gives a rationale for

---

[1] Reprinted in Boden (1990: 49). From here referred to as B49.

maintaining these boundaries and shows how we deal with those who threaten to transgress them. In the following section I look at the ways in which boundary maintenance is played out in artificial intelligence. In this, the work of Brian Bloomfield and Theo Vurdubakis (1995) has proved insightful.

The boundary options for human and machine include the following. We can side with the position that Searle seems to take in making the boundary impossible to cross while preserving humanity's superior status. Alternatively we may maintain the human–machine boundary where it is and let cultural forces move it gradually as societies bend to accommodate machines further. Thirdly, through demonstrations of virtuosity such as the Loebner prize or chess games between human experts and computers we may push the boundary towards the machine. Finally we can stand the whole thing on its head and let the machines take the superior role. As I discuss below, the latter view is taken by some prominent AI and robotics scientists motivated by appeals to technological advances in robotics and evolution. Yet none of these positions is somehow satisfactory, as a boundary is always drawn somewhere, thus always maintaining the separation of human and machine. This separation mirrors the widely accepted mind–matter Cartesian dualism. But the point seems to be not to find ways of finally and once and for all doing away with this split and the boundary implied by it. Rather it is a question of finding new ways of looking at the boundary and ways of viewing the issues raised in a different light rather than trying to resolve them. In particular, the reason why people seem to set so much store in maintaining the distinction is of much interest. In the remainder of the chapter I describe two recent attempts to approach these distinctions in a substantially different way. Importantly, these alternatives attempt to blur the human–machine distinction rather than trying to maintain it.

My first area involves research from the domain of science and technology studies, often termed actor-network theory (ANT for short). ANT is rather a definite term for what is covered by a broader 'seamless web' approach; indeed one of its major proponents, Bruno Latour (1999) now tries to disown the term altogether! For my argument the most important aspect of the seamless web approach is that it offers a way of blending the distinction between human and object. However, this is not the only area to offer interesting and potentially useful views with which to inspect the human–object relationship. Feminist studies of technoscience, particularly Donna Haraway's cyborg feminism, offer an alternative way to blur the boundary between human, animal, and machine as all are blended into the image of the cyborg or cybernetic organism. Both these approaches identify interesting resonances with the intentionality problem in AI. Before exploring this it is necessary to take a longer look at borders and their transgression.

Boundaries and Border Crossings

Questions of the nature of the relationship between machines and humans (and indeed animals too—see papers from *Science, Technology and Human Values*, 23/4 (1998)) form an important part of debates in contemporary philosophy. Stemming from Descartes's description of the mind–body problem and his development of the mechanical philosophy, the contemporary form of this debate can be found in discussions on the nature and possibility of artificial intelligence. As I have suggested above, philosophers such as Searle and Dreyfus are ranged on the side which argues against the possibility of truly artificial intelligence by computational means and AI scientists such as Moravec (1988, 1998) are lined up on the other side, with his argument that the human race will have downloaded itself into the robot brains of our 'mind children' within a few generations.

The plausibility of arguments for or against is not my concern in this chapter. Rather it is the question of why such passion is raised over the creation of true intentionality via artificial intelligence in the first place. Much of the reason for the continuing interest in this lies in our concern with making and maintaining certain fundamental boundaries—here the boundary between human and non-human, between mind and matter, *res cogitans* and *res extensa*. Thus, although, much of the action in the Chinese Room debate revolves around a concern with the potential boundary between understanding and non-understanding, I argue that this is a manifestation of a deeper concern with the human–non-human boundary. Understanding and humanity are not the same thing, but considering the understanding–non-understanding boundary leads directly to a consideration of the human–non-human boundary, as Searle holds that only humans have the special quality of intentionality.

Writing from within the domain of anthropology, Douglas's (1966) *Purity and Danger* is one of those rare works in the humanities and social sciences which continues to exert influence beyond its time and far beyond its original scope. It is not difficult to understand why this happens here, as, in this book, Douglas describes some very fundamental ways in which human societies organize themselves. It continues to be one of the best descriptions of the maintenance of boundaries in human culture. Originally written as a study of 'primitive' cultures, its influence has extended well beyond its own boundaries, notably into various versions of science and technology studies, emerging from the 1970s onwards, which emphasize cultural and sociological approaches (Barnes 1974; Bloor 1976).

Douglas's writing identifies the categorization and marking of boundaries as a fundamental aspect of the way we organize our social world. She argues that we have a strong need to categorize and order our world. As social animals this appears to be one of our strongest driving forces. Rituals of purity and impurity create order and unity in experience. That which steps outside this order pollutes, and sanctions are applied to bring the polluter and the pollution back into line. These are used to reinforce a moral order, upheld by appeals to nature. So the moral order of a society is maintained by dangers which threaten transgressors and which force its members into good citizenship (Douglas 1966: 2): '[I]deas about separating, purifying, demarcating and punishing trans- gressions have as their main function to impose system on an inherently untidy experience' (ibid. 4). There are strong religious overtones embedded in this process of ordering and boundary marking. Douglas points to the way that rules of separation are the distinguishing marks of the sacred, which is the polar opposite of the profane. Sacred relations are expressed by the rituals of separa- tion and demarcation and '. . . beliefs in the danger of crossing forbidden boundaries' (ibid. 22).

As a culture develops, much revolves round its systems of classification: 'As time goes on and experiences pile up, we make a greater and greater investment in our system of labels . . . Uncomfortable facts which refuse to be fitted in, we find ourselves ignoring or distorting so that they do not distort these estab- lished assumptions' (ibid. 36–7). The sacred–profane boundary maps onto the holy–unholy distinction in human action. In many societies people are seen to prosper when they conform to holiness and to perish when they deviate from it (ibid. 50). Holiness carries with it the idea of wholeness and completion. Douglas argues that this concept is given physical expression in the wholeness of the body seen as a perfect container. Holiness requires that the individual completes his or her work and knows and conforms to his or her class or station in life. As in Leviticus, holiness requires that different classes of things shall not be confused (ibid. 53). Hence, by dietary rules and rules of avoidance, by ritual, we frame, select, and order our experiences and by correct observance of these rules and rituals we become holy. Transgress the rules and we pollute and become unholy.

How do these considerations map onto the ways that boundaries and boundary transgression is played out in respect of the artificial intelligence debate? And importantly how does it relate to the non-human–human boundary which is manifest in the Chinese Room and reactions to it? As David Noble (1997) argues, although we view the progress of technology as a rational and increasingly secular enterprise, notions of religion have never left it throughout its history. The way that the sacred–profane, holy–unholy boundary is manifest in commentaries on AI is an example of this. Those who wish to preserve human intentionality as unique are not just preserving the human–machine boundary but through it the sacred–profane boundary. This connection is not necessarily an intentional one (i.e. intentional in the non-Searlian everyday sense). Rather I am arguing, through a reading of Douglas, that it is a manifestation of the way that so many apparently secular distinctions we make in the world reduce, at bottom, to religious or proto-religious distinctions. The human may be seen as the sacred and the machine profane. The complete human body is holy in that it is the perfect container for the human soul and human intentionality. The machine threatens to transgress, to be unholy as it is not the vessel which can contain human intentionality. The machine must know and conform to its place in the order of nature.

The distinction between sacred and profane and the pollution which occurs when the boundary between the two is transgressed is one aspect of the story of boundaries which accords with our treatment of humans and machines. A second aspect relates to what happens in the very boundaries or margins themselves. What happens at these very boundaries and margins we create? In making social order we are not just condemning disorder—we are recognizing that disorder is both dangerous and, at the same time, potent. For instance, someone who goes beyond the ordinary limits of society, perhaps into the disordered regions of the mind, and who comes back may bring a power not available to those who have remained in control of themselves and within the bounds of society.

This suggests that those whose position in society is marginal enjoy an indefinable status even though they may be doing nothing morally wrong. Douglas suggests that examples can be found in the unborn child or the perceived transition from childhood to adulthood in some societies. To be in a marginal condition is to be in a dangerous condition but it is also a source of power: 'It is consistent with the ideas about form and formlessness to treat initiands coming out of seclusion as if they were themselves charged with power, hot, dangerous, requiring insulation and a time for cooling down'

(Douglas 1966: 94). We must not assume that such ideas are confined to so-called 'primitive' societies. In Western societies we treat marginal people similarly, for example, problems resettling ex-offenders seem to rest with the way that society regards them as permanently 'outside'. A similar story can be told with those who spend time in institutions for the treatment of mental illness. As long as they stay at home their eccentricities may be tolerated but once admitted to an institution they cross a tolerance threshold and are correspondingly treated differently. Many of these ideas on power conform to a notion of society seen as a source of forms surrounded by non-form: 'There is power in the forms and other power in the inarticulate area, margins, confused lines and beyond the external boundaries' (ibid. 98). Those who hold specific office in society have well-defined powers by dint of that office but those in the margins may also hold power, albeit of an unconscious and uncontrollable nature. So the unstructured areas of society contain energy in the margins, albeit of a potentially dangerous kind. Margins and boundaries are powerful symbols, no more so than in the human body which can represent the precarious boundaries of society. The body can represent, in miniature, the power and danger of society and it can also represent social pollution pressing on external boundaries or internal contradictions within. Pollution rules serve to reinforce moral concerns and in so doing help to preserve the social order. Social sanctions serve to enforce these pollution rules and thereby preserve the social order.

As I have suggested above, one line of reasoning would see artificial intelligence as outside the human body, therefore potentially profane and unholy. This accords with the first notion of boundary crossing described above. But an alternative reading of machines in our society would include them as marginal members rather than complete outsiders. Viewing machines as marginal members of our society once again offers an explanation of why they are potentially threatening when read against Douglas's reading of power and danger in the margins. As marginal members of human society they stand outside and threaten the moral order. As they are not fully enfranchized humans they need not follow our moral codes. Indeed in the following section I shall suggest that some future predictions suggest that they will not even recognize our 'human rights' at all when they take over the world. Their 'take-over' story also follows the line of thought which says that, just as the margins contain danger, they contain power, as these machines are seen, in the roboticists' predictions, to become more powerful than us. This suggests that we might not be able to trust them—we must remember to switch them off as we leave the laboratory every night.

Boundaries in AI

How do these, and other considerations on boundaries, manifest themselves in relation to the AI project?

I have already claimed that the Chinese Room Argument turns on the question of whether the boundary between human and machine is to be maintained or not. Lynch and Collins (1998) and others recognize this as the old Cartesian split. Although she did not consider AI explicitly, Douglas's discussion of boundaries provides anthropological or cultural explanations for old philosophical problems.

Bloomfield and Vurdubakis (1995) have extended some of Douglas's arguments to look at how claims for the maintenance of the boundaries between humans and other entities especially animals, and, more pertinently for present purposes, machines are represented in the public arena. This reaffirms Douglas's assertion that the maintenance of these boundaries expresses a moral ordering—entities which are ascribed agency in one moral universe exclude and marginalize those kept in another. Claims made, and challenged, on behalf of AI, Bloomfield and Vurdubakis see as part of the discourse which asserts and reinforces its boundaries.

For instance, they see the often well-publicized chess matches between human experts and computers as challenges to and affirmations of the boundary between humans and machines. I would argue that these stand in an analogous position to the Chinese Room.

> . . . conceding esoteric skills to machines could be read as an indication of the creation of 'artificial' intelligence or, alternatively as a pointer to the mechanical basis of reason—therefore it is not simply the human-machine boundary represented by esoteric skills such as chess that is at stake, but the very distinctiveness of the human in the evolutionary order of things. (ibid. 4–5)

Following Steve Woolgar (1989) Bloomfield and Vurdubakis argue that claims that AI machines can display intelligent behaviour pose a potential threat to the moral order of representation. Many, if not most, people do not regard these displays of machine virtuosity as displays of actual intelligence, although some prominent commentators such as Ray Kurzweil do seem to see Deep Blue as evidence of superior intelligence in the computer (Searle 1999, sect. 1). Whether or not people *believe* that these programs are more intelligent than people does not seem to weaken the arguments of Bloomfield and Vurdubakis. It is, rather, the rhetoric, the public spectacle, and media circus which are important. Clearly it is taken very seriously by Kasparov, IBM, and Searle him-self who devotes several detailed columns of his review of Kurzweil's book to discussing the Deep Blue phenomenon. It may be just a game but it is one which excites much passion. It is perhaps better seen as a game of drawing and redrawing the human–machine boundary.

This is in accord with Douglas's assertions on the way that moral ordering is part of the societal consensus on the relationship of things in the world, here the relationship between humans and machines. AI machines threaten to disturb the boundary between human and machine which we take to be part of a natural moral order. As we can see from Douglas's writing, disturbances at the boundaries are potential sources of pollution and sanctions must be applied to bring the polluter into line. At the same time, disturbances at the boundary are potent sources of energy, albeit of a dangerous kind. The marginal role of artificial intelligences, real or imagined, is a potential source of dangerous energy. We can see this in the predictions of the robot scientists outlined below where the machines are predicted to take over human society. This variety of dangerous power in the margins is frighteningly portrayed in fictional settings where our fears are played out in films such as *Terminator* when robots threaten to destroy the human race.[2]

Chess matches between computers and human experts are very public dis-plays of the continual renegotiation of the boundary between human and machine. A similar, but perhaps less newsworthy display of boundary challen-ging can be found in the annual Loebner (http://www.loebner.net) contest where a prize is awarded to the AI program which comes closest to passing the Turing Test with the promise of a grand prize of $100,000 and a gold medal for the system that finally and conclusively passes. But as Collins (1985) points out, what counts as passing the Turing Test, indeed what counts as replicating any scientific experiment, is subject to continual renegotiation, that is why so many controversies in the history of science have been so convoluted. Turing (1950) originally articulated this test but, of course, did not lay down strict guidelines as to *exactly* how it was to be conducted. It would have been impossible for him to do so.

---

[2] It is not entirely clear whether Terminator is a robot or a cyborg. Indeed it can be seen as poten-tially blurring the distinction between the two, thereby, ironically, contributing to the essentially feminist project of cyborg boundary blurring. Thanks to John Preston whose late-night research on cable channels enabled him to offer this suggestion.

Scientific proof is no simple matter, which somehow stands outside the confines of society—it is socially negotiated (MacKenzie 1996). This means that it is perfectly consistent for Searle, say, never to be convinced of a demonstration of a machine supposedly passing the Turing Test, while others may accept a very minimal demonstration as success. But then it becomes almost impossible to say exactly what constitutes a once-and-for-all Turing Test and what constitutes passing it. To be consistent with his position Searle could *never* accept the Turing Test as a test of machine intelligence anyway, no matter what the experimental conditions.

Some commentators, most notably Moravec (1988, 1998), argue for the abandonment of any boundary between machine and human at all. In his book *Mind Children*, Moravec argues for the tide of evolution to wash us onto a 'post-biological' era where having downloaded our minds into computers, our children will be virtual rather than flesh and blood. His more recent work, *Robot: Mere Machine to Transcendent Mind*, extends and updates his earlier book. This is a position similar to that of Kurzweil (1999) and which Searle himself (1999) has criticized. For Moravec, the story of the machine in the decade between his two books is one of unmitigated success. They have defeated the world chess champion, driven vehicles across thousands of miles of public roads, found theorem proofs, composed music, and made many medical, scientific, and financial decisions. Moravec holds that this success demonstrates the natural course of evolution, showing that the human race will evolve into robots via our irresistible choice to download our minds. A more pragmatic version of this idea is found in research on evolutionary robotics (Wheeler 1996). The underlying concept is the same although only a few roboticists make ambitious claims about their machines' success. Successive generations of robots are made to 'evolve', thus apparently carrying out in a short space of time a process that nature would undertake over billions of years. But Moravec does not see robot evolution as a metaphor for biological evolution—it is just as real an evolution as the human form. Rather he views the process as a continuum, where humans will choose to evolve themselves into machines compelled by the logic of the machines' superiority.

Kevin Warwick (1997) paints a similar scenario, suggesting clip-on chips to the brain rather than downloading it into a machine, as a less far-fetched alternative to Moravec's plan. But he also has a vision of the evolutionary potential of robots, suggesting that we may eventually become second-class citizens to more intelligent machines just as we, as more intelligent organisms, currently dominate apes. In terms of evolution we can just hand over to the machines and he sees no reason why the new dominant life form should treat humans with respect just as we do not now treat animals with respect (although this is a position which might be difficult to maintain in the face of much recent discussion and activity on animal rights issues):

It is because of our intelligence that we humans are the dominant life form on Earth, and should there arise a more intelligent life form then the chances are that it will dominate humans, in the same way that humans dominate less intelligent species. There appears to be nothing to stop machines becoming more intelligent than humans in the not-too-distant future. So what can we conclude other than that machines will dominate the Earth? Not only this, but it will not be very long before they do so. (ibid. 232)

Bloomfield and Vurdubakis (1995: 10) see this kind of rhetoric as offering a different moral order of representation where the evolutionary vector moves from animal to human to machine. In this chain the machine has moved position from humble tool to the pinnacle of creation; in the words of Moravec's (1998) book title from 'mere machine to transcendent mind'. Hence it would seem that Moravec and Warwick do not just envisage pushing the human–machine boundary a little more towards the machine side, they either see the boundary disappearing or, if it does remain, machines replacing humans on top. The two positions are, either that we download our minds into robots (Moravec) and thereby continue evolution that way or that machines evolve as our 'technological' offspring and eventually take over (Warwick). The 'gods' of this machine age, should it ever happen, will of course be the robot and AI scientists. Perhaps their artificial offspring will feel some filial affection and will therefore be kinder to them than they will be to the rest of humanity. In any case if the intelligence of the machines is superior to ours, must it be a gloomy future for the human race? May we not assume that their moral senses will be more advanced than ours? Pushing the human–machine boundary so that machines come out on top, whether by downloading minds or letting the robots take over, is a substantially different position from what is being suggested in this chapter. In that case the boundary may disappear, but only because it has been pushed off the scale at the machine end. Blurring boundaries advocates making the boundary disappear but in a substantially different way and for different reasons. By boundary blurring I am not suggesting that humans retain superiority nor that machines become superior, rather, that there are good reasons for blurring the distinction and celebrating that blurring. This is the position I explore below.

Boundaries Blurred

This, then, represents the spectrum of views on the human–machine boundary. Searle's Chinese Room Argument places that border as a firm line of demarcation between the two and this is part of a spectrum of possible boundary positions. In the final sections, although I can hardly do justice to the richness of their approaches in a short space, I consider briefly two contemporary intellectual currents which blur the human–machine boundary rather than move it or transgress it and therefore offer a different reading to the problem of intentionality raised by the Chinese Room. These are actor-network theory (ANT) and cyborg feminism. In emphasizing the blurring rather than the transgression of boundaries, I do not wish to suggest that these approaches are better than those outlined above. Nor will they somehow 'solve' the human–machine problem. In any case I have argued that it should not be seen as a problem to be solved. However they do offer an alternative reading of the human–machine boundary which acknowledges its cultural aspects, thus getting away from both polarized 'for or against' arguments and 'doom and gloom' futuristic scenarios.

ANT is part of a new style of research in science and technology studies fermenting over the last twenty-five or so years. This is represented in a move away from the rationalist philosophy of science, epitomized by Popper and Lakatos, as the dominant paradigm; an approach which saw its job in terms of analysing the internal logic and rationality of the scientific enterprise rather than getting into laboratories with scientists and describing what they do on a day-to-day basis. Science and technology studies began to undergo a 'social turn' towards sociological, ethnographical, and cultural studies which, to paraphrase Bruno Latour (1987), 'follows scientists and engineers around'. From the 1970s' debates on 'internal' and 'external' factors in the history of science (Barnes 1974) and discussions of treating true and false beliefs symmetrically for explanatory purposes (Bloor 1976), the human gradually became reinstated in science and technology studies. But ANT goes further in attempting to enfranchise non-humans as objects of interest for sociological study. This involves looking at the process of creating scientific and technical knowledge in terms of a network of actors or actants, where power is located throughout the network rather than in the hands of individuals and may equally well reside with non-humans as with humans (Callon 1986; Latour 1992).

ANT extends David Bloor's symmetry requirement, logically following on from earlier arguments to plead for a symmetrical, sociological treatment of human and non-human actors. In particular Latour (1991) argues against the dualist paradigm which describes two separate ontological universes. Under this view, in a study of technology, there is no realm of 'sociality' confronting one of unmixed 'materiality'; all relations are sociotechnical. There are clear resonances between ANT and the concerns of those studying the possibility of true AI, in terms of intentionality and agency. The granting of 'as if' intentionality to a computer in the sense which Dennett implies and ANT's treatment of agency appear to be very similar.

Unsurprisingly ANT has been subject to some criticisms. In the UK, Collins has been one of ANT's most forceful critics from within the ranks of the sociology of science. In the now infamous 'Chicken Debate' (after Harry Collins's and Steve Yearley's (1992) paper 'Epistemological Chicken'), he explains the difference in style between the two main approaches. The dominant Anglo-American approach puts the human at the centre of the natural world, while the Continental approach treats natural 'actants' and human actors symmetrically, as part of the semiotic extension of the question about representation, which apparently has no centre.

Collins and Yearley (ibid.) stress the primary role of human action in constructing the agency of non-human actors, and the perceived symmetry they see as an artefactual creation of the researchers. Scallops, door-closers, electric vehicles, and all the other things that have been the subject of ANT studies cannot speak for themselves the way humans do. Yet Michel Callon and Bruno Latour (1992) criticize the social sciences, and in particular sociology as being too human-centred and socially realist. But from whatever side of the symmetry dualism, it is important to note that ANT researchers clearly see the possibility of including machines alongside other entities not usually accorded the status of agents (e.g. animals and young children), for sociological analysis.

The upshot is that rather than moving the boundary between human and machine about in the hope of finding somewhere comfortable to put it, ANT tries to abandon the distinction, to blur the boundary altogether. This is not to say that ANT ignores the distinction between humans and non-humans; it remains clear what is a human and what a non-human actor. Rather humans and non-humans are to be treated symmetrically in our descriptions of the world, especially with regard to the agency of non-humans, an agency which may or may not have been designed or inscribed by human actors.

I argue that there are particular resonances between ANT's position on intentionality and Dennett's intentional stance. The latter offers a 'get-out clause' for the problem of original intentionality, and suggests a way of acting as if certain objects have intentionality without worrying about whether they actually do have. Taking an intentional stance towards something is a way of granting it some level of agency. I believe that Dennett's position strikes a significant chord with recent research in and around actor-network theory although the two bodies of work do not seem to have discovered each other. By adopting an intentional stance we no longer have to worry about whether a machine or other object can really think or display original intentionality; we worry instead about the appropriateness of designating it an intentional system, or in the language of ANT we worry about granting it agency. ANT sets attempts to enfranchize the world of objects, although the process of delegation is done by humans—to argue that knowledge and sociability are not properties just of humans but of humans accompanied by those objects that are delegated humanity—so that the job that sociologists have, up to now, only done for humans, ANT must attempt for the masses of non-humans that coexist with us in our societies (Johnson (Latour) 1988). Returning to Douglas's (1966) religious metaphors, it is, perhaps, the agnosticism of ANT that may be unsettling. Whereas Searle appears to be a believer in the sacredness of the human category, ANT seems unconcerned about whether it is a human or a machine in the Chinese Room.

Cyborg Feminism

Actor-network theory is one important thread in contemporary science and technology studies which offers an alternative reading of the human–machine boundary; cyborg feminism offers another. In considering cyborg feminism it may seem that we have moved a long way from the Chinese Room and 'good old-fashioned AI.' Nevertheless I have argued elsewhere (Adam 1998) that feminism has much to offer an analysis of AI. For the present discussion, it is cyborg feminism's blurring of boundaries which offers important congruences with ANT's similar treatment of the human–machine boundary. This offers an alternative reading to the impasse which is created by attempts to preserve that boundary.

The cyborg, or cybernetic organism, is one of the most powerful images to emerge from the upsurge of interest in the cultures surrounding new information and communications technologies. The concept of the cyborg owes much to the 'cyberpunk' genre of science fiction and film, but also predates it in older images of the fusion of human and machine. Although, in this case it has been taken up by a branch of feminism, the cyborg is hardly a feminist invention; indeed in its manifestation in films such as *Terminator* and *Robocop*, whether it is a true cyborg or a robot or a blurring of both, it epitomizes masculine destruction. Nevertheless, it has been appropriated as a feminist icon for the blurring of several sorts of boundaries, most famously in Donna Haraway's 'A Cyborg Manifesto' (1991). It is difficult to overestimate the influence of her essay for contemporary feminism and beyond. In any piece of contemporary academic writing it seems impossible to talk of cyborgs without, in the same breath, talking of the Cyborg Manifesto. Indeed John Christie (1993: 172) describes it as having 'attained a status as near canonical as anything gets for the left/feminist academy'.

In Haraway's hands the cyborg works as an ironic political myth originally developed in the 1980s with the continuing threat of Cold War and nuclear proliferation, stretching into and finding its full force in the next decade and beyond as the information technologies become available which just might make some of the futuristic pronouncements feasible if not realities. This version of feminism built round the image of the cyborg involves a blurring, transgression, and deliberate confusion of boundaries of the self, a concern with what makes us human and how we define humanity. In any case, with our reliance on spectacles, hearing aids, heart pacemakers, dentures, dental crowns, artificial joints, not to mention computers, faxes, modems, mobile phones, and networks, we are all cyborgs, 'fabricated hybrids of machine and organism' (Haraway 1991: 150).

The cyborg is to be a creature of a post-gendered world. So for feminists, the notion of a boundary between the genders begins to blur and disappear, offering the promise of something different and better. Clearly gender is not the only, nor indeed necessarily the most important boundary blurring which Haraway's writing offers. As the boundary between human and animal has been thoroughly breached, and the boundaries between species are disturbed by the cloning, so too has the boundary between human and machine. This transgression of boundaries and shifting of perspective signals a lessening of the dualisms which have troubled many writers, not least those writing as feminists. The notion of leaving dualisms behind is a particular feature of postmodern writing within which tradition cyborg feminism locates itself. But with the lessening of dualisms and blurring of boundaries Haraway sees that we do not necessarily have to seek domination of the technology nor must we accept the gloomy futuristic scenarios painted by commentators such as Moravec and Warwick. Cyborg imagery offers a way to walk away from troubling dualisms and the boundaries we have set ourselves, to embrace deliberate blendings and the ambiguities these throw up.

The manner in which Haraway's picture blurs boundaries between machine/human/animal strikes a significant chord with actor network theory research which emerged at around the same time in the science and technology studies arena. All this has heralded an upsurge of academic interest in the programme of cyborg postmodernism where all boundaries are up for grabs. All boundaries may be inspected and transgressed. So the human/machine boundary stands as a metaphor for all the boundaries we have constructed in organizing our social worlds and its treatment in the hands of ANT and cyborg feminism demonstrates that no boundary may now be taken for granted.

Conclusion

In this chapter my concern has been to look afresh at Searle's brilliant but troubling Chinese Room thought-experiment. Asking the question, 'what lies at the heart of the Chinese Room?' leads to the ancient boundary between human and not-human and, more particularly, to the boundary between human and machine. To answer the further question of why the maintenance of this boundary should matter so much to us, I turn to the work of Douglas (1966). This research suggests that the making and maintaining of boundaries, and application of sanctions when these are transgressed, is an essential part of our means of ordering and making sense of our worlds. Such a view provides a convincing approach towards understanding why we concern ourselves with pushing to and fro the human–machine boundary. On the one hand, preserving human superiority at all costs, which is what Searle appears to be doing, is difficult in a world where our perceptions of humans versus other creatures are changing and where we have already accommodated machines into our social networks with great ease. But the 'machines on top' view of the roboticists does not mount a real challenge to the boundary question, it merely reverses the roles. The alternatives I offer in the shape of ANT and cyborg feminism offer no magic fix. But they do offer different ways of viewing the human–machine relationship, ways which no longer see the boundary as something to be maintained or breached; rather they offer the prospect of blurring the old boundaries so that machines may be further accommodated into our culture in ways which we find comfortable rather than threatening.

References

ADAM, A. (1998) *Artificial Knowing: Gender and the Thinking Machine* (London and New York: Routledge).

BARNES, B. (1974) *Scientific Knowledge and Sociological Theory* (London and Boston: Routledge & Kegan Paul).

BLOOMFIELD, B. P., and VURDUBAKIS, T. (1995) 'The Outer Limits: Humans, Animals, Machines and Attributions of Agency', Paper presented to Fourth Bath Quinquennial Science Studies Workshop: Humans, Animals, Machines, 27–31 July.

BLOOR, D. (1976) *Knowledge and Social Imagery* (London: Routledge & Kegan Paul).

BODEN, M. A. (ed.) (1990) *The Philosophy of Artificial Intelligence* (Oxford: Oxford University Press).

CALLON, M. (1986) 'Some Elements of a Sociology of Translation: Domestication of Scallops and the Fishermen of St Brieuc Bay', in J. Law (ed.), *Power, Action and Belief: A New Sociology of Knowledge* (London: Routledge & Kegan Paul) (Sociological Review Monograph), 196–229.

—— and LATOUR, B. (1992) 'Don't Throw the Baby out with the Bath School! A Reply to Collins and Yearley', in A. Pickering (ed.), *Science as Practice and Culture* (Chicago and London: University of Chicago Press), 343–68.

CHRISTIE, J. R. R. (1993) 'A Tragedy for Cyborgs', *Configurations*, 1: 171–96.

COLLINS, H. M. (1985) *Changing Order: Replication and Induction in Scientific Practice* (London, Beverly Hills, Calif., and New Delhi: Sage).

—— (1990) *Artificial Experts: Social Knowledge and Intelligent Machines* (Cambridge, Mass.: MIT Press).

—— (1996) 'Embedded or Embodied? A Review of Hubert Dreyfus' *What Computers Still Can't Do*', *Artificial Intelligence*, 80: 99–117.

—— and YEARLEY, S. (1992) 'Epistemological Chicken', in A. Pickering (ed.), *Science as Practice and Culture* (Chicago and London: University of Chicago Press), 301–26.

DENNETT, D. C. (1987) *The Intentional Stance* (Cambridge, Mass.: Bradford/MIT Press).

—— (1994) 'The Myth of Original Intentionality', in E. Dietrich (ed.), *Thinking Computers and Virtual Persons: Essays on the Intentionality of Machines* (San Diego and London: Academic Press), 91–107.

DOUGLAS, M. (1966) *Purity and Danger: An Analysis of the Concepts of Pollution and Taboo* (London and New York: Ark).

DREYFUS, H. L. (1979) *What Computers Can't Do: The Limits of Artificial Intelligence*, 2nd edn. (New York: Harper and Row).

—— (1992) *What Computers Still Can't Do: A Critique of Artificial Reason* (Cambridge, Mass. and London: MIT Press).

—— (1996) 'Response to my Critics', *Artificial Intelligence*, 80: 171–91.

HARAWAY, D. (1991) 'A Cyborg Manifesto: Science, Technology and Socialist-Feminism in the Late Twentieth Century', *Socialist Review*, 80 (1985), 65–107, and reprinted in her

Simians, Cyborgs and Women: The Reinvention of Nature (London, Free Association Books), 149–81.

JOHNSON, JIM (a.k.a. Latour, Bruno) (1988) 'Mixing Humans and Non-Humans Together: The Sociology of a Door-Closer', *Social Problems*, 35: 298–310.

KURZWEIL, R. (1999) *The Age of Spiritual Machines: When Computers Exceed Human Intelligence* (New York: Viking).

LATOUR, B. (1987) *Science in Action: How to Follow Scientists and Engineers through Society* (Cambridge, Mass.: Harvard University Press).

—— (1991) *We Have Never Been Modern* (London and New York: Harvester Wheatsheaf).

—— (1992) 'Where are the Missing Masses? The Sociology of a Few Mundane Artifacts', in W. E. Bijker and J. Law (eds.), *Shaping Technology/Building Society: Studies in Sociotechnical Change* (Cambridge, Mass. and London: MIT Press), 225–58.

—— (1999) 'On recalling ANT' in J. Law and J. Hassard (eds.), *Actor Network Theory and After* (Oxford and Malden, Mass.: Blackwell), 15–25.

LYNCH, M., and COLLINS, H. M. (1998) 'Introduction: Humans, Animals, and Machines', *Science, Technology & Human Values*, 23/4: 371–83.

MACKENZIE, D. A. (1996) *Knowing Machines: Essays on Technical Change* (Cambridge, Mass.: MIT Press).

MORAVEC, H. P. (1988) *Mind Children: The Future of Robot and Human Intelligence* (Cambridge, Mass. and London: Harvard University Press).

—— (1998) *Robot: Mere Machine to Transcendent Mind* (New York: Oxford University Press).

NOBLE, D. F. (1997) *The Religion of Technology* (New York: Knopf).

SEARLE, J. R. (1980) 'Minds, Brains, and Programs', *Behavioral and Brain Sciences*, 3: 417–24.

—— (1999) 'I Married a Computer' (Review of R. Kurzweil, *The Age of Spiritual Machines: When Computers Exceed Human Intelligence*), *New York Review of Books* (8 Apr.), 34–8.

TURING, A. M. (1950) 'Computing Machinery and Intelligence', *Mind*, 59: 433–60. Reprinted in Boden 1990.

WARWICK, K. (1997) *March of the Machines: Why the New Race of Robots Will Rule the World* (London: Century).

WHEELER, M. (1996) 'From Robots to Rothko: The Bringing Forth of Worlds', in Boden 1990: 209–36.

WOOLGAR, S. (1989) 'Reconstructing Man and Machine: A Note on Sociological Critiques of Cognitivism', in W. E. Bijker, T. P. Hughes, and T. J. Pinch (eds.), *The Social Construction of Technological Systems: New Directions in the Sociology and History of Technology* (Cambridge, Mass. and London: MIT Press), 311–28.

18

Change in the Rules: Computers, Dynamical Systems, and Searle

Michael Wheeler

Introduction

The Chinese Room Argument (described elsewhere in this volume) is directed against what John Searle calls *strong artificial intelligence (Strong AI)*, an intellectual position according to which 'the computer is not merely a tool in the study of the mind; rather, the appropriately programmed computer really *is* a mind, in the sense that computers given the right programs can be literally said to *understand* and have other cognitive states' (Searle 1980: 417[1] (B67), emphasis in original). Searle is thus famously opposed to the view that computation is sufficient for mind. Recently, some equally vocal opposition to the computational orthodoxy in AI and cognitive science has come from another quarter, namely the emerging *dynamical systems approach to cognition* (henceforth *DSC*), which is the view that '[natural] cognitive systems are dynamical systems and are best understood from the perspective of dynamics' (van Gelder and Port 1995: 5).

I carried out the bulk of this research during my time as (simultaneously) a Junior Research Fellow in Philosophy at Christ Church, Oxford, a member of the Department of Experimental Psychology at the University of Oxford, and a Post-doctoral Research Fellow of the Oxford McDonnell-Pew Centre for Cognitive Neuroscience. I completed the final revisions during my time as a Post-doctoral Research Fellow in the Department of Philosophy at the University of Stirling. Many thanks to Martin Davies, Phil Husbands, Derek Stacey, Tim van Gelder, the editors of this volume, and two anonymous referees for important comments and/or discussions.

[1] Reprinted in Boden (1990: 67). From here referred to as B67.

Work within DSC (an example of which is described later) ranges from the analysis of neural network control systems which have been evolved to control walking in insect-like artificial agents (Beer 1995*a,b*) to the modelling of human decision-making (Townsend and Busemeyer 1989, 1995).[2] Given that the archetypal supporter of DSC agrees with Searle that the mind is not, or perhaps not merely, a computer, one might wonder just how deep the agreement goes. Are the two perspectives mutually supporting, or is there some sense in which DSC too falls foul of the Chinese Room? And either way, does the adoption of a dynamical systems perspective provide any new insights into Searle's position? These are the principal questions that will exercise us in this chapter, and I shall begin by providing some conceptual background necessary to answer them. In the next section I shall introduce dynamical systems and dynamical systems theory, lay out DSC as I see it, and identify the relationship that exists between computational systems and dynamical systems.[3]

Is the Brain's Mind a Dynamical System?

What is a dynamical system? One answer which I have endorsed in the past (e.g. in Wheeler 1998*a*) is that a dynamical system is a state-determined system, where a system is state-determined just in case the current state of the system always determines a unique future behaviour. Although this approach was in tune with a certain common practice in the wider scientific community, it was mistaken. At root the science of dynamics is about characterizing the ways in which real-world systems change over time, and, given what we know about such change, any decent definition of 'dynamical system' must leave conceptual room for the existence of dynamical systems which are stochastic rather than deterministic. The concept of a state-determined system allows no such room (van Gelder 1998*a*). A better view is that a dynamical system is any system in which there is *state-dependent change over time*, where systemic change is state-dependent just in case the future behaviour of the system depends

---

[2] In addition to the authors just mentioned, DSC has been developed and defended by, among others, Elman (1995), Giunti (1991, 1995), Husbands *et al.* (1995), Kelso (1995), Port *et al.* (1995), Smithers (1995), Thelen and Smith (1993), van Gelder (1992, 1994, 1995, 1998*a,b*), and Wheeler (1994, 1998*a*, forthcoming). The canonical introduction to the field is the collection edited by Port and van Gelder (1995).

[3] The lengthy set-up is, I think, necessary. Many readers will be unfamiliar with DSC. Moreover, certain details of my interpretation of DSC matter to my eventual treatment of Searle's arguments.

causally on the current state of the system.[4] Given this definition, just about any natural system we meet will count as a dynamical system, since just about any natural system we meet will change over time in a state-dependent way. But even if the bulk of natural systems are, ontologically speaking, dynamical systems, the task of explaining them as such remains far from trivial, since to make a system intelligible *as* a dynamical system, one needs to provide a satisfying mathematical analysis of the distinctive ways in which that system changes over time in a state-dependent fashion. Notice that if a system counted as having some property of interest (e.g. intentionality) by virtue of achieving a particular kind of state-dependent change over time, then the sort of mathematical analysis I have in mind would constitute a specification of a set of sufficient conditions for the presence of that property. This will be important later.

The first goal of a dynamical systems analysis is to find a collection of *state variables* which, allowing for appropriate idealizations, adequately captures the overall state of the target system at a given time. The scientist can then produce a *state space*, a geometric model of the set of all possible states of the system. A state space has as many dimensions as there are state variables for the system, and each possible state of the system (each possible combination of values for the state variables) is represented by a single point in that space. The next requirement is a set of *state space evolution equations* (e.g. differential equations) describing how the values of the state variables change with time in a state-dependent way. (Certain values in such equations specify quantities that affect the behaviour of the target system without being affected in turn; these are called the *parameters* of the system.) Given a set of state space evolution equations, plus some initial conditions (a point in the state space), subsequent changes in the state of the system can be plotted as a curve in the state space. Such a curve is called a *trajectory* of the system, and the set of all such trajectories is the system's *phase portrait*. Phase portraits often contain one or more *attractors*. Attractors represent states of the system to which trajectories passing nearby tend to converge, and they come in a number of different varieties. For example, *point* attractors represent constant states of convergence, whilst *periodic* attractors are oscillatory in nature. The set of states such that, if the system is in one of those states, the system will evolve to a particular attractor, is called that attractor's

---

[4] This idea (or something very like it) is at work in Beer's dynamical systems approach to robotics (see Beer 1995*a*: 129). Many thanks to Tim van Gelder (personal communication) for helping me to see sense on the issue of stochastic change, and for suggesting the term 'state-dependent'. Van Gelder does not himself think that the term 'dynamical system' should be defined in such terms (see van Gelder 1998*b*).

basin of attraction, and the trajectories which pass through points in the basin of attraction on the way to the attractor, but which do not lie on the attractor itself, are called *transients*. The complementary concept to that of an attractor is that of a *repellor*, a state of the system from which trajectories passing nearby tend to move away.[5]

So how might a dynamically minded cognitive scientist proceed? We can get a feel for the approach by considering some work by Elman in which a particular kind of connectionist network—what Elman calls a *simple recurrent network*—is used to study aspects of language processing (Elman 1991, 1995). Roughly speaking, the term 'connectionist network' picks out that class of systems in which a (typically) large number of interconnected units process information in parallel. In as much as the brain is made up of a large number of interconnected units (neurons) that process information in parallel, connectionist networks are 'neurally inspired', although at a massive level of abstraction. Each unit in a connectionist network has an activation level regulated by the activation levels of the other units to which it is connected, and the effect of one unit on another can be positive (if the connection is excitatory) or negative (if the connection is inhibitory). The strengths of these connections are known as the network's weights, and it is usual to think of the network's 'knowledge' as being stored in its set of weights. The values of these weights are (in most networks) modifiable, so, given some initial configuration, changes to the weights can be made which improve the performance of the network over time. In other words, within all sorts of limits imposed by the way the input is encoded, the specific structure of the network, and the weight-adjustment algorithm, the network may 'learn' to carry out some desired input–output mapping.

One widely used connectionist architecture has three layers of processing units—an input layer, a hidden (intervening) layer, and an output layer. In a simple recurrent network, as used by Elman, this three-layer arrangement is supplemented with a group of context units. These context units store the

---

[5] Abraham and Shaw (1992) and Norton (1995), among others, offer more detailed (yet novice-friendly) explanations of the dynamical systems concepts mentioned in the text, plus others that I have omitted, such as bifurcation points, coupling, and chaos. It is important to note that although the framework of dynamical systems theory already provides the mathematical backbone for many areas of science, the development of that framework is far from complete. For example, there exist serious problems in applying our present stock of dynamical systems concepts to stochastic systems, and, as we have seen already, the class of dynamical systems certainly includes such systems (see also Crutchfield 1998; Jaeger 1998). Whether dynamical systems theory will eventually run out of explanatory steam is anyone's guess, but given the apparently endless ingenuity of scientists, we can be optimistic.

activation values of the hidden units at any one time-step, and then feed that information back to the hidden units at the following time-step. The present state of the network is thus a function of both the present input and the network's previous state. As Elman shows, this allows such systems to succeed at certain predictive tasks. For example, given a corpus of simple sentences, constructed from a small set of nouns and verbs, and presented so that the only information explicitly available to the network is distributional information concerning statistical regularities in the input strings, a simple recurrent network can be trained to predict words in complex sentences that contain long-distance sequential dependencies. Thus, for instance, the network is able to predict correctly (for novel as well as familiar sentences) whether a main verb ought to be singular or plural, even given the presence of intervening clauses (between the noun and the verb) that might or might not conflict with that number.

To understand such successes, Elman adopts a dynamical systems perspective. Connectionist networks are naturally understood as dynamical systems (see e.g. Smolensky 1988), and one key notion in such an understanding is the concept of a network's *activation space*. The most general activation space of a network will have as many dimensions as there are units in the network, and a point in that space will be defined by the simultaneous activation values of those units. During its performance phase, the network follows a trajectory in this space, as determined by the initial conditions (the point in activation space at which the network is placed when it receives input) and the appropriate evolution equation. The post-training numerical values of the weights on the network's connections are fixed parameters of that equation. Building on the basic idea of an activation space, Elman shows that the sequential dependencies about which his network 'knows' are represented in trajectories in the hidden unit activation space along which the network travels as it processes input sentences. In fact, the hidden unit activation space here has seventy dimensions—far beyond the limits of human visualization—so, in order to obtain a geometric model of the dynamics, Elman uses principal component analysis to discover the dimensions along which there is variation in the hidden unit activation vectors, and thus produces a series of two-dimensional state spaces. Important grammatical features (e.g. agreement in number, degree of embedding) are shown to be captured by various positional differences and displacements in these spaces.

Where do we go from here? Searle's Chinese Room thought-experiment is supposed to undermine the idea that a machine could have a mind simply by virtue of running the 'right' computer program. We also know that supporters of DSC conceptualize mental phenomena as state space evolution in certain forms of dynamical system. So, to see whether or not the dynamical systems approach to cognition lends support to Searle's position on computation and cognition, we need to find out how computational systems and dynamical systems are related.

Computational systems are dynamical systems. This is a trivial consequence of my favoured definition of a dynamical system (as any system in which there is state-dependent change over time), and it doesn't tell us very much. What matters is precisely what *kind* of dynamical system a computational system is. Here is my view: computational systems are dynamical systems that (i) realize well-defined input–output functions by accessing, manipulating, and/or transforming representations, and (ii) feature a distinctive lack of richly temporal phenomena.[6] To see why my position is at least a plausible one to occupy, consider first a kind of semi-intuitive, somewhat pre-theoretical use of the term 'computation', according to which a computational system is any system that can be understood as realizing some well-defined input–output function (or some set of such functions). The problem with this definition is that it fails to exclude from the class of computational systems those systems in which *computable* behaviour (for present purposes, behaviour which can be calculated as the output of some well-defined function) is produced by non-computational means. For example, as both Beer (1995a: 126) and van Gelder (1998b: 625) observe, we should not conclude from the fact that the behaviour of the solar system is computable that the planets compute their orbits. The solar system is a computable dynamical system, but it is not a computer. It seems to me that the way forward here is to remind ourselves that when we describe some target system as a computer, we are surely trying to say something about the *states and processes within that system* which actually guide its behaviour. Given this, one piece of 'tightening-up' which suggests itself is to add the condition that representation is necessary for computation, such that to be a computer, a system must not simply realize some well-defined input–output function, it must realize

---

[6] Other versions of the view that computational systems form a subset of dynamical systems are defended by Beer (1995a), Giunti (1991, 1995), Horgan and Tienson (1994), and van Gelder (1992). There are alternative positions according to which the class of computational systems and the class of dynamical systems either (a) don't intersect at all (e.g. van Gelder 1994, 1995; van Gelder and Port 1995), or (b) do intersect, but only in theoretically uninteresting cases (e.g. van Gelder 1998a,b). I do not have the space here to consider these alternatives (for discussion, see Wheeler forthcoming, ch. 4).

that function by accessing, manipulating, and/or transforming representa-tional states (something which the solar system does not do). This is an improve-ment, but we are not yet home, because there is no reason to think that every representation-using process is a computational one. What is still missing is a method for distinguishing between computational and non-computational representation-using processes.[7]

This is where the concept of *Turing machine computation* (Turing 1936) comes in handy, because it supplies us with a theoretically principled and independently motivated set of constraints on what constitutes a computational process.[8] Of course, most computers are not actually Turing machines, so we should not *identify* the notion of computation-in-general with that of Turing machine computation. Nevertheless, legions of researchers working on the theory of computation take the Turing machine concept to be an anchor of that theory, and some have even insisted that Turing machine equivalence is the only *well-defined* concept of computation we have.[9] Thus it seems highly plausible that the notion of computation-in-general is *intimately connected with* that of Turing machine computation, at least to the extent that the deep properties of Turing machines will provide a guide to the deep properties of computational systems in general. So what are the deep properties of Turing machines? Turing machines are certainly systems in which there is state-dependent change over time, so (like all computational systems) they are dynamical systems.[10] Moreover, Turing machines realize well-defined input-output functions by accessing, manipulating, and transforming representations (in this case, symbols). But these properties, however deep they may be, simply underwrite our existing analysis of computation. The news arrives when one considers the distinctive features of a Turing machine's processing profile. Here is a list of such features (for a related analysis, see van Gelder 1992): Turing machine computation is digital, deterministic, discrete, effective (in the technical sense that behaviour is always the result of an algorithmically specified finite number of operations), and temporally austere (in that time is reduced to

---

[7] It is worth noting that a non-computational representation-using system might still be a dynamical system. There is no in-principle tension between dynamical systems and representation. However, dynamical systems do not have to be representational in nature, whereas computational systems do.

[8] For a brief, non-technical introduction to Turing machines, see Johnson-Laird (1988: 48–51).

[9] For an expression of the latter view in a cognitive-scientific context, see Sloman (1996).

[10] A second and complementary route to the conclusion that Turing machines are dynamical systems is provided by Giunti (1991) who demonstrates technically that the notions of a state space and a state space evolution equation apply to Turing machines.

mere sequence). This last property requires some explanation. When talking about change in Turing machines, the received language is one of successive 'time-steps'. But this way of talking is potentially misleading, since, in Turing machines, the so-called 'time-steps' are nothing more than indices which allow us to specify the order of the steps in a particular sequence of state transitions. The fact is that, in a Turing machine, there is simply no *theoretical* sense in which (i) state transitions take any time to complete, (ii) there is a time interval between states, or (iii) the states themselves persist for any length of (real) time (cf. van Gelder 1992). In short, in a Turing machine, state-dependent change over time is reduced to mere state-dependent sequential update. Of course, state-dependent change over time can be *much* more complex than mere sequence, involving richly temporal phenomena such as *rates of change* and *intrinsic rhythms*.

Each of the properties of Turing machines mentioned above probably contributes, to some extent, to our core idea of a computational process. However, in the present, *cognitive* context, it is the property of being temporally austere which, I think, most clearly separates computational dynamical systems from non-computational ones. I'll say why in a moment. First let's just see the idea through. By deploying the proposed link between Turing machines and computational systems in general, we now have a licence to say that computational systems will, paradigmatically, be temporally austere. So if richly temporal phenomena are present in some dynamical system of interest, then we can conclude that that dynamical system is not a computational system. Now notice that whilst the computational architectures proposed within computational cognitive science require that inner events happen in the right order, and (in theory) fast enough to get a job done, there are, in general, no constraints on how long each operation within the overall cognitive process takes, or on how long the gaps between the individual operations are (cf. van Gelder and Port 1995). Moreover, the transition events that characterize those inner operations are not related in any systematic way to the real-time dynamics of either neural biochemical processes, non-neural bodily events, or environmental phenomena (dynamics which surely involve rates and rhythms). All of this explains why we should focus on temporal austerity as a deep theoretical feature of computation, for once we do so, a striking fact about computational cognitive science falls neatly into place.

This completes my analysis of the relationship that exists between computation and dynamics. Notice that it is an analysis which leaves ample conceptual space for the view that mind and cognition are constituted by state space evolution trajectories in certain *non-computational* dynamical systems. According to such a view, not only are psychological phenomena essentially dynamical, but the specific kinds of dynamics involved are non-computational in form. Call this the *radical DSC claim*. The radical DSC claim will be true, for some property of interest, if, according to our best science, the dynamics underlying that property (a) do not realize any well-defined input-output function, and/or (b) do not involve the manipulation of representations, and/or (c) feature richly temporal phenomena.[11] So once a proper philosophical articulation of DSC (an articulation to which I hope to have contributed here) is in place (alongside, I might add, a proper philosophical explication of the concept of representation), it is up to ongoing scientific research to decide whether or not the radical DSC claim is correct. But sorting out the empirical truth or otherwise of the radical DSC claim is not on the agenda for today. All we need right now is for it to be the case that there is conceptual room for such a claim—and there is. With that, it is high time that we turned explicitly to Searle.

Rooms, Gyms, and Dynamical Neural Networks

It might seem that Searle should be sympathetic to the radical DSC claim, since its message is that computation is neither necessary nor sufficient for mind. However, things are not so simple. For starters, there is a sense in which Searle's own brand of a prioristic anti-computationalism is weaker than the empirical variety promoted by the radical DSC claim. The most that the Chinese Room demonstrates is that computation is not sufficient for mind. Strictly speaking, it leaves open the possibility that computation is necessary, although Searle himself regards this outcome as wildly unlikely (Searle 1980: 418 (B70)). A more telling observation, however, is that to the extent that the Chinese Room argument succeeds in burying the idea that computation is sufficient for mind, it does so by undermining the more general thought that any purely *formal* process (Searle sometimes says '*syntactic* process') could ever constitute a mind. When Searle describes an element, state, or process as 'formal', he means both

---

[11] For accounts of neural systems which suggest that (a) might be satisfied, see e.g. Keijzer (2001); Varela *et al.* (1991). For my views on (b), see e.g. Wheeler (1998b); Clark and Wheeler (1998); Wheeler and Clark (1999). And for a compelling case of (c), see Port *et al.* (1995). My present bet (for what it's worth) is that while many psychological phenomena (especially those involving real-time environmental interaction) are plausibly the result of non-computational dynamics, others (such as deliberative planning) are likely to be computational in nature (Wheeler forthcoming).

that it has no intrinsic content (meaning), and that it is hardware independent (see Searle 1990: 21–2). The second of these features will be important later. For now let's concentrate on the first, and consider the following formulation of Searle's argument against strong AI:[12] (i) computer programs are purely formal in character; (ii) minds have semantic contents; (iii) no formal process is sufficient for semantics; so (iv) computer programs are not sufficient for mind. Searle takes premise (i) to be part of our technical understanding of what computation is, and premise (ii) to be obvious. The Chinese Room thought-experiment is designed to establish premise (iii), via the pumped intuition that the person in the room plainly does not understand Chinese, even though she is, by hypothesis, running a formal program which enables her to pass the Turing test for that cognitive domain. From these three premises, (iv) follows. But now since Searle's argument turns on the formal character of computation (rather than, say, the fact that it is temporally austere), any camaraderie between Searle and the supporter of the radical DSC claim is destined to be short-lived. The positive side of the radical DSC claim is that mental properties are constituted by state space evolution trajectories in certain non-computational dynamical systems. From this perspective, the relevant dynamical systems analysis emerges as a specification of conditions which are sufficient for the presence of mind. But any such dynamical systems account, couched in terms of geometric structures such as state spaces, trajectories, attractors, and phase portraits, remains a *purely formal* story. So, at the deeper level at which Searle's arguments function—the level at which the focus is on the purely formal character of the processes concerned—there is simply no significant difference between certain strong versions of the computational and the dynamical approaches. Both maintain that meeting some set of formal criteria is sufficient for mind. One might even add some Searlian colour to this point by constructing a dynamical systems variant of the Chinese Room in which the imprisoned person feverishly manipulates certain formal elements (e.g. the values of numerical variables) in accordance with a set of state space evolution equations.

It turns out, then, that far from being united against the common enemy, champions of the radical DSC claim and Searle are at loggerheads. The underlying reason is that the supporter of any version of DSC shares one of her deep commitments with the computationalist. This fact also explains why one

---

[12] This sort of formulation appears in chapter 2 of *Minds, Brains and Science* (Searle 1984) and in Searle (1990).

response to Searle that a particular sort of dynamical systems theorist might be tempted to make, as well as what one can confidently predict would be Searle's reply, both track moves already familiar from the extant Chinese Room literature. The computationalist response to Searle that I have in mind concedes that the Chinese Room Argument might undermine a certain style of Strong AI—one which involves classical, symbolic, serial computation, and which buys into a language-based model of thought far removed from straightforwardly biological considerations. However, goes the response, the Chinese Room Argument loses its force once we turn to connectionist models of thought, with their more biologically motivated, subsymbolic, highly distributed style of parallel computation (see e.g. Churchland and Churchland 1990; Clark 1989). Searle's counter-measure is to introduce the *Chinese gym*, a hall in which many interacting monolingual English speakers perform the kind of state-transition functions and message-sending operations standardly performed by the units in a connectionist network. Although the gym could be set up so as to pass the Turing test for understanding Chinese, '[no one] in the gym speaks a word of Chinese, and there is no way for the system as a whole to learn the meanings of Chinese words' (Searle 1990: 22).[13]

The dynamical systems version of this response to Searle concedes that an appropriate variant of the Chinese Room Argument might undermine one dynamical systems version of the Strong AI claim—a version, that is, which claims that having a mind is a matter of realizing the right *abstract* dynamical profile, where an abstract dynamical profile is one whose evolution equations determine state-dependent change over time in certain 'high-level' psychological variables (e.g. the attentional weights, valences, and preferences that figure in the work of Townsend and Busemeyer 1989, 1995). Such variables are far

---

[13] In some ways, the Chinese gym is foreshadowed by Searle's established reaction to the earlier brain-simulator response (see e.g. Searle 1980). There Searle imagines a system of water pipes that recreates the formal activity of the brain thanks to the activity of a person operating the valves in an appropriate manner. I should add that the Chinese gym and its older relation do not exhaust Searle's replies to the connectionist move. He also argues that since '[any] function that can be computed on a parallel machine can also be computed on a serial machine', the shift to parallel computation, as championed by connectionism, is no defence against the Chinese Room (see Searle 1990: 22). As it stands this argument is suspect for at least two reasons. First, it fails to rule out the possibility that some other aspect of connectionist computation (e.g. its distributed or continuous nature) might be crucial for mind. Secondly, it threatens to confuse simulation with duplication in precisely the manner that, in other contexts, Searle is quick to warn against (see e.g. Searle 1980: 84). It is true that any parallel system can be *simulated* on a serial machine. But that does not mean that the serial simulation will necessarily *duplicate* all the properties that the properly parallel system enjoys. For one thing, the serial simulation will presumably be slower.

removed from any straightforwardly biological considerations. However, goes the response, the dynamically oriented Chinese Room Argument loses its force once we turn to so-called *dynamical neural networks*, networks which feature properties not found in their conventional computational relations, properties such as asynchronous processing, real-valued time delays on connections, non-uniform activation functions, deliberately introduced noise, and connectivity which is not only both directionally unrestricted and highly recurrent, but also not subject to symmetry constraints. Such properties underlie the capacity of dynamical neural networks to generate richly temporal non-computational behaviour. They also reflect, to some extent, the generic architectural properties and dynamical complexity of real biological nervous systems.[14] This is all very exciting for cognitive science; but does the introduction of dynamical neural networks block Searle's argument? I don't think so. The counter-move that we might expect from Searle would be a simple re-staging of the Chinese gym as the dynamical Chinese gym, a hall in which many interacting monolingual English speakers perform the kinds of varied state-transition functions and time-dependent message-sending operations standardly performed by the units in a dynamical neural network. One can almost hear Searle's scorn: no one in the dynamical gym speaks a word of Chinese, and there is no way for the system as a whole to learn the meanings of Chinese words.

The reason why the shift to dynamical neural networks runs headlong into the dynamical Chinese gym is, of course, that that shift, as radical as it may be, still leaves us firmly within the formalist conceptual framework identified earlier. It is worth unpacking this point. The connectionist-computation and the dynamical-systems responses to Searle that we have just considered share the general thought that formal processes of some sort will be sufficient for producing minds. Moreover, both responses agree that the defining characteristic of the formal processes that are mind-producing will be that they feature some particular subset of the low-level structural properties of real neural machinery. Where the two approaches differ is over what that subset will be, with the computationalist focusing on, for example, distributedness or parallelism, and the fan of dynamical neural networks focusing on, for example,

---

[14] Dynamical neural networks featuring various subsets of the properties mentioned in the text have been deployed by, for example, Beer and colleagues (see e.g. Beer 1995*b*; Beer and Gallagher 1992) and members of the Sussex evolutionary robotics group (see e.g. Cliff *et al.* 1993; Husbands *et al.* 1995). I discuss the generic architectural restrictions placed on orthodox connectionist networks in Wheeler (forthcoming, ch. 3) and pursue the parallels between dynamical neural networks and biological nervous systems in Wheeler (1998*b*: 102–3).

temporal complexity or high degrees of recurrency. But the Chinese Room Argument targets not merely computation, but formal processes in general, so the extra demand that the formal processes at issue be grounded in what we know of biological nervous systems is beside the point. Given this, we should expect the thought experiment itself to be flexible enough that it can be adjusted so as to apply to *any* particular subset of formal processes that might be up for consideration—computational or dynamical, biologically grounded or not. So it is unsurprising that the Chinese Room can be modified so as to apply to orthodox connectionist networks or, with a further twist, to dynamical neural networks. And while it is true that the Chinese Room itself targets a style of formal process that is (in the relevant sense) abiological, the Chinese gym can be set up so that it realizes formal processes that enjoy a proud biological heritage. It seems, then, that Chinese-room-style considerations apply equally to any computationalist version of Strong AI (classical or connectionist) and to any claim to the effect that realizing the right set of dynamical systems is sufficient for mind (whether those dynamical systems are abstract in nature or dynamical neural networks).

The Rediscovery of the Brain

So far Searle is in the ascendancy, but now there is a serious worry to be recorded, one which resides at the very heart of the positive position on mind and brain that Searle himself develops in the wake of the Chinese Room Argument. Whilst this worry might conceivably be exposed by other means, we shall see that it becomes highly visible once one adopts a dynamical systems perspective.

A far-too-crude (and, as we shall see, ultimately misleading) statement of Searle's positive position might be to say that he believes it to be stuff (hardware) and not structure that really matters for mind. For example, he argues that we find it natural to ascribe mentality to certain other animals because (*a*) we find it impossible to make sense of their behaviour without using intentional language, and (*b*) 'we can see that the beasts are made of similar stuff to ourselves—that is an eye, that a nose, this is its skin, and so on' (Searle 1980: 421 (B80)). We know that (*a*) alone cannot be sufficient for the presence of mind, because of the Chinese Room. However, as it stands, the added appeal to stuff in (*b*) does not tell us nearly enough. We need to unearth Searle's explanation of precisely what it is about organic stuff that matters. The first step towards a better interpretation here comes if we highlight Searle's claim that the brain has *specific causal properties* that endow it with the ability to produce mental states (see e.g. Searle 1980: 421 (B78)). But what are these causal properties? Searle is adamant that they cannot be tied up with any formal features of the brain, since formal features 'have by themselves no causal power except the power, when instantiated, to produce the next stage of the formalism when the machine is running' (Searle 1980: 422 (B82)), and the most important message to come out of the Chinese Room was supposed to be that purely formal processes are not sufficient for generating psychological phenomena. If we add this rejection of formal properties to the claim that 'actual human mental phenomena [are causally] dependent on actual physical-chemical properties of actual human brains' (Searle 1980: 423 (B86)), then we get the straightforward result that, for Searle, *the causal properties that matter for mind are certain specific, non-formal, physical-chemical properties of human brains.* This appeal to physical-chemical properties needs to be unpacked with care, since Searle is not a carbon chauvinist who thinks that systems made out of different stuff simply could not have minds. His claim is that to cause a mind, any system (natural or artificial) would have to have causal powers equivalent to those of human brains. So a silicon brain (for example) could cause a mind, if it had the right causal powers. That said there is still something missing from the explanation. The negative point is clear: the relevant causal powers are not formal in nature. What we are still owed from Searle is a decent positive account of the nature of those powers. Were there no sign of such an account, Searle would seemingly be open to the charge that he has left the causal connection between brains and minds entirely mysterious. Fortunately Searle does have a story to tell. Unfortunately it lands him in trouble.

The first thing to note here is that Searle holds consciousness to be the pivotal psychological phenomenon, in the strong sense that all the other mental phenomena (cognition, intelligence, intentionality, etc.) can be understood *as mental* only by way of their connections with consciousness. For an unconscious neurophysiological process going on in my brain right now to be genuinely mental, that process must be a candidate for consciousness in that, under the right circumstances, it will generate a conscious state (for more details, see Searle 1992, ch. 7). This indicates that, for Searle, whatever goes for consciousness goes for mental states in general. So what does go for consciousness? To answer this question, we need to understand what Searle means by the phrase 'causally emergent system features'. System features are those features of systems of components that are not also features of the components individually.

So an object (one type of system of molecules) might weigh ten pounds, but the molecules that make up that object do not each weigh ten pounds. Some system features (e.g. weight) can be calculated from facts about the system components and the way in which those components are structurally related to each other and, possibly, to the environment. However, others (e.g. solidity and liquidity) have to be explained in terms of the causal interactions among the components. These are what Searle calls 'causally emergent system features', and he proceeds to claim that *consciousness is a causally emergent feature of systems of neurons*:

[Consciousness] is a causally emergent property of systems. It is an emergent feature of certain systems of neurons in the same way that solidity and liquidity are emergent features of systems of molecules. The existence of consciousness can be explained by the causal interactions between elements of the brain at the micro level, but consciousness cannot itself be deduced or calculated from the sheer physical structure of the neurons without some additional account of the causal relations between them. (Searle 1992: 112)

If I am right that, for Searle, whatever goes for consciousness goes for mental states in general, then Searle's position is that mental states are causally emergent features of certain systems of neurons in exactly the same way that solidity and liquidity are causally emergent features of certain systems of molecules.

At this point Searle and DSC renew their relationship, with spectacular results. To see why, we need to add a further dimension to our understanding of dynamical systems. Certain complex dynamical systems display *self-organization*, a phenomenon in which the components of the system interact with each other (and possibly with the environment) in non-linear ways so as to produce the emergence and maintenance of new structured order, without the orchestrating influence of any controlling executive. Popular examples of the phenomenon include lasers, slime moulds, activity patterns in ants, and flocking behaviour in creatures such as birds. Flocking provides a good illustration of what to expect. Using computer simulations, Reynolds (1987) demonstrates that no central executive or external controller is needed to coordinate flocking behaviour in a group of individuals. Rather, if each participating individual follows just three local rules—keep a minimum distance from other objects, move at roughly the same speed as those around you, and move towards the perceived centre of the mass of those around you—then that group of agents will self-organize into a robust flock, one which is capable of maintaining its integrity when faced with obstacles. (Upon encountering an obstacle, the flock breaks up into sub-flocks, which then pass on either side of the object, before reforming into a single flock.)

Dynamical systems theory is the natural theoretical framework within which to characterize self-organization, and appeals to self-organization are often pivotal in core examples of DSC (see e.g. Kelso 1995; Thelen and Smith 1993). But now as soon as one thinks about self-organization, it seems clear that the concept is deeply intertwined with Searle's notion of causal emergence. In fact, I suggest, the term 'causally emergent system feature' is simply another name for the distinctive kind of property that, as the outcome of self-organization, I have glossed as 'new structured order'. In effect, then, Searle is telling us that mental states are causally emergent properties of certain self-organizing neural dynamical systems in exactly the same way that solidity and liquidity are causally emergent properties of certain self-organizing molecular dynamical systems.[15]

Given the self-organization-based understanding of mental states that appears to be on offer from Searle, one might wonder about the specific causal properties that neural stuff would need, in order to produce mental states so understood. There is an answer that, in the interests of consistency, Searle ought to give. Think again about flocking. Using Searle's language, flocks (as revealed by Reynolds's compelling explanation) are causally emergent features of certain systems of individuals. They come about because each contributing individual follows certain local rules of interaction (e.g. keep a specified minimum distance from other objects). In other words, flocks are higher-level system properties that can be explained by the causal interactions between individuals at a lower level. Now recall that when Searle describes an element as 'formal', he means both (i) that it has no intrinsic content, and (ii) that it is hardware-independent. By these dual criteria, the processes that are sufficient for flocking in the real world count as being formal in character. The first condition is satisfied because the rules that specify the lower-level causal inter-actions constitute a computational algorithm, and thus (from a Searlian perspective) have no intrinsic content. The second condition is met, in what is surely an appropriate way, because the only causal power that the relevant hardware elements—certain spatially located physical individuals—need here is the capacity to follow the intrinsically content-free rules of interaction, that

---

[15] Anyone who thinks that properties such as solidity are too 'inert' to be the products of self-organization should seek out Harper's (1995) account of rocks as self-organizing dynamical systems.

is, to *instantiate* those rules. Of course, only certain sorts of physical elements will be capable of instantiating the particular rules in question, and thus of generating flocks, but that doesn't prevent flocks, where they do occur, from being correctly identified as the products of purely formal processes. It simply indicates that a particular generic pattern of self-organization is not universally realizable.[16] In principle at least, a similar story can be told for solidity. Solidity is a causally emergent system feature generated by the vibratory movements of molecules in lattice structures. These movements can be specified by mathematical rules—rules which have no intrinsic content—and the only causal power each individual molecule needs is the property of being able to enter into the right kinds of interactions by instantiating those rules.

So what? There seems to be little doubt that Searle means us to take seriously the parallel that he draws between mental states and other less controversial causally emergent phenomena such as solidity and, we can now add, flocking. But if the forgoing analyses of solidity and flocking are right, then this parallel seems to commit him to the following view. The specific causal properties that neural components need, in order to produce minds, are purely a matter of having the capacity to instantiate the appropriate, intrinsically content-free rules or equations of interaction. Of course, only certain sorts of physical components will be capable of following the particular rules or equations that matter for mind—rules or equations which, if DSC is right, will involve all sorts of fine-grained temporal complexities. But that doesn't prevent minds, where they do occur, from being the products of purely formal neural processes. This interpretation of Searle allows us to give an entirely unmysterious reading to his claim that the existence of consciousness—and, by extension, mental states in general—'can be explained by the causal interactions between neural components at the micro level'. So there is a line of reasoning, *present in Searle's own account*, which propels us towards the conclusion that the physical processes sufficient for causing minds are, in transgression of the Chinese Room Argument, purely formal in nature. But if this is so, then there is a serious internal tension lurking in Searle's account of mind, a tension that becomes visible once one adopts a dynamical systems perspective.

At this juncture one might be tempted to complain that I have read too much into the parallel that Searle draws between mental states and, say, solidity, and that he avoids the supposed difficulty that I have tried to lay at his door

[16] In his discussion of how the definition of computation might be tightened up so as to prevent universal realizability, Searle himself is clear that the fact that a process is not universally realizable is not, in itself, enough to stop that process from being a formal one (see Searle 1992: 209).

because he holds there to be something uniquely different about mental states, namely that they, unlike other physical phenomena, possess subjectivity. To see why this potential escape-route is not available to Searle, we need to understand the distinction that he draws between two different types of reduction.[17] In *causal reductions* one demonstrates that the causal powers of the reduced phenomenon can be explained entirely in terms of the causal powers of the reducing phenomenon. Causally emergent system features can be causally reduced. Solidity is causally reducible to vibratory movements of molecules in lattice structures, and mental states are causally reducible to patterns of neuronal firings. Where one has completed a causal reduction, one can often go on to perform an *ontological reduction*, in which the surface features of the reduced phenomenon—features which will typically include certain subjective appearances—are (to use Searle's phrase) 'carved off', and the target phenomenon redefined in terms of the underlying causes. For example, certain surface aspects of solidity, such as impenetrability, might be carved off, and the phenomenon of solidity then redefined as the vibratory movements of molecules in lattice structures.

According to Searle, the practice of ontological reduction, as just characterized, is inappropriate in the case of mental states, even though, in the psychological case, the pattern of facts in the world remains basically the same as in instances of successfully established ontological reduction. Thus in the psychological context too there exist particular lower-level physical (neurophysiological) events, and these are the underlying causes of certain surface phenomena such as subjective experiences. The difference, however, is that in psychological explanation it is precisely the subjective surface phenomena in which we are primarily interested; so although carving them off to be ontologically reduced (and thus excluded from a new definition of the mental) would be possible in principle, it would constitute a seriously counter-productive strategy. Here is not the place to enter into a detailed discussion of this claim. In the present context the key points are that, according to Searle, (i) the pattern of causal reduction familiar from the non-psychological cases goes through in exactly the same way in the psychological case, and (ii) the ontological irreducibility of the mental is not a deep metaphysical fact, but, as Searle himself puts it, a 'trivial consequence of our definitional practices' with 'no untoward scientific consequences whatever' (Searle 1992: 124). Nothing about this

---

[17] My exegesis of Searle on reductionism is necessarily brief. The details are in (Searle 1992, ch. 5). For the reasons given previously, I continue to take the liberty of substituting 'mental states' for 'consciousness' in the argument.

treatment of subjectivity undermines the thought that minds are caused by purely formal processes. Indeed, in a way the opposite is true: the sense of scientifically oriented demystification that drives Searle's approach threatens to encourage that very thought.

Conclusions

At today's close of play, this is how things stand. If the Chinese Room Argument is successful against the idea that computation (biologically oriented or not) is sufficient for mind, then an appropriate variant of that argument will be successful against the idea that realizing the right set of dynamical systems (biologically oriented or not) is sufficient for mind. This is because (i) what the Chinese Room actually establishes, if successful, is the more general claim that no purely formal process could ever constitute a mind, and (ii) computation and dynamical state space evolution are both formal processes. However, once one approaches things from a dynamical systems perspective, it seems that Searle's own positive theory of mind—turning, as it does, on the concept of causal emergence—is itself revealed as being most readily and consistently interpreted as a formal account. In other words, the anti-formalist conclusion of the Chinese Room Argument appears to be contradicted by the very concrete account of mind that Searle himself develops. This should be worrying for Searle. Tomorrow should provide a fascinating day's play.

References

ABRAHAM, R. H., and SHAW, C. D. (1992) *Dynamics—The Geometry of Behavior* 2nd edn. (Redwood City, Calif.: Addison-Wesley).

BEER, R. D. (1995a) 'Computational and Dynamical Languages for Autonomous Agents', in Port and van Gelder 1995: 121–47.

——— (1995b) 'A Dynamical Systems Perspective on Agent-Environment Interaction', *Artificial Intelligence*, 72: 173–215.

——— and GALLAGHER, J. G. (1992) 'Evolving Dynamic Neural Networks for Adaptive Behavior', *Adaptive Behavior*, 1: 91–122.

BODEN, M. A (ed.) (1990) *The Philosophy of Artificial Intelligence* (Oxford: Oxford University Press).

CHURCHLAND, P. M., and CHURCHLAND, P. S. (1990) 'Could a Machine Think?' *Scientific American*, 262/1: 26–31.

CLARK, A. (1989) *Microcognition: Philosophy, Cognitive Science, and Parallel Distributed Processing* (Cambridge, Mass. and London: MIT Press/Bradford Books).

—— and WHEELER, M. (1998) 'Bringing Representation Back to Life', in Pfeifer *et al.* 1998: 3–12.

CLIFF, D., HARVEY, I., and HUSBANDS, P. (1993) 'Explorations in Evolutionary Robotics', *Adaptive Behavior*, 2: 73–110.

CRUTCHFIELD, J. (1998) 'Dynamical Embodiments of Computation in Cognitive Processes', *Behavioral and Brain Sciences*, 21: 635.

ELMAN, J. L. (1991) 'Distributed Representations, Simple Recurrent Networks, and Grammatical Structure', *Machine Learning*, 7: 195–225.

—— (1995) 'Language as a Dynamical System', in Port and van Gelder 1995: 195–225.

GIUNTI, M. (1991) 'Computers, Dynamical Systems, Phenomena, and the Mind', Ph.D. thesis, Department of History and Philosophy of Science, Indiana University. Published as a Ph.D. dissertation microfilm, University Microfilms Inc., Ann Arbor, 1993.

—— (1995) 'Dynamical Models of Cognition', in Port and van Gelder 1995: 549–71.

HARPER, T. (1995) 'Dead or Alive: Two Concepts of Rock Behaviour', in P. Day & C. R. A. Catlow (eds.), *Proceedings of the Royal Institution of Great Britain*, 66: 43–64.

HORGAN, T., and TIENSON, J. (1994) 'A Nonclassical Framework for Cognitive Science', *Synthese*, 101: 305–45.

HUSBANDS, P., HARVEY, I., and CLIFF, D. (1995) 'Circle in the Round: State Space Attractors for Evolved Sighted Robots', *Robotics and Autonomous Systems*, 15: 83–106.

—— and MEYER, J.-A. (eds.) (1998) *Evolutionary Robotics: Proceedings of the First European Workshop, EvoRobot98, Lecture Notes in Computer Science*, vol. 1468 (Berlin: Springer Verlag).

JAEGER, H. (1998) 'Today's Dynamical Systems are too Simple', *Behavioral and Brain Sciences*, 21: 643–4.

JOHNSON-LAIRD, P. N. (1988) *The Computer and the Mind: An Introduction to Cognitive Science* (London: Fontana).

KEIJZER, F. (2001) Representation and Behavior (Cambridge, Mass.: MIT Press).

KELSO, J. A. S. (1995) *Dynamic Patterns* (Cambridge, Mass. and London: MIT Press/Bradford Books).

NORTON, A. (1995) 'Dynamics: An Introduction', in Port and van Gelder 1995: 45–68.

PFEIFER, R., BLUMBERG, B., MEYER, J.-A., and WILSON, S. (eds.) (1998) *From Animals to Animats 5: The Fifth International Conference on Simulation of Adaptive Behavior* (Cambridge, Mass.: MIT Press/Bradford Books).

PORT, R. F., CUMMINS, F., and McAULEY, J. D. (1995) 'Naive Time, Temporal Patterns, and Human Audition', in Port and van Gelder 1995: 339–71.

—— and van GELDER, T. (eds.) (1995) *Mind as Motion: Explorations in the Dynamics of Cognition* (Cambridge, Mass.: MIT Press/Bradford Books).

REYNOLDS, C. W. (1987) 'Flocks, Herds, and Schools: A Distributed Behavioral Model', *Computer Graphics*, 21: 25–34.

SEARLE, J. R. (1980) 'Minds, Brains, and Programs', *Behavioral and Brain Sciences*, 3: 417–24. Reprinted in Boden 1990.

—— (1984) *Minds, Brains and Science—The 1984 Reith Lectures* (London: Penguin).

—— (1990) 'Is the Brain's Mind a Computer Program?' *Scientific American*, 262/1: 20–5.

—— (1992) *The Rediscovery of the Mind* (Cambridge, Mass. and London: MIT Press/Bradford Books).

SLOMAN, A. (1996) 'Beyond Turing Equivalence', in P. Millican and A. Clark (eds.), *Machines and Thought: the Legacy of Alan Turing, Volume 1* (Oxford: Clarendon Press), 179–219.

SMITHERS, T. (1995) 'Are Autonomous Agents Information Processing Systems?' in L. Steels and R. Brooks (eds.), *The Artificial Life Route to Artificial Intelligence* (Hillsdale, NJ: Lawrence Erlbaum), 123–62.

SMOLENSKY, P. (1988) 'On the Proper Treatment of Connectionism', *Behavioral and Brain Sciences*, 11: 1–74.

THELEN, E., and SMITH, L. B. (1993) *A Dynamic Systems Approach to the Development of Cognition and Action* (Cambridge, Mass.: MIT Press).

TOWNSEND, J. T., and BUSEMEYER, J. (1989) 'Approach-Avoidance: Return to Dynamic Decision Behaviour', in C. Izawa (ed.), *Current Issues in Cognitive Processes* (Hillsdale, NJ: Lawrence Erlbaum), 107–33.

—— —— (1995) 'Dynamic Representation of Decision-Making', in Port and van Gelder 1995: 101–20.

TURING, A. M. (1936) 'On Computable Numbers, with an Application to the *Entscheidungsproblem*', *Proceedings of the London Mathematical Society*, series 2, 42: 230–65.

VAN GELDER, T. (1992) 'What Might Cognition be, if not Computation?' (original version). Indiana University, Cognitive Sciences technical report no. 75.

—— (1994) 'What Might Cognition be, if not Computation?' (revised version). Indiana University, Cognitive Sciences technical report no. 75.

—— (1995) 'What Might Cognition be, if not Computation?' *Journal of Philosophy*, 91: 345–81.

—— (1998a) 'Disentangling Dynamics, Computation, and Cognition', *Behavioral and Brain Sciences*, 21: 654–65.

—— (1998b) 'The Dynamical Hypothesis in Cognitive Science', *Behavioral and Brain Sciences*, 21: 615–28.

—— and PORT, R. (1995) 'It's about Time: An Overview of the Dynamical Approach to Cognition', in Port and van Gelder 1995: 1–43.

VARELA, F. J., THOMPSON, E., and ROSCH, E. (1991) *The Embodied Mind: Cognitive Science and Human Experience* (Cambridge, Mass. and London: MIT Press).

WHEELER, M. (1994) 'From Activation to Activity: Representation, Computation, and the Dynamics of Neural Network Control Systems', *Artificial Intelligence and Simulation of Behaviour Quarterly*, 87: 36–42.

—— (1998a) 'An Appeal for Liberalism, or why van Gelder's Notion of a Dynamical System is too Narrow for Cognitive Science', *Behavioral and Brain Sciences*, 21: 653–4.

—— (1998b) 'Explaining the Evolved: Homunculi, Modules, and Internal Representation', in Husbands and Meyer 1998: 87–107.

—— (forthcoming) *Reconstructing the Cognitive World: The Next Step*. (Cambridge, Mass.: MIT Press).

—— and CLARK, A. (1999) 'Genic Representation: Reconciling Content and Causal Complexity', *British Journal for the Philosophy of Science*, 50: 103–35.

19

Dancing with Pixies: Strong Artificial Intelligence and Panpsychism

Mark Bishop

In 1994 John Searle stated (Searle 1994: 11–12) that the Chinese Room Argument (CRA) is an attempt to prove the truth of the premise:

(1) Syntax is not sufficient for semantics

which, together with the following:

(2) Programs are formal
(3) Minds have content

led him to the conclusion that 'programs are not minds' and hence that computationalism, the idea that the essence of thinking lies in computational processes and that such processes thereby underlie and explain conscious thinking, is false.

The argument presented in this chapter is not a direct attack or defence of the CRA, but relates to the premise at its heart, that syntax is not sufficient for semantics, via the closely associated propositions that semantics is not intrinsic to syntax and that syntax is not intrinsic to physics.[1] However, in contrast to the CRA's critique of the link between syntax and semantics, this chapter will explore the associated link between syntax and physics.

---

[1] See Searle (1990, 1992) for related discussion.

The main argument presented here is not significantly original—it is a simple reflection upon that originally given by Hilary Putnam (Putnam 1988) and criticized by David Chalmers and others.[2] In what follows, instead of seeking to justify Putnam's claim that, 'every open system implements every Finite State Automaton (FSA)', and hence that psychological states of the brain cannot be functional states of a computer, I will seek to establish the weaker result that, over a finite time window, every open system implements the trace of a particular FSA Q, as it executes program (p) on input (x). That this result leads to panpsychism is clear as, equating Q (p, x) to a specific Strong AI program that is claimed to instantiate phenomenal states as it executes, and following Putnam's procedure, identical computational (and *ex hypothesi* phenomenal) states (ubiquitous little 'pixies') can be found in every open physical system.

The route-map for this endeavour is as follows. In the first part of the chapter I delineate the boundaries of the CRA to explicitly target all attempts at machine understanding—not just the script-based methods of Schank and Abelson (1977). Secondly, I introduce *Discrete State Machines*, DSMs, and show how, with input to them defined, their behaviour is described by a simple unbranching sequence of state transitions analogous to that of an inputless FSA. Then I review Putnam's 1988 argument that purports to show how every open physical system implements every inputless FSA. This argument is subsequently applied to a robotic system that is claimed to instantiate genuine phenomenal states as it operates.

Thus, unlike the CRA, which primarily concerns the ability of a suitably programmed computer to understand, this chapter outlines a reductio-style argument against the notion that a suitably programmed computer *qua* performing computation can ever instantiate genuine phenomenal states. I conclude the chapter with a discussion of three interesting objections to this thesis.

The Chinese Room

The twenty-one years since its inception have seen many reactions to the Chinese Room Argument from both the philosophical and cognitive science communities.

[2] See Chalmers (1994, 1996*a,b*) and also the special issue, *What is Computation?* of *Minds and Machines* (4/4, Nov. 1994).

Comment in this volume ranges from Bringsjord, who asserts the CRA to be 'arguably the twentieth century's greatest philosophical polarizer', to Rey who claims that in his definition of Strong AI, Searle, 'burdens the [Computational Representational Theory of Thought (Strong AI)] project with extraneous claims which any serious defender of it should reject'. Yet the CRA is not a critique of AI *per se*—indeed it is explicit in 'Minds, Brains, and Programs', as in other of his expositions, that Searle believes that there is no barrier in principle to the notion that a machine can think and understand. The CRA is primarily a critique of *computationalism*, according to which a machine could have genuine mental states (e.g. genuinely understand Chinese) purely in virtue of its carrying out a series of computations.

In the CRA Searle presented a rebuttal of the then computationalist orthodoxy that viewed cognition and intelligence as nothing more than symbol manipulation and search.[3] Following work on the automatic analysis of simple stories, a cultural context emerged within the AI community that appeared comfortable with the notion that computers were able to 'understand' such stories, a concept which can be traced back to the publication of Alan Turing's seminal paper 'Computing Machinery and Intelligence' (Turing 1950).

For Turing, emerging from the fading backdrop of Logical Positivism and the Vienna Circle, conventional questions concerning 'machine thinking' were too imprecise to be answered scientifically and needed to be replaced by a question that could be unambiguously expressed in scientific language. In considering the metaphysical question, 'Can a machine think?', Turing arrived at the other, distinctly empirical, question of, whether, in remote interaction via teletype with both a computer and a human, a human could identify which was which as accurately as by chance. If so, the computer is said to have passed the Turing Test.

It is now more than fifty years since Turing published details of his test for machine intelligence and although the test has since been discredited by several commentators (e.g. Bringsjord 1992; Kelly 1993), the notion of a thinking machine continues to flourish. Indeed, the concept has become so ingrained in popular culture by science fiction books and movies that many consider it almost apostate to question it. And yet, given the poverty of current AI systems on relatively simple linguistic comprehension problems,[4] it is

---

[3] e.g. Newell and Simon (1976).

[4] As illustrated by the poor quality of the entrants to the annual Loebner prize (an award made to the program that can best maintain a believable dialogue with a human. See http://www.loebner.net/Prizef/loebner-prize.html).

hardly surprising that, when writing on the subject, a phrase from Hans Christian Andersen slipped into Roger Penrose's mind (Penrose 1989). None the less, throughout the 1970s and early 1980s, Searle and Hubert Dreyfus (Dreyfus 1972) remained isolated voices that surfaced above the hegemony of symbolically Strong AI. Still today, partly due to the (apparent) simplicity of its attack, the CRA is perhaps the best-known philosophical argument in this area.

In the CRA Searle argues that understanding of a Chinese story can never arise purely as a result of the state transforms caused by 'following the instructions' of any computer program. His original paper offers a first-person tale outlining how Searle could instantiate such a program, produce correct internal and external state transitions, pass a Turing Test for understanding Chinese, and yet *still* not understand a word of Chinese. However, in the twenty years since its publication, perhaps because of its ubiquity and the widespread background perception that, if it succeeds at all, its primary target is Good Old-Fashioned AI (GOFAI), the focus of AI research has drifted into other areas: connectionism, evolutionary computing, embodied robotics, etc. Because such typically cybernetic[5] approaches to AI are perceived to be the antithesis of formal, rule-based, script techniques, many working in these fields believe the CRA is not directed at them. Unfortunately it is, for Searle's rule-book of instructions could be precisely those defining learning in a neural network, search in a genetic algorithm, or even controlling the behaviour of a humanoid-style robot of the type beloved by Hollywood.

But what does it mean to genuinely understand Chinese? That it is not simply a matter of acting in the behaviourally correct way is illustrated if we consider Wittgenstein's illustration of the difference between following a rule and merely acting in accordance with it.[6] Although rule-following requires regularity in behaviour, regularity alone is not enough. The movements of planets are correctly described by Kepler's laws, but planets do not *follow* those laws in a way that constitutes rule-following behaviour.

It is clear that the CRA employs a similar rhetorical device. It asks: 'Does the appropriately programmed computer follow the rules of (i.e. understand) Chinese when it generates "correct" responses to questions asked about a story, or is it merely that its behaviour is correctly described by those rules?' This difference between genuinely following a rule and merely acting in accordance

---

[5] Cybernetic AI is characterized by emphasis on 'subsymbolic knowledge representation' and a 'bottom-up' approach to problem-solving.   [6] Wittgenstein (1953, §§207–8, 232).

with it seems to undermine Turing's unashamedly behaviouristic test for machine intelligence.

That the CRA addresses both phenomenal and intentional aspects of understanding and intelligence is clear from the introduction to Searle's original paper, where we find Searle's definition of Strong AI:

But according to Strong AI the computer is not merely a tool in the study of the mind; rather the appropriately programmed computer really *is* a mind, in the sense that computers given the right programs can be literally said to *understand* and have other cognitive states. (Searle 1980: 417[7] (B67))

An axial statement here is that, 'the appropriately programmed computer really is a mind'. This, taken in conjunction with, '[the appropriately programmed computer] can be literally said to understand' and hence have associated 'other cognitive states', implies that the CRA also, at the very least, targets some aspects of machine consciousness—the phenomenal infrastructure that goes along with 'really having a mind'.

However it is also clear from literature on the CRA that many philosophers do not believe that prestigious practitioners of AI take the idea of machine phenomenology and artificial consciousness seriously and hence that, in this aspect at least, the CRA is supposed to target a straw man. Yet several eminent cognitive scientists such as Minsky, Moravec, and Kurzweil have already speculated widely on the subject.[8] Further, as Searle makes clear, it was precisely such statements, emerging from a vociferous bunch of proselytizing AI-niks discussing Schank and Abelson's work, that originally led him to formulate the CRA.

The idea that the appropriately programmed computer really is a mind is eloquently outlined by Chalmers. Central to Chalmers's non-reductive functionalist theory of mind is the Principle of Organisational Invariance (POI). This asserts that, 'given any system that has conscious experiences, then any system that has the same fine-grained functional organisation will have qualitatively identical experiences' (Chalmers 1996b: 249). To illustrate the point Chalmers imagines a fine-grained simulation of the operation of the human brain—a massively complex and detailed neural network. If the outputs of each simulated neuron were identical to those found in a real brain, then, via 'Dancing Qualia' and 'Fading Qualia' arguments, Chalmers argues

---

[7]   Reprinted in Boden (1990: 67). From here referred to as B67.
[8]   See e.g. Minsky (1985), Moravec (1988), and Kurzweil (1998).

that the neural network must have the same qualitative conscious experiences as the brain.

What is clear from Chalmers, and indeed any of the prophets of computationally instantiated consciousness, is that the system's phenomenal states must somehow be realized by the formally generated sequence of computational state transitions that arise as the program executes. But, following Turing, we must rid ourselves of a popular intuition:

Importance is often attached to the fact that modern digital computers are electrical, and that the nervous system also is electrical. Since Babbage's machine was not electrical, and since all digital computers are in a sense equivalent, we see that the use of electricity cannot be of theoretical importance. (Turing 1950: 439 (B46))

Indeed, in 1976 Joseph Weizenbaum described a game-playing 'computer' that could be constructed from toilet rolls and coloured stones (Weizenbaum 1976: 51ff.). Certainly functionalism, as a philosophy of mind, remains silent on the underlying hardware that causes computational state transitions— whether a program is executed on a PC or a MAC the results of its execution, the computational states it enters, are functionally the same.[9]

Discrete State Machines

In 'Computing Machinery and Intelligence', Turing defined DSMs as, 'machines that move in sudden jumps or clicks from one quite definite state to another' (Turing 1950: 439 (B46)), and explained that modern digital computers are a subset of them. An example DSM from Turing is that of a wheel machine that clicks round through $120°$ once a second, but may be stopped by the application of a lever-brake mechanism. In addition, if the machine stops in one of the three possible positions it will cause a lamp to come on. Input to the machine is thus the position of the lever-brake, {*brake on; brake off*}, and the output of the machine is the lamp state, {*lamp on; lamp off*}.

Such a machine can be described abstractly in the following manner. Its internal (computational) state is labelled (arbitrarily) by a mapping function f that maps from the *physical state* of the machine (i.e. what position the wheel is in) to the *computational state* of the machine, $q \in \{q_1\ q_2\ q_3\}$. The input to the DSM, the brake position, is described by an input signal, $i \in \{i_0\ brake\ off;\ i_1\ brake\ on\}$.

---

[9] *Modulo* temporal constraints.

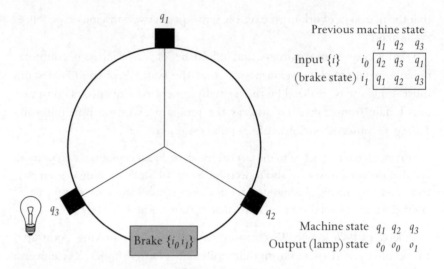

Fig. 19.1 Turing's 'discrete state wheel machine'.

Hence the next state of the machine is determined solely by its current state and its current input as follows:

	q_1	q_2	q_3
i_0	q_2	q_3	q_1
i_1	q_1	q_2	q_3

With its output being determined by:

State	q_1	q_2	q_3
Output	o_0	o_0	o_1 (lamp on)

Thus, with input to the machine either $\{i_0\}$ or $\{i_1\}$ (input undefined), the branching state transition diagram shown in Fig. 19.2 describes the DSM's behaviour. Figure 19.2 has several branch points where the next state of the machine is determined by a state transition contingent on the current input. However, as shown below, for any specific input value there are no such branching state transitions. The machine's output (lamp on/off) is determined purely by its initial state, ($q \in \{q_1\ q_2\ q_3\}$), and the system input value, ($i \in \{i_0\ i_1\}$). Knowledge of the specific input to the machine's state transition table (program) has thus *collapsed its combinatorial structure*. Further, over a given time period,

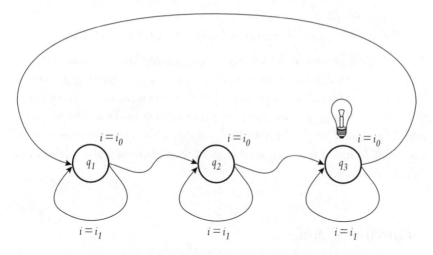

Fig. 19.2 State transition diagram of Turing's wheel machine—input undefined.

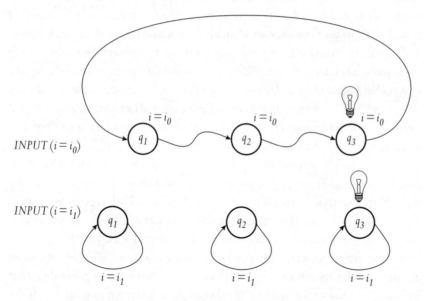

Fig. 19.3 State transition diagram of Turing's wheel machine—input defined.

say $[t_1 \ldots t_7]$, all loops can be removed from the state diagram to form a linear path of state transits. The machine now functions *like clockwork*, for example:

INPUT STATE 0:

$<q_1 q_2 q_3 q_1 q_2 q_3 q_1>$ OR $<q_2 q_3 q_1 q_2 q_3 q_1 q_1>$ OR $<q_3 q_1 q_2 q_3 q_1 q_2 q_3>$

INPUT STATE 1:

$<q_1 q_1 q_1 q_1 q_1 q_1 q_1>$ OR $<q_2 q_2 q_2 q_2 q_2 q_2 q_2>$ OR $<q_3 q_3 q_3 q_3 q_3 q_3 q_3>$

The following argument aims to show that for any Discrete State Machine which, it is claimed, instantiates mental (phenomenal) states purely in virtue of its execution of a suitable computer program, we can generate a corresponding state transition sequence using any open physical system. That this conclusion leads to a form of panpsychism is clear, as if such state transition sequences are effectively found in most material objects, then phenomenal states must be equally ubiquitous.

Putnam's Claim

Hidden away as an appendix to Hilary Putnam's 1988 book *Representation and Reality* is a short argument that endeavours to prove that every open physical system is a realization of every abstract Finite State Automaton and hence that functionalism fails to provide an adequate foundation for the study of the mind.

Central to Putnam's original argument is the observation that every open physical system, S, is in different *maximal states*[10] at every discrete instant and is characterized by a discrete series of *non-cyclic*[11] modal state transitions, $[s_1, s_2 \ldots s_t \ldots s_n]$. To simplify the following discussion of Putnam's claim and with minimal loss of generality,[12] I will replace Putnam's arbitrary physical system, S, with a *counting machine*, generating the non-cyclic state sequence $[c_1, c_2 \ldots c_t \ldots c_n]$ in place of $[s_1, s_2 \ldots s_t \ldots s_n]$ (see Fig. 19.4). It is clear that given counter state (c_k) at time $[t_k]$, it is trivial to predict its next state $[c_{k+1}]$ at time $[t_{k+1}]$. Note that this transition from state $[c_k]$ to $[c_{k+1}]$ is both regular and carries full modal force—that the counting machine is in state $[c_k]$ defines and contains the provision to force it to transit to $[c_{k+1}]$ at the next clock interval.

Any inputless FSA is characterized by its state transition table, defining, given its current state, its subsequent state. Imagine, without loss of generality, that the state transition table for FSA **Q** calls for the automaton to go through the following sequence of states in the interval $[t_1 \ldots t_6]$:

<A B A B A B>

---

[10] Putnam (1988: 122).   [11] ibid. 121.

[12] Chalmers argues that for Putnam's open physical system to reliably transit a sequence of states it must include a natural clock (such as a source of radioactive decay), however he concedes that, '[p]robably most physical systems satisfy such a requirement' (1996a: 316).

ORIGINAL COUNTER STATE $[C_t]$

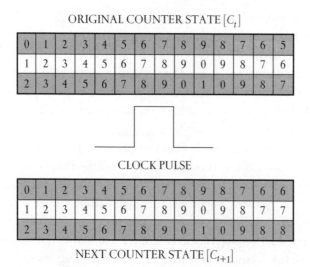

CLOCK PULSE

NEXT COUNTER STATE $[C_{t+1}]$

Fig. 19.4 A 'non-cyclic' counting machine.

Next let us suppose we are given a counting machine, **C**, which goes through the sequence of states, $[c_1, c_2, c_3, c_4, c_5, c_6]$ in the interval $[t_1 \ldots t_6]$. We wish to find a mapping between counter states $[c_a]$ and $[c_b]$ and FSA states $[A]$ and $[B]$ such that, during the time interval under observation, the counting machine obeys **Q**'s state transition table by going through a sequence of states which the state mapping function will label $[A\ B\ A\ B\ A\ B]$.

Putnam's Mapping

It is trivial to observe that if we map FSA state $[A]$ to the disjunction of counting machine states, $[c_1 \lor c_3 \lor c_5]$, and FSA state $[B]$ to the disjunction of counting machine states, $[c_2 \lor c_4 \lor c_6]$, then the counting machine will fully implement **Q**. Further, given any counting machine state $[c_a] \in \{c_1, c_3, c_5\}$, at time $[t_a]$, we can predict it will enter state $[B]$ at time $[t_b]$.

To show that being in state $[A]$ at time $[t_1]$ caused the counting machine to enter state $[B]$ at $[t_2]$ we observe that at $[t_1]$ the counting machine is in state $[c_1]$, (which the mapping function labels FSA state $[A]$), and that being in state $[c_1]$ at $[t_1]$ causes the counting machine to enter state $[c_2]$, (which the mapping function labels FSA state $[B]$) at $[t_2]$. Hence, given the current state of the counting machine at time [t], we can predict its future state and hence how the states of **Q** evolve over the time interval under observation.

Note, after Chalmers, that the counting system above will only implement a particular execution run of the FSA—there may be other state transition sequences that have not emerged in this execution trace. To circumvent this problem Chalmers posits a (counting) system with an extra dial—a subsystem with an arbitrary number of states [$c_{[dial\text{-}state,\ counter\text{-}state]}$].

Now, as Chalmers suggests, we associate dial-state [1] with the first run of the FSA. The initial state of the counting machine will then be [$c_{[1,\ 1]}$] and we associate this with an initial state of the FSA. We then associate counting-machine states [$c_{[1,\ 2]}$], [$c_{[1,\ 3]}$] with associated FSA states using the Putnam mapping described earlier. If at the end of this process some FSA states have not come up, we choose a new FSA state, [**C**], increment the dial of the counting machine to position [2] and associate this new state [$c_{[2,\ 1]}$] with [**C**] and proceed as before. By repeating this process all of the states of the FSA will eventually be exhausted. Then, for each state of the FSA there will be a non-empty set of associated counting-machine states. To obtain the FSA implementation mapping we use Putnam's mapping once more and the disjunction of these states is mapped to the FSA state as before. Chalmers remarks:

It is easy to see that this system satisfies all the strong conditionals in the strengthened definition of implementation [above]. For every state of the FSA, if the system is (or were to be) in a state that maps onto that formal state, the system will (or would) transit into a state that maps onto the appropriate succeeding formal state. So the result is demonstrated. (Chalmers 1996a: 317)

Chalmers remains unfazed at this result because he states that inputless FSA's are simply an 'inappropriate formalism' for a computationalist theory of mind:

To see the triviality, note that the state-space of an inputless FSA will consist of a single unbranching sequence of states ending in a cycle, or at best in a finite number of such sequences. The latter possibility arises if there is no state from which every state is reachable. It is possible that the various sequences will join at some point, but this is as far as the 'structure' of the state-space goes. This is a completely uninteresting kind of structure, as indeed is witnessed by the fact that it is satisfied by a simple combination of a dial and a clock. (ibid. 318)

But Putnam extends his result to the case of FSAs with input and output, by arguing that an FSA with input and output is realized by every open physical system with the right input–output dependencies—if the physical system has the right input–output then it instantiates the FSA correctly. Patently this is a restriction on his original claim, but none the less it remains a significant result that, if correct, suggests that functionalism implies behaviourism.[13]

Putnam's original argument, using an open physical system to generate a series of non-repeating system states equivalent to the non-cyclic counting machine states described earlier, runs as follows. For any arbitrary FSA, take an open physical system with the right input–output dependencies, for example, a rock with a number of marks on it encoding the input vector, $(\mathbf{x})$, (where $(\mathbf{x})$ encodes the finite set of input values, $\{x_1, x_2 \ldots x_n\}$) and another set of marks encoding the output vector $(\mathbf{o})$, (where $(\mathbf{o})$ encodes the finite set of output values, $\{o_1, o_2 \ldots o_n\}$). Associate rock state $[s_1]$ at $[t_1]$ with the relevant initial state of the FSA, and rock state $[s_2]$ at $[t_2]$ with the subsequent state of the FSA etc. Putnam claims that it is clear that by mapping each FSA state with the disjunction of associated rock states we ensure the system goes through the relevant state sequence $[s_1, s_2, s_3]$ that corresponds, using this mapping, to the relevant FSA state sequence, $[A, B, C]$, with system output encoded by the other marks on the rock.[14]

However, as for Turing's DSM, the addition of input now makes the formalism non-trivial. There can now be branching in the execution trace, as the next FSA state is contingent upon its current state and the input. This gives the system a combinatorial structure. But, as Chalmers states, Putnam's revised construction does not fully encapsulate this structure—rather it merely manifests one trace of the FSA with a specific input-output dependency. So we are left with the counter-intuitive notion that, for example, when using say a rock to implement a *two plus two program*, we mark *two* on the input area of the rock and *four* on the output and credit the rock with computing the result . . .

In his 1996 paper, Chalmers introduces a more suitable FSA formalism, which makes explicit such input/internal-state dependencies, the Combinatorial State Automaton, CSA. A CSA is like (and no more powerful than) a conventional FSA except that its internal states $[\mathbf{S}]$ are structured to form a set, $\{s_1, s_2 \ldots s_n\}$, where each element $\{s_i\}$ can take on one of a finite set of values or substates and has an associated state transition rule.

---

[13] Putnam (1988: 124–5). Any open system with the correct input–output dependencies implements the FSA with input–output. Hence every FSA with input (i) and output (o) is implemented by any physical system with the same input–output dependencies. Hence mentality is contingent only on input and output and functionalism implies behaviourism.

[14] As before, we can use Chalmers's *extra dial* construction to ensure that all initially uninstantiated FSA states are generated by the system.

Chalmers then demonstrates how to map a CSA onto a physical system in such a way as to deal with such input/internal-state dependencies correctly and preserve the internal functional organisation of the original program, but only at the price of a combinatorial increase in the number of states required for the implementation. In fact, as he illustrates in his paper, executing even the most trivial FSA with input and output, over a small number of time steps would rapidly require a physical system with more states than atoms in the known universe to implement it. So it seems that, 'we can rest reasonably content with the knowledge that the account as it stands provides satisfactory results within the class of physically possible systems' (Chalmers, 1996: 329), and functionalism is preserved.

The problem that the CSA makes explicit is that of fully encapsulating the complex inter-dependencies between machine state and the input. To implement these using an open physical system requires an astronomical number of internal states, whereas the simple implementation of an inputless FSA that Putnam describes functions only because of the subsequent loss of generality. However, as we observed with Turing's DSM, when input is defined over a specific time interval the combinatorial state structure collapses to a bounded linear path which can be simply generated using Putnam's mapping and any open physical system.

A Small Constriction

Consider a mobile robot whose behaviour is controlled by a program (p), acting upon input states (x), generating output states (o), running on computer hardware (Q). Consider the operation of the robot over a specified time interval $[t_1 \ldots t_k]$. Assume that after switch-on at time $[t_1]$, the robot experiences a series of phenomenal states until it is switched off at time $[t_k]$.

During the specified interval, $[t_1 \ldots t_k]$, the robot's input states are defined by data from its sensors forming the input set (x) $= \{i_1 \, i_2 \, i_3 \ldots i_k\}$ with its output states defining the actuator commands controlling its external behaviour, which together form the output set (o) $= \{o_1 \, o_2 \, o_3 \ldots o_k\}$. Let us now concede that the robot's control program (p) instantiates a series of phenomenal states in Q, caused by interaction with its environment as the program executes. But what is it in the robot that manifests this property? Unless we allow mind to extend beyond the physical extent of the controlling computational hardware, Q, it must be manifested solely by that hardware, that is, the claimed phenomenal properties of the system must be realized solely by $Q(p, x)$; CPU, Q, executing program (p), on input (x).

Now as Q executes (p) over the interval $[t_1 \ldots t_k]$, $Q(p, x)$ generates a specific set of computational states, S, $(S = \{s_1, s_2 \ldots s_t\})$, at the discrete clock intervals of the CPU, Q. Due to the universal realizability of Turing machine programs, the particular underlying computational engine, Q, is irrelevant to the generation of the computational states $\{s_1, s_2 \ldots s_t\}$. Whether Q had at its heart a CPU made from toilet rolls or a 600 Mz Intel Pentium P3, the associated computational states are the same, yet it is the system's generation of these computational states that must result in its instantiation of phenomenal experience.

But we have already seen from Putnam how the computational states resulting from the execution of any given FSA, Q (with specific input-output), can be mapped onto an open physical system (e.g. a simple counting machine). Thus, by relaxing the requirement that the physical system instantiates the full combinatorial state structure of a program with general input, to the relatively trivial requirement that it just instantiate the correct state transitions for a specific execution trace, we side-step the need for an exponential increase in state space. Over the specified time interval $[t_1 \ldots t_k]$ and with the input set defined, we are thus able to replicate the computational states governing the robot's behaviour (and hence the claimed phenomenal states), via an open physical system.

Three Objections

(1) Hofstadter: This is not Science

Douglas Hofstadter, in his 1981 critique of the CRA, objects that we can only perform a Putnam-style mapping a posteriori, that is, we can only map the robot's computational states onto the physical states of the system after the program has been executed and hence when we know the computational states it generates. Hence the Putnam construct is not a real mapping and this type of technique is 'not science'.

But Hofstadter is a little too harsh in his taxonomy of science and non-science. Unlike say, the intrinsic relationship between the solidity of a substance and the laws of physics, the relationship between the logical state of a computer variable and its physical implementation as a set of voltage levels is observer-relative. That is, in Searle's formulation, 'Syntax is not intrinsic to physics'

(Searle 1992: 207, 208). A computer variable cannot be uniquely identified from purely physical measurements without first knowing the mapping between the two domains (e.g. 5v = logic TRUE).

Following Turing's observations on universal realizability, if we repeat the robot's program execution with the same input on any suitable hardware, the resulting computational states are the same. Hence there is no substantive difference between equating physical system state $[c_i]$ with FSA state $[s_i]$, compared to equating the logical state TRUE with the physical state of $+5v$.

Clearly, once we know the computational states encountered in a given trace of a program, we can map them onto, and later read them off, the state transitions of an open physical system.

That Putnam's mapping can only be applied a posteriori is irrelevant to this discussion. Consider the experiment being repeated using the same FSA over the same length time interval $[t'_1 \ldots t'_k]$, with the same input, $[i'_1 \ldots i'_k]$. The computationalist would continue to claim that the robot instantiated phenomenological states over this period. It is clear that a posteriori knowledge of system input does not impact upon this claim.

(2) The Execution of a Series of State Transitions is not Sufficient to Attribute Phenomenal Properties to a Physical System[15]

This objection runs as follows. Putnam claims that his argument shows that any physical system realizes any finite automaton's state transition table, but in fact it merely realizes any desired sequence of states. Suppose an FSA recognizes a simple (regular) language—given any input string, the machine enters a phenomenal state contingent upon the string being in the language or not being in it. It seems that because the automaton has gone through a sequence of states $[s_1, s_2 \ldots s_n]$, where each state causes the next, by using a Putnam mapping function, f, to map from open physical system states to automaton states, the physical system can be viewed as going through the same sequence of states. Hence the physical system also 'recognizes' the string. But this is a false intuition. Going through a certain sequence of states is not sufficient for a system to recognize a particular string, s. What matters is not just the sequence of states the automaton went through on this occasion, but the sequences of states it would have gone through if it had been presented with other strings.

---

[15] Objection based upon a discussion with Peter Fletcher, lecturer in Computing and Mathematics at the University of Keele, UK.

This argument conflates two distinct properties: that of a system recognizing the string *s* and that of a system experiencing phenomenal states. Input-sensitive counterfactual reasoning may or may not be a necessary property of any system which it is claimed understands a language (and hence recognizes the string *s*); however it does not constitute a necessary condition of any system that experiences phenomenal states—see below.

(3) Lack of Counterfactuals[16]

The open physical system described above does not genuinely replicate an FSA with input. In particular, it lacks the ability to correctly implement counterfactuals. As such it is not a full functional isomorph of an FSA system with input. Even though specific computational states may not be entered on a particular execution run of the FSA, the mere possibility that they could be if system input was different is required in any genuine functional isomorph of the FSA, and is a necessary condition for both systems to have identical phenomenal states.

The first point to note in this response is that it seems to require a non-physical causal link between non-entered machine states and the resulting phenomenal experience of the system over the given time interval.

Secondly, we can use a type of Fading Qualia Argument (FQA)[17] to show that, in the context of FSA behaviour with input defined, counterfactuals cannot be necessary for phenomenal experience.

Consider the operation of two robots over the time interval $[t_1 \ldots t_k]$, with defined input $[i_1 \ldots i_k]$. One robot, R1, is controlled by a program designed to Chalmers's specification, replicating the fine-grained functional organization of a system known to have phenomenal states; the second, R2, generates the computational states of R1 via an open physical system using Putnam's mapping. Hence, although the external behaviour of the two systems over the time interval is identical, for Chalmers, only R1 would experience genuine phenomenal states.

Yet even for R1, contingent on the defined input vector I (I $= [i_1 \ldots i_k]$), only a small subset of potential machine states will be transited during the particular execution trace of state transitions, T_{R1} (I).

Now, with reference to system input, consider what happens if at each branch point in T_{R1} (I) we delete a state transition sequence that is not entered[18],

---

[16] Objection based upon a discussion with David Chalmers at the ASSC4 conference, Brussels, June–July 2000.   [17] Chalmers (1996b: 255).

[18] This is achieved by replacing one input-sensitive branching state transition (cf. Fig. 19.2), with a simple linear state transition contingent on the input (cf. Fig. 19.3).

then iteratively repeat this procedure until Chalmers's robot, R1, with full input-sensitivity, is step-by-step transformed into a second robot R2 whose behaviour is determined solely by a linear series of state transitions. We can imagine that throughout this replacement procedure R1 is repeatedly asked to report the colour of a red square placed within its sensor field.

Initially, R1 would both enter a phenomenal state corresponding to red, and report that it perceived red. But what happens to the phenomenological experience of R1 as it incrementally undergoes the above transformation? In the spirit of Chalmers's exposition of the Fading Qualia Argument, imagine R1 to be at a basketball game, surrounded by shouting fans, with all sorts of brightly coloured clothes. Specifically, imagine R1 focusing on the bright red of the players' uniforms. Imagine also R2 in its final state (functioning as R1 without input-sensitive branching behaviour, that is, simply performing a linear series of state transitions), being the same system but, by hypothesis, not experiencing any phenomenal states.

Between R1 and R2 there are a number of intermediate robots {R′}—what is it like to be them? As we transform R1 into R2, how does its phenomenal perception vary? Either its experience of phenomenal states must gradually fade (Fading Qualia) or it must switch abruptly at some point (Suddenly Disappearing Qualia). We can rule out the latter possibility by observing that it would imply that the removal of one such privileged branching state transition instruction would result in the complete loss of the robot's phenomenal experience.

Imagine then, that initially R1 was having bright red experience, which, as it transmutes to R2, must vanish. At some point R″'s experience must stop being bright, yet the only difference between R1 and R′ is that a sequence of non-entered machine states has been deleted.

It is clear that this fading qualia scenario is implausible, for otherwise we have a system, R′, whose phenomenal experience is contingent upon non-physical interactions with sections of its control program that are not executed—a form of dualism. Hence, if phenomenal states are purely physical phenomena, the phenomenal experience of the two robot systems, R1 and R2, must be the same.

Yet is this rendering of the FQA valid? David Chalmers has argued that it is not[19]. In contrast to his version of the FQA, in this scenario although the first robot, R1, is sensitive to its input, the second, R2, is not ('it merely acts like a

[19] Discussion with David Chalmers at ASSC5 Durham, North Carolina, May 2001.

clockwork toy'). Yet it is clear that decreasing input sensitivity *per se* cannot affect R''s phenomenal experience, for consider what would happen to R1's qualia if the link between its frame store[20] and its visual sensor is damaged, such that its frame store constantly maintains a red image, irrespective of the colours processed by its optical sensor. This will result in R1, like R2, becoming insensitive to the colours of its visual input. When asked, R1 will now 'act like clockwork' and always report that the objects in its visual field are red, irrespective of their true hue.

This lack of input sensitivity will either deflate the phenomenal experience of R1 or have no effect (with any phenomenal states in the latter case analogous to the human experience of a red hallucination). But as R1's control program is unchanged and the data it reads from its frame store is of exactly the same form (a set of binary numbers), whether it is an accurate representation of the world or is erroneous, R1 will function as it always has and its phenomenal experience will be unchanged (i.e. constantly 'red').

Hence, in the execution of a computer program with known input, input-sensitive state transition branching behaviour (counterfactual reasoning) is not a necessary condition for phenomenal states to be instantiated by a computational system.

Conclusion

For any computing machine, Q, executing program (p), with known input (x), over the specified time interval $[t_1 \ldots t_k]$, only a formal (and repeatable) series of state transitions occurs within its hardware. The generation of these state changes must be responsible for the generation of the machine's phenomenal properties. In this chapter we have seen why, following Turing's observations on universal realizability, the underlying hardware that instantiates computational state transitions is unimportant and hence, following Putnam, that a series of such transitions could be implemented by any open physical system. Thus if, over a specified time interval, Q (p, x) has phenomenal awareness purely as a result of its execution of a Strong AI computer program, then so does any open physical system, and we find little pixies dancing everywhere . . .

---

[20] A device that maintains a digital representation of an image obtained by a visual sensor such as a TV camera.

References

BODEN, M. A. (ed.) (1990) *The Philosophy of Artificial Intelligence* (Oxford: Oxford University Press).

BRINGSJORD, S. (1992) *What Robots Can and Can't Be* (Dordrecht: Kluwer).

CHALMERS, D. J. (1994) 'On Implementing a Computation', *Minds and Machines*, 4: 391–402.

—— (1996a) 'Does a Rock Implement Every Finite-State Automaton?' *Synthese*, 108: 309–33.

—— (1996b) *The Conscious Mind: In Search of a Fundamental Theory* (Oxford: Oxford University Press).

DREYFUS, H. (1972) *What Computers Cannot Do* (New York: Harper & Row).

HOFSTADTER, D. (1981) 'Reflections', in D. Hofstadter and D. C. Dennett (eds.), *The Mind's I: Fantasies and Reflections on Self and Soul* (London: Penguin), 373–82.

KELLY, J. (1993) *Artificial Intelligence: A Modern Myth* (Chichester: Ellis Horwood).

KURZWEIL, R. (1998) *The Age of Spiritual Machines: When Computers Exceed Human Intelligence* (New York: Viking).

MINSKY, M. (1985) *The Society of Mind* (New York: Simon & Schuster).

MORAVEC, H. P. (1988) *Mind Children: The Future of Robot and Human Intelligence* (Cambridge, Mass.: Harvard University Press).

NEWELL, A., and SIMON, H. A. (1976) 'Computer Science as Empirical Enquiry: Symbols and Search', *Communications of the ACM*, 19: 113–26.

PENROSE, R. (1989) *The Emperor's New Mind: Concerning Computers, Minds, and the Laws of Physics* (Oxford: Oxford University Press).

PUTNAM, H. (1988) *Representation and Reality* (Cambridge, Mass.: MIT Press/Bradford Books).

SCHANK, R. C., and ABELSON, R. P. (1977) *Scripts, Plans, Goals and Understanding* (Hillsdale, NJ: Lawrence Erlbaum).

SEARLE, J. R. (1980) 'Minds, Brains, and Programs', *Behavioural and Brain Sciences*, 3: 417–24.

—— (1984) *Minds, Brains and Science* (London: BBC Publications).

—— (1990) 'Is the Brain a Digital Computer?' *Proceedings of the American Philosophical Association*, 64: 21–37.

—— (1992) *The Rediscovery of Mind* (Cambridge, Mass.: MIT Press).

—— (1994) *The Mystery of Consciousness* (London: Granta Books).

TURING, A. M. (1950) 'Computing Machinery and Intelligence', *Mind*, 49: 433–60.

WEIZENBAUM, J. (1976) *Computer Power and Human Reason: From Judgement to Calculation* (San Francisco: W. H. Freeman).

WITTGENSTEIN, L. (1953) *Philosophical Investigations* (Oxford: Blackwell).

20

Syntax, Semantics, Physics

John Haugeland

The Chinese Room

In introducing his famous 'Chinese Room' thought-experiment, Searle articulates a methodological maxim, which he proposes to follow: 'A way to test any theory of mind is to ask oneself what it would be like if one's own mind actually worked on the principles that the theory says all minds work on'. Unfortunately, the question that Searle in fact goes on to ask is not this. Rather, he asks himself what it would be like if he were *part of* a mind that worked according to the principles that strong AI says all minds work on—in particular, what it would be like if he were the central processing unit (or the 'interpreter', as it is called in some systems). In other words, he imagines himself as a homunculus inside the complete AI system, self-consciously doing the work that the central processor (i.e. a part of the implementation or 'hardware') would normally do.

More specifically, as everybody knows, Searle considers a hypothetical system that meets the usual fluency tests for understanding Chinese, and then asks whether he, as its central processor, would *ipso facto* also understand Chinese. Plausibly, he maintains that he would not. But neither the question nor the answer is very interesting, since no one would ever have argued otherwise. So what could he have been thinking?

The form of his argument is a *modus tollens*. Thus, from the premises that (i) the hypothetical system understands Chinese, and (ii) if the system understands Chinese, then Searle himself does too, it would follow that (iii) Searle himself understands Chinese. Since the conclusion is false, one of the premises must be false. In order to show that it's the first premise that's false, Searle must argue that the second—the conditional—is true. How can he do that?

Well, in the first version of his thought-experiment, he simply *slides* from characterizing himself as a *part* of the system—namely, its central processor—to speaking of himself as if he were the *whole*. Thus, in the paragraph where he draws the moral from his initial example, he writes: 'I have inputs and outputs that are indistinguishable from those of the native Chinese speaker'; and, even more blatantly: 'in the Chinese case, the computer is me'. Of course, if Searle just *were* the system—all of it, not just part of it—then the above conditional would be trivial, as would the whole argument, by the indiscernibility of identicals. But that simply *isn't* the case that Searle initially described.

The argument resting on the slide from part to whole is an obvious fallacy. Thus, it's not surprising that Searle's early interlocutors pointed it out to him—a point that survives in his published text as what he calls 'the systems reply': it isn't the central processor that they say understands conversations or stories, but rather the system as a whole. But Searle's response to this obvious objection is very odd. He claims that he could *internalize* the whole system, by simply memorizing all of its code and data, and then carrying out all of the operations in his head.

Notice first that this still isn't a case of Searle asking what it would be like if *his own* mind worked as the theory says. Rather, what he now asks is what it would be like if he, in his own mind, were consciously to implement the underlying formal structures and operations that the theory says are sufficient to implement *another* mind. And to that question, he replies, again plausibly, that he himself wouldn't *ipso facto* understand whatever that other mind supposedly does—namely, Chinese. But this is again irrelevant, and for a similar reason: the claim was never that the implementing hardware and/or software would understand anything, but rather the systems implemented in them. In other words, Searle has simply shifted from a part–whole fallacy to a level-of-description fallacy.

In his response to the systems reply, however, Searle also offers another argument, one that might be thought to address the level-of-description issue. So we had better look at this response a little more closely. What we are to imagine in the internalization fantasy is something like a patient with multiple personality disorder. One 'personality', Searle, is fluent in English (both written and spoken), doesn't know a word of Chinese, and is otherwise perfectly normal (except that he has the calculative powers of a mega idiot savant). The other ostensible personality—let's call him Hao—is fluent in Chinese (though only written, not spoken), has no English, and, moreover, apart from seeming to be able to read and write, is deaf, dumb, blind, and paralysed. Indeed, it's worse than that: for, were Hao's Chinese interlocutor to present the (written Chinese) characters for 'Could you please write a little larger?', Hao's response (also in written Chinese) would have to be something like 'Gee, so far as I can tell, I'm communicating with you by mental telepathy; I have no knowledge of any *writing* at all'.

Searle seems to think this would be pretty bizarre; and who could disagree? But why, exactly, should we conclude that Hao doesn't *understand* the Chinese that he appears to be reading and writing ('automatically', as it were)? According to Searle's new argument, it's 'because there isn't anything in the system [Hao] which isn't in him [Searle]', and *he* doesn't understand Chinese. Let's spell this out. From the premises that (i) whatever is *in* Hao is *in* Searle, and (ii) there is some understanding *in* Hao, it follows that (iii) that very understanding is *in* Searle too. But what does this conclusion mean? One all too easy way to take it is: Searle himself *has* that understanding—thus, that he himself understands whatever Hao does. In particular, if Hao understood Chinese, so would Searle—which is exactly the conditional he needs for his *modus tollens* refutation of the premise that Hao understands Chinese.

But taken in that way, the argument equivocates on the word 'in'. When we say that the understanding that a person has is 'in' that person, what we mean by 'in' is something like 'is a capacity or feature of'. (Surely we mean more than that; but all that's needed to establish an equivocation is enough specificity in the two senses to show their difference.) But, when we agree that whatever is in Hao is 'in' Searle, we mean by the latter 'in' something like 'is implemented in some of the internal processes in'. So, if the argument is not to equivocate, this is what the 'in' in the conclusion must mean. Since this second sense is manifestly not the same as the first, Searle is not entitled to conclude that, were Hao to understand Chinese, so would he. Hence, the *modus tollens* still fails, for lack of the needed conditional.

The only way to rebut this diagnosis (or to have overlooked it) would be to maintain that being 'implemented in some of the internal activities in' something entails being 'a capacity or feature of' that *same* something. But that's just the level-of-description fallacy all over again. It would be like inferring from the fact that some of the internal activities in a cockroach implement the ability to seek out and recognize hostile viruses, that the cockroach itself can seek out and recognize hostile viruses; or like inferring from the fact that some of the internal processes in an engine implement the feature of rotating, that the engine itself is rotating.

In sum, the Chinese Room Argument fails, due to a part–whole fallacy, a level-of-description fallacy, a fallacy of equivocation, or some combination of the three.

Syntax and Semantics

In later writings, Searle claims that the Chinese Room Argument shows or rests on the fact that syntax *by itself* is not sufficient for semantics. In his APA Presidential Address, for instance, he says:

Since programs are defined *purely* formally or syntactically and since minds have an intrinsic mental content, it follows immediately that the program *by itself* cannot constitute the mind. The formal syntax of the program does not *by itself* guarantee the presence of mental contents. I showed this a decade ago in the Chinese Room Argument. . . . The argument rests on the simple logical truth that syntax is not the same as, nor is it *by itself* sufficient for, semantics. (Searle 1990: 21, 1992: 200, emphasis added)

This passage (like many others to the same effect) is carefully formulated, particularly in the qualifiers 'purely' and 'by itself' that I have emphasized. But that very carefulness becomes misleading and even irresponsible when, four paragraphs later (and obviously referring back to the quoted passage), Searle defines what he calls 'strong AI' as 'the view that all there is to having a mind is having a program'.

This is misleading because it insinuates that what one might call *serious* AI is committed to denying the claim about syntax and semantics put forward in that passage. And it's irresponsible to the extent that Searle believes he is entitled to discount serious AI on the basis of his ability to refute the straw position that he here attributes to strong AI.

In undertaking to raise fundamental questions about a major intellectual or scientific point of view, it is incumbent on one to confront that point of view in its most credible version—even if, as Descartes did for epistemological skepticism, one has first to articulate that version oneself. Accordingly, I would like to outline, very briefly, a version of the conceptual foundations of AI—in particular, the relevant conception of the relation between syntax and semantics—that I believe is considerably more credible, and also closer to what its serious proponents really believe, than the one Searle attacks. Then we can see what purchase his arguments have against that conception.

Searle is certainly right that *one* way of describing any digital computer program or data is as a formal structure of formal tokens—that is, purely syntactically. It is an *essential* feature of them that they can be so described; and this has many important consequences, including that they can in principle be implemented or realized in an open-ended variety of different physical media. There are also, however, substantial *further* constraints on any adequate implementation—that is, on any concrete instance of them in which they can actually be the program and data that they are supposed to be.

Above all, any implementation *must* be such that the operations on the data, including input and output operations, that are explicitly prescribed in the program, are reliably carried out as prescribed. Since in general these operations will involve modifications to the (concretely implemented) data structures, carrying out the operations must be a *causal* process. (It doesn't affect this point, or any that follow, that in some computer architectures the distinction between program and data is fluid or context-relative—there are always prescribed operations to be carried out on designated operands.)

So, *another* way to describe computer programs and data structures is that there must be possible concrete implementations of them such that they inter-act causally in the right way—in other words, such that they have 'the right causal powers'. That there can be such implementations is just as *essential* a feature of them, *qua* programs and data, as that they can be described formally. Indeed, in the light of this second essential feature, it becomes clear that the purely syntactical descriptions (which must also be possible) must, strictly speaking, be regarded as *abstractions* from the various possible concrete causal implementations.

Without *actual* causal implementation there is no *actual* program or data, but only an abstract specification of the kind of causal implementation that it would take to actualize them. This is exactly like the relation between engineering drawings or diagrams for a pump or an electronic circuit and the various pos-sible actualizations of such pumps or circuits. The only difference (so far) is that, given the kind of causal system being specified, the abstract specification itself (at one level of abstraction) is a formal syntactical structure rather than a drawing or a diagram.

This puts us in position to appreciate yet a *third* way in which computer programs, whether in the abstract or in concrete implementations, must be describable. I said above that programs explicitly *prescribe* operations on the data, including input and output operations. It is precisely the reliable carrying out of *whatever* these prescriptions explicitly prescribe that must be causally implemented in any implementation.

The 'whatever' is crucial here. Programs are written in a *general* code with a *compositional* structure—a structure that can be, and often is, recursive. The components out of which basic program elements are built include general terms for the operations to be performed, singular terms and variables for their operands, second-order devices for forming indirect or complex singular or general terms from given ones, conditional devices for letting what is prescribed next be a function of the current state, and so on. So, though what can be specified in a program is limited to operations on formal tokens, the possibilities for what these can be are in principle unbounded.

And whatever is specified is what the processor (or processors) should *do*. *Implementing* a processor is nothing other than constructing a device that will respond to programs (in a certain code) as specifications of what to do—namely, by *actually doing* that, *whatever* it is. If programs were not specifications of what to do, the notion of implementation would make no sense, and there would be no such things as computers or computer programs. But, of course, there are. This is why I used the word 'prescription'.

Specifications and prescriptions as such, however, have a *semantics*—that is, meanings—complete with modes of presentation, conditions of satisfaction, and directions of fit. In particular, singular terms *denote* operands (which can also be denoted in other, non-equivalent ways), general terms *denote* operations to be performed, program elements have the illocutionary force of declarations or imperatives, and conditional devices permit genuine conditional declarations or imperatives. If programs are not understood in this way, they are not intelligible *as programs* at all.

So the third way in which computer programs must be describable is *semantically*. This is just as essential to them as that they be describable syntactically and as concretely implementable. And, that allows us to introduce some further technical terminology: the *program* tokens, in the complex code described earlier, can also be called *symbols*. (Symbols, in this sense, are just tokens with a semantics.) By contrast, however, the *operand* or *data* tokens are (so far) *just* tokens: within the system *qua* computer, they have no relevant semantics at all. Or, to put it another way, the only semantics they could have would be 'derivative' (as conferred upon them by some outside observer or user, say).

But this raises a question. If the program consists of symbolic expressions with a semantics—which is to say, meanings—then to whom (or what) are they meaningful? From one obvious and familiar point of view, it is the human programmer (assuming there was one) who has performed the illocutionary act of explicitly prescribing what the processor is to do. So the prescriptions would have to be meaningful to her. But, on the face of it, this act would make no sense unless those prescriptions were meaningful to the processor itself as well. You can't sensibly *give* a command to something that can't understand and follow it; and it is that processor that must respond to these prescriptions as such and carry them out.

Now, one can certainly maintain that the processor doesn't 'understand' in the same sense that the programmer does; and there is surely something right about that. For instance, the processor has no clue as to the point of the operations it is carrying out, or even any inkling of the meta-concepts of prescription, operation, operand, and the like. And, no doubt, there are other important differences as well.

But it would be a mistake to dismiss, on such grounds, the first-order semantics of computer programs as merely 'as-if' semantics—an anthropomorphizing metaphor—on a par with saying that water 'seeks' its own level, or that setting a thermostat is 'telling' it what temperature to maintain. The difference in the computer case is that we have explicit prescriptions, expressed in a *general* symbolic code, with denotation, conditionals, and all the rest, that the processor responds to *as prescriptions with those semantics*. For comparison, a human being could seek its own level in a salt lake, and maintain its own body temperature, while in a coma and understanding nothing. But she could not execute a computer program, given to her as a text, without *understanding* its expressions as prescriptions specifying particular operations to be performed on specified operands, and so on.

Here is another way to put the point that may be better. The *only* way that we can *make sense of* a computer *as executing a program* is by understanding its processor as responding to the program prescriptions as meaningful. This is a level of description without which computers *as such* would be unintelligible to us. To be sure, we may *also* have a physical account of how such a system is possible (i.e. reliably implementable). But that does not undermine the point, as can be seen in two ways. First, it is analogous to the case of pumps and circuits, the operation of which we cannot understand except in *functional* terms, even if (as may be) we also know how those functions are physically implemented. And secondly, it will surely always be legitimate and necessary to understand human capacities semantically, even if (as may some day be) we come to know how they are physically implemented. In other words, no matter how well we understand such an implementation, that can never obviate the need for a distinct, 'higher-level' understanding of what is implemented—such as a semantic one.

Similarly, it is important never to confuse the specifications (prescriptions) that a computer program consists of with any of *our* descriptions of it, or

386 / John Haugeland

specifications for implementing it. The program prescriptions are *part of* the system itself, and, as such, part of what we describe and implement—and, moreover, must describe and implement *as prescriptions*. And this means further that, even at the level of an abstract specification of a computational system, a purely formal or syntactical description, though necessarily possible, is essentially incomplete. To describe the system fully, even in abstraction from any implementation, the *semantics* of its program part must also be specified.

Such descriptions are therefore also fundamentally different from engineering drawings or diagrams of ordinary pumps or circuits. The latter specify how the pump or circuit is to be constructed, and they do so with a view to how it is intended to behave. But they do not specify any part of the pump or circuit as *itself* explicitly prescribing what a second part of it is to do to a third part. The same can be said, incidentally, of telephone switchboards and hydraulic systems—which is why these aren't really comparable to computer systems as possible models for the mind. (This doesn't mean, of course, that certain specialized circuits, or even hydraulic systems, can't be used to implement computers. But, if they are, then they will also have to be describable in the terms outlined above; and it will be as describable in those terms, if any, that they are relevant to psychology.)

Semantics and *Serious* AI

Now, at last, we can begin to address Searle's point about syntax and semantics, and see what bearing it has on serious AI. Certainly, syntax *by itself* is never sufficient for semantics. But neither is it sufficient for computer programs as computer programs. What else is required is (at least) implementability in a system with the right causal powers. Moreover, these must be the right causal powers *for semantics*, because, if the system as implemented isn't intelligible— and, at the relevant level, *only* intelligible—as *actually having* those semantics, then it isn't intelligible as a *programmed computer*.

It is worth remarking that this point is completely compatible with the original Chinese Room example. In the Chinese Room, the program part of the system is in meaningful English, and the central processor—Searle—has the right causal powers for carrying out its prescriptions as prescriptions. And, finally, considering the system only at this level of description, the data tokens—the Chinese characters—are *just* meaningless tokens.

But, of course, this is *only* a beginning. The semantics of the computer program itself—with its singular and general terms denoting data tokens and operations—is not really what is at issue in serious AI. Rather, what is at issue is the possibility of semantics about 'the outside world'. These meanings, if any, would be attributed not to the *program* tokens (which already have their semantics) but rather to the *data* tokens—including symbolic inputs and outputs, if any—that the program prescriptions denote. Nevertheless, the discussion of the internal semantics of computers has been worthwhile for two reasons. First, it demonstrates that computer technology really can have the right causal powers for semantics, at least of a certain sort. And secondly, it can serve as a kind of model for how the states of computer systems in a larger sense might be able to have semantics of a further sort.

Here's how that model could work. Call the whole computer as we've described it so far the *narrow* system; and then think of it as just *part of* a wider and more comprehensive computational system. In this reconception—in effect, an even higher-level description—the narrow system's processor and program *together* are regarded as a single unit, which is the (much more sophisticated) *processor* of the wider system. The narrow system's data—for instance, the scripts, in Schank's old designs, along with certain input and output tokens— then serve as the *program* in this larger system, telling it how to deal with external objects, and also just keeping track of them and what they're like. Accordingly, though these internal data have no semantics when considered only as data for the narrower system, when considered as the program for the wider system, it is precisely they that must be understood semantically—namely, as denoting objects and properties in the world. Thus, finally, it is these worldly objects (which aren't part of the narrow system at all) that are playing the role of 'data' in the larger system.

But a very important lesson from the *internal* semantics case is this: not only does the *processor* have to have the right causal powers, but so also do the program symbols (which actually have the semantics) *and* the data tokens (which make up their extensions). For, after all, the capacity to be causally affected or responded to is just as much a causal power as the capacity to affect or respond. In other words, the causality that this internal semantics depends on is really an elaborate pattern of causal interactions among the processor, the meaningful program symbols, *and* the data tokens that they are about. Accordingly, if the internal case is to serve as a model for a larger system with semantics about objects in the outside world, then those objects themselves will have to be included in a correspondingly larger pattern of causal interactions. But since these outer objects are not themselves tokens within the narrow system (the computer itself), the necessary causal interactions with them will have to be mediated by special facilities called 'transducers'.

Now this is not quite the way that Schank's and most other early AI systems actually worked; nor, indeed, do many work this way today. Rather, the systems' designers avail themselves of a questionable (if often unavoidable) shortcut. Instead of building and using the requisite transducers for causal interaction with the worldly 'data' (objects), they either do the transduction themselves, or, more often, simply pretend that they do, by providing contrived 'symbolic' inputs to their systems and being satisfied with 'symbolic' outputs. Though this expedient can be justified within limits, it does inevitably deprive the systems of the actual causal interaction with objects that, according to the model, is a necessary prerequisite to any genuine semantics about them. Still, suitable transducers are not obviously impossible; and, with them in place, the model would not be altogether implausible.

(Needless to say, that same expedient is what inspired the form of the Chinese Room thought-experiment, and also what makes Hao's predicament so bizarre. And this, of course, is also why those who appreciated its status as a mere expedient responded with what Searle called 'the robot reply'.)

Searle is perfectly clear that, in his view: (i) only material objects, and, moreover, objects that are in some sense machines, can have minds and genuine semantics; (ii) it does not matter, in principle, what materials these machines are made of, or whether they are natural or artificial; and (iii) what does matter is whether those material machines have the right causal powers. *Serious AI fully agrees with all of these claims.* The only point of contention is what the right causal powers are, and what would suffice to have them. Indeed, serious AI is nothing other than a theoretical proposal as to the genus of the requisite causal powers, plus a concrete research program for homing in on the species. Therefore, the observation that syntax *by itself* (without causal powers) is insufficient for semantics is, though true, entirely beside the point.

Just for the record, I too would like to be perfectly clear about something. I myself do not believe that anything like the model just sketched on behalf of serious AI has any hope at all of homing in on the causal powers that are prerequisite for genuine intelligence and semantics. Thus, I agree, in effect, with Searle's conclusion—though for quite different reasons. I maintain (and have argued elsewhere—1998, chs. 10–13) that genuine intelligence and semantics presuppose the capacity for a kind of commitment in *how* one lives, a commitment that cannot be understood as any kind of propositional attitude or interactive facility, and that is essentially akin to love. Accordingly, I call the species of intentionality that is appropriately attributable to serious AI systems—at any rate, those with transducers and robotic 'bodies'—*ersatz* intentionality.

Syntax and Physics

Searle's Presidential Address, from which the quotation at the beginning of the second section of this chapter was taken, is not mainly about the relation of syntax to semantics, but rather about a new topic: the relation of syntax to *physics*. This topic arises in the context of asking whether the brain itself might be a digital computer. Searle's response to that question is that it is not well-defined. The reason that it's not well-defined is that it is not a straightforward matter of fact whether any given physical object exhibits the syntactical structure that is prerequisite to being a computer. Or, as he also puts it, 'syntax is not intrinsic to physics', and, even more forcefully, 'the really deep problem is that syntax is essentially an observer relative notion' (Searle 1990: 27, 1992: 209).

The basis for these contentions is the multiple realizability of syntactical structures (and the operations on them) that I mentioned earlier. In support of his point, Searle recounts an amusing litany of the fanciful implementations of computers that various popularizers have used to illustrate the idea of multiple realizability. But he seems to infer from such examples that virtually *anything* would do as an implementation. Here is a typical formulation:

For any program there is some sufficiently complex object such that there is some description of the object under which it is implementing the program. Thus for example the wall behind my back right now is implementing the Wordstar program, because there is some pattern of molecule movements which is isomorphic with the formal structure of Wordstar. (Searle 1990: 27, 1992: 208–9)

The first sentence would be fine (modulo issues of scale) if both occurrences of 'there is' were replaced by 'there could be'. But the astonishing conclusion in the second sentence is worth further examination, for it goes to the heart of what I think are several deep misconceptions about syntax and computation.

Let us begin with an essentially simpler case. Might some pattern of molecules or molecular movements in the wall behind Searle—presumably an ordinary plaster wall—implement an inscription of the *Book of Psalms* in the

King James version (specified purely syntactically)? We are all familiar with the remarkable micro-inscriptions of, say, the twenty-third psalm on a small medallion, or even the head of a pin. But we don't just take some hawker's word for such a marvel before we part with our money. Rather, we verify the claim empirically by examining the object under a lens or microscope, and confirming that we can actually *read* the text as inscribed there.

This readability—and the writability that is in general its counterpart—is non-trivial and essential to inscriptions as such. A further example will bring out the point. A century ago, it would have seemed incredible that the *Book of Psalms* could be 'inscribed' on a small magnetic disk. What would it take to convince a skeptic from that era that we can now do that? Just this, I think. Allow the skeptic to choose (or compose) *any* text of roughly that length, write it in secret to the disk, and then take that disk to someone else—who could have no prior idea what was written on it—and let her read it. (Writing and reading are here to be understood purely syntactically.) It doesn't matter what tools or techniques are required for the writing and reading (disk drives and video terminals, for instance). All that matters is that, *from the inscription itself*, the reader can reliably recover *whatever* was written there. This is what shows that *that text* is actually inscribed on the disk.

To put it another way, the very idea of a complex syntactical token—in a sense that is independent of any particular technology—presupposes specified processes of writing and reading, such that any number of different tokens of any number of different syntactical types could be written, and whatever type of token is written in any particular instance can reliably be recovered from that token. Though in one sense this definition is technology-independent, in another sense it is not—because not just anything will do. For instance, a cubic inch of pure liquid water would *not* do (not for long, anyway) since it has no modifiable structure or features that are persistent enough to permit later recovery of the type from the 'token'.

What about the patterns of molecules in Searle's wall? No doubt, a short text could be scratched into them with a screwdriver; and perhaps finer inscriptions could be achieved with lasers, or something. But is there any chance that the *Book of Psalms* is inscribed in them *now*? I am highly confident that there is not. For, in order for it to be so, there would have to be a *general* and *reliable* reading procedure (or device) such that: (i) it could, given any suitable wall, read off *whatever* text (if any) is inscribed into its molecular patterns; and (ii) given Searle's wall in particular, it would in fact read off the *Book of Psalms*. By a *general* procedure or device, I mean one that could be devised on general principles of wall reading, without knowledge of any particular wall or text; and in calling it *reliable*, I mean at least that there are specified feasible ways of carrying it out (or using it) such that it comes up with the same result from the same well-formed token almost every time. (Properly, of course, reliability and well-formedness should be specified together in terms of the write/read cycle.) This is what real inscriptions, such as books and disk recordings, are like; and it is what I am confident there is no chance of with regard to Searle's wall and the *Book of Psalms*.

Searle, of course, was not talking about text inscriptions, but rather about implementations of computer programs (such as Wordstar). Nevertheless, the forgoing has been to the point, since basic writing and reading technology—*and more*—is essential to any digital computer implementation. In other words, it is qualitatively *harder* to implement a computer than to produce a readable inscription. As we saw earlier, what else is required is a processor with the causal power (ability) to respond to some of the inscribed tokens as explicit prescriptions, and reliably carry them out by making prescribed modifications to other inscribed tokens. Needless to say, there is even less—if there can be less—reason to believe that the molecules in Searle's wall have these powers than that they contain a readable inscription of the *Book of Psalms*.

So, is syntax an essentially 'observer-relative' notion—in a way that, for instance, being a pump is not? No, not at all; and here's why. Something is a concrete token of a certain syntactical type, or a pump of a certain type, if and only if it can (in principle) be *correctly* described as a token or pump of that type. Whether any such description is correct is subject to empirical test, based on more or less stringent specifications of what it takes to be such a token or pump—in effect, definitions of them. And, whether any given description would actually pass that test is not relative to any observers. (I have just finished spelling out such a test for Searle's description of his wall, and have made an empirical prediction about how it would come out.)

Notice further about these empirically testable specifications—as much for syntactical tokens as for pumps—that (i) they will include specific required causal powers in the concrete implementations (reading tokens, for instance, is a causal process, and tokens must be readable); (ii) they will be neutral as to the materials of any particular implementation, provided only that the materials are consistent with the required causal powers; and (iii) the effects of these causal powers will (according to physicalists anyway) always be physical effects.

Now, it may be useful in some contexts to point out that an empirical description can only be given by an 'observer', and that it will always be 'relative' to that observer's chosen level of description. But these points are banal, and, in any event, apply equally to inscription tokens and to pumps. What's important here is rather this. Whether the definitive specifications are *actually satisfied* in any given case—again equally for an inscription or a pump—is a *straightforward matter of fact*. So, being an inscription with a certain syntax, *a fortiori* a computer with a certain program and data, is no more observer-relative than is being a pump—which is to say, it's not observer-relative in any pertinent sense at all. Consequently, Searle's contention that the question of whether the brain might be a digital computer is ill-defined is unfounded.

References

HAUGELAND, J. (1998) *Having Thought* (Cambridge, Mass.: Harvard University Press).
SEARLE, J. R. (1990) 'Is the Brain a Digital Computer?' *Proceedings and Addresses of the American Philosophical Association*, 64: 21–37.
—— (1992) *The Rediscovery of the Mind* (Cambridge, Mass.: MIT Press).

A SHORT BIBLIOGRAPHY
ON SEARLE'S ARGUMENTS

Only books, chapters, and articles primarily concerned with Searle's arguments are listed here. In addition, most introductory books on the philosophy of mind or cognitive science have a few pages on the Chinese Room Argument. Another major source for material on Searle's arguments against Strong AI is the internet. Websites dealing with the Chinese Room Argument are plentiful, although since they are easy to find, but come and go, are changed, and change location so much, no list has been attempted here. A wall-chart entitled 'Can Chinese Rooms Think?', mapping the debate, appears in the excellent series 'Mapping Great Debates: Can Computers Think?', published by MacroVU Inc (http://macrovu.com).

ABELSON, R. P. (1980) 'Searle's Argument is Just a Set of Chinese Symbols', *Behavioral and Brain Sciences*, 3: 424–5.

ANDERSON, D. (1987) 'Is the Chinese Room the Real Thing?' *Philosophy*, 62: 389–93.

BAILEY, A. (1994) 'Representations versus Regularities: Does Computation Require Representation?' *Eidos*, 12: 47–58.

BALDNER, K. (1990) 'Transcendental Idealism from the Chinese Room: Does God Speak Chinese?' *Proceedings of the Heraclitean Society*, 15: 9–15.

BAUMGARTNER, P., and PAYR, S. (eds.) (1995) *Speaking Minds: Interviews with Twenty Eminent Cognitive Scientists* (Princeton: Princeton University Press).

BECKERMANN, A. (1988) 'Language Understanding Machines', *Erkenntnis*, 28: 65–85.

BEN-YAMI, H. (1993) 'A Note on the Chinese Room', *Synthese*, 95: 169–72.

BIERWISCH, M. (1990) 'Perspectives on Mind, Brain, and Language: Linguistics as a Cognitive Science, or, Touring the Chinese Room', in A. Burkhardt (ed.), *Speech Acts, Meaning and Intentions: Critical Approaches to the Philosophy of John R. Searle* (Berlin and New York: de Gruyter), 391–428.

BLOCK, N. J. (1980) 'What Intuitions about Homunculi Don't Show', *Behavioral and Brain Sciences*, 3: 425–6.

—— (1990a) 'Consciousness and Accessibility', *Behavioral and Brain Sciences*, 13: 596–8.

—— (1990b) 'The Computer Model of the Mind', in D. N. Osherson and E. E. Smith (eds.), *Thinking: An Invitation to Cognitive Science*, iii (Cambridge, Mass.: MIT Press), 247–89.

BODEN, M. A. (1989) 'Escaping from the Chinese Room', in her *Artificial Intelligence in Psychology: Interdisciplinary Essays* (Cambridge, Mass.: MIT Press), 82–100.

BOYLE, C. F. (1991) 'On the Physical Limitations of Pattern Matching', *Journal of Experimental and Theoretical Artificial Intelligence*, 3: 191–217.

BRIDGEMAN, B. (1980) 'Brains + Programs = Minds', *Behavioral and Brain Sciences*, 3: 427–8.

—— (1990) 'Intention itself will Disappear when its Mechanisms are Known', *Behavioral and Brain Sciences*, 13: 598–9.

BRINGSJORD, S. (1992) *What Robots Can and Can't Be* (Dordrecht: Kluwer).

—— (1997) 'Strong AI is Simply Silly', *AI Magazine*, spring, 19–22.

BUTTON, G., COULTER, J., LEE, J. R. E., and SHARROCK, W. (1995) *Computers, Minds and Conduct* (Oxford: Polity Press).

—— —— —— —— (2000) 'Re-entering the Chinese Room: A Reply to Gottfried and Traiger', *Minds and Machines*, 10: 145–8.

CAM, P. (1990) 'Searle on Strong AI', *Australasian Journal of Philosophy*, 68: 103–8.

CARLETON, L. R. (1984) 'Programs, Language Understanding, and Searle', *Synthese*, 59: 219–30.

CARLSON, R. A. (1990) 'Conscious Mental Episodes and Skill Acquisition', *Behavioral and Brain Sciences*, 13: 599.

CHALMERS, D. J. (1992) 'Subsymbolic Computation and the Chinese Room', in J. Dinsmore (ed.), *The Symbolic and Connectionist Paradigms: Closing the Gap* (Hillsdale, NJ: Lawrence Erlbaum), 25–48.

—— (1994) 'On Implementing a Computation', *Minds and Machines*, 4: 391–402.

—— (1996a) 'Does a Rock Implement Every Finite-State Automaton?' *Synthese*, 108: 309–33.

—— (1996b) *The Conscious Mind: In Search of a Fundamental Theory* (Oxford: Oxford University Press), ch. 9.

CHOMSKY, N. (1990) 'Accessibility "In Principle" ', *Behavioral and Brain Sciences*, 13: 600–1.

CHURCHLAND, P. M., and CHURCHLAND, P. S. (1990) 'Could a Machine Think?' *Scientific American*, 262: 32–9.

CLARK, A. (1990) 'Aspects and Algorithms', *Behavioral and Brain Sciences*, 13: 601–2.

COHEN, L. J. (1986) 'What Sorts of Machines can Understand the Symbols they Use?' *Proceedings of the Aristotelian Society*, suppl. vol. 60: 81–95.

COLE, D. (1984) 'Thought and Thought Experiments', *Philosophical Studies*, 45: 431–44.

—— (1991a) 'Artificial Intelligence and Personal Identity', *Synthese*, 88: 399–417.

—— (1991b) 'Artificial Minds: Cam on Searle', *Australasian Journal of Philosophy*, 69: 329–33.

COPELAND, B. J. (1993a) *Artificial Intelligence: A Philosophical Introduction* (Oxford: Blackwell).

—— (1993b) 'The Curious Case of the Chinese Gym', *Synthese*, 95: 173–86.

—— (1998) 'Turing's O-Machines, Penrose, Searle, and the Brain', *Analysis*, 58: 128–38.

CZYZEWSKA, M., HILL, T., and LEWICKI, P. (1990) 'The Ability versus Intentionality Aspects of Unconscious Mental Processes', *Behavioral and Brain Sciences*, 13: 602.

DANTO, A. C. (1980) 'The Use and Mention of Terms and the Simulation of Linguistic Understanding', *Behavioral and Brain Sciences*, 3: 428.

DARDIS, A. (1993) 'Comment on Searle: Philosophy and the Empirical Study of Consciousness', *Consciousness and Cognition*, 2: 320–33.

DARTNALL, T. (1996) 'Illuminating the Chinese Room', *Manuscrito*, 19: 13–43.

DENNETT, D. C. (1980) 'The Milk of Human Intentionality', *Behavioral and Brain Sciences*, 3: 428–30.

—— (1982) 'The Myth of the Computer: An Exchange' (reply to Searle's review of *The Mind's I*), *New York Review of Books*, 29 (24 June), 56.

—— (1984) 'The Role of the Computer Metaphor in Understanding the Mind', in H. R. Pagels (ed.), *Computer Culture: The Scientific, Intellectual, and Social Impact of the Computer* (New York: The New York Academy of Sciences), 266–75.

—— (1985) 'Can Machines Think?' in M. Shafto (ed.), *How We Know* (San Francisco: Harper & Row), 121–45.

—— (1987) 'Fast Thinking', in his *The Intentional Stance* (Cambridge, Mass.: MIT Press), 323–37.

—— (1990) 'The Myth of Original Intentionality', in K. A. Mohyeldin Said, W. H. Newton-Smith, R. Viale, and K. V. Wilkes (eds.), *Modelling the Mind* (Oxford: Oxford University Press), 43–62, reprinted in Dietrich, 1994: 91–107.

—— (1991) *Consciousness Explained* (London: Allen Lane).

—— (1993) Review of J. R. Searle, *The Rediscovery of the Mind*, *Journal of Philosophy*, 60: 193–205.

—— (1995a) 'In Defense of AI', in Baumgartner and Payr, 1995: 59–69.

—— (1995b) 'The Mystery of Consciousness: An Exchange', *New York Review of Books*, (21 Dec.), 83.

DIETRICH, E. (ed.) (1994) *Thinking Computers and Virtual Persons: Essays on the Intentionality of Machines* (San Diego: Academic Press).

DOUBLE, R. (1983) 'Searle, Programs, and Functionalism', *Nature and System*, 5: 107–14.

—— (1984) 'Reply to Fields', *Nature and System*, 6: 55–7.

DRESHER, B. ELAN, and HORNSTEIN, N. (1990) 'Language and the Deep Unconscious Mind: Aspectualities of the Theory of Syntax', *Behavioral and Brain Sciences*, 13: 602–3.

DREYFUS, H. L. (1990) 'Searle's Freudian Slip', *Behavioral and Brain Sciences*, 13: 603–4.

DYER, M. G. (1990) 'Intentionality and Computationalism: Minds, Machines, Searle and Harnad', *Journal of Experimental and Theoretical Artificial Intelligence*, 2: 303–19.

ECCLES, J. C. (1980) 'A Dualist-Interactionist Perspective', *Behavioral and Brain Sciences*, 3: 430–1.

EDELSON, T. (1982) 'Stimulating Understanding: Making the Example Fit the Question', *Behavioral and Brain Sciences*, 5: 338–9.

FELLOWS, R. (1995) 'Welcome to Wales: Searle on the Computational Theory of Mind', in R. Fellows (ed.), *Philosophy and Technology* (Cambridge: Cambridge University Press), 85–97.

FIELDS, C. A. (1984) 'Double on Searle's Chinese Room', *Nature and System*, 6: 51–4.

FISHER, J. A. (1988) 'The Wrong Stuff: Chinese Rooms and the Nature of Under-standing', *Philosophical Investigations*, 11: 279–99.

FODOR, J. A. (1980) 'Searle on What Only Brains Can Do', *Behavioral and Brain Sciences*, 3: 431–2.

—— (1991) '*Afterthoughts*: Yin and Yang in the Chinese Room', in D. M. Rosenthal (ed.), *The Nature of Mind* (Oxford: Oxford University Press), 524–5.

FOTION, N. (2000) *John Searle* (London: Acumen).

FREEMAN, W. J. (1990) 'Consciousness as Physiological Self-Organizing Process', *Behavioral and Brain Sciences*, 13: 604–5.

FREIDIN, R. (1990) 'Grammar and Consciousness', *Behavioral and Brain Sciences*, 13: 605–6.

GLOBUS, G. G. (1991) 'Deconstructing the Chinese Room', *Journal of Mind and Behavior*, 12: 377–91, reprinted as chapter 2 of his *The Postmodern Brain* (Amsterdam: John Benjamins Publishing Company, 1995).

GLYMOUR, C. (1990) 'Unconscious Mental Processes', *Behavioral and Brain Sciences*, 13: 606–7.

GOEL, V. (1993) 'Comments on the Connection Principle', *Behavioral and Brain Sciences*, 16: 189–90.

GOTTFRIED, G., and TRAIGER, S. (1997) 'Review of G. Button *et al.*, *Computers, Minds and Conduct*', *Minds and Machines*, 7: 129–33.

GOZZANO, S. (1997) 'The Chinese Room Argument: Consciousness and Understanding', in M. Gams, M. Paprzycki, and X. Wu (eds.), *Mind versus Computer: Were Dreyfus and Winograd Right?* (Amsterdam: IOS Press), 231–5.

GREGORY, R. L. (1987) 'In Defence of Artificial Intelligence—A Reply to John Searle', in C. Blakemore and S. Greenfield (eds.), *Mindwaves* (Oxford: Blackwell), 235–44.

HARMAN, G. (1990) 'Intentionality: Some Distinctions', *Behavioral and Brain Sciences*, 13: 607–8.

HARNAD, S. (1982) 'Cognition—An Afterthought', *Cognition and Brain Theory*, 5: 29–47.

—— (1989) 'Minds, Machines and Searle', *Journal of Experimental and Theoretical Artificial Intelligence*, 1: 5–25.

—— (1990) 'The Symbol-Grounding Problem', *Physica D*, 42: 335–46.

—— (1991) 'Other Bodies, Other Minds: A Machine Incarnation of an Old Philosophical Problem', *Minds and Machines*, 1: 43–54.

HARVEY, R. J. (1985) 'On the Nature of Programs, Simulations, and Organisms', *Behavioral and Brain Sciences*, 8: 741–2.

HAUGELAND, J. (1980) 'Programs, Causal Powers, and Intentionality', *Behavioral and Brain Sciences*, 3: 432–3.

HAUSER, L. (1993*a*) 'Searle's Chinese Box: The Chinese Room Argument and Artificial Intelligence', Michigan State University Doctoral Dissertation.

—— (1993*b*) 'Reaping the Whirlwind: Reply to Harnad's "Other Bodies, Other Minds" ', *Minds and Machines*, 3: 219–37.

—— (1993c) 'Why Isn't My Pocket Calculator a Thinking Thing?' *Minds and Machines*, 3: 3–10.

—— (1993d) 'The Sense of "Thinking" ': Reply to Rapaport, *Minds and Machines*, 3: 12–21.

—— (1997) 'Searle's Chinese Box: Debunking the Chinese Room Argument', *Minds and Machines*, 7: 199–226.

HAYES, P. J. (1997) 'What is a Computer? An Electronic Discussion', *The Monist*, 80: 389–404.

HEINAMAA, S. (1995) 'On Thoughts and Emotions: The Problem of Artificial Persons', *Acta Philosophica Fennica*, 58: 269–86.

HIGGINBOTHAM, J. (1990) 'Searle's Vision of Psychology', *Behavioral and Brain Sciences*, 13: 608–10.

HOBBS, J. R. (1990) 'Matter, Levels, and Consciousness', *Behavioral and Brain Sciences*, 13: 610–11.

HODGKIN, D., and HOUSTON, A. I. (1990) ' "Consciousness" is the Name of a Non-entity', *Behavioral and Brain Sciences*, 13: 611–12.

HOFSTADTER, D. R. (1980) 'Reductionism and Religion', *Behavioral and Brain Sciences*, 3: 433–4.

—— (1981) 'Reflections', in D. R. Hofstadter and D. C. Dennett (eds.), *The Mind's I: Fantasies and Reflections on Self and Soul* (New York: Basic Books), 373–82.

HOLENDER, D. (1990) 'On Doing Research on Consciousness without being Aware of it', *Behavioral and Brain Sciences*, 13: 612–14.

HORL, C. (1991) 'Semantik und Handlungskausalität: Zur Diskussion über die künstliche Intelligenz', *Theologie und Philosophie*, 66: 192–215.

HUBBARD, T. L. (1996) 'The Importance of a Consideration of Qualia to Imagery and Cognition', *Consciousness and Cognition*, 5: 327–58.

JACQUETTE, D. (1989a) 'Adventures in The Chinese Room', *Philosophy and Phenomenological Research*, 49: 605–23.

—— (1989b) 'Searle's Intentionality Thesis', *Synthese*, 80: 267–75.

—— (1990) 'Fear and Loathing (and other intentional states) in Searle's Chinese Room', *Philosophical Psychology*, 3: 287–304.

JAHREN, N. (1990) 'Can Semantics be Syntactic?', *Synthese*, 82: 309–28.

JORION, P. (1997) 'Jean Pouillon et le mystère de la chambre chinoise', *L'Homme*, 143: 91–100.

JULESZ, B. (1993) 'Consciousness and Focal Attention: Answer to Searle', *Behavioral and Brain Sciences*, 16: 191–3.

KELLY, J. (1993) *Artificial Intelligence: A Modern Myth* (Chichester: Ellis Horwood).

KOBER, M. (1998) 'Kripkenstein Meets the Chinese Room: Looking for the Place of Meaning from a Natural Point of View', *Inquiry*, 41: 317–32.

KORB, K. B. (1991) 'Searle's AI Program', *Journal of Experimental and Theoretical Artificial Intelligence*, 1: 283–96.

KULLI, J. C. (1990) 'Is Searle Conscious?' *Behavioral and Brain Sciences*, 13: 614.

LAKOFF, G., and JOHNSON, M. (1999) *Philosophy in the Flesh: The Embodied Mind and its Challenge to Western Thought* (New York: Basic Books).

LEIBER, J. (1991) *An Invitation to Cognitive Science* (Oxford: Blackwell).

—— (1992) 'The Light Bulb and the Turing-Tested Machine', *Journal for the Theory of Social Behavior*, 22: 25–39.

LENZEN, W. (1997) 'Searles chinesischer Zauber oder Wahrnehmung, Sprachver-ständnis und der Turing-Test', in A. Burri (ed.), *Sprache und Denken/Language and Thought* (Berlin and New York: De Gruyter), 93–111.

LEPORE, E., and VAN GULICK, R. (eds.) (1991) *John Searle and his Critics* (Oxford: Blackwell).

LIBET, B. (1980) 'Mental Phenomena and Behavior', *Behavioral and Brain Sciences*, 3: 434.

LIMBER, J. (1990) 'What's It Like to be a Gutbrain?' *Behavioral and Brain Sciences*, 13: 614–15.

LLOYD, D. (1990) 'Loose Connections: Four Problems in Searle's Argument for the "Connection Principle" ', *Behavioral and Brain Sciences*, 13: 615–16.

LUDWIG, K. (1993) 'A Dilemma for Searle's Argument for the Connection Principle', *Behavioral and Brain Sciences*, 16: 194–5.

LYCAN, W. G. (1980) 'The Functionalist Reply (Ohio State)', *Behavioral and Brain Sciences*, 3: 434–5.

LYONS, W. (1985) 'On Searle's "Solution" to the Mind–Body Problem', *Philosophical Studies*, 48: 291–4.

—— (1986) *The Disappearance of Introspection* (Cambridge, Mass.: MIT Press).

McCARTHY, J. (1980) 'Beliefs, Machines, and Theories', *Behavioral and Brain Sciences*, 3: 435.

McDERMOTT, D. (1982) 'Minds, Brains, Programs and Persons', *Behavioral and Brain Sciences*, 5: 339–41.

—— (1990) 'Zombies are People, Too', *Behavioral and Brain Sciences*, 13: 617–18.

McKEVITT, P., and CHENGMING, G. (1996) 'From Chinese Rooms to Irish Rooms: New Words on Visions for Language', *Artificial Intelligence Review*, 10: 49–63.

MacLENNAN, B. J. (1994) 'Words Lie in Our Way', *Minds and Machines*, 4: 421–37.

McMULLIN, B. (1997) 'Computing Machinery and Mentality', *Brain and Cognition*, 34: 28–47.

MacQUEEN, K. G. (1990) 'Not a Trivial Consequence', *Behavioral and Brain Sciences*, 13: 163–4.

MALONEY, J. C. (1987) 'The Right Stuff', *Synthese*, 70: 349–72.

MARCONI, D. (1997) *Lexical Competence* (Cambridge, Mass.: MIT Press).

MARSHALL, J. C. (1980) 'Artificial Intelligence—The Real Thing?' *Behavioral and Brain Sciences*, 3: 435–7.

MATTHEWS, R. J. (1990) 'Does Cognitive Science Need "Real" Intentionality?' *Behavioral and Brain Sciences*, 13: 616–17.

MAXWELL, G. (1980) 'Intentionality: Hardware, not Software', *Behavioral and Brain Sciences*, 3: 437–8.

MEINI, C., and PATERNOSTER, A. (1996) 'Understanding Language through Vision', *Artificial Intelligence Review*, 10: 37–48.

MELNYK, A. (1996) 'Searle's Abstract Argument against Strong AI', *Synthese*, 108: 391–419.

MENZEL, JR., E. W. (1980) 'Is the Pen Mightier than the Computer?' *Behavioral and Brain Sciences*, 3: 438–9.

MICHIE, D. (1997) ' "Strong AI": An Adolescent Disorder', in M. Gams, M. Papryzcki, and X. Wu (eds.), *Mind versus Computer: Were Dreyfus and Winograd Right?* (Amsterdam: IOS Press), 1–8.

MINSKY, M. (1980) 'Decentralized Minds', *Behavioral and Brain Sciences*, 3: 439–40.

MOODY, T. C. (1993) *Philosophy and Artificial Intelligence* (Englewood Cliffs, NJ: Prentice-Hall).

MOOR, J. H. (1988) 'The Pseudorealization Fallacy and the Chinese Room Argument', in J. H. Fetzer (ed.), *Aspects of Artificial Intelligence* (Dordrecht: Kluwer), 35–53.

MOTZKIN, E. (1989) 'Artificial Intelligence and the Chinese Room: An Exchange', *New York Review of Books*, 36 (16 Feb.), 44–5.

NARAYANAN, A. (1991) 'The Chinese Room Argument: An Exercise in Computational Philosophy of Mind', in I. Mahalingam and B. Carr (eds.), *Logical Foundations: Essays in Honour of D. J. O'Connor* (New York: St. Martin's Press), 106–19.

NATSOULAS, T. (1980) 'The Primary Source of Intentionality', *Behavioral and Brain Sciences*, 3: 440–1.

NEWTON, N. (1988) 'Machine Understanding and the Chinese Room', *Philosophical Psychology*, 1: 207–15.

OBERMEIER, K. K. (1983) 'Wittgenstein on Language and Artificial Intelligence: The Chinese Room Thought Experiment Revisited', *Synthese*, 56: 339–49.

PAPINEAU, D. (1984) 'The Significance of Squiggles' (Review of Searle, *Minds, Brains and Science*), *Times Literary Supplement*, (14 Dec.), 1442.

PARBERRY, I. (1994) *Circuit Complexity and Neural Networks* (Cambridge, Mass.: MIT Press), ch. 1.

PENROSE, R. (1989) *The Emperor's New Mind: Concerning Computers, Minds, and the Laws of Physics* (Oxford: Oxford University Press).

—— (1994) *Shadows of the Mind: A Search for the Missing Science of Consciousness* (Oxford: Oxford University Press).

PFEIFER, K. (1992) 'Searle, Strong AI, and Two Ways of Sorting Cucumbers', *Journal of Philosophical Research*, 17: 347–50.

—— (1993) 'Causal Dispositions, Aspectual Shape and Intentionality', *Behavioral and Brain Sciences*, 16: 196–7.

PIATELLI-PALMARINI, M. (1990) 'Somebody Flew over Searle's Ontological Prison', *Behavioral and Brain Sciences*, 13: 618–19.

PINKER, S. (1997) *How the Mind Works* (New York: Norton).

PUCCETTI, R. (1980) 'The Chess Room: Further Demythologizing of Strong AI', *Behavioral and Brain Sciences*, 3: 441–2.

PYLYSHYN, Z. W. (1980) 'The "Causal Power" of Machines', *Behavioral and Brain Sciences*, 3: 442–4.

RACHLIN, H. (1980) 'The Behaviorist Reply (Stony Brook)', *Behavioral and Brain Sciences*, 3: 444.

—— (1982) 'Minds, Pains, and Performance', *Behavioral and Brain Sciences*, 5: 341.

RAPAPORT, W. J. (1986) 'Searle's Experiments with Thought', *Philosophy of Science*, 53: 271–9.

—— (1988a) 'Critical Review of John Searle, *Minds, Brains and Science*', *Nous*, 22: 585–609.

—— (1988b) 'Syntactic Semantics: Foundations of Computational Natural-Language Understanding', in J. H. Fetzer (ed.), *Aspects of Artificial Intelligence* (Dordrecht: Kluwer), 81–131.

—— (1993) 'Because Mere Calculating Isn't Thinking', *Minds and Machines*, 3: 417–24.

—— (1995) 'Understanding Understanding: Syntactic Semantics and Computational Cognition', in J. E. Tomberlin (ed.), *AI, Connectionism and Philosophical Psychology* (Atascadero: Ridgeview), 49–88.

REBER, A. S. (1997) 'Caterpillars and Consciousness', *Philosophical Psychology*, 10: 437–49.

REY, G. (1986) 'What's Really Going on in Searle's "Chinese Room" ', *Philosophical Studies*, 50: 169–85.

—— (1990) 'Constituent Causation and the Reality of Mind', *Behavioral and Brain Sciences*, 13: 620–1.

—— (1996) *Contemporary Philosophy of Mind: A Contentiously Classical Approach* (Oxford: Blackwell), ch. 11.

RINGLE, M. (1980) 'Mysticism as a Philosophy of Artificial Intelligence', *Behavioral and Brain Sciences*, 3: 444–5.

RORTY, R. (1980) 'Searle and the Special Powers of the Brain', *Behavioral and Brain Sciences*, 3: 445–6.

ROSENBERG, A. (1983) 'Fitness', *Journal of Philosophy*, 80: 457–73.

ROSENTHAL, D. M. (1990) 'On Being Accessible to Consciousness', *Behavioral and Brain Sciences*, 13: 621–2.

RUSSOW, L.-M. (1984) 'Unlocking the Chinese Room', *Nature and System*, 6: 221–7.

RYCHLAK, J. F. (1991) *Artificial Intelligence and Human Reason: A Teleological Critique* (New York: Columbia University Press), esp. ch. 1.

SAMET, J. (1982) 'Understanding and Integration', *Behavioral and Brain Sciences*, 5: 341–2.

SAVITT, S. (1982) 'Searle's Demon and the Brain Simulator', *Behavioral and Brain Sciences*, 5: 342–3.

SCHANK, R. C. (1980) 'Understanding Searle', *Behavioral and Brain Sciences*, 3: 446–7.

SCHULL, J. (1990) 'When Functions are Causes', *Behavioral and Brain Sciences*, 13: 622–4.

SCHWEIZER, P. (1994) 'Intentionality, Qualia, and Mind/Brain Identity', *Minds and Machines*, 4: 259–82.

SEARLE, J. R. (1980a) 'Minds, Brains, and Programs', *Behavioral and Brain Sciences*, 3: 417–24.

—— (1980b) 'Intrinsic Intentionality', *Behavioral and Brain Sciences*, 3: 450–6.

—— (1982a) 'The Chinese Room Revisited', *Behavioral and Brain Sciences*, 5: 345–8.

—— (1982b) 'The Myth of the Computer' (review of D. Hofstadter and D. C. Dennett (eds.), *The Mind's I: Fantasies and Reflections on Self and Soul* (New York: Basic Books, 1981)), *New York Review of Books*, 297: 3–6.

—— (1982c) 'The Myth of the Computer: An Exchange' (reply to Dennett's reply to Searle's review of *The Mind's I*), *New York Review of Books*, 29 (24 June), 57.

—— (1984a) *Minds, Brains and Science* (London: BBC Publications and Cambridge, Mass.: Harvard University Press).

—— (1984b) 'Panel Discussion: Has Artificial Intelligence Research Illuminated Human Thinking?' (with H. L. Dreyfus, J. McCarthy, M. L. Minsky and S. Papert), in H. R. Pagels (ed.), *Computer Culture: The Scientific, Intellectual, and Social Impact of the Computer* (New York: The New York Academy of Sciences), 138–60.

—— (1985) 'Patterns, Symbols, and Understanding', *Behavioral and Brain Sciences*, 8: 742–3.

—— (1987) 'Minds and Brains without Programs', in C. Blakemore and S. Greenfield (eds.), *Mindwaves* (Oxford: Blackwell), 208–33.

—— (1987b) 'Turing the Chinese Room', in T. D. Singh and R. Gomatam (eds.), *Synthesis of Science and Religion: Critical Essays and Dialogues* (San Francisco and Bombay: The Bhaktivedenta Institute), 295–301.

—— (1989a) 'Artificial Intelligence and the Chinese Room: An Exchange [with Elhanan Motzkin]', *New York Review of Books*, 36 (16 Feb.), 45.

—— (1989b) 'Reply to Jacquette's "Adventures in the Chinese Room" ', *Philosophy and Phenomenological Research*, 49: 701–7.

—— (1990a) 'Is the Brain's Mind a Computer Program?' *Scientific American*, 262 (Jan.), 20–5.

—— (1990b) 'Is the Brain a Digital Computer?' *Proceedings and Addresses of the American Philosophical Association*, 64: 21–37.

—— (1990c) 'The Causal Powers of the Brain: The Necessity of Sufficiency', *Behavioral and Brain Sciences*, 13: 164.

—— (1990d) 'Consciousness, Explanatory Inversion, and Cognitive Science', *Behavioral and Brain Sciences*, 13: 585–96.

—— (1990e) 'Who is Computing with the Brain?' *Behavioral and Brain Sciences*, 13: 632–40.

—— (1990f) 'Ist der menschliche Geist ein Computerprogramm?' *Spektrum der Wissenschaft*, Mar., 40–7.

—— (1991) 'Yin and Yang Strike Out', in D. M. Rosenthal (ed.), *The Nature of Mind* (Oxford: Oxford University Press), 525–6.

—— (1992) *The Rediscovery of the Mind* (Cambridge, Mass.: MIT Press).

—— (1993a) 'Consciousness, Attention and the Connection Principle', *Behavioral and Brain Sciences*, 16: 198–202.

—— (1993b) 'The Problem of Consciousness', *Social Research*, 60: 3–16.

—— (1993c) 'The Failures of Computationalism', *Think*, 2: 68–71.

SEARLE, J. R. (1994) 'Searle, John R.', in S. Guttenplan (ed.), *A Companion to the Philosophy of Mind* (Oxford: Blackwell), 544–50.

—— (1995) 'Ontology is the Question', in Baumgartner and Payr 1995: 202–13.

—— (1997) *The Mystery of Consciousness* (London: Granta), esp. chs. 1 and 5.

—— (1998) 'The Explanation of Cognition', in J. M. Preston (ed.), *Thought and Language* (Cambridge: Cambridge University Press), 103–26.

—— (1999a) 'Chinese Room Argument', in R. A. Wilson and F. C. Keil (eds.), *The MIT Encyclopedia of the Cognitive Sciences* (Cambridge, Mass.: MIT Press), 115–16.

—— (1999b) Interview (with Julian Moore), *Philosophy Now*, winter, 37–41.

SEIDEL, A. (1989) 'Chinese Rooms, A, B, and C', *Pacific Philosophical Quarterly*, 70: 167–73.

—— (1997) 'Searle's New Argument', *Dialogue*, 36: 575–82.

SHANON, B. (1993) 'What Next? Ramifications for Empirical Psychology', *Behavioral and Brain Sciences*, 16: 197–8.

SHARVY, R. (1985a) 'Searle on Programs and Intentionality', *Canadian Journal of Philosophy*, suppl. vol. 11: 39–54.

—— (1985b) 'It Ain't the Meat, it's the Motion', *Inquiry*, 26: 125–85.

SHEVRIN, H. (1990) 'Unconscious Mental States Do Have an Aspectual Shape', *Behavioral and Brain Sciences*, 13: 624–5.

SIMON, H. A. (1991) 'The Computer as a Laboratory for Epistemology', in L. Burkholder (ed.), *Philosophy and the Computer* (Oxford: Westview Press), 3–23.

SKARDA, C. A. (1990) 'The Neurophysiology of Consciousness and the Unconscious', *Behavioral and Brain Sciences*, 13: 625–6.

SKOKOWSKI, P. G. (1994) 'Can Computers Carry Content "Inexplicitly"?' *Minds and Machines*, 4: 333–44.

SLOMAN, A. (1986a) 'What Sorts of Machines Can Understand the Symbols They Use?' *Aristotelian Society*, suppl. vol. 60: 61–80.

—— (1986b) 'Did Searle Attack Strong Strong or Weak Strong AI?' in A. G. Cohn and J. R. Thomas (eds.), *Artificial Intelligence and its Applications* (Chichester: John Wiley and Sons), 271–88.

—— and CROUCHER, M. (1980) 'How to Turn an Information Processor into an Understander', *Behavioral and Brain Sciences*, 3: 447–8.

SMYTHE, W. E. (1980) 'Simulation Games', *Behavioral and Brain Sciences*, 3: 448–9.

—— (1982) 'Rule-Following and Rule-Reduction', *Behavioral and Brain Sciences*, 5: 343–4.

STERELNY, K. (1990) *The Representational Theory of Mind: An Introduction* (Oxford: Blackwell), ch. 10.

TAYLOR, C. (1990) 'The Possibility of Irreducible Intentionality', *Behavioral and Brain Sciences*, 13: 626.

TEIXEIRA, J. DE F. (1991) 'Robots, Intentionality, and Artificial Intelligence', *Trans Form Acao*, 14: 109–21.

TER MEULEN, A. (1990) 'The Causal Capacities of Linguistic Rules', *Behavioral and Brain Sciences*, 13: 626–7.

THAGARD, P. (1986) 'The Emergence of Meaning: How to Escape Searle's Chinese Room', *Behaviorism*, 14: 139–46.

TICHY, M. (1987) 'Auf der Suche nach dem Subjekt in der Maschine: Zu John Searles Kritik am Computermodell des Denkens', *Zeitschrift für philosophische Forschung*, 41: 429–43.

ULEMAN, J. S., and ULEMAN, J. K. (1990) 'Unintended Thought and Nonconscious Inferences Exist', *Behavioral and Brain Sciences*, 13: 627–8.

UNDERWOOD, G. (1990) 'Conscious and Unconscious Representation of Aspectual Shape in Cognitive Science', *Behavioral and Brain Sciences*, 13: 628–9.

VAN GULICK, R. (1988) 'Consciousness, Intrinsic Intentionality, and Self-Understanding Machines', in A. Marcel and E. Bisiach (eds.), *Consciousness in Contemporary Science* (Oxford: Oxford University Press), 78–100.

—— (1998) 'Chinese Room Argument', *Routledge Encyclopedia of Philosophy*, ii (London: Routledge), 328–9.

VELMANS, M. (1990) 'Is the Mind Conscious, Functional, or Both?' *Behavioral and Brain Sciences*, 13: 629–30.

WALTER, D. O. (1980) 'The Thermostat and the Philosophy Professor', *Behavioral and Brain Sciences*, 3: 449.

WARFIELD, T. A. (1999) 'Searle's Causal Powers', *Analysis*, 59: 29–32.

WEISS, T. (1990) 'Closing the Chinese Room', *Ratio* (new series), 3: 165–81.

WILENSKY, R. (1980) 'Computers, Cognition and Philosophy', *Behavioral and Brain Sciences*, 3: 449–50.

WILKS, Y. (1982) 'Searle's Straw Man', *Behavioral and Brain Sciences*, 5: 344–5.

YEE, R.-W. (1993) 'Turing Machines and Semantics Symbol Processing: Why Real Computers Don't Mind Chinese Emperors', *Lyceum*, 5: 37–59.

YOUNG, A. W. (1990) 'Consciousness, Historical Inversion, and Cognitive Science', *Behavioral and Brain Sciences*, 13: 630–1.

ZELAZO, P. D., and REZNICK, J. S. (1990) 'Ontogeny and Intentionality', *Behavioral and Brain Sciences*, 13: 631–2.

INDEX